THE
SECOND
COMING

THE SECOND

SEX AND THE NEXT GENERATION'S FIGHT OVER ITS FUTURE

COMING

CARTER SHERMAN

GALLERY BOOKS

New York   Amsterdam/Antwerp   London
Toronto   Sydney/Melbourne   New Delhi

G

Gallery Books
An Imprint of Simon & Schuster, LLC
1230 Avenue of the Americas
New York, NY 10020

For more than 100 years, Simon & Schuster has championed authors and the stories they create. By respecting the copyright of an author's intellectual property, you enable Simon & Schuster and the author to continue publishing exceptional books for years to come. We thank you for supporting the author's copyright by purchasing an authorized edition of this book.

No amount of this book may be reproduced or stored in any format, nor may it be uploaded to any website, database, language-learning model, or other repository, retrieval, or artificial intelligence system without express permission. All rights reserved. Inquiries may be directed to Simon & Schuster, 1230 Avenue of the Americas, New York, NY 10020 or permissions@simonandschuster.com.

Copyright © 2025 by Carter Sherman

All rights reserved, including the right to reproduce this book or portions thereof in any form whatsoever. For information, address Gallery Books Subsidiary Rights Department, 1230 Avenue of the Americas, New York, NY 10020.

First Gallery Books hardcover edition June 2025

GALLERY BOOKS and colophon are registered trademarks of Simon & Schuster, LLC

Simon & Schuster strongly believes in freedom of expression and stands against censorship in all its forms. For more information, visit BooksBelong.com.

For information about special discounts for bulk purchases, please contact Simon & Schuster Special Sales at 1-866-506-1949 or business@simonandschuster.com.

The Simon & Schuster Speakers Bureau can bring authors to your live event. For more information or to book an event, contact the Simon & Schuster Speakers Bureau at 1-866-248-3049 or visit our website at www.simonspeakers.com.

Interior design by Lexy East

Manufactured in the United States of America

10 9 8 7 6 5 4 3 2 1

Library of Congress Control Number: 2025933543

ISBN 978-1-6680-5245-7
ISBN 978-1-6680-5247-1 (ebook)

For my family.
Thank you for your unwavering support,
even after I told you the title of this book.

CONTENTS

Introduction.. I

1. A Nation of Virgins 15
Welcome to the Sex Recession

2. Generation Guinea Pig.. 39
The Billion-Dollar Campaign for Abstinence-Only Sex Ed

3. Classroom Culture Wars 6I
How the Pandemic Upended the Fight over Sex Ed

4. "There Is Porn of It. No Exceptions." 87
Internet Porn, Romance Novels, and the Legacy of *Fifty Shades of Grey*

5. Internet Sexplorers II7
The Rise of Young LGBTQ+ Americans

6. The Fuckability Trap 137
How Social Media Turns Us into Sex Objects

7. "Of Course He's Gonna Send You Dick Pics".................. I6I
Nudes and the Manosphere in a Post-#MeToo World

8. A Disturbing Rite of Passage 189
Sexual Violence and the Destruction of Title IX

VIII | CONTENTS

9. *Roe* v. Your Sex Life **215**
Sex and Abortion After *Roe v. Wade*

10. The *Dobbs* Domino Effect **241**
The Rights Now Under Threat

Conclusion 259
Notes on Interviews and Sources 267
Acknowledgments 269
Glossary 271
Notes 275

THE
SECOND
COMING

INTRODUCTION

The journalist perched on a stool in the corner of the bedroom, pen in hand, ready to jot down the most intimate details of our sex lives.

Her name was Peggy Orenstein, and I knew exactly three facts about her. First: She knew my favorite journalism professor. Second: She wrote for the *New York Times*, where, as an aspiring reporter myself, I desperately wanted to work. Third: She was writing a book about girls and sex.

As a twenty-year-old college sophomore, I apparently still qualified as a girl, and I was having sex. So, one night in late 2013, I agreed to let Orenstein hang out at my sorority house.

We swanned about the tiny bedroom, dodging piles of clothes and admiring one another's earrings in the mirror, while Orenstein quizzed us on boys and parties and relationships. She listened attentively as we detailed the precise alchemy of a "going-out outfit." (You could wear a tight skirt to show off your legs or a tight shirt to show off your boobs, but never both. The goal was to look available, not like a sure bet.) I could feel her eyes taking in all the pink in the room—the hot pink carpeting, the pale pink walls. Elle Woods would have been jealous. I mostly felt like a stereotype.

As we continued to answer her questions, I could sense her slow deflation. Our sex lives were not what she was looking for. We weren't having sex often enough, with enough boys. Frankly, we weren't slutty enough. (There's no such thing as a slut, but I was years away from realizing that.) After Orenstein left, I couldn't shake my suspicion that we had been drawn into playing a rigged game. While it was clear that Orenstein did not want to claim that young women were immoral for sleeping around, I felt like she had wanted to frame my sorority sisters and me as victims of "hookup culture," the 2000s moral panic that posited that young Americans were having sex so casual that it bordered on indifferent.

Like practically every other adult we encountered, she had wanted to prove that we were doing sex wrong.

Orenstein's book *Girls and Sex* was published in 2016, during my senior year of college. My sorority sisters and I did not make the final draft. But although the book was much more nuanced than my impression of her would have suggested, it also adopted the tone I had expected: that of a hand-wringing mom. "The girls I talked to often spoke of 'going crazy' as an integral part of the 'college experience'; they sounded like they were all quoting from the same travel brochure," Orenstein wrote. In her day, she said, "the college experience" involved less alcohol and more friendship, love, and "exposure to alternative music and film."[1]

In addition to being immature self-saboteurs addicted to lattés and avocado toast, millennials also evidently invented college binge drinking and one-night stands.

I did end up becoming a reporter—and because I cover gender and sexuality, I have spent a lot of time thinking about the stories we tell about sex and why they matter. I have traveled all over the United States, interviewing teenage and twentysomething Americans of all backgrounds about sex and its byproducts, and I've come to a conclusion: There is no point in trying to map the sexual landscape facing "girls" so that parents can counsel their daughters in private about how to be safe. We have no less of a need to understand today's sexual landscape; in fact, it's even more critical that we do. But we do not live in a country or world where one-on-one discussions about sex are enough to improve young people's experience of it. We might have spent a few generations telling ourselves that we did, just like we told millennials that their Starbucks habits were to blame for their inability to afford homes. In reality, however, young people are being buffeted by enormous and oppositional forces, powered by changes in politics and technology, that no birds-and-the-bees talk can fix.

Since that night in my sorority house, almost everything about how young Americans have sex has changed. We are post-#MeToo, post-pandemic, and post–*Roe v. Wade*. Kink has gone mainstream. More American adults than ever—almost 8 percent—now identify as LGBTQ+.[2] (That's likely one reason why my sorority sisters weren't hooking up with too many boys: Quite a few have since come out as gay.) We spend our days swiping through a TikTokian carousel of porn, borderline porn, Face-tuned influencers, potential dates, and more and more and more—all governed only by algorithms and Section 230 of the Communications Decency Act. It's a brain-melting infinite scroll of promises of better sex, better relationships, a better life. It is also a mass social experiment with no antecedent and whose results we are just now beginning to see. From our very first stirrings of puberty, millennials and Gen Z have had access to basically the entirety of human knowledge, nearly every other person on Earth, and, increasingly, the ability to explore every sexual whim we could want online.

Sometimes this fire hose of content helps young people find information that their schools have deprived them of, as well as communities that make them feel less alone. Other times it reinforces their darkest impulses, leading them to hate themselves and others.

As young Americans navigate unprecedented access to sex, they are simultaneously and increasingly at the mercy of activists, politicians, and institutions that have not only failed to keep up with the times but are actively working to turn back the clock. These actors have razed access to abortion, comprehensive sex ed, pornography, information about LGBTQ+ identities, and tools to combat sexual assault—to name just a few of their favorite areas of attack—on behalf of a movement that I call sexual conservatism. And, over the past twenty-five years, this movement has steadily amassed power to the point that it has dramatically restricted young Americans' sex lives and imperiled their ability to grow up safely and happily.

Sexual conservatism has been a cultural, political, and legal force in American life for centuries, yet its existence, the connections between its various wings, and its overarching goals are all too often overlooked or obscured. Specifically, sexual conservatism aims to implement policies that make it difficult and dangerous to have any kind of sex that is not heterosexual, married, and—as it seeks to limit access to abortion and birth control—potentially procreative. In addition to elevating heterosexual and married sex, American sexual conservatism tries to enforce specific ideas about gender, about what makes a man and what makes a woman. It wants to turn the United States back to a pre-internet age—to, say, the 1950s, before the Sexual Revolution and second-wave feminism of the 1960s and '70s, a time when a (white) man was expected to have a (white) wife, 2.5 (white) kids, and a suburban home on a single salary.

Sexual conservatism is not anti-sex. (White evangelical churches that oppose premarital sex have, for example, long urged their married members to go crazy in the bedroom.) Instead, it uses sex as a cudgel to force Americans into a way of life where some types of people have more power—but everybody has fewer choices.

This is not a short-term plot. It is a slow-drip corrosion of community- and state-level attacks that normalizes the loss of freedoms and ultimately clears the path for national action. The destruction of *Roe v. Wade* exemplified this strategy. Conservatives started taking over state legislatures in 2010, passed hundreds of abortion restrictions that gnawed away at access to the procedure, and wrote laws with the explicit purpose of teeing up a Supreme Court challenge to *Roe*—which, of course, succeeded. Sexual conservatives' defeat of *Roe* was a thrilling proof of concept. They now know what they can achieve, and they know how to endure.

People who work to advance sexual conservatism may not say all this to your face; they may not even say it to themselves. They may disagree with some of the aspects of sexual conservatism that I've identified. But individuals' specific beliefs or intentions matter less, in this book and to young Americans' lives, than the outcomes of the policies they push. And those outcomes are already here.

Although sexual activity among young people has been on the decline for years, the eradication of *Roe* is further endangering sex among single Americans, whose sexual activity is by definition unmarried. There are more than a hundred million single adults in the United States, and almost 90 percent of those under fifty say *Roe*'s demise has changed their dating and sex lives. In particular, 13 percent of Gen Z and 11 percent of millennials say the end of *Roe* has led them to have less sex. The same percentages say that, when they *do* have sex, they are more anxious. Sixteen percent of Gen Z are now more nervous to even date.[3]

"Not only is it impacting behavior, it's also impacting the meaning and the quality of the experience that people are having. It's really remarkable that legislation is making people feel more nervous or worried or less comfortable with their sexual lives," Justin Garcia, the executive director of the Kinsey Institute, the leading sexuality research center on the planet, told me. The loss of *Roe* threatens people's ability to form partnerships, he said. "You're not gonna connect that well if you're feeling anxious the whole time."[4]

Being able to choose if, when, and how to have sex—and what to do afterward—is not just a matter of being able to bang people without fear of consequences. Making young people afraid of sex, afraid of having the wrong kind of sex, afraid of even being *perceived* to be interested in one another—all of that robs them of their ability to pursue pleasure, self-knowledge, and connection, both sexual and nonsexual. It places relationships of every kind under a microscope and turns them into a potential avenue for persecution. It undermines their right to their own bodies, at a time when individuals are just discovering what their bodies can do or how they want their bodies to be. It denies them a full life.

Under that kind of pressure, people cannot trust their own desires, much less form trusting communities with one another—communities that could be a source of power, including political power. "The sharing of joy, whether physical, emotional, psychic, or intellectual, forms a bridge between the sharers which can be the basis for understanding much of what is not shared between them, and lessens the threat of their difference," the feminist Audre Lorde wrote in her seminal essay "The Uses of the Erotic: The Erotic as Power."[5] "In touch with the erotic," Lorde continued, "I become less willing to accept powerlessness, or those other supplied states of being which are not native to me, such as resignation, despair, self-effacement, depression, self-denial."[6]

Sex has always been political, but it is today at the white-hot center of our country's "culture wars." I use quotation marks for a reason. It's a useful shorthand, but these are not fights over some amorphous "culture." Culture wars are disputes about the very meaning of the United States, about which huddled masses deserve to breathe free on U.S. shores. Democracy is rule of the people, by the people, for the people—but who gets to count as "people"? Who gets to have power and autonomy, including sexual and reproductive autonomy? Who doesn't? And what do our answers to those questions say about the future of our democracy?

With *Roe* gone, the next phase of our culture wars is beginning.

6 | CARTER SHERMAN

* * *

In January 2023, six months after *Roe v. Wade* fell, I sat in a darkened hotel ballroom in Washington, D.C., and watched a man in a perfectly hemmed suit rile up a crowd of high school– and college-age anti-abortion activists. His name was Roger Severino. He was a vice president at the Heritage Foundation, a think tank that sets much of the right's political agenda and the group behind Project 2025, an infamous playbook of conservative policies. As he paced the stage, a microphone headset wrapped around his oil slick of dark hair, Severino gestured expansively, confidently.

He wanted his audience to have sex. But only the right kind: married, heterosexual, procreative.

"We're in it for the long haul. And the other side is on the side of death. They literally do not reproduce," Severino told the hundreds-strong crowd, who had gathered at the hotel for the daylong National Pro-Life Summit. Severino paused for laughter, then continued, "So that gives us a built-in advantage. But it means you have to do your part. Get married. Have kids. Lots of them."

The audience erupted in applause.

To his credit, Severino has taken his own advice: He and his wife, Carrie Severino, have six kids, he told the crowd. The pair are a power couple who operate in the highest echelons of the American political right. Roger was a key figure in Donald Trump's Department of Health and Human Services from 2017 to 2021, while Carrie's work as a judicial activist helped install the Supreme Court conservative majority that overturned *Roe*.

A few months after the 2023 National Pro-Life Summit, the Heritage Foundation made its agenda on sex crystal clear. "Conservatives have to lead the way in restoring sex to its true purpose, and ending recreational sex and senseless use of birth control pills," the organization posted on X, the platform formerly known as Twitter. Roger Severino's boss, Heritage Foundation president Kevin Roberts, has also praised the leadership of Viktor Orbán, the prime minister of Hungary. Orbán is an open Christian nationalist who has bragged about turning Hungary into an "illiberal democracy,"[7] has a fanatical obsession with halting immigration, and is so convinced that couples need to be heterosexual and procreative that his political party amended Hungary's constitution to declare that "Hungary shall protect the institution of marriage as the union of one man and one woman. . . . The mother shall be a woman, the father shall be a man."[8]

"Modern Hungary is not just *a* model for conservative statecraft," Roberts has said, "but *the* model."[9]

As I watched Severino bask in the crowd's cheers, I wondered whether I was watching a man housebreak a generation for authoritarianism.

But that ballroom is not a comprehensive snapshot of Gen Z. Outside those hotel walls, more than 60 percent of eighteen-to-twenty-nine-year-olds lean left,[10] and around a quarter[11] of Gen Z identify as LGBTQ+ (depending on whom you ask and how you ask the question). They are also increasingly secular. Like millennials, more than a third of Gen Z identify as religiously unaffiliated, which is far more than Gen X or baby boomers.[12] Gen Z's secularity is, however, distinct from millennials': While men are historically more likely to disaffiliate from religion than women are, most members of Gen Z who have disaffiliated from religion are women.[13] Relatedly, Gen Z women might just be the most progressive cohort ever documented in U.S. history. Since 2008, they have veered hard to the left on the issues like the environment, gun control, and, yes, abortion.[14]

Early exit polling from the 2024 election indicated Democrat Kamala Harris won 51 percent of the vote among eighteen- to twenty-nine-year-old voters. No other age demographic supported her as strongly; voters between the ages of eighteen and twenty-four, in particular, swung hard for Harris. But 2024 also saw a massive gender gap open up among voters between the ages of eighteen and twenty-nine: 58 percent of female voters in that age range voted for Harris, while 56 percent of young male voters backed Trump, an accused sexual predator who appointed three of the Supreme Court justices who overturned *Roe*. This gender gap is wider than that found in the all-ages electorate as well as wider than the gap between youth voters in the 2020 election, when Joe Biden won 56 percent of young men. Between 2020 and 2024 alone, young men swung almost 30 points to the right.[15]

As striking as these statistics are, this story is more complicated than it may appear (and it already looks plenty complicated). While they may be voting Republican, since 2008 young men have become more liberal, not less, on almost every issue, including abortion rights and same-sex marriage.[16] There is a baffling disconnect between young men's political stances and their voting patterns—one that can be explained in large part by the sexual and gendered landscape in which they have been raised.

Gen Z grew up watching and attending the kind of mass protests that break out only once in a lifetime, such as the Women's March of 2017 and the Black Lives Matter protests of 2020. They also grew up on social media, which has given them an extraordinary ability to access information and energize one another. In the 2020 election, half of eighteen-to-twenty-nine-year-olds voted, notching one of the highest rates of youth electoral participation since 1971, when the voting age was lowered from twenty-one to eighteen.[17] This was no one-off, either: The 2018 and 2022 midterms also saw record-breaking youth turnout.[18]

In 2022, their top issue was abortion, more so than any other age group.[19] Thanks to outrage over *Roe*'s demise, the much-heralded "red wave" of Republican victories never materialized. GOP candidates floundered and failed.

Youth voter turnout dropped in 2024, but that may say more about Gen Z-ers' growing distrust of elected politicians than it does about their commitment to social change. Compared to other generations, Gen Z adults are more likely to have attended a rally, volunteered, or posted online about a social issue that mattered to them. And when Trump defeated Harris, left-leaning young people immediately converted their political fury into personal action—namely, by proposing a sex strike. Searches for the feminist South Korean "4B" movement, in which women pledge to swear off heterosexual dating, sex, marriage, and childbirth, exploded online in the hours after Trump's victory. "GIRLS IT'S TIME TO BOYCOTT ALL MEN!" one TikTok creator wrote in a video with more than 3.4 million views. "YOU LOST YOUR RIGHTS, AND THEY LOST THE RIGHT TO HIT RAW!"

Frankly, I doubt we'll see a lasting *Lysistrata* in the United States. But one thing is clear: Young Americans intrinsically understand that sex, its consequences, and control over both are political weapons.

For much of the last quarter century, most ignored the erosion of sexual and reproductive freedoms, thanks in no small part to a puritan queasiness about the very existence of sex, especially among the young. Now, a generation is ready to do battle over those freedoms. They are fighting about many of the very same rights that progressives and conservatives warred over in the 1960s and '70s—and to fight over some new ones, too, as Gen Z is the most diverse generation yet in terms of race, ethnicity, gender identity, and sexual orientation. As sexual conservativism overtakes schools, courthouses, legislatures, and the White House, countless young people are working to advance a cause that I define as sexual progressivism.

Unlike sexual conservatism, which has long been aligned with Republicans, sexual progressivism has no political home. Democrats are rarely the champions of sexual, reproductive, and gendered rights that they like to portray themselves as; for example, they spent years stigmatizing abortion by claiming it should be "safe, legal, and rare" and rarely mentioned the procedure until *Roe*'s demise revealed that abortion rights can be an election-winning issue. Accordingly, sexual progressivism is less of an articulated, organized movement than sexual conservatism. Nobody ever used the words "sexual progressivism" in interviews with me—but they so often espoused a similar set of values that I had to give it a name. Many of my interviewees wanted to do more than expand access to things like sex ed, birth control, and sexual assault resources; they also sought to dismantle and reimagine traditional concepts of sex and desire so that they no longer feel so entrenched or suffocating. And they felt this way largely because they had grown up as citizens of the borderless community of the internet, with its endless depictions of sex and unparalleled ability to infuse that sex with political meaning.

As these individuals seek to revolutionize sex and the expectations that surround it, they are revolutionizing gender, too. This is by necessity. We have long expected—or forced—people of particular genders to approach sex in particular ways. By the light of these expectations, women should be its gatekeepers, forever pushing off men, who are unfailingly horny; any fallout from sex is the woman's fault; she should bear the trauma, stigma, pregnancy, childrearing, or any of the other countless consequences that sex has had through the millennia. (Forget about folks outside of the gender binary.) Casting off these expectations is, I've found, a key part of young people's sexual progressivism.

Over the course of reporting this book, I have come to understand that the battle between sexual conservatism and progressivism is the defining feature of young Americans' sex lives—and that, while they started off the twenty-first century as casualties in this clash, they are increasingly its warriors. The changes that we have witnessed in young Americans' sex lives over the past twenty-five years, and especially over the past ten, can be traced back to or have been folded into the struggle between those who believe the American family should be heterosexual, married, and procreative—and those who think individuals deserve a broader range of choices. Age alone does not determine what side someone falls on; the battle between sexual conservatism and progressivism is both intergenerational and intragenerational, as straight and cisgender young men appear to be heading down a political path that has diverged sharply from their female and LGBTQ+ peers. Age also does not insulate you from this clash. It affects us all.

In short, we are living through nothing less than the second coming of the sexual revolution. Pun intended.

*   *   *

This book is a portrait of young Americans' sexual and romantic desires and habits, how they were formed, and what they mean for the future of this country. It is an exploration of the societal forces that have shaped this new sexual revolution, such as the 2010s rise of sex positivity, the "sex recession," the anti-Trump fervor for social justice, and the mental health crisis generated by a recent series of minor apocalypses (as well as the scars left behind by the trauma of surviving said apocalypses). It is a history of how reactionary activists and politicians, aided by stagnating institutions—which they pushed into failure and then blamed for failing—have driven us to this point. And it is a book about growing up on the internet, because the internet has redefined everything we know and value about intimacy.

This is adamantly not a book about how young people are doing sex right or wrong. I'm not advocating in favor of no-holds-barred sex or against it. It is not wrong to be celibate, if that is somebody's informed choice or an expression of their sexuality. Sex before you're ready, sex with the wrong person, or bad sex can feel ruinous. (And there are many, many types of sex that can fall under the banner of "bad.") If someone wants to have only heterosexual, married, and procreative sex—I support them. As I've said, this book is far more concerned with the impact of sexual conservatism as a movement than as an individual belief.

I want consenting young people to be free to do what they want, to possess the knowledge needed to do it fearlessly, and to have access to resources that can help if anything goes wrong. I wish that wasn't controversial.

I decided to write this book because, as a millennial, I'm living in it. I grew up alongside the internet, before we used the words "me too" but after "catfishing" became commonplace. I have been slut-shamed online, flirted with non-monogamy, and survived sexual harassment and assault. I cannot say that my life experience is representative of all millennials, much less all members of Gen Z. But to shore up my own experiences, I have interviewed more than a hundred people under thirty about their experiences with, thoughts on, and hopes for sex—for their peers and in their own lives.

I talked to white people, Black people, Latinx/e people, Asian people, Indigenous people, mixed people. I talked to an individual who cheerfully described themselves as "a girl but only at Easter and Christmas" and to people who would probably have been offended had I even asked them to describe their gender identity. I talked to people who grew up in New York City, to people from towns with eight hundred inhabitants, to people with disabilities, even to one twenty-one-year-old who grew up Mennonite. I talked to people who had never had sex, including some who never want to, and at least one individual who has had sex with more than a hundred partners. I heard stories that made me cackle with recognition or vicarious joy. I also heard stories that made me cry because of how much buried pain they contained.

Most of my interviewees were Gen Z, a demographic typically thought to have been born between 1997 and 2012. However, a number were "late millennials," or people like myself, a cohort born toward the end of the millennial era whose sexual lives and attitudes have far more in common with Gen Z than is usually recognized.[*]

---

[*] People born on the border between millennials and Gen Z have also been said to be on the "cusp" or "zillennials," but I avoid those words because, honestly, I think they're ugly.

The line where one generation ends and another begins is always fungible and, frankly, mostly a matter of marketing. The Pew Research Center, one of the country's leading polling groups, has defined millennials as anyone born between 1981 and 1996. However, I believe that time frame is too wide to be meaningful, because someone born in 1981 would have been as old as twenty-two in 2003, when Myspace launched, and twenty-five in 2006, when Facebook let members of the general public register for accounts. If the point of labeling a group of people as one "generation" is to imply that they have a shared set of experiences, then the experience of coming of age alongside mainstream social media—arguably the defining force of modern life—is too fundamental to ignore. Thus, I consider late millennials to be anyone born between 1990 and 1996. Put another way: You fall into this group if you're a millennial but younger than Taylor Swift, who was famously born just a few weeks before the end of 1989 and whose career has dovetailed with the rise of social media.

I tried to make my pool of interviewees as broad as possible, although I'm sure I missed some critical viewpoints and voices. The goal, however, was not to represent every possible perspective, because that's just impossible. Instead, I prioritized interviewing Gen Z individuals who are engaged in activism, on both sides of the aisle, because I wanted to understand why and how they are driven to influence their peers' sexual and reproductive lives. This led my interview pool to skew toward people who are in college or have gone to it, because higher education is linked to increased political engagement.

To ensure interviewees could speak freely about private and stigmatized matters, I have changed their names—some to a pseudonym they selected—or used only their first names, except in cases where someone is an established public figure. Interviews usually lasted well over an hour. In several cases, I interviewed people multiple times. Sometimes I talked to individuals whom I'd spoken to numerous times in the course of my work as a journalist. Others were total strangers whom I met through online spaces like Reddit and X. A handful were friends.

Many of sexual conservatism's attacks are being waged in young people's names, as parents and (increasingly elderly) politicians claim that children need to be defended from drag queens, descriptions of sex in books, and anything that seems even remotely fun. While sexual conservatism zeroes in on "protections" for young Americans, I wanted to ask about their *rights*. As the group whose futures are now being debated and decided, what do they want to happen? What do they want for the next generation, Generation Alpha?

What happens to young people matters because *they* matter. If they head out into the world without adequate sex ed or with a belief that porn accurately depicts sex, for example, they may end up hurt or hurt others. But if you're older and feel like the culture war between sexual conservatism and progressivism is interesting to watch from afar, know this: When it comes to the future of sexual, reproductive, and gendered freedoms, minors and young adults are the canaries in the coal mine. Because older Americans are so uncomfortable with young people's sex lives, sexual conservatives have long used them to test-drive rhetoric and restrictions that they would like to eventually place on all Americans—or used them to justify the implementation of policies that, from the start, surreptitiously limit the rights of Americans of all ages. What happens to and among young people is a harbinger for everybody else in the United States.

When I think back to that time Peggy Orenstein stopped by my sorority house, I wish I had then understood how cloistered my pink-filled world was. How much that world was about to change. How moving it would be to watch people—my age and younger—fight for what they believe in.

That sorority house, with its endless hallways filled with portraits of white girls with white smiles, is empty now. Amid the 2020 Black Lives Matter protests, thousands of college students left their sororities and fraternities, calling for an end to Greek life in light of its centuries of racism, sexism, homophobia, and sexual violence. Members of my sorority voted to simply shut the entire chapter down. It was the kind of declaration that Gen Z has been making more and more frequently, on all kinds of topics: They weren't going to stand for it any longer.

The stool where Orenstein once sat has, I'm sure, long since been tossed into the trash.

I.

A NATION OF VIRGINS
Welcome to the Sex Recession

The text I had been dreading for months, if not years, lit up my phone during sixth period. One of my best friends had left school early to hang out with a male classmate of ours—and, she texted me excitedly, she had just lost her virginity to him on her laundry room floor.

It was not exactly the dreamiest of introductions to sexual intercourse. Romeo and Juliet would certainly have disapproved. But this was Seattle in 2011, not fair Verona, and it was the height of the era of sex positivity. Although we were only juniors in high school, treating sex as flippantly as Samantha from *Sex and the City* was evidence of being a modern, self-assured woman, which my female friends and I desperately wanted to be. By losing her virginity before me, my friend was leaving me behind.

I congratulated my friend and managed to keep it together for the rest of school. But when my mom arrived to drive me home, I burst into tears. My mom, understandably alarmed, demanded to know what was wrong. Between sobs, I gasped out an explanation: I was the last virgin among my friends. I could end up being the last virgin in senior year. Maybe I was the last seventeen-year-old virgin on the entire planet.

"When you were my age, were you still a virgin?" I asked my mom.

She grimaced. "Well, no," she admitted.

I cried harder.

Where did this obsession with my own virginity come from? Why was I so convinced that everybody my age was having sex without me? I partially blame TV shows like *Gossip Girl* and *Skins*, where teenagers slobbered over each other in swimming pools and then had sex so gymnastic they threw each other into walls. But as much as I longed for someone to lust after me like that, I also knew these shows were fantasy. What I read in the newspaper every morning or watched on the news at night was real—and day after day, I absorbed these outlets' moral panic over "hookup culture." The journalists, politicians, and miscellaneous moralists of the 2000s and early 2010s couldn't let it go: They were consumed by the idea that by losing our virginities so unceremoniously, young people were losing themselves.

As I came of age during George W. Bush's and Barack Obama's presidencies, books with titles like *Unhooked: How Young Women Pursue Sex, Delay Love, and Lose at Both* and *The End of Sex: How Hookup Culture Is Leaving a Generation Unhappy, Sexually Unfulfilled, and Confused About Intimacy* filled bookshelves. The *New York Times* ran numerous articles trying to demystify this apparently unprecedented phenomenon, bemoaning how hookup culture led students to smother their emotions and turned orgasms into an endangered species. Some outlets went even further. In a 2015 suite of stories about sex on college campuses, *New York* magazine suggested that many schools were little more than "great drunken bacchanals in which men and women can choose to participate in no-strings-attached, or at least few-strings-attached, experimentations in lust."[1] The stories, which covered the links between hookup culture and the high rates of sexual assault on college campuses, were nuanced and empathetic—but when the TV show *The View* interviewed one of the story's writers, the hosts were immediately condescending. Nobody said out loud that young women were "asking for it"—but, the hosts wanted to know, why couldn't college students understand that hookup culture was *obviously* an invitation to rape? "Where did the disconnect come in," Whoopi Goldberg asked, "when hookups and sexual assault have now really become sort of synonymous?"[2]

A lot of the discourse about hookup culture, however, conveniently skirted statistics that revealed many young millennials weren't having much sex at all. In 2011, the year my friend lost her virginity, the Centers for Disease Control and Prevention (CDC) asked more than fifteen thousand high school students whether they had ever had sexual intercourse as part of the agency's biennial Youth Risk Behavior Survey. More than half the millennial respondents had not.[3] I would have given a limb to know that statistic back in high school, when I kept Googling "average age of virginity loss American" and hoping for a different answer.

A sizable chunk of millennials did not even have sex in college. One 2012 study discovered that a fifth of female college seniors reported still being virgins,[4] while even the *New York* magazine story that called campuses "great drunken bacchanals" found that, in its poll of more than seven hundred college students, almost 40 percent were virgins.[5] (Neither the study nor magazine offered a firm definition of "virgin.") The vagueness of the term "hookup culture" also obscured the fact that only about a third of college students said they'd had intercourse during a hookup.[6]

Millennials were in fact having sex later and less than past generations, including the generation behind the screeds about how hookup culture was killing intimacy and safety. Late millennials—those born between 1990 and 1996—were particularly likely to go without. Compared to millennials born in the '80s, or elder millennials, late millennials were 41 percent more likely to report having had zero sexual partners between the ages of eighteen and twenty-four.[7] Between 2000 and 2002, about 19 percent of men and 15 percent of women aged eighteen to twenty-four—a cohort that captures the end of Gen X and the beginning of elder millennials—said they had gone without sex for the past year.[8] But by 2018, when late millennials were in their early twenties and Gen Z was nearing them, those numbers had shot up to 31 percent of men and 19 percent of women.[9] Casual sex fell off, too. In 2007, roughly a third of men and women between the ages of eighteen and twenty-three said they had indulged in casual sex in the last month.[10] Ten years later, only about a quarter said the same.[11]

"I started my career writing about hookups. I wrote about it for years. The data is changing," Justin Garcia, executive director of the Kinsey Institute, told me. "Casual sex is still happening, but it appears to be not as in vogue as it was just a decade ago."

Ultimately, the only living generation who enjoyed less sexual activity than young millennials were Americans born in the 1920s.[12] That generation's sex lives were, I imagine, somewhat hampered by the fact that the birth control pill hadn't been invented yet. And by the Great Depression. And World War II.

Millennials have now aged out of our sex lives being a matter of national interest. We're wandering into our thirties and forties, doing exactly what media outlets thought we would never do if we spent our teens and twenties in a frenzy of casual sex: getting married and having babies. Granted, we're doing it at later ages and lower rates than past generations, but by 2019, more than half of millennials were living with families of their own.[13] That's hardly indicative of "a generation that's terrified of and clueless about the ABCs of romantic intimacy," as one college professor dubbed millennials in a 2014 *New York Times* story.[14]

Yet the American urge to tell a story about how young people have sex—and, especially, how they're doing it wrong—hasn't disappeared. It's just been transplanted onto those mysterious creatures known as Gen Z.

Today, we tell a different story about Gen Z and sex: Rather than having too much impersonal sex, they are not having sex at all. It's called the "sex recession."

While I felt like a virginal freak in the early 2010s, I would have fit right in by the late 2010s and 2020s. "Why Are Young People Having So Little Sex?" a headline in *The Atlantic* wailed in 2018. Coronavirus pandemic-era lockdowns may have temporarily justified sexlessness, but concerns about it came roaring back to life alongside restaurants and concerts. In 2023, a *New York Times* opinion essay linked young Americans' poor mental health and stunning levels of loneliness to their lack of sex. "Have More Sex, Please!" the headline pleaded.

Although the hookup culture narrative that surrounded millennials as they came of age was flawed, there is more evidence that Gen Z is having even less sex than millennials had in our youth. (Really, it seems like public discourse has just caught up with the science—a generation too late.) In 2021, when the CDC again conducted its Youth Risk Behavior Survey, only 30 percent of the Gen Z respondents said they'd had sexual intercourse, according to data released in 2023.[15] That's a 17 percent drop from when I was in high school. In a 2022 survey conducted in part by the Kinsey Institute, one in four Gen Z adults also said they had never experienced partnered sex.[16]

Even masturbation is somehow on the decline. Between 2009 and 2018, the share of adolescent men who had never experienced partnered *or* solo sexual activity rose from 29 percent to 50 percent.[17] Among adolescent women, the share increased from 43 percent to 74.[18]

The story about Gen Z proclaims that they are more than sexless—

they are also allegedly *opposed* to sex and even to relationships. According to the internet, Gen Z is full of "puriteens," a portmanteau of "puritan" and "teenager" that Urban Dictionary defines as an "(almost always) young person on the internet who thinks that the internet has to conform to being entirely SFW," or safe for work. These puriteens and their supposed concerns—age gaps between partners, displays of kink at Pride parades, irredeemably tilted power dynamics in relationships that might have been once perceived as equal—typically hail not from the political right, where reservations about sexual exploration may seem more naturally at home, but from the left. News story after news story has worried over Gen Z's apparent turn away from "sex-positive" feminism and toward "sex negativity."

"I think because they've waited for so long, they're nervous about finally engaging with other people," Kristen, a twenty-four-year-old in Iowa, told GQ of two virgin friends of hers. "They'll joke about wanting to go out, hook up, put themselves out there, but in reality, they're so uncomfortable."[19]

Gen Z is so terminally online, so addicted to pathologizing normality through therapy-speak, and speeding so far to the left that they've lost their ability to navigate the nuances of human relationships. Further addled by the isolation of the pandemic, they've thrown their hands up and escaped back into their bedrooms-cum-bunkers, alone, their faces aglow with blue light.

Or so the lore goes, anyway.

Why are we so obsessed with crafting narratives around how young people have sex? Because they can be used to push agendas. For sexual conservatives, all these statistics boil down into pronatalist fears over the United States' declining birth rate (and especially the declining birth rate among white women). Several countries have reported declines in sexual activity in recent years; Japan, in particular, is frequently held up as a cautionary tale. Like the United States, Japan has seen its sexual activity, marriage, and births all drop, leading its prime minister to warn that the country's falling population is "the biggest crisis Japan faces."[20]

The sex recession enables sexual conservatives to portray sexual progressivism as an existential threat to the United States, as they argue that it has led to a breakdown in gender roles—especially women's roles—that prevents men and women from pursuing relationships and, more importantly, families. "Our people aren't having enough children to replace themselves. That should bother us," JD Vance, the vice president of Donald Trump's second administration, once told a conservative conference.[21] Vance, infamously, has a long track record of denigrating single, child-free women.[22] In his view, these women are so dangerous that we must take political action to stop them. The United States, Vance claimed in a 2021 *Fox News* interview, is being run by "a bunch of childless cat ladies who are miserable at their own lives and the choices that they've made and so they want to make the rest of the country miserable, too."

Neither sexual conservatism nor progressivism alone has caused the sex recession, although the recent successes of sexual conservativism have certainly complicated sex for young people. Instead, the sex recession is the result of a constellation of factors that have been heavily influenced by both movements. And it is the result of forces that date back to long before the first millennials and Gen Z were ever born—to the sexual and political tumult of the 1960s and '70s. To begin to understand how the sex recession came to be, we need to reckon with how Americans' approaches to sex have shifted over the decades, the movements that have led those shifts—like feminism—and how those shifts have sped up rapidly over the past ten to fifteen years.

Perhaps most importantly, as we look to the future of sex, we need to ask: What stories are young people telling *themselves* about sex and the sex recession? Just as the hookup culture narrative led me to castigate myself, I've found that many people are still punishing themselves—or even one another—over failing to meet imagined ideals that don't match the generational reality.

THE NATURE(S) OF VIRGINITY

Before I go further, I have to address a vital question: What is sex, anyway?

By the time of my breakdown in my mom's car, I had experienced a wide range of sexual activity. I'd given blow jobs and hand jobs. Boys had fingered me. (No one had gone down on me, nor did I expect them to.

THE SECOND COMING | 21

I'll return to that inequality later.) However, I never considered that those experiences might constitute "sex," because I believed sex happened only when a penis penetrated a vagina. I thought I was a virgin until I experienced that and only that.

I'm far from the only person to believe that penis-in-vagina sex is the One True Sex. Although young Americans have become more accepting of homosexual sex, most adolescents and college students have long thought penis-in-vagina intercourse is the most surefire way to lose your virginity.[23] When I asked interviewees how they defined "virginity" and "sex," many had, like me, believed vaginal intercourse was the only way to swipe your V-card—even if they were not interested in having that form of sex.

"I definitely thought that I had to have sex with a cis man," said Ciné, a twenty-two-year-old queer, transgender Floridian. "And there had to be penetration involved."

"I didn't think that you had to have an orgasm, that you had to bleed or anything like that," added Kate, a queer, cis twenty-one-year-old woman from Wisconsin. "But I did consider 'losing your virginity' as penetrative sex."

When I asked Ethan, a twenty-year-old straight cis man from Ohio, how he would define losing his virginity, he was plainspoken: "Probably dick in vagina."

The endurance of this belief across geography and sexual orientation isn't exactly surprising. We are force-fed depictions of heteronormative sex and relationships from the moment we can turn on a screen. Penis-in-vagina sex is also primarily responsible for sex's most famous lasting consequence: pregnancy.

The association between virginity and the threat of pregnancy originally arose out of economic utility. Before we could prove paternity using a DNA test, marrying a virgin was the only way to ensure that your wife's child was definitely yours, and that you weren't handing off your property to some bloodline imposter. Virginity was thus linked to being "untouched" and "pure," and far more important for women. If they were discovered to not be virgins, their social value would plummet. Their chances of survival might, too.

Yet the hymen, that vexing bit of skin that has been held up as proof of female virginity, the "cherry" that gets popped in a burst of blood, is a misunderstood piece of anatomy. Although almost everybody who is assigned female at birth[*] is born with a hymen, it can be broken long before someone engages in penetrative sex. Even if a hymen *does* break during penetrative sex, it may leave no evidence behind. Some hymens do not bleed because they are made out of tissue with relatively few blood vessels, according to virginity scholar Hanne Blank.

"Short of catching someone in the act of sex, virginity can be neither proven nor disproven. We cannot prove it today, nor have we ever been able to," Blank wrote in her book *Virgin: An Untouched History*. "Barring some unprecedented quantum leap in diagnostic techniques, we are equally unlikely to be able to do so in the future."[24]

All of this is to say: Virginity is and always has been a social construct. Individuals can and should feel free to define it however they wish. But the fact that virginity is socially constructed does not mean that it doesn't carry life-altering, mind-poisoning importance.

I finally lost my virginity—as I understood it then, through vaginal intercourse—at nineteen, when I was a freshman in college. It didn't feel particularly special or particularly disappointing. Really, I was so relieved to finally get it over with that I barely paid attention to how it felt.

I was in the midst of falling in love with the man who took my virginity, but I didn't tell him that it was my first time. I didn't even tell my newfound college friends. Sure, I told them I had started having sex with my boyfriend, but I intimated that I had already done "it" before. The day afterward, when I sat with my friends in their dorm room, nestled into denim-blue beanbags, one friend pressed me for the details. Another exclaimed, "It's not like she lost her virginity!"

Her clueless words hit with the precision of a drone strike. Outrageous embarrassment flooded my body. I couldn't make the words, the truth, come out. I hunched into the beanbag and willed myself to just get through it.

---

[*]Someone who is "assigned female at birth" is socially perceived, thanks to their body and/or to societal norms at their birth, to be female, but that perception may not align with their gender identity. "Assigned female at birth" can be abbreviated to the shorthand AFAB, just like its companion term "assigned male at birth," or AMAB. If you encounter other terms you're not familiar with, there is a glossary included at the end of this book.

I'm far from the only virgin of my generation to view virginity not as a prize, as it may have been viewed in the past, but as an albatross that blocks people from forging relationships and independent identities. In 2016, Kinsey Institute researchers discovered that heterosexual male and female adults who were sexually inexperienced considered themselves more stigmatized than people who do have sexual experience. Young adults were especially unlikely to want to date virgins—which leaves virgins in something of a catch-22, because they can't lose their virginity and become desirable if they can't find someone who already desires them enough to take it. Virgins, the study showed, didn't even want to date other virgins.[25]

I'm an independent woman, Rachel, a twenty-two-year-old from Ohio, likes to tell herself when she thinks about the fact that she has not had sex. *It doesn't matter. Society built this construct about virginity.*

But she doesn't really believe it.

"It makes me feel like I'm not cool and I'm not where I should be as a twenty-two-year-old," Rachel said. "When I graduated high school, I was like, 'Oh, I'll go to college, I'll start dating someone, I'll have sex—blah, blah, blah, all this stuff—by the time I've graduated college.' I'm not there. Now that I'm not in school anymore, I feel like there's fewer opportunities for me to meet people and go on dates and expand my horizons. It has impacted my mental health in that I feel like I'm behind the ball for where I should be for someone my age—which, who defines that?"

Rachel, who is bisexual, doesn't want to find some random stranger on Tinder and just lose her virginity to them. She wants to feel comfortable. But in a vicious irony, Rachel's inexperience is undercutting her confidence and ability to pursue experience.

"In my head, I'm gonna go on a date and they'll be like, 'Do you want to have sex?'" Rachel said. "And I'll be like, 'I've never had sex before.' And they'll be like, 'Oh, that's really weird,' and then never want to talk to me ever again."

If virginity is historically a feminine trait, then to be a virgin can feel embarrassing to the point of being emasculating among people who are assigned male at birth, or AMAB. Sam, a twenty-one-year-old from Texas, started feeling anxious about being a virgin as early as fourteen. "Dudes will make fun of other students in school, like, 'Oh, you're a virgin, bro.

Shut up. What are you even talking about?' It's definitely a playground insult," he told me. Being a male virgin, he said, means "you're a loser and you're lame."

Virginity flies in the face of what masculinity researchers like to call "hegemonic masculinity," which the internet would probably label as "toxic masculinity" and which generally stereotypes men as big, strong, emotionless, high status, and (of course) straight. That narrow mold of masculinity—which is, by the way, impossible for anyone to shrink themselves into—reinforces traditional gender roles, because it portrays men as being nothing like women. And it dictates that men should not possess virginity, but should rather take it.

This attitude was alive and well in Sam's conservative hometown, which was rife with the belief that men should *love* having sex with virgins. "If you have sex with a virgin, that's the best thing ever," Sam said. "You're claiming this land or whatever—some weird ideals like that."

In this worldview, women are property that loses value through sex, while men gain.

"There is this expectation for men to be pursuing sex, because we assume that's just how men biologically exist," explained Colby Fleming, a sociologist who's studied virginity, gender, and masculinity. "If you're not having sex with women—more recently, you can't attract them, or before, you couldn't land one through money or whatever—that means that you are not masculine. You're doing something wrong that's reflecting something about you. Because if you were really a man, you would be doing this. And if you're not, that's suspect."

Ethan likes to call himself "culturally gay," as if his heterosexuality is a surprise. For a time, as a kid, Ethan thought he might be gay; he questioned his sexuality again when he started dating someone who was nonbinary. He even watched gay porn to gauge his own reaction. His verdict: "Meh. Not for me."

He now identifies as straight because he's just not that into penises. "Conventionally, for societal standards, I'm a straight guy," Ethan said. "It's just the easiest for me to go with."

But even for someone who wears his sexuality and masculinity as lightly as Ethan does, virginity was a weight around his neck. Like the men in Sam's hometown, his friends would tease him for being "a fucking virgin."

THE SECOND COMING | 25

"I feel like the way toxic masculinity functions, you have to operate in this alpha position," Ethan said. "You can't be this fucking virgin wimp, whatever the fuck."

He was determined to lose his virginity as soon as possible after he got to college—and he did. After Ethan finally had "dick-in-vagina" sex, as he put it, he went to the bathroom and did a Michael Jordan–style fist pump all by himself. Then Ethan texted his closest friends: "Guess who's done?" ("Did you really just text me post-sex?" one replied.)

"Getting that out of the way, for me, was an aspect of growing up," Ethan said. "I noticed I was just more confident in myself and my life the minute I got it over with."

THE FIRST COMING OF THE SEXUAL REVOLUTION

How has virginity become so stigmatized? Well, sexual conservatives aren't totally wrong to blame sexual progressivism.

In 1972, researchers at the University of Chicago launched the General Social Survey, a biennial survey that, over the last half century, has become one of the best indicators of how Americans view and do sex. The researchers' timing was serendipitous, because at the time of the survey's launch, sex was in the midst of becoming untethered from pregnancy and childbirth. The Food and Drug Administration (FDA) had approved the birth control pill in 1960, and by 1970, 60 percent of all American women—married and unmarried alike—were on the pill, had an IUD, or had been sterilized.[26] Two years later, the Supreme Court ruled that single people had the right to access contraception. Some states were also loosening their restrictions on abortion, while in states that still banned the procedure, people were taking matters into their own hands. In Chicago, the General Social Survey's home, a secret network of women known as "Jane" performed more than eleven thousand illegal abortions in the late 1960s and early '70s.[27] In 1973, a year after the General Social Survey started, the Supreme Court legalized abortion nationwide in *Roe v. Wade*. And the year after *that*, women gained the legal right to own a credit card in their own name.

All the while, the median marriage age in the United States, which had dropped to a record low of just over twenty for women and twenty-two for men in 1955, began to creep back up.[28] No-fault divorce laws emerged. Rather than being tied to a partner due to pregnancy or economic necessity, people were able to make more and more time in their lives for experimenting with flirtation, relationships, and sex. The United States had already weathered a sexual revolution in the first few decades of the twentieth century,[29] but when someone mentions the "Sexual Revolution" today, it is this era of rapid social and legal change that we think of.

The sexual progressivism of the Sexual Revolution, combined with the second-wave feminism of the 1960s and '70s, stunned and infuriated conservative Christians across the country. They started to organize—against *Roe*, of course, but also against issues like porn, homosexuality, the banning of school prayer, and sex education.[30] Defeating the feminist cause of the Equal Rights Amendment (ERA) was a particular clarion call, with conservatives arguing that establishing a constitutional right to gender equality would disrupt "the beautiful way men treat women in this country," as Phyllis Schlafly, a doyenne of twentieth-century conservatism and the activist most responsible for defeating the ERA, once told the *New York Times*.[31]

Hoping to channel this groundswell of activism, evangelical pastor Jerry Falwell Sr. in 1979 founded the Moral Majority, an organization designed to register conservative Christians as voters in service of a "holy war"[32] against proponents of abortion rights, porn, sex ed, and other assorted left-wing causes. "We are economically, politically, and militarily sick because our country is morally sick," he wrote.[33] Falwell thus established the religious right as a political force and outlined one of its core missions: to defend his version of Christian family values against sexual progressivism and thus save the United States. The religious right isn't synonymous with sexual conservativism, but the values and actors of the two movements continue to overlap significantly.

For the first three decades or so of the General Social Survey, sexual conservatism kept winning in one crucial way: Researchers usually found that only about half of eighteen-to-thirty-four-year-olds believed sex between unmarried adults was "not wrong at all." But starting around 2006, support for premarital sex began to climb at an astonishing pace. By

2022, a record 77 percent of eighteen-to-thirty-four-year-old respondents thought sex before marriage was "not wrong at all." More than three-quarters said that homosexual sex was "not wrong at all," either.

This was a sea change in U.S. life. Perhaps anxiety about changing attitudes toward sex, rather than actual behaviors, inspired all those breathless stories about hookup culture in the 2000s and 2010s. After all, teenage sex has been common for decades: By the 1970s, more than half of Americans had had premarital sex by the time they turned twenty.[34] But maybe that status quo was acceptable only as long as we felt guilty about it.

Today, Americans tend to get married for the first time around thirty—older than ever before.[35] More unmarried people in their twenties are cohabitating with partners,[36] but the change in people's timeline for marriage remains a foundational factor in the sex recession. "That sets the stage for all the other questions," Garcia said. "When we're thinking about what's happened with hookup culture, what's happening with the sex recession—there's a bigger demographic shift. We're seeing more and more single people, more and more young people who are not thinking about starting a marriage in the next few months, or few years even."

We tend to imagine that single people get laid more, but partnered people have more sex because they have a guaranteed source of it. Today, almost half of U.S. adults under thirty are single.[37] If young Americans don't feel compelled to pursue committed relationships and marriage—because sexual progressivism has enabled them to have sex outside of those strictures, because its ally feminism has helped women make their own way without a husband—they are potentially setting themselves up to go without sex, for better or worse.

SEX AND THE SINGLE #GIRLBOSS

As the United States has become far more accepting of sex over the past seventy-five years, we have not grown more accepting of sexlessness—as young people's (and my) abhorrence of our own virginities demonstrates. Since the 1960s, "what has passed as liberation has often been liberalization," the critic Mark Greif wrote in a 2006 essay.[38]

"A test of liberation, as distinct from liberalization, must be whether you have also been freed to be free from sex, too—to ignore it, or to be asexual, without consequent social opprobrium or imputation of deficiency," Greif continued. "One of the cruel betrayals of sexual liberation, in liberalization, was the illusion that a person can only be free if he holds sex as all-important and exposes it endlessly to others—providing it, proving it, enjoying it."[39]

Ironically, feminism, the movement that helped champion sexual progressivism in the 1960s and '70s, might be partially responsible for this state of affairs among millennials and Gen Z. Or at least the worst version of feminism might be.

In the 1980s, as second-wave feminism receded from its high-water mark following the ERA's demise, prominent feminists skirmished over pornography in a series of battles now known as "the sex wars." On one side were "sex-negative" feminists, who believed that porn replicates and reinforces the degradation of women. (They had a famous motto: "Pornography is the theory. Rape is the practice."[40]) Sex-negative feminists' rivals were "sex-positive" feminists, who saw state intervention in sexual pleasure as a tool of male dominance, given that men tend to run the state.[41] I think these labels are rather reductive, even unfair, but when people claim Gen Z is "sex-negative," they are—maybe unwittingly—invoking this lineage.

Sex-negative feminists sought to pass government ordinances to limit porn, a move that found them in bed with sexual conservatives who opposed porn for very different reasons. But courts shut down those ordinances, and by the mid-1990s, the sex wars were over. Sex-positive feminists won. Pornography was here to stay. (Or so we thought, anyway.)

Feminism's stature in pop culture largely faded until the late 2000s, when trenchant feminist blogs like *Jezebel* and *The Hairpin* began generating takes on pop culture and issues like sexual assault, reproductive rights, and office sexism; an online feminist ecosystem developed as social media platforms then disseminated those takes even further, but often erased the takes' nuances in the process. In 2013, Sheryl Sandberg aimed directly for these blogs' professional-class audience when she published *Lean In*, a guide for working women so instantly controversial that I had to read it for a college gender studies class. Sandberg came to represent what the popular notion of feminism ended up calcifying into: If a woman chooses to do it, it's feminism. She might even be a #girlboss.

This "pop" feminism, as I think of it, celebrates rather than challenges; it suggests that people combat injustice not with structural changes but with self-help. Brands ate it up and spit it out as what Andi Zeisler, founder of Bitch Media, has called "empowertising," as in: *Spend fifty dollars on a "The Future Is Female" T-shirt!* White women, especially straight and cisgender women with some degree of wealth, benefit most from pop feminism—which could also be called white feminism.

By 2014, feminism's edges had been sanded down enough that A-list celebrities were ready to claim the title. Taylor Swift declared herself a feminist in an interview with the *Guardian*,[42] while Beyoncé stood in front of a neon screen that blazed the word "FEMINIST" at the MTV Video Music Awards. Feminism was officially cool again.

Which, when it came to sex, was a problem.

Thanks to its victory in the 1980s sex wars, sex positivity was still the default mode among feminists. At its best, sex positivity does not hold that sex is a unilateral force for good, but rather that we should strive to have a good relationship with sex through the normalization of practices like consent and comprehensive sex education. This idea is critical to sexual progressivism. But within 2010s pop culture, the sex positivity movement's deep thinking and ardent politics were watered down into a general belief that to be feminist was to have sex and vice versa.

This approach to sex meshed quite well with pop feminism's consumerism, because brands could fold sex into their empowertising and sell more sex-related goods. Virgins weren't just politically and culturally behind the times; they were bad capitalists. Furthermore, if feminism meant acquiring goods that boosted girl power, then women should treat sex itself like a good and acquire as much of it as possible.

Yet for many young women in the 2010s, sex was supposed to be so liberating, it weighed them down.

Francesca, a twenty-nine-year-old woman from Michigan, identified as a feminist from her adolescence. But she didn't connect it to her sex life "until it became a defense mechanism."

"Against?" I asked her.

"Having hurt feelings about being perceived as a slut. It was like,

30 | CARTER SHERMAN

'Actually, I'm just very, very radical and cool and you guys don't know about it,'" Francesca replied. "It wasn't until years later that I considered: 'Wait, if you were having sex as an empowered woman, wouldn't you have been thinking about yourself and your body and how you fit within sex more?'"

Instead, she was stuck "having sex to see the reaction of other people.

"It was still all a performance. It all went back to: 'How can I exist in a way that is most soothing to men, erotic to men, least offensive to men, and most interesting to men?' With sending nudes and everything like that—the only thing I got out of that was compliments, which seemed like fair currency. But they got all the power. I just told myself that it was mine."

The problem, as Francesca's experience makes clear, is that a string of one-night stands doesn't exactly lead to political change, respect, or even pleasure. A 2012 study found that, for female undergraduates, "a hookup with intercourse" led to an orgasm just 24 percent of the time. Without intercourse, they orgasmed 8 percent of the time.[43]

Many of the men who participated in the study said they wanted to make sure their girlfriends orgasmed because it made them feel manly. (Remember, "real" men are supposed to be good at obtaining and doing sex.) But men didn't feel as obligated to women with whom they'd had casual sex. One man in the study confidently informed researchers, "I'm all about just making her orgasm."

"The general her or like the specific her?" a researcher asked.

"Girlfriend her," he replied. "In a hookup her, I don't give a shit."[44]

Men got to enjoy women's desire to be "good, giving, and game," as popular sex advice columnist Dan Savage put it, but rarely acted like they owed their partners anything in return. (Remember how no one performed oral sex on me in high school?) And because 2010s pop feminism was so committed to uplifting casual and adventurous sex, it strengthened the hookup culture narrative and obscured its inaccuracies.

By the mid-2010s, some feminist writers had started to publicly question this setup. "Young feminists have adopted an exuberant, raunchy, confident, righteously unapologetic, slut-walking ideology that sees sex—as long as it's consensual—as an expression of feminist liberation," Rebecca Traister wrote in *New York* magazine in 2015. "A vast expanse of bad sex—joyless, exploitative encounters that reflect a persistently sexist culture and can be hard to acknowledge without sounding prudish—has gone largely uninterrogated, leaving some young women wondering why they feel so fucked by fucking."[45]

This feeling has not gone away. It may even be part of the explanation for the sex recession among millennials and Gen Z. What if, rather than submitting to "joyless, exploitative encounters," people—and in particular women—are just abstaining? Debby Herbenick, a professor at the Indiana University School of Public Health–Bloomington, proposed a version of this theory in the *Washington Post* in 2017, around the time more late millennials were reporting having less sex. "In my research, while some say they would like more frequent sex, what most people say they want is greater connection and meaning within sex," Herbenick wrote, adding, "More women now initiate sex or decline sex they don't want, even with their spouse."[46]

I would like to believe that Herbenick is right—that the hand-wringing over the sex recession is an overblown reaction to a positive development, that young people's relative sexlessness is because they are thoughtfully postponing or declining sex out of a refusal to compromise themselves, that puriteens (such as they exist) are onto something. I would like to dismiss the whole narrative as fearmongering, just like the hookup culture narrative. And it is true that, in the 2020s, more women have publicly spoken up about embracing celibacy, often in response to men who treat them poorly. But while media reports of this phenomenon have largely focused on young women, recent Kinsey Institute research indicates that, while about one in six American women are "single by choice" and avoiding sexual activity, most of those women are fifty-five or older; younger women were also more likely to be dissatisfied with their nonexistent sex lives.[47] When a woman named Mahkaylah started college, she told *The Cut* in 2024, she found most of her female peers had zero interest in celibacy. "So honestly, it's looking like it's only a me thing," Mahkaylah said.[48]

In my own interviews, I found that the sex recession was hurting people. That's not because sex is inherently good for us, but because *not* having sex remains so profoundly stigmatized. Sixty-one percent of Gen Z women, raised in the era of 2010s pop feminism and its aftermath, now identify as feminists,[49] but despite that embrace—or because of it—many still feel like virginity is a personal failure.

Like me, twenty-year-old Maddy has cried because she was so convinced she would never have sex. The very word "virgin," with its shroud of purity culture, felt so outdated. Still, Maddy couldn't shake the conviction that "if you had sex, you were cooler.

"I felt very undesirable because I grew up in a very white community. I didn't ever have a crush. No one liked me," continued Maddy, who is of Chinese descent and grew up in Michigan. Their pronouns are she/they. "I was the funny kid, and that's how I was identified by my friends. Because of that, I was viewed as asexual by my friends. It was very much like: 'Oh yeah, Maddy's a *virgin*. Maddy's the *virgin* of the group." Maddy spat the word "virgin," as if the label still rankled.

Even people who truly have no interest in sex can't escape the stigma of virginity. Sarah, a twenty-four-year-old who is embarking on a career as a neuroscientist, has never had any kind of sex and never plans to. An asexual woman raised in rural New York, Sarah has always found the idea of sex repulsive, like biting into a jellyfish. Sure, she's idly curious what it would taste like. But really, she knows it would be disgusting.

"The logical part of my brain is like, 'It doesn't matter.' But people do infantilize me," Sarah said. "People think that I have less wisdom about life, that I don't know love, I don't know what it is to be an adult despite having supported myself for almost ten years now. There's a sense that I'm still a child because I haven't had sex."

"SYSTEMS ARE FALLING APART"

Pop feminism, so obsessed with women's sexual freedoms, failed to do anything lasting to protect them. While it was telling female late millennials to solve their problems by leaning in or hooking up, the GOP had devised a plan—code-named "REDMAP"—to retake state legislatures in the 2010 midterms, in the hopes that Republicans could control states' redistricting in 2011[50] and give themselves an electoral edge for years to come. The plan was extraordinarily successful: By the time the curtains closed on the 2010 midterms, Republicans controlled 53 percent of the nation's legislative seats, more than at any point since 1928.[51] Then they got to work. Between 2010 and 2016, state legislatures enacted 334 abortion restrictions, which—at the time—accounted for 30 percent of all abortion restrictions since the Supreme Court decided *Roe* in 1973.[52] These restrictions laid the groundwork for demolishing *Roe* and, ultimately, making sex seem too complicated for comfort.

While politicians push narratives around sex and the sex recession to further their own goals, touting sexual conservatism as a fix to the supposed excesses of sexual progressivism, they are skating over the possibility that their own rhetoric may be contributing to the sex recession. The tumultuous state of post-2016 U.S. politics itself might just be making people who would like to have sex too depressed to do so, which isn't exactly great for the mental health of those who already feel isolated by their inexperience.

U.S. youth are mired in a terrifying mental health crisis. In the CDC's latest Youth Risk Behavior Survey, 42 percent of high school students said they experienced "persistent feelings of sadness or hopelessness."[53] One in ten had attempted suicide.[54] These statistics are on the rise and notably dire among students who are female, Black, or Indigenous, or who identify as LGBQ+.* Male students may also be underreporting their own feelings, because boys are so often encouraged to bury their emotions or channel sadness into other outlets, such as rage.

This mental health crisis is arguably even worse among young adults. About a third of young adults between the ages of eighteen and twenty-five experience anxiety and depression, roughly double the share of teenagers.[55] Millennials tended to have better mental health at that age,[56] but between 2007 and 2017, suicide rates among eighteen-to-thirty-four-year-olds—millennials and the beginning of Gen Z—increased by 35 percent.[57]

This mental health crisis has political dimensions. Adult Gen Z-ers who are Democrats are twice as likely as their Republican peers to experience depression, anger, loneliness, and anxiety.[58] And when Harvard researchers asked young adults why they felt so anxious and depressed, they brought up political issues. More than a third pointed to school gun violence, abortion bans, and climate change as a reason for their poor mental health. Thirty percent blamed "corrupt politicians." Almost half cited the "sense that things are falling apart."[59]

---

*The survey didn't include information about participants who identified as trans or nonbinary.

Gen Z also knows it can't rely on political and legal institutions to fix things. Less than a quarter trust the Supreme Court, 14 percent trust the presidency, and 12 percent trust Congress.[60] It's not hard to see why. I'm sure that every generation believes that they were born at the end of the world, but millennials and Gen Z really were. If the frenzied growth of artificial intelligence doesn't kill us, the rapidly changing climate will.

"In terms of the mammalian social behavior and physiology, if you're in a threat response or a fear response, it's not conducive to mating psychology," said Garcia, who is an evolutionary biologist by training. "You don't see two gazelles mating in front of a lion." Our country's unstable politics, Garcia hypothesized, may have turned us all into gazelles. In 2024, internet It Girl Julia Fox, a millennial, voiced this sentiment on *Watch What Happens Live*. "With the overturning of *Roe v. Wade* and our rights being stripped away from us, this is a way that I can take back the control," she told host Andy Cohen of her decision to be celibate. "It just sucks that it has to be in that way. But I just don't feel comfortable until things change."

While politics makes some people too stressed out to be turned on, poor mental health, a lack of social connection, and sexlessness are simultaneously linked in a chicken-or-egg cycle. The more depressed you are, the more likely you are to stay home alone; the more you stay home alone, the deeper you tend to sink into depression. It's not clear whether the loneliness crisis has caused the mental health crisis, although mental health issues spiked among young people starting around 2010, when smartphones and social media started to become far more common. We also know that if you are lonely and unpartnered, you are almost certainly having less sex.

Over and over, interviewees told me that their anxiety and depression—and the medications required to treat both—had negatively impacted their sex lives or their ability to navigate the kind of interpersonal dynamics needed to have partnered sex. "The world fucking sucks," said Ethan, the twenty-year-old from Ohio. "Your generation came into this as being the first to do worse than the generation before you. We're continuing that pattern. And that's not really fucking fine. Everything around us is getting worse. Systems are falling apart. A fucking extinction event is gonna fucking come, because no one can get their shit together."

He has anxiety and depression. In case it's not obvious, I do too.

THE HOUSE OF VIRGINITY

Despite these less-than-encouraging circumstances, there is reason to hope. Sure, most Americans will have partnered sex at some point and stop agonizing over their virginities. But far more importantly, some young people are embracing sexual progressivism by reconceptualizing sex in ways that evince an inclusive outlook on sex and its place in society. Even if the sex recession spreads in coming years, these efforts will hopefully lead individuals to feel better about their sex lives (or lack thereof). And as these young people age and acquire more influence in U.S. society— or seize it through activism—their sexual progressivism may lessen our national conviction that, regardless of whether young people are having too much or too little sex, they are always doing it wrong. Sexual conservatives' critiques might be drained of their power.

Although interviewees usually said they had once believed that losing your virginity meant having penis-in-vagina sex, many also said their definition of sex had evolved and expanded as they got older. This was in part due to the fact that around a quarter of Gen Z identifies as LGBTQ+.[61] Frequently, interviewees' realization of their own queerness or their interactions with LGBTQ+ peers had led them to reassess how they saw sex.

"Definitely having sex, like penetrative sex with a man—that was [the definition of] virginity [loss] to me. And so I graduated high school thinking, 'Oh my God, I'm a virgin in college. This is the worst thing ever,'" recalled Molly, a twenty-one-year-old Texan. But as she surrounded herself with more people who identified as LGBTQ+, she stopped fixating on it so much and came out as queer. She hasn't had sex with a man—she's no longer sure she's even attracted to them—but she has had sex with a woman, "depending on the definition there."

Molly also began to reframe her sexual experiences from high school. "I wasn't having penetrative sex with my boyfriend in high school, but we were having oral sex," she said. "That also was sex."

It was the LGBTQ+ interviewees who, rather than overly fixating on virginity, most often felt at peace with their sexual status, regardless of whether they had had it, were having it, or none of the above. For LGBTQ+ people, people with disabilities, and other individuals whose bodies and desires may not match Hallmark depictions of romance, the definition of "virginity" has long been elastic. It has to be—or else plenty of people with firsthand experience of penises, vaginas, and other assorted genitalia would still be virgins.

"It's a weird social concept that's very tied to purity culture," Clare, a queer nineteen-year-old from Montana, said of virginity. "I always felt a little weird in high school because I'd never been in a relationship. It felt like a thing I needed to do." Quietly, she added, "I didn't talk to anyone about this, because God forbid."

She still has not had sex. But now that Clare is in college, she's realized, "No one actually cares that much. And if it's something I want to do for me, then sure. But it's not like a box you need to check off on the Normal Teenager Checklist."

Up until recently, there was very little research into LGBTQ+ folks' thoughts on virginity. But in 2014, in one of the first studies to examine the topic, people were split: Many thought penetration was key to losing your virginity, but others believed virginity loss could be a multistep event.[62] Maybe you lose your virginity through heterosexual sex, before losing it again through homosexual sex. Or maybe you lose it a little more each time you experiment with a new sex act.

"Virginity is like a house," one man told researchers. "The front door is kind of that very first time that you're no longer playing doctor and have the intention of intimate contact with another person, no matter what the degree. Once you pass that doorway then you get into the main hall, then there's side doors where each room is giving a different experience via mutual masturbation for the first time, oral sex—giving or receiving, anal sex—giving or receiving. There's different virginal experiences."[63]

Generally, though, there was a sense among study participants that virginity didn't matter all that much, that virginity was a heterosexual concept shoved down LGBTQ+ people's throats. Having sex for the "first time," knowing what to do with someone else's body—that mattered. But, researchers noted, participants didn't use the term "virginity" on their own. They had to be prompted.[64] "Virginity" was just not part of their vocabulary.

I admire that focus on sexual exploration rather than achievement. Clearly, an obsession with virginity imperiled the mental health of people like Ethan, Maddy, and me. Although I have zero complaints about the night I lost my virginity, I wish I could have let myself open up about my sexual history with both my then-partner and my friends. Rather than pretending the experience was nothing new, I could have celebrated a milestone that was, right or wrongly, important to me. If I had let myself be vulnerable much earlier in my sex life, I might have set myself up to have not only much better sex, but a better time living in my own skin—regardless of whether I was between the sheets.

To return to a question I posed earlier: What is sex, exactly? In my interviews, people agreed that to lose your virginity, there had to be another person (or persons) present; you can't masturbate your way out of being a virgin. But they often struggled to come up with an answer when I asked them to define what sex looks like to them now. Even among straight people, other forms of sex have begun to count more frequently. Most college students believe anal intercourse counts toward losing your virginity,[65] despite the long-standing belief that anal can be a way to get laid while staying a virgin. A majority of young people say oral sex counts, too.[66]

My interviewees frequently avoided giving a concrete answer.

"It's like a *vibe*," said Jessie, a queer nonbinary nineteen-year-old from New Jersey, their voice shivering with innuendo. "I'm using so many words to try to describe this, because as I'm saying it to you, I'm also trying to process it in my head. What does it actually mean? I don't know!"

In all my conversations for this book, my favorite definition of sex came from Clare.

"What, to you, would count as sex?" I asked.

Clare thought about it. "If there's pants on the floor," she said. She paused. "Intentionally."

Without ever quite articulating it to myself, that's the definition of sex that I've used for years. The intention makes the difference. When I sleep with my partner, we may fool around for a while before potentially indulging in penetrative sex—or we might not ever get to that point. At what point do those activities start to count as "sex"? And when does the sex end? If I were fooling around with someone else, my actions might be the same, but my answers to these questions might not be. I am telling myself an ouroboros of a story: *I'm having sex with my partner. Everything we're doing right now is sex.*

It's sex because I say it is. Sex is always whatever we say it is. Politicians and pundits can map all kinds of narratives onto how generations are or aren't having sex, in order to push all kinds of agendas. But as individuals, having sex or not having sex doesn't need to matter all that much if we say it doesn't—as long as we are equipping young people with a quality education that helps them make informed choices about sex.

Spoiler: We're not.

2.

GENERATION GUINEA PIG
The Billion-Dollar Campaign for Abstinence-Only Sex Ed

Pretty much every scene in the 2004 film *Mean Girls* could claim cinematic immortality, but just one runs through my head every time I think of the term "sex ed." In the scene, Coach Carr, the wildly incompetent gym teacher (and secret sexual predator), stands in front of a whiteboard that reads, "SAFE SEX." The word "abstinence" is circled beneath it. "Don't have sex, 'cause you will get pregnant and die," he warns a group of dead-eyed students. "Don't have sex in the missionary position. Don't have sex standing up. Just don't do it, promise?"

Carr pauses. "Alright, everybody take some rubbers."

In about fifteen seconds, *Mean Girls* skewered the fundamental premise of sex education in the United States: Sex is dangerous because pregnancy. Also, we can't really stop you from having it, but let's pretend.

Coach Carr's fumble of a lecture was supposed to be a parody. But in interview after interview, as Gen Z and late millennials recited the lessons they'd learned from their schools' sex ed, their teachers sounded uncannily like Coach Carr.

"Don't do it. You'll get pregnant. You'll get chlamydia," one nineteen-year-old from Massachusetts said she was told. "And it's gonna hurt. You're gonna bleed. They're gonna pop your cherry."

"Don't have sex. You'll be shamed for life," another woman, a twenty-year-old from the Southeast, recalled hearing. "You should not have sex. Don't do that till you get married." (I spoke to this unmarried woman at an abortion clinic, shortly before she underwent the procedure.)

Several of my interviewees' sex ed instructors were, in fact, gym teachers. Cameron, a nineteen-year-old from Florida, said he had to listen to

40 | CARTER SHERMAN

his gym teacher tell his class that having sex was "a very poor choice and it will lead to further poor choices," including but not limited to non-virgins' going to jail, becoming a drain on the state government, contracting a sexually transmitted infection, and ultimately having their genitalia amputated.

Images were supplied.

"There wasn't anything about safe sex. To my knowledge, there wasn't anything about contraceptives or anything like that. There wasn't even the token condom presentation with whatever banana. Just abstinence only. Just the negative things that can happen," Cameron said. "Just the most repulsive kind of traditionalism."

From its earliest days, American sex ed has been overtly hostile to the actual practice of sex. Formalized, government-sponsored sex ed in schools emerged in the aftermath of World War I, when national support for sex ed skyrocketed amid concerns about STIs and children born out of wedlock. But those pressing public health crises weren't enough to make people cast aside sexual conservatism, according to public health historian Alexandra Lord's history of U.S. sex ed, *Condom Nation*. The sex ed of the era believed that "properly educated young adults would follow 'a life of continence [or abstinence] before marriage'; after marriage, fidelity would follow naturally," Lord wrote, quoting 1918 government documents about sex ed. "Fundamentally, good sex education, newspapers sternly reminded their readers, taught that 'there is no compromise with vice in the nationwide effort toward higher morality.'"[1]

We are now more than a century into the era of government-sponsored sex ed in American schools, and stunningly little has changed—even though the needs of sex ed have been utterly redefined as attitudes around sex have evolved and sex has become inescapable online. If anything, the government's approach to sex ed has even become more sexually conservative, more committed to the impossible goal of stamping out premarital and non-heterosexual sex. In 1995, more than 80 percent of adolescents said they were formally educated about birth control. By 2013, between 55 and 60 percent said the same.[2]

Although there is no nationwide curriculum that all U.S. schools must teach students when it comes to sex, the federal government plays an enormous role in setting the tone of the national conversation around sex

THE SECOND COMING | 41

ed because it has directed billions of dollars toward supporting it. And over the past twenty-five years, late millennials and Gen Z-ers have become the guinea pigs of a national experiment to champion abstinence-only-until-marriage sex ed to an unprecedented degree—an experiment that some red states have taken even further. While other Western democracies have moved away from abstinence-only sex ed in recent years, the United States' continued devotion to it means the country has, in philosopher Lauren Bialystok's words, "mirrored and joined hands with global conservative movements, traditional sexist cultures, and even theocracies."[3]

A lack of formal education in how to have safe, consensual sex can change someone's life forever. When Grace, a twenty-two-year-old from Oklahoma, was diagnosed with herpes in college, she asked her provider, "Oh, so I'll just take an antibiotic, right?" It was not until the provider started to detail a yearslong medication regime that Grace realized: *Oh my God, this is for life.*

"I had no idea," she told me. "It was at that point where I was like, 'Wow, sex ed failed me.'"

Sex ed is determined by a patchwork of federal, state, and local laws and initiatives. As of this writing, thirty-eight states and Washington, D.C., require schools to educate students about sex, HIV, or both, according to the Guttmacher Institute, which tracks sexual and reproductive health laws. When schools do offer sex ed, twenty-nine states—more than half the country—require that abstinence be stressed, while nineteen states insist teachers emphasize the importance of sex occurring within a marriage. Only sixteen states require that, when provided, sex ed must be medically accurate. Just four say sex ed cannot promote religion.

Regardless of what's written into the law, there's often very little oversight or enforcement of schools' approach to sex ed. This is true even in places believed to be liberal havens, like New York City. "The New York City public school system is enormous. It is notoriously bureaucratic," said Rachel Lotus, a New York City public school teacher turned sex educator. "I can't imagine how many people would have to be employed to really oversee what is happening at each individual school."

Every two years, the CDC surveys states, territories, tribal lands, and major school districts to evaluate what students are learning about health in middle and high school. In 2022, the most recent year for which data is available and which included info from forty-four states, about 69 percent of middle schools nationwide taught about the benefits of being sexually abstinent.[4] Taken at face value, this fact isn't exactly damning. Abstinence is the only sexual lifestyle that completely prevents pregnancy and STIs, so students should learn about that option. More than 80 percent of adults—regardless of their political persuasion—support schools providing what is known as "abstinence-plus," a model of sex ed that frames abstinence as the best choice but that also provides information about other ways of preventing pregnancy and STIs.[5] This model, one sex educator told me, is more popular than apple pie.

However, only a fraction of schools ever get around to the "plus," the CDC found. Less than half teach students that it's important to use condoms consistently and correctly. Only 37 percent teach them how to actually obtain condoms.[6]

In total, a quarter of middle schools in 2022 taught about all twenty-two sexual health topics recommended (but, again, not required) by the U.S. government. While more high schools teach these topics, just 45 percent teach them all.[7] Moreover, many interviewees told me that by the time high school rolled around, their sex ed felt even more out of touch. Sexual mores had already emerged and set in. By that age, they needed not rhetoric but resources: how to find and use birth control, how to report sexual assault.

On paper, my home state of Washington has strong sex ed policies. In 2007—the year I entered seventh grade, where I received my second round of public school sex ed—Washington state legislators enacted a law requiring public schools to teach comprehensive, scientifically accurate sex ed that did not just focus on abstinence and that recognized that students hail from a diversity of backgrounds. (One crucial caveat: This law applied only to schools that already taught sex ed.) But all I remember from my high school sex ed is making a PowerPoint about the dangers of syphilis and watching a video of a woman giving birth to a thirteen-pound baby. I have no memory of learning about consent. No one ever told me what to do if my boundaries were violated. And although I grew up in the liberal mecca of Seattle, where support for LGBTQ+ rights was and remains widespread, there wasn't even a whisper about the possibility that we students might one day have non-heteronormative sex.

My teachers did not morally condemn the concept of premarital or LGBTQ+ sex. They didn't overtly shame people who were interested in it. But they did their best to scare us out of sex, to pathologize it.

Years after I moved out of Seattle, Macy went to high school on the opposite side of Washington state, in a conservative, sports-obsessed small town. That town had almost nothing in common with Seattle, other than the fact that both were bound by Washington's relatively progressive sex ed laws. But in Macy's town, as in mine, those laws weren't enough to guarantee quality sex ed.

Unlike me, Macy did get a lesson on consent. It was adamant, if truncated: She was taught that "no means no." But while that mantra might be easy enough to mouth, it ignores the complexity of sexual assault, especially within the cloistered hierarchy of high school. Macy was never told about her rights and options if someone were to ignore that mantra—and someone did.

Because Macy lived in what she called "the boonies," she depended on a classmate, an athlete, for rides to school and cheerleading practice, which she saw as a lifeline out of a desperately unhappy home life. The price of those rides was putting up with repeated sexual assaults, Macy said.

"He was very much 'no does *not* mean no,'" she said. When they drove home, he would grab Macy's hand and put it on "himself," as Macy put it, while Macy stared out the window. She wanted to leave her body behind.

One night, the pair drove back from a game. It was late—after midnight, as Macy recalled it. At some point along the dirt road, the athlete suddenly stopped the car. He unbuckled Macy's seat belt, picked her up out of her seat, and pinned her between the driver's side door and the steering wheel. He then forcefully penetrated her with his fingers, said Macy, who recalled telling him "no," "stop," and "take me home." He didn't listen.

She managed to get out of the car. Pissed off, the athlete drove away, abandoning her in the dark. Macy cried throughout the mile-long walk back to her house. She kept crying as she got home, got in the shower, and rubbed her skin raw.

Reporting him to the school was never a serious possibility. She wasn't even totally sure how that process would work, anyway. Some of the few people she did confide in about what had happened suggested that she was "doing it for attention," Macy said.

No one's gonna believe me over him, because he's older than me, because he's more respected than I am, Macy thought at the time. Now, looking back, she knows: "In my teenage, traumatized brain, I was more scared of what could happen to me than of what would happen to him."

Sex ed alone cannot solve sexual assault. But Macy's experience brings up one of the fundamental questions about sex ed that emphasizes abstinence to the exclusion of in-depth information about, well, everything else: If you only ever tell students to say no to sex, what are they supposed to do when someone hears "no" and does not stop?

A FEDERAL VIRGINITY CAMPAIGN

The modern era of federally funded, abstinence-only sex ed dates back to 1981, when two Republican senators, Jeremiah Denton of Alabama and Orrin Hatch of Utah, rammed the Adolescent Family Life Act through Congress. Embedded in that year's Omnibus Budget Reconciliation Act and signed into law by President Ronald Reagan, the Adolescent Family Life Act passed with zero hearings but redefined American sex ed by directing millions of federal dollars[8] toward programs intended "to promote chastity and self-discipline."[9] In 1988, one in fifty sex ed teachers taught in abstinence-only programs. By 1999, one in four did.[10] The American Civil Liberties Union (ACLU) accused the law of using government money to "subsidize religious indoctrination as a means of opposing premarital sex, abortion, and birth control for teenagers,"[11] and took the case all the way to the Supreme Court. The law survived, but a settlement later restricted the Adolescent Family Life Act from funding sex ed that referenced religion.[12]

Under George W. Bush's administration, which came to power as late millennials were entering K-12 school, funding for abstinence-only sex ed exploded in a way that was "unprecedented in American history and unique among the nations of the contemporary world," in the words of virginity scholar Hanne Blank.[13] Between 2001 and 2005, the annual federal funding of abstinence-only programs more than doubled, with hundreds of millions of dollars gushing into programs devoted to incentivizing states to promote abstinence.[14] By the end of Bush's presidency, the feds had spent more than $1 billion on abstinence-only sex ed.[15]

This was, according to Blank, a massive virginity program. Sure, these sex ed programs did not publicly label themselves as pro-virginity. (The word "virginity" itches with religion.) But if a government is supporting a program intended to convince people who have not yet had sex to remain abstinent until marriage, that government is supporting a virginity program.

In other words: While I was desperate to lose my virginity, the federal government was running a billion-dollar campaign to convince me to keep it.

It did not work. Rather than being rehabilitated, virginity has become instead more uncool. More importantly, numerous studies have found that abstinence-only sex ed does not lead young people to delay their "sexual debut"—as researchers call it—or to have fewer sexual partners.[16] The federal government should know this: A study supported by the Department of Health and Human Services found that students who underwent federally funded abstinence-only sex ed were likely to lose their virginity at the same time as people who did not undergo that sex ed.[17] The two groups even had a similar number of sexual partners.[18] (The sex recession thus cannot be chalked up to abstinence-only sex ed.)

Concerningly, some studies have discovered that people who receive abstinence-only sex ed are more likely to practice unsafe sex or to be made to feel bad about themselves. Compared to female students who got more inclusive sex ed, female students who underwent abstinence-only sex ed are less likely to use condoms the first time they have sex.[19] Students of color in states with abstinence-focused sex ed have also said their teachers often assumed that they were sexually active, incapable of abstinence, and uninterested in or already informed about safe sex practices. "Why are we assuming that everyone knows about sex?" one Black student asked researchers.[20]

In 2004, a report prepared for Rep. Henry Waxman, a California Democrat, found that over 80 percent of the abstinence-only curricula that had been funded by a U.S. government program were riddled with "false, misleading, or distorted information."[21] One curriculum told students that up to 10 percent of women who get legal abortions become sterile.[22] (They do not.) Another said condoms do not stop the spread of STIs.[23] (They do.) Yet another called a forty-three-day-old embryo a "thinking person."[24] (An embryo at that stage of pregnancy doesn't even have a fully developed heart, much less a brain.)

Several curricula reinforced sexist stereotypes. One told students that women need "financial support" and "devotion" from men, while men want "domestic support" and "admiration" from women.[25] Another featured the story of a knight who refuses to marry a princess because she is better than him at killing dragons. "Moral of the story: Occasional suggestions and assistance may be alright, but too much of it will lessen a man's confidence or even turn him away from his princess," the curriculum declared.[26] These lessons frame men as sexual aggressors and women as the grateful gatekeepers of sex and domesticity, reinforcing attitudes that contribute to sexual assault, domestic violence, and other horrifying relationship dynamics.

It turned out that the federal agency tasked with doling out hundreds of millions of dollars to sex ed programs did very little to review those programs' scientific accuracy.[27] Even after Waxman's report unleashed widespread outrage, the feds merely asked sex ed programs to attest that their materials were medically accurate. Many kept right on using inaccurate materials.[28]

After Barack Obama won the presidency in 2008 with his glossy promises of "hope and change," his administration defunded the Adolescent Family Life Act. Still, the Obama administration couldn't give up on the country's century-long love affair with abstinence. Because Democrats have never been reliable advocates of sexual progressivism, the Obama administration continued to dump hundreds of millions of dollars into abstinence-only education through new programs, including through sneaky pathways in Obama's signature piece of legislation, the Affordable Care Act.[29]

In 2009, Obama signed into law a groundbreaking initiative called the Teen Pregnancy Prevention Program. The program boosted funding for evidence-based sex ed programs, a qualification that knocked almost all abstinence-only programs out of competition for funding and, instead, prioritized abstinence-plus sex ed as well as what is known as "comprehensive sex ed."

Given the anemic state of U.S. sex ed, abstinence-plus sex ed is better than what's on offer in many classrooms, but many sex ed experts—including several major medical groups and the World Health Organization—recommend that students receive comprehensive sex ed. Originally conceived in 1991,[30] making it about as old as late millennials, this umbrella term refers to age-appropriate sex ed that can include a range of information about everything from STI and pregnancy prevention to healthy relationships to media literacy. When done right, these kinds of programs have been shown to increase use of contraception,[31] reduce sexism and intimate partner violence, and prevent child sex abuse.[32] They can also lead students to have sex later on in life and with fewer partners.[33]

Between 2010 and 2015, half a million teenagers participated in sex ed funded by the Teen Pregnancy Prevention Program.[34] And, over the course of the Obama administration, teen birth rates took a steep plunge.[35]

Abstinence-only education did not suddenly start working. Rather, the opposite happened: Adolescents started using contraception a lot more.[36] Obama and the Teen Pregnancy Prevention Program deserve a lot of the credit for that change.

Enter Donald Trump.

Trump has never been a paragon of sexual conservatism. After all, the man has publicly waffled on issues like abortion, been married three times, and was criminally convicted for his role in a scheme to pay off a porn star who said they'd had sex. But he has been more than willing to carry water for the cause. Mere months after Trump took over the White House in 2017, his administration abruptly yanked more than $200 million worth of programs from eighty-plus institutions around the country.[37] Courts later found that Trump's actions were unlawful, but the turbulence was deeply destabilizing.

The Trump administration also pumped stunning amounts of money into abstinence-only education. However, rather than saying they're teaching "abstinence," the federal government now likes to say it's educating kids about "sexual risk avoidance."

The feds didn't dream up this term on their own. The government's adoption of "sexual risk avoidance" was the result of a yearslong campaign by activists who realized that reports like Henry Waxman's had made the term "abstinence" radioactive. In 2012, the National Abstinence Education Association, the preeminent advocacy organization for abstinence-only sex ed, changed its name to the girlboss-esque "Ascend" and transitioned to talking about "sexual risk avoidance." In fiscal year 2016, while Obama was still president, Congress started using the term in a grant program—which speaks to sexual conservatism's ability to gain traction even under a liberal president.[38] After Trump moved into the White House, his administration hired Valerie Huber, Ascend's president, to work at the Department of Health and Human Services. Between 2017 and 2020, the federal government spent $520 million on "sexual risk avoidance education,"[39] or abstinence-only education by another name.

The Trump administration also proselytized for "sexual risk avoidance" overseas. In a secretive United Nations meeting, Huber said women should learn sexual "refusal skills." "She spoke of 'trying to get women to make better choices in the future,' which is that terrifying and outmoded idea that women make bad sexual choices and that what happens to them is their fault," one meeting attendee told *Buzzfeed News*.[40]

In her 2007 book *Virgin*, written when the word "abstinence" was still in vogue, Blank marveled at the strategic brilliance of abstinence advocates' swerve away from the word "virginity." Virgins need someone to initiate them into sex; such powerlessness is embarrassing. "Abstinence, on the other hand, is associated with virtuous self-control. Critically, it offers the impression of choice," Blank wrote. "One *is* a virgin, but one *chooses* to abstain. Using the word 'abstinence' in this context suggests the quintessentially American ideal of self-determination and choice. It verbally transforms compliance with government propaganda into a celebration of personal liberty."[41]

The same philosophy undergirds the modern use of the phrase "sexual risk avoidance." While the nasally "abstinence" can evoke caricatures of nerds who can't get laid or sister-wives in sack-like skirts, "sexual risk avoidance" sounds so much more genteel and scientific, like a call to both safety and action.

The end result, though, is the same: a Coach Carr telling kids not to have sex.

THE SECOND COMING | 49

After Joe Biden defeated Trump in the 2020 presidential election, Biden reversed the Trump administration's changes to the Teen Pregnancy Prevention Program. But even as it distributed more than $100 million in program grants to dozens of organizations looking to implement evidence-based sex ed, the Biden administration continued to champion abstinence, like the Obama administration before it. In fiscal year 2023, $110 million in federal dollars flowed to "sexual risk avoidance" sex ed.[42]

By that point, the United States had already spent more than $2.15 billion on abstinence-only education,[43] and it still had one of the highest rates of teen pregnancy among rich countries.[44] Between 2018 and 2024, cases of syphilis, a disease once nearly eliminated in the United States, soared by 80 percent, marking the highest rate of recorded new infections since 1950[45] (which is even more striking in light of the sex recession).

Sexual conservatism, always a guiding principle of government-sponsored sex ed in the United States, is now lodged so deeply in the federal approach to sex ed that I doubt a president will ever stop dumping tax dollars into abstinence-only-until-marriage programs. And as sexual conservatism continues to tighten its grip on U.S. education, red states offer a preview of what it looks like when sexual conservatism has the government in a white-knuckle hold. Texas, in particular, reveals how sexual conservatism can come to dominate sex ed, what this domination means for students growing up there—especially in conjunction with other sexually conservative policies—and how sexually progressive young activists are already pushing back.

OUR FUTURE IS TEXAS

Let's time-travel to summer 2008. George W. Bush was on his way out. Barack Obama had just cinched the Democratic nomination for president. I was fourteen, convinced I had no friends, and far more interested in the politics of my middle school than those of the White House. I spent many of my summer afternoons daydreaming on my bedroom floor, listening to a Michelle Branch CD and longing for my real life to begin. Despite my best efforts, I was still a child.

50 | CARTER SHERMAN

More than two thousand miles away, in the sunlit concrete swamp that is Houston, Justine Ang Fonte was teaching summer school to eighth graders. Although her students were roughly my age, many had already been forced to leave childhood behind. According to Fonte, two of her twenty-four students were parents, two were pregnant, and one student missed two of the five weeks of summer school.

When the student returned, Fonte asked her where she had been.

"I'm sorry, miss," the student said, as Fonte recalled it. "I was really sick."

"What happened?" Fonte asked.

"Well, I was bleeding a lot."

"Where?"

"You know, down there."

"What do you mean, 'down there'?"

"Well, I don't know," the student said. "It just happens every month. And I don't know what's wrong with me." The bleeding had begun back when she was in sixth grade.

During lunch, Fonte went to the principal's office.

"You have a sixteen-year-old eighth grader who has failed eighth grade two years in a row and is gone for half the year because she's on her period and doesn't know it," Fonte told the principal.

"Oh, you're talking about Maria?" The principal sighed. "Yeah, that's a tough one."

That defeatist response astounded and enraged Fonte. "If you want me to teach math, I can't do it if students don't show up to school, so it sounds like you need to be teaching more than just math," Fonte argued. She wanted to know: Do the kids here get any lessons about puberty?

"Well, that falls under sex ed, and it's an abstinence-only state here in Texas," the principal said. (Texas does permit educators to teach sex ed beyond abstinence—it's just not welcoming to it.) The principal continued, "So, it's a slippery slope."

"It's also really bad if students aren't even showing up to school, because they can't do all the other subjects that you have not politicized," Fonte replied.

Fonte asked if she could teach sex ed rather than math for the last

THE SECOND COMING | 51

week of summer school. The principal said she could, so long as she avoided the words "homosexuality," "contraception," and "abortion."

"Well, I have a thesaurus," Fonte retorted.

Texas is something of a Rorschach test for northern liberals. Sometimes it is the starring character in a *West Wing*–level fantasy, a place that Democrats dream of flipping blue by electing toothy men like Beto O'Rourke. But when Texas does something that northern liberals are less than thrilled about, they choose to shrug it off rather than address it: *That's just Texas being Texas. What can you expect?*

"We like to look to the horizon instead of to the soil because we bury the people we do not care about in the South. It is where we have put migrants and poor people and sick people. It is where we put the social problems we are willing to accept in exchange for the promise of individual opportunity in places that sound more sophisticated," sociologist Tressie McMillan Cottom once wrote. "But the South is still a laboratory for the political disenfranchisement that works just as well in Wisconsin as it does in Florida. Americans are never as far from the graves we dig for other people as we hope."[46]

If we want to know what the future of young Americans' sexual and reproductive health holds, we should look to Texas. Home to thirty million people, including one in ten American women of reproductive age, Texas has long been sexual conservatives' favorite testing site for initiatives and restrictions that then get exported to other states. What starts off in Texas does not stay there.

In the early 2010s, Texas moved to become the first state in the country to effectively defund Planned Parenthood,[47] one of the foremost sex ed and sexual health providers in the country. In 2013, Texas passed a sweeping package of abortion restrictions that led half the state's abortion clinics to close their doors,[48] many to never return. And in 2021, when *Roe v. Wade*—a case that just so happened to originate in Texas—was still the law of the land, Texas became the first state to finagle a way around *Roe* and ban abortion past six weeks of pregnancy by allowing ordinary Texans to sue people they suspected of "aiding and abetting" illegal abortions. (If an abortion provider gets sued every time they "aid and abet" an abortion, they'll be too tied up in court and drowning in legal costs to do their job.)

Researchers later linked the six-week ban to the births of almost ten thousand babies over a nine-month period, indicating that those babies would not have been born had the ban never existed.[49] It was an early look at what has since happened to the rest of the country now that *Roe* has fallen.

Texan conservatives rejoiced at the news of increased births. "This new study highlights the significant success of our movement in the last two years, while we look forward to helping the mothers and families of our state care for their children," Texas Right to Life president John Seago told the *Texas Tribune*.[50]

By drawing a line between "mothers" and "children," Seago neatly elided an uncomfortable truth about Texas: Many of the people who give birth there are themselves children. Texas, which has a teen birth rate 33 percent higher than the national rate, has one of the United States' highest rates of "repeat teen births." About one in six Texas teenagers who gave birth in 2023 was already a parent. More than half of unmarried twenty-to-twenty-four-year-olds who gave birth were already parents, too.[51]

Given Texan politicians' interest in handicapping abortion providers and anybody who works with them, you might have imagined that the state invests in comprehensive sex ed to help prevent pregnancy. You might have also already guessed, correctly, that it does not. In her San Antonio–area middle school, Elle's sex ed consisted of an instructor bringing in a blind wheelchair user who warned them that his disabilities were due to HIV/AIDS. In her high school, educators flashed photos of STIs to scare them out of ever having sex. "Not once did they say, 'This is how you should put on a condom,'" said Elle, who is twenty-two. "I went to school with people who were mothers at the age of fifteen."

In fiscal year 2021, right around the time Texas kneecapped *Roe* with its six-week ban, Texas took home more than $7.5 million in federal funding to teach "sexual risk avoidance," more than any other state in the nation.[52]

Again, what starts off in Texas does not stay there. Because a tenth of all U.S. public school students live in Texas,[53] the state has long played an outsize role in setting the educational agenda for the entire United States. For decades, if the Texas State Board of Education didn't approve a textbook for its public school students, then the rest of the country was unlikely to see it, because publishers wanted to keep the massive Texas textbook market happy. Texas's command over the national market has weakened as it has become easier for publishers to customize books to states' preferences, but the sexual conservatives who hijacked the Texas textbook approval process in the 1960s proved that states can demand publishers rewrite history, science, and other topics to suit partisan politics—and publishers still continue that practice today. If your school textbook taught you that evolution was "just a theory," you might have Mel and Norma Gabler of Longview, Texas, to thank.

In 1962, the year the Supreme Court ruled that state-sponsored prayer in public schools violated the First Amendment, Norma Gabler made her first appearance at a Texas State Board of Education hearing.[54] Norma and her husband, Mel, had discovered that their son's encyclopedia had omitted the words "under God" from the Gettysburg Address.[55] When they examined his 1954 textbook, they were offended that the information inside had been updated from information contained in nineteenth-century textbooks.

"I'm Irish, and that got my Irish up," Norma told a reporter.[56]

The Gablers took a legitimate complaint—the Gettysburg Address *does* include the words "under God"—and turned it into a decades-long crusade, one whose focus was less about remedying inaccuracies and more about making sure American students could never again avoid the Christian God. By continuing to show up at state board of education hearings, the Gablers became what historian Andrew Hartman called "trusted fixtures" in the textbook approval processes.[57] Remarkably adept at throwing wrenches into the approval processes of books they did not like, the Gablers effectively convinced textbook and curriculum authors to start censoring themselves rather than risk their wrath.

In the Gablers' eyes, teaching kids about Robin Hood would encourage stealing.[58] When a textbook read, "The law that allowed slavery in America was wrong, so people could break the law," they said it sanctioned insubordination.[59] The couple seemed curiously incurious—and wanted everybody else to be, too. Any curriculum that left students with thought-provoking questions, rather than ironclad answers and values, was not to be trusted. In their view, there was no such thing as moral relativism; right and wrong were absolutes no matter the circumstances or epoch.

"What some textbooks are doing is giving students ideas, and ideas will never do them as much good as facts," Norma complained. But she also did not appear to want students to look up said facts on their own, once objecting to a fourth-grade book that suggested students should double-check facts. "It could lead to very dangerous information," she told the Texas State Board of Education, adding, "I just don't think questions should be asked unless the information has already been covered in the text."[60]

The Gablers' impact stretched far beyond the classroom. They shipped their materials out across the country and amassed influence within the conservative movement known as the "New Right," which effectively morphed into what we would now recognize as the religious right. (Jerry Falwell Sr. was a fan of the Gablers' work.) By the early 1980s, one censorship expert marveled that the Gablers were "the two most powerful people in education today."[61]

The Gablers understood that the way to a nation's political future lay through its children—and through stoking fear in families *about* their children. It's a lesson that modern-day conservatives still clutch as tightly as their pearls. The Gablers also understood that an unrelenting campaign by a dedicated minority can change the course of the entire United States. And that, not coincidentally, is exactly how the anti-abortion movement toppled *Roe*.

Unsurprisingly, the Gablers were no fans of school-based sex ed. They believed that marriage is a lifelong commitment between men and women,[62] that women should primarily aspire to become "mothers molding young lives," and that parents have the right to provide information about sex—or not. "Silence is a most underrated virtue," they said of sex ed. "Talk in the classroom is no substitute for a quiet example at home."[63]

Translation: God forbid anybody have a straightforward conversation about sex.

Today, Texas does not require that schools teach sex ed. If a school offers it, that sex ed course is not required to be medically accurate but must stress abstinence. And while high school educators who teach sex ed are able to discuss birth control methods other than abstinence, health class—and thus sex ed—became an elective in Texas high schools in 2009.[64] Between 2016 and 2020, less than a third of Texas high school students took a health class.[65]

During Paxton Smith's years in Dallas K-12 public schools, the only thing the Texas native ever learned about sex was that she should feel ashamed for wanting it. "The presenters only ever presented about abstinence," said Paxton, who is twenty. "That was the only thing they talked about."

In elementary school, during Paxton's first taste of sex ed, teachers divided her class up into boys and girls, then taught each class separately about puberty. I'd heard this story before. I had a similar sex ed class in fifth grade, and almost everybody I spoke to said their first sex ed class consisted of being split up into two genders in order to learn about their changing bodies and, sometimes, the science of reproduction. (Girls also usually learned about menstruation. "The boys got to play outside," one twenty-year-old from Houston recalled.) Paxton, however, offhandedly used a specific term to describe this kind of class, one I had never thought to use: She called it "gender education."

When people say the words "gender education," it's usually to kick off a heated battle over LGBTQ+ students and their rights. But dividing up children into two stereotypical genders and giving them stereotypical information about each gender is indeed an education in how to *be* a particular gender. It excludes the very real existence of children who exist outside the gender binary and can inculcate self-loathing in cisgender boys and girls. An analysis of Texas sex ed programs in the 2015–16 school year—which found that more than 80 percent of school districts taught abstinence-only sex ed or no sex ed at all—discovered that many programs portrayed men as "natural leaders, protectors, and sexual beings." Women, meanwhile, were taught to "look to men for rescue and 'shut up and be mysterious.'" (Remember the knight who left a princess because she dared to be competent?) The programs also depicted women who are interested in sex as "manipulative, unnatural, and not respectable."[66]

"Growing up in Dallas, Texas, of all places—your entire life, you're thrown into these gender categories," Paxton said. "They teach little girls how to act and they teach little boys how to act and they constantly divide them and group them and push them in certain ways.

56 | CARTER SHERMAN

"I hated being treated the way a girl was treated. I wanted to be treated like a boy. I wanted people to think that I was smart," she continued. Paxton started to oppose not only feminism, but girls and women in general. "I wasn't friends with girls, and I didn't play with girls. Done deal, didn't matter: Girls were bad and boys were good."

Paxton's middle school sex ed turned out to be less about sex and more about how to avoid it. One young female instructor spoke about being a virgin and turning down her prom date's pleas for sex. "I was like, 'Yeah, girl, you tell him no!'" said Paxton, her Texan twang clanging with each word. "She was talking about her friends in college who had sex before marriage, and she was talking about how almost all of them, if not all of them, regretted their choice, and that it had some kind of negative emotional impact that stuck with them over long periods of time."

Paxton's teachers talked about sex like it was a psychological STI. "They had this diagram that they showed us," she recalled. "If you have sex with two people, and if those two people have sex with two more people, and they have sex with two more people, *you* have been in contact with thousands of people. It was this weird idea of when you have sex with someone, that person sticks with you always and it comes with you into all of your future sexual encounters. You have no control over where the other person has been—so save it for marriage."

Paxton signed a virginity pledge in middle school. She then had zero sex ed in high school.

All this abstinence-only education has not led Texan teens to avoid "sexual risk." If anything, compared to high school students in the rest of the country, young Texans' sex lives are riskier. They are more likely to have had sex before the age of thirteen, more likely to have had sex with four or more people, and more likely to have forgone contraception the last time they had heterosexual sex.[67] Nationwide, students who take virginity pledges—which became common in abstinence-only education in the 1990s thanks to Christian evangelicals—lose their virginity around the same time as students who don't make such pledges.[68] Pledgers are also more likely to get pregnant outside marriage,[69] which isn't surprising, given that they are less likely to report using birth control or condoms in the past year.[70]

In 2021, Texas became one of a handful of states to decree that students could take sex ed only if their parents signed permission slips—

and the only state that required permission slips for abuse prevention education.[71] These kinds of requirements make it less likely that students will get sex ed;[72] the students who miss out on it may be the ones who need it the most, such as those facing sexual abuse. "Abusers will not grant permission to abused children," one Texas school district employee pointed out to researchers.[73]

There is at least one major other arena where Texas is blazing a trail in attacking sex ed: its Alternatives to Abortion program, which aims to persuade people not to have abortions. Founded in 2005,[74] the program has become the country's largest state-level, taxpayer-supported funding stream for crisis pregnancy centers, faith-based facilities whose main mission is convincing pregnant people not to get abortions. Between 2005 and 2021, Alternatives to Abortion's biennial funding spiked by 1,900 percent, to $100 million, as lawmakers stuffed its budget with tens of millions of dollars originally earmarked for programs that helped with air quality and health technology.[75] The fall of *Roe* further turbocharged that spending. In 2023, the Texas state legislature renamed the program "Thriving Texas Families" and approved sending it $165 million over the next two years.[76]

Crisis pregnancy centers, including at least fourteen funded by the Alternatives to Abortion program, have taught sex ed across dozens of Texas school districts, according to an investigation by the nonprofit newsroom the Hechinger Report. These centers usually stress abstinence above all else. One center's curriculum has told high school students that people who "go from sex partner to sex partner" could develop brain damage to the point that they struggle to form long-term relationships. Another center has performed ultrasounds in front of students. It's so obviously anti-abortion the center doesn't bother trying to hide it. "When we are able to show them a baby moving in the womb, it becomes a lot more tangible," its executive director told the Hechinger Report.[77]

In a 2019 tax return, one center that has taught sex ed in more than a dozen Texas school districts[78] said it gave almost nineteen thousand students "education presentations about sexual purity." That number far outstrips the roughly five hundred people to whom the center gave services like "crisis counsel," pregnancy testing, and STI screenings. Teaching sexual conservatism to young people may thus be how crisis pregnancy centers make their greatest impact.

Sam, the twenty-one-year-old Texan I mentioned in chapter one, went to a high school that outsourced its sex ed to a crisis pregnancy center. Mostly, he recalled, his sex ed focused on the dangers of STIs. He said the instructors showed gruesome pictures and told students that while some infections were curable, others were not, emphasizing the difficulty of treating even curable infections.

"I remember walking away terrified," Sam said. "I felt like I didn't have like any real information. What if I have already had sex, and I already had some [STI], and I don't know how to solve it? Now, I'm just supposed to feel bad about myself?

"It definitely made me not want to have sex or do anything because I was like, 'Oh, there's no options if this happens to me,'" Sam continued. He has no memory of any discussion of consent. Even pregnancy barely merited a mention. "It was just like, 'You don't have to worry about it if you maintain abstinence.' That was their number one message."

Texas isn't the only state where schools have invited crisis pregnancy centers to teach sex ed. Around 2016, Andrea Swartzendruber, a University of Georgia professor who studies crisis pregnancy centers, got a phone call from parents whose children went to a large public school district in Georgia. The parents were enraged: They had just learned that a crisis pregnancy center had been teaching their kids' sex ed.

"What they didn't know at that time was that the local crisis pregnancy center had been teaching in their school district for the past sixteen years," Swartzendruber recalled.

In 2022, more than half a million students attended "sexual risk avoidance education" taught by crisis pregnancy centers, according to the anti-abortion organization the Charlotte Lozier Institute.[79] That number is likely to go up. Since the overturning of *Roe*, at least sixteen states have sent more than $250 million of taxpayer money to programs that support crisis pregnancy centers.[80]

AN ACCIDENTAL ACTIVIST

I first talked to Paxton Smith not for this book, but because she went viral.

In 2021, Paxton's Dallas-area high school named her valedictorian, an honor that afforded Paxton the opportunity to make a speech to her graduating class. As she told a football field full of spectators—their seats spaced feet apart with Covid carefulness—Paxton had originally planned to give a speech about "TV, and media, and content." But she tossed out that speech to talk about something else: abortion. Namely, Texas's then-impending plan to ban abortion past six weeks of pregnancy.

"I have dreams and hopes, and ambitions. Every girl graduating today does. And we have spent our entire lives working toward our future, and without our input and without our consent, our control over that future has been stripped away from us," Paxton said, as the crowd burst into cheers. "I am terrified that if my contraceptives fail, I am terrified that if I am raped, that my hopes and aspirations and dreams for my future will no longer matter."

When videos of Paxton's speech hit social media, they garnered hundreds of thousands of views. "This took guts," Hillary Clinton posted on Twitter, now known as X. "Thank you for not staying silent, Paxton."

The speech instantly transformed Paxton, who was then just eighteen years old, into a kind of folk hero. She became a standard-bearer for Texas teen girls as well as for their parents and peers who were bewildered by their state legislature's hard-line opposition to abortion. Paxton had publicly turned her body, the thing that anti-abortion lawmakers had sought to legislate, into a warning: *I am what's at stake.*

That's the warning Paxton meant to give, anyway. But as the recipient of abstinence-only sex ed, she inadvertently gave another: *Abstinence-only sex ed will not keep young people from speaking out against sexual conservatism.*

Paxton really did plan to save sex for marriage. There was no single, grand moment where she changed her mind. Instead, it was a slow-dawning realization that abstinence-only advocates had not quite been telling her the truth. Her friends had sex; their lives weren't ruined. "All these things that they were saying just didn't really seem realistically true," Paxton told me. "Or true enough to deter me from doing it."

Plus, she wanted to have sex. Really badly.

"I always had a very, very, very strong sex drive. And so by the time I was fifteen, I was ready. I was still going with the purity culture, waiting till marriage—I was still having that internal conflict. But I wanted to have sex. I didn't care who it was with, honestly, at that point," Paxton said. She was done trying to weigh her virginity against her desirability, trying to figure out what society wanted from her. She wanted to follow her *own* desires. "It's a status symbol to not be a virgin, as well as a status symbol to be a virgin. It's weird, but I just wanted it gone."

Her trust in herself is also what led Paxton, a few years later, to make her public plea for abortion rights. She was done with people telling her what to do. "I really couldn't fathom how somebody else could be allowed to make a life-changing decision for me like that—like becoming a parent—and that what I wanted for myself and for my life would literally have zero role in that decision," she told me. "It felt incredibly dehumanizing to me, so I wanted to do something about it."

For a year after her barnstorming speech, Paxton could scarcely get through the day without someone mentioning it. In college, she joined a number of pro–abortion rights groups, where she continued to advocate for reproductive rights and expanding access to information about sexual health.

She also came out as pansexual, meaning she is attracted to people of any gender. By the time we reconnected, more than two years after her speech, Paxton was casually seeing a couple she had met on a dating app. "I'm not dating them," she told me wryly. "But we're friends, you know. With benefits."

So much for that abstinence-only sex ed.

3.

CLASSROOM CULTURE WARS
How the Pandemic Upended the Fight over Sex Ed

From its opening minutes, the hearing of the Texas State Board of Education was unusual.

The board members' desks were arranged in a circle, each one placed about three feet away from the next. Although it was November 2020 and the coronavirus pandemic had locked down much of the United States, few of the board members and staffers who appeared in person bothered to wear a mask. This wasn't the rest of the United States, after all—this was Texas.

Still, there were some concessions to the deadly virus. Although the board hearing was open to the public, concerned citizens would not be appearing in person. Instead, they would have two minutes to talk on Zoom, their comments broadcast through screens hoisted throughout the cavernous, gray-carpeted boardroom. And there sure were a lot of people who wanted to speak, because there was another reason this meeting was unusual: For the first time in more than two decades, the Texas State Board of Education was set to update the minimum curriculum standards that guide sex ed in the state.

Sex ed advocates had high hopes for the process. They wanted to require schools to teach students about consent and eliminate state provisions that effectively forced educators to demonize LGBTQ+ people. Texas is one of a handful of states with a so-called No Promo Homo law, which requires sex ed materials to emphasize that "homosexuality is not a lifestyle acceptable to the general public and that homosexual conduct is a criminal offense" (as the Texas version declares). In addition to being bigoted, this law is misleading to the point of being alarmist, because the Supreme Court invalidated all same-sex sodomy bans in the 2003 case *Lawrence v. Texas.*

"What we're advocating for is age-appropriate, medically accurate information, and at the earliest levels, that really looks like dignity and respect for all," said Patrick Hanley, who works for a north Texas LGBTQ+ organization called Resource Center, which was heavily involved in the fight over the Texas sex ed standards. "We want to talk about consent. The whole point of teaching consent is about acknowledging someone's bodily autonomy; it's about the basic level of dignity and respect for other people's choices."

Texans wanted that, too. In a March 2020 poll of Texas voters, 75 percent said they supported abstinence-plus sex ed and agreed that "to help prevent bullying of LGBTQ youth, Texas public schools should include standards around cultivating respect for all people, regardless of their sexual orientation or identity." Almost 90 percent agreed that "it's important for students to learn about consent." A majority of Republican voters backed all these stances.[1]

Just 9 percent supported abstinence-only sex ed. Another 9 percent wanted zero sex ed.

This minuscule minority, however, seemed to have the loudest voice at Texas State Board of Education meetings and hearings over the updates, which quickly morphed into a microcosm of the national battle over sex ed. The CEO of Ascend, the national abstinence organization that helped popularize the term "sexual risk avoidance," showed up to argue that Texans should "begin to normalize sexual delay as the optimal behavior"—as if this hasn't been something that abstinence-only advocates have been trying to do for a hundred years, to lackluster results.

But if conservatives had spent much of the first two decades of the twenty-first century fanning the flames of the controversy over sex ed, giving it just enough oxygen to keep their cause burning but generally beneath most people's notice, then the coronavirus pandemic turned those flames into a full-on conflagration. When the coronavirus trapped people at home, after nearly four years of the maddening Trump administration and with only their computers for company, rage and conspiratorial thinking soared. Protests against lockdown and mask mandates radicalized new converts to right-wing causes, including sexual conservatism. After 2020, fights that might have once been skirmishes between professional advocates of abstinence-only and comprehensive sex ed spiraled into all-out culture wars over LGBTQ+ rights, sexual violence, and the future of public education itself.

These wars took sexual conservatism to extremes that would have been unthinkable just a few years before, with states and schools seeking to enact novel restrictions not just on sex ed but also on teachers and books that touched on topics like race and gender. In sum, outrage over sex ed became a Trojan horse for attacks on free speech.

The tone of public arguments changed, too. It became far more hateful.

In that November hearing, Texas—as it usually does—provided an early glimpse into how pandemic-era and post-pandemic fights over sex ed fused Gabler-era homophobic stereotypes with thoroughly modern, deeply online conspiracy theories about vast networks of sexual predators looking to gobble up children. Speakers at the hours-long board of education hearing talked about sex ed as if it were a scheme jointly dreamed up by pedophiles, human traffickers, the gays, and Planned Parenthood (who may or may not all be one and the same). One mom, who said she was volunteering with "local organizations, law enforcement, FBI, and Texas Rangers as they combat child predators and all forms of sex trafficking," urged the board of education to fight back against "manipulative mental tricks that can turn our public school system into a marketplace for the abortion pharmaceutical industries." Another said sex ed had led the classroom to become a "grooming field" for teachers. "Remember that some of the most vocal about the need for more sex ed are those who will benefit financially, because they know increased sexual activity will follow," one grandmother admonished.

One speaker, Connie Wyatt Coleman, told the board that comprehensive sex ed "is a passive term which serves to make sexual content a part of kids' education much earlier and seeks to normalize and neutralize any type of sexual relationship. Who does this benefit? Not the kids."

She repeatedly urged the board: "Follow the money." Planned Parenthood, she intimated, was behind everything.[2]

It's no secret that Planned Parenthood supports comprehensive sex ed, given that it's the biggest sex ed provider in the United States. But I followed Coleman's money, too. She led an anti-abortion crisis pregnancy center located near the Dallas–Fort Worth area, which, as she told board members, "partner[s] with our schools to encourage our youth to make wise choices that will empower their future." In fiscal year 2021, that center received more than $45,000 from Texas's Alternatives to Abortion program. Coleman quit working at that center in 2021, according to her LinkedIn, but the following fiscal year, the Alternatives to Abortion program gave that crisis pregnancy center more than $125,000.

This is the paradox of the demonization of sex ed: If there is a moneyed conspiracy tilting the field of sex education, it's not on the left.

The undercurrent of homophobia that coursed through the Texas hearings sometimes surfaced in confounding ways. Comprehensive sex ed, one Austin community group leader declared, involves "reading picture books to four-year-olds about boys wearing girls' dresses, celebrating gay pride for an entire week by having parades and cross-dressing, scheduling student band members to perform in the city gay pride parade and loading buses with students to attend, sharing 'consent' videos with twelve-year-olds that depict adults taking their clothes off and teaching them to negotiate for sex, otherwise known as consent." After this word salad of a speech, the woman then addressed the board of education: "I want to thank all of you for voting to protect students and not forcing teachers to teach consensual sex, or negotiating for sex, and LGBT indoctrination."[3]

Texas schools are not pursuing some mythical gay agenda. Besides being restrained by the state's "No Promo Homo" law, they're profoundly unsupportive of individual LGBTQ+ students. Nearly 70 percent of LGBTQ+ students in Texas say they've been verbally harassed at school over their sexual orientation, and 10 percent say the harassment has graduated to physical assault.[4] Only a quarter say that their school administration supports LGBTQ+ students.[5] Suicide attempts among young LGBTQ+ people, which are appallingly common, are linked to a lack of support in schools.[6] The lives of the estimated 150,000 LGBT youth who live in Texas are, quite literally, at risk.[7]

The belief that the word "consent" was somehow a pedophiliac password was not limited to the everyday Texans who testified at hearings. Although the board of education gathered groups of working experts to piece together the new curricula, one Republican board member said in a meeting that he had consulted people "back home" about "consent." They allegedly told him that "consent" was a "gateway word."

"It's a very important word to Planned Parenthood and their friends," the member, Ken Mercer, told the group. He threw his hands into the air as he spoke, as if Planned Parenthood's involvement was evidence enough of wrongdoing. "I was cautioned by experts in the field who work with people in prisons, who work with pedophiles, who've interviewed NAMBLA, other places—it's a gateway word."[8] (NAMBLA, if you've been lucky enough to never encounter the organization, is the North American Man-Boy Love Association, and yes, it's a pedophilia advocacy group.)

People's willingness to air these harebrained beliefs at school board meetings, in open view of their neighbors, is evidence of just how far formerly fringe ideas have now migrated into mainstream discourse. Before the coronavirus pandemic, these meetings were often sleepy, sparsely attended affairs. But between May 2021—when in-person school board meetings resumed in much of the United States—and November 2022, there were nearly sixty incidents at these meetings that led to arrests or charges, according to an analysis by the news outlet ProPublica. Almost everybody involved in the incidents was white, and many were enraged by what they saw as schools' support of sexuality and LGBTQ+ rights. "You are indoctrinating them to hate their bodies the way that they were born, the way that they were made!" one woman shouted at a New York school board meeting, to cheers from the crowd.[9] Blue states are just as susceptible as their red neighbors to misinformation and alarmism.

It is impossible to quantify the toll that this rhetoric has taken on LGBTQ+ young people, particularly those involved in activism. During that November hearing in Texas, one LGBTQ+ rights advocate who said they had survived sex trafficking—the very thing that so many pro-abstinence advocates used to fearmonger about—told the board members that the debate over the sex ed standards had left them "heartbroken."

"I have no [illusions] that sex education would have prevented the abuse my stepfather put me through from age six to age eight. But maybe if I had been taught in elementary school when and how to find a trusted adult, I wouldn't have waited until I was seventeen to tell my mother what happened," the activist said. "And maybe if I had learned early on

66 | CARTER SHERMAN

that my body is my own, and only I have the right to say what happens to it, when my uncle started to sexually abuse me at age thirteen, I might have known I could say no."[10]

In the end, the Texas State Board of Education voted to let middle school teachers tell students about birth control methods other than abstinence, as high school teachers had already been allowed to do. (With an important caveat, which I mentioned earlier: Health class is only an elective in Texas high schools.) But the board rejected efforts to explicitly teach students about consent and LGBTQ+ rights.

"Because things are so glacially slow here, it's really going to be an entire extra generation of students that won't have access to this information," Patrick Hanley, the Resource Center staffer, told me. He grimaced. "Which is criminal."

DON'T SAY GAY (OR ANYTHING ELSE)

In the years after 2020, parents' and politicians' slurry of bigotry, confusion, and self-righteousness was codified into sexually conservative legislation with remarkable speed and efficiency. The free expression organization PEN America has a term for this legislation: It's the "Ed Scare."

In 2021, as in-person school board meetings resumed, state legislators across the country started introducing what PEN America calls "educational gag orders." Filed in the months after George Floyd's 2020 murder and the national eruption of Black Lives Matter protests, the first wave of these bills largely focused on curtailing discussion of race in public schools, colleges, and state agencies by proposing to ban discussion of concepts like "critical race theory." But by 2023, these "gag orders" had multiplied and reoriented to focus on sex and gender rather than race. Out of the 110 educational "gag orders" introduced in 2023, thirty-nine aimed to block educators from talking about sexual orientation or gender identity.[11] This strand of legislation is known as "Don't Say Gay" legislation, and it's a younger cousin of "No Promo Homo" laws.

On top of those gag orders, states have also introduced nearly four hundred "educational intimidation" bills, as PEN America has dubbed them.

Rather than directly banning educators from speaking about particular subjects, "educational intimidation" bills chill free speech by incentivizing teachers into censoring themselves, such as by expanding definitions of obscenity and making it easier for parents and students to file complaints (including by creating tip lines that people can call to report teachers, as if educators are criminals).[12] In 2022, Missouri passed a law banning people "affiliated with a public or private elementary or secondary school" from providing "explicit sexual material" to students, which the law defined as virtually any pictorial depictions of sexual activity, "sadomasochistic abuse," or "postpubertal human genitals." People who broke the law could end up in jail for up to a year. According to a 2022 tally by PEN America, that law led Missouri schools to ban nearly three hundred books, including a Batman comic book, several books about art, and a graphic novelization of *The Handmaid's Tale*.[13] At one Missouri school board meeting, one parent even suggested adding two school librarians to the sex offender registry, the news outlet Coda reported.[14]

All but fifteen of these "educational intimidation" bills were introduced by Republican legislators, and most were based on model legislation, or legislation that is prewritten for lawmakers, usually by special interest groups. In this case, a handful of conservative think tanks crafted the "educational intimidation" bills.[15]

Spurred by the Ed Scare, book bans also started to spread across the United States. These bans tried to smother any whiff of relationships, intimacy, and sex in schools—even the fictional sort, and especially any kind that involves people who are not cisgender, straight, and married.

In the 2022–23 school year, public K-12 schools enacted more than 3,300 book bans—an increase of 33 percent from the previous school year.[16] Thousands of books were banned due to "hyperbolic and misleading rhetoric about 'porn in schools' and 'sexually explicit,' 'harmful,' and 'age-inappropriate' materials," according to PEN America, which also found that banned books' authors were most often women or people of color, or people who identified as LGBTQ+.[17] The true scale of the book bans, PEN America cautioned, is incalculable, because several states enacted "wholesale bans" that led to entire classrooms and school libraries to be "suspended, closed, or emptied of books."[18]

In 2024, Utah became the first state in the country to pass a law that

68 | CARTER SHERMAN

effectively created a statewide banned books list.[19] When considering whether to ban books, the law instructed educators to "prioritize protecting children from the harmful effects of illicit pornography over other considerations in evaluating instructional material."

Attacks on sex ed also didn't stop after the pandemic. In fact, they increased. In 2024, at least 135 sex ed bills swirled through state legislations, more than any other year since 2018—but back in 2018, most of those bills were on the side of comprehensive sex ed, proposing to teach topics like consent and dating violence prevention. By 2024, most sex ed legislation had pivoted to favor sexual conservatism. They suggested restricting the information that could be included in sex ed, adding anti-abortion content to it, or requiring more parental oversight. Bills that proposed teaching about consent-related topics dwindled dramatically, and many bills suggested banning teaching sex ed altogether to younger students.[20]

PEN America estimates that, conservatively, about 1.3 million public school teachers as well as one hundred thousand public college faculty members have been impacted by "gag orders,"[21] while about 140 million Americans live in states with one or more "educational intimidation provisions" in force. Who knows how many students have been impacted?

A nineteen-year-old with shaggy, champagne-colored hair and an infectious grin, Cameron Driggers grew up on Florida's eastern coast. He was the guy whose gym teacher told him that having sex would lead people to make "further poor choices," go to jail, and contract an STI so serious that their genitals would be amputated.

Stigmatizing STIs like that would stun anybody, but for Cameron, it held a specific kind of terror. His great-uncle had died of AIDS complications, and, as a gay teenager, Cameron was—perhaps irrationally—choked by the fear that something similar would happen to him. He felt like he didn't know a single person he could ask about safe sex; while his family accepted his sexuality, his hometown did not.

"I've never been in an area where I had friends who would give me that insight or advice," he said. "There really wasn't a resource to learn what is normal, what isn't.

"What I would have loved to have, really, is representation and reassurance that I wouldn't end up like my uncle," Cameron continued.

"When stuff like that happens, I guess some people are more eager to explore their sexual identity than others. For me, I didn't think about it and pushed it away. I don't think anybody should have to do that just because they don't have any resources to talk about who they are, how to be safe and feel comfortable in their own skin."

A girl outed Cameron at a pool party in middle school. Afterward, he could be out as gay, but not *too* gay—whatever that meant. With his higher-pitched voice, Cameron was always standing on the edge of acceptability, petrified of being pushed off. "I tried to not express my sexuality and to be the least queer that I could," he said. Cameron didn't date and he didn't have sex. By the time we talked, he still had not.

"It's hard, even if it's not outright hate crimes and bullying and stuff like that—you're shunned and treated as an 'other,'" Cameron said. More than 60 percent of LGBTQ+ students in Florida say they have been discriminated against in school.[22] At least once, Cameron did face outright hate: "I was called a faggot by one of my teachers my freshman year of high school," he recalled.

In 2022, when he was seventeen, Cameron learned that Florida's Republican governor, Ron DeSantis, was pushing the nation's first Don't Say Gay bill. A lightbulb went off. *I'm already doing the work for him!* Cameron realized.

I'm literally doing exactly what he wants me to do, what this legislation asks a gay person to do, which is to bury themselves and to ignore who they are, Cameron thought. He told me: "That disgusted me and really made me do some soul-searching about where I was at and my priorities."

Enough is enough, he thought. *I'm not going to silence myself for the governor. I'm going to do the opposite of that from now on.*

In March 2022, the week after the Florida House passed the Don't Say Gay bill, Cameron and his friends organized a massive walkout at their high school, in an effort to keep DeSantis from signing it into law. More than five hundred students joined.[23] So did hundreds of other students at more than twenty other schools across Florida. "Say gay!" they chanted. "Say gay! Say gay!"

To hold the protest, the students at Cameron's school had to defy school administrators, who tried to stop them from distributing Pride flags and attempted to cut the peaceful protest short, despite school policies that should have allowed it, the *Daytona Beach News-Journal* reported. One student was later suspended for his role in organizing it.[24]

Cameron found the whole walkout surreal. He'd heard people talk about the power of the youth "voice," but he'd never before felt that voice inflate his lungs or those of his friends. "As a generation, we've experienced very historic moments—negative historic moments, just [one disaster] after another, that I feel like has completely eroded our faith and trust in institutions," Cameron said. His family lost their house in the 2008 recession. He grew up watching the never-ending wars in Iraq and Afghanistan, which fostered, he said, "this constant reflection and awareness that the United States is sponsoring violence across the globe." More recently, Cameron's world was shaken by the pandemic and "this skyrocketing of GOP extremism around the country."

Plus, Cameron added wryly, "it's hard to take your government seriously when you're led by Donald Trump."

Despite the efforts of Cameron and his friends, DeSantis signed Florida's Don't Say Gay bill into law in March 2022. The law's scope was later curbed by a legal settlement,[25] but bigots everywhere seemed to see its passage as a seal of approval. In the month after its passage, there were upward of six thousand daily posts on Twitter, as the platform X was then known, that both mentioned the LGBTQ+ community and used slurs.[26] That's an increase of more than 400 percent from the month prior to the bill's passage.[27]

After the walkout, Cameron joined a rally against book bans. Members of the Three Percenters, an anti-government militia movement that had a presence at the January 6 insurrection, showed up, Cameron said. They were dressed in Darth Vader–like tactical gear, complete with face masks. "I got called 'faggot' and told they were gonna make me suck [one of their] genitalia, that they were going to follow me home," Cameron said. He condemned "the utter hypocrisy of this culture war, which is masked by the so-called effort to protect children and protect their innocence—but their fiercest proponents are literally threatening violence, sexual violence, on children. It's mind-boggling."

The fight over the Don't Say Gay bill also revived the use of the word "groomer" as a homophobic slur suggesting that LGBTQ+ people, particularly gay men, are pedophiles. Weeks before DeSantis signed the Don't

Say Gay bill into law, his press secretary posted on Twitter that anybody who opposed it was "probably a groomer or at least you don't denounce the grooming of 4-8 year old children." Her words evoked the 1970s Save Our Children campaign by former beauty queen Anita Bryant, who argued that LGBTQ+ people were dangerous to children and that, as a Christian mother, she had the right to keep LGBTQ+ people away from her kids. "Homosexuals cannot reproduce, so they must recruit," Bryant infamously announced. "And to freshen their ranks, they must recruit the youth of America."[28]

After the Don't Say Gay bill became law, far-right Congresswomen Marjorie Taylor Greene of Georgia and Lauren Boebert of Colorado sent out their own "grooming" tweets.[29] Greene even called Democrats a "party of pedophiles."[30]

The rhetoric that once echoed from Zoom screens into a Texas State Board of Education hearing room was being echoed everywhere. Since 2022, at least seven other states have enacted their own versions of Don't Say Gay laws.[31]

PARENTAL RIGHTS

The official name of Florida's Don't Say Gay law is the Parental Rights in Education Act. Cries of "parental rights" pop up again and again in post-2020 fights over sex ed and the Ed Scare, as well as in many other theaters where the culture war between sexual conservatism and progressivism rages. "I believe the state's only business in sex education should be teaching basic information about anatomy and reproduction. Morals and values should remain the parents' domain," one speaker at the Texas State Board of Education hearing in November 2020 declared. "Comprehensive sex education flies in the face of parental rights."

The parental rights movement dates back at least a century. In the 1920s, a Christian-led movement to outlaw the teaching of human evolution in public schools rooted its arguments in the importance of parental rights. That effort led to the sensational Scopes "monkey trial" of 1925, which saw the ACLU square off against the state of Tennessee over a young biology teacher, John Scopes, who had been arrested for teaching the theory of evolution.[32] (Scopes lost, and Tennessee's ban on teaching evolution in educational institutions remained on the books for decades.) In the wake of the 1954 Supreme Court case *Brown v. Board of Education*, evangelicals argued that parents have the right to send their white kids to tax-exempt, private Christian "segregation academies."[33] The academies' tax-exempt status was revoked in 1970,[34] but the loss lent strength to the emerging religious right. Fights over parental rights continued to roil school boards throughout the next decade. Like the Gablers in Texas, parents were horrified not only by changing mores around sexuality and race, but by the very idea that what is "right" can depend on the circumstances. After a 1970 battle over West Virginia's plan to have students read texts that reflected the United States' multiethnic composition, one parent complained, "They were teaching my kids socialism, homosexuality, and situational ethics."[35]

Each of these surges in parental rights activism coincided with eras in U.S. history when sexual progressivism was on the rise, sexual norms were in the midst of great change, and groups such as youths, people of color, women, and LGBTQ+ people were gaining greater public visibility and freedoms. Each surge was a backlash.

The 2020s iteration of the parental rights movement originally convened around parents' protests against Covid restrictions in schools, such as mask mandates. But in the years that followed, the movement grew into a widespread anti-government campaign that has pushed a mishmash of sexually conservative policies, like the Ed Scare, that undermine students' ability to learn about issues facing people of color, women, and LGBTQ+ folks. It has even led to attempts to restrict the general public's ability to learn about sex, gender, and race. In the first eight months of 2023, the American Library Association (ALA) recorded attempts to ban almost two thousand books from *public* libraries. Many of the attempts were the result of coordinated efforts to ban a hundred or more books at once—a sharp break from past years, when people usually tried to ban a single book.[36]

In total, the ALA recorded more attempts to ban books in 2023 than in any year in the past two decades.[37] Beyond demolishing sex ed and teachers' ability to talk about sexual and gender diversity in the classroom, these efforts try to cut young people off from being able to even look up such things on their own, just like Norma Gabler had wanted.

There is also a distinct anti-science bent within the parental rights movement. In 2023, the Indiana state legislature blocked Indiana University from using state dollars to fund the prestigious Kinsey Institute after one legislator suggested that Kinsey's founder sexually experimented on children and that Kinsey researchers might be "hiding" something.[38] These categorically untrue claims were pushed by an Indiana-based parental rights organization that the Southern Poverty Law Center had deemed an anti-government extremist group. But regardless of their veracity, the defunding undermined a school's ability to conduct research on sex—to merely ask questions—and painted scientific inquiry as sinister. Once again, the Gablers would have been proud.

Taken together, the restrictions on sex ed, school curricula, books, and teachers paint a disturbing portrait of the future of free speech and expression. Young people can't learn about sex or other "controversial" topics from their teachers; they can't find books on the subject; their only option is to scour the internet for information. (Which comes with its own benefits and drawbacks.) Meanwhile, educators and researchers who have dedicated their lives to helping the next generation are running for cover. Between the 2020 and 2022 school years, more than 160 teachers lost their jobs over culture war–related disputes, a *Washington Post* analysis found.[39] The analysis concluded before the parental rights movement came into its full power—and even then, the *Post* warned that its statistics were "probably a significant undercount."[40]

That analysis, by the way, included teachers who lost their jobs for espousing traditionally conservative viewpoints. Demands that we all think and act the same way—including the sexual conservatism movement's insistence that all Americans act *their* way—strike at both sides of the aisle.

Every sex educator I interviewed agreed: While teaching sex ed has never been easy, it's never been this bad.

Lynn has worked as an Iowa health teacher for more than two decades, so she's used to the occasional public uproar. But nothing prepared her for the bedlam she accidentally unleashed in 2022, when she showed her class a short cartoon about intersectionality.

The cartoon is charmingly clunky. In it, three stick figures sit around a table, looking at photos from a relative's wedding. Two of the figures are a Black woman and her Black daughter. The other is a white boy.

"Wow, a lot of different types of people came together for your aunt's wedding!" the boy exclaims.

"Definitely! That sort of reminds me of what you were telling me about intersectionality, Mom," the girl replies. Her mom then jumps into a rudimentary discussion of the concept, which recognizes that because people can belong to multiple social categories, they can face overlapping systems of oppression at once. For example, a Black woman faces both racism and sexism.

The cartoon is made by Amaze, a website that produces age-appropriate content about puberty and sex ed. Lynn showed it because she wanted to amble into a talk about differences and similarities, and then gently transition into discussing sexual orientation and gender identity. At the time, that discussion was perfectly legal under Iowa law, she said.

"Everything I do is, like, t's are crossed, i's are dotted. I'm not going to deviate. I'm following what the guidance is," Lynn told me. As she spoke, her melodious voice gently twirled around her words. She had a teacher's cadence, one that was used to rising and falling to draw in children's attention. "And the parents just absolutely lost their marbles."

The parents of one boy in the class were offended by the video's mention of the scholar Kimberlé Crenshaw, who coined the term "intersectionality" and whose name has now become a trigger for right-wing rage. The parents met with Lynn's curriculum director, with the school principal, with school board members, and with an attorney for the school. One of the parents started regularly emailing Lynn and asked her to explain, in minute detail, how each part of her curriculum aligned with Section 279.50 of the Iowa code, which involves teachers' ability to instruct students about human growth and development.

"They were so mad at me, *so* mad at me," Lynn recalled. "They wanted to take my license away, because how dare I indoctrinate their children with all of this rhetoric?"

It made her want to quit teaching altogether.

"I almost feel like there's a conscious effort trying to literally disband public education," Lynn said. "It's like, 'We're gonna throw spaghetti at the wall and see what sticks!' A couple of years ago, it was critical race theory, and that didn't stick so much. But now we're throwing sexual orientation and gender identity at the wall, and that's starting to stick a little bit."

After her experience in Houston in 2008, Justine Ang Fonte left math behind and devoted her career to sex ed. She ended up teaching it to the offspring of some of the wealthiest, most powerful people in the country. For seven years, Fonte worked as the director of health and wellness at Manhattan's Dalton School, an exclusive K-12 school where yearly tuition costs more than $60,000. By 2021, Fonte was a sought-after sex educator, and she gave two talks over Zoom about pornography and consent to Columbia Grammar and Preparatory School, another Manhattan school where tuition tops $60,000.

Days later, the *New York Post* ran a headline about it. "Columbia Prep students and parents reel after class on 'porn literacy,'" the newspaper blared. About a week later, the *Post* reported that its story on Columbia Prep had led Dalton parents to "bombard" the school with complaints about Fonte.[41]

Multiple sex educators told the *New York Times* that Fonte's work aligned with national and international standards for sex ed.[42] (Porn literacy is a real thing, which I'll discuss in the next chapter.) The furor unleashed by parents and the press was so crazed, however, that Fonte left Dalton altogether.

When I asked Fonte why this scandal happened in New York City and not while she was working in Houston, she had only one answer: money. New York may be more liberal, but thanks to their wealth, an aggrieved minority of critics were able to yell loudly enough.

"In Texas, I was in a Title I school, which means half to 100 percent of the students are on a free or reduced lunch. And it's a public school," Fonte said. "Even though the state as a whole may have more critics of sex ed than New York state, I was working in a school that does not have families of such privilege and access to amplify their criticism."

While the families of Fonte's Texan students may have little in common economically or politically with those of her New York students, Texans and New Yorkers have been targeted by the same messaging. The summer of the scandal around Fonte, trucks with billboards with messages like "Woke School? Speak Out" wheeled around New York private schools, including Dalton.[43] The billboards directed onlookers to a website, supposedly run by a group of "concerned parents," that bemoaned how "the new orthodoxy has emerged at our schools, dividing our communities based on immutable characteristics such as race, ethnicity, gender, and sexual orientation."[44] It all sounded a lot like what happened at the Texas hearing, just dressed up in fancier language for people who believed themselves to be fancier.

I do have a caveat about this chapter and the previous one, which you may have already noticed: I am largely focusing on K-12 public schools, not private schools. The sex ed in private schools can be far from ideal—Grace, the Oklahoman I mentioned in chapter two who was diagnosed with herpes, went to private school. Nor are these institutions free of restrictions or from the parental rights movement, as Fonte's experience shows; parents' obsession with controlling what their kids learn is arguably why we have private schools in the first place.

Yet interviews with people who attended or are attending private schools convinced me that private schools, unbeholden to local school boards, at least possess the capacity to give their students a much more comprehensive sex education—one that includes adequate information about LGBTQ+ issues and consent. The minuscule number of my interviewees who had no complaints about their sex ed overwhelmingly went to private school.

This is not an advertisement for private schools. It's a reminder that, like virtually everything else in this country, the quality of your sex ed depends on your income bracket.

Mya grew up just a few miles away from me, in Seattle, but we only connected by chance once I started doing interviews for this book. A year younger than me, Mya attended the same public middle school that I went to, where we had the same seventh-grade sex ed teacher—a science teacher whom she described as the "worst teacher I've ever had, bar none."

Mya's memory of his approach to sex ed matched mine: He generally bumbled his way through a course that he presumably taught every year and thus should have been much better at teaching, but he sometimes veered into great, discomforting detail. During Mya's time in his class, he demonstrated how to put a condom on a banana and went on a lengthy rant about Pap smears. ("I was terrified for the next ten years," Mya said.) This incompetence does not foster the kind of reassuring environment that encourages learning among teenagers, who are generally just trying to keep their heads down amid the trench warfare that is puberty.

"If I had questions," Mya said, "I was not thinking about them in that class."

After middle school, Mya went to a private all-girls high school. Even though the school was Catholic, the sex ed that Mya, who is gay, received there was far more comprehensive than what she got in public school. They even talked about respecting LGBTQ+ identities in religion class—something that virtually none of my interviewees who went to public school told me they experienced, and certainly not something I remember receiving from my public high school, which was just twenty minutes away from Mya's private one.

Cami Armijo-Grover teaches sex ed in both public and private schools in Bozeman, Montana, which does not require that students learn sex ed. After the pandemic enabled ultrarich parents to work remotely and thus move their families wherever they wanted, wealth gushed into Montana. In 2021, Montana's Republican governor, multimillionaire Greg Gianforte, signed into law a PEN America–designated "educational intimidation" bill, which requires public schools to let parents inspect any sex ed curricula and allows parents to opt their kids out of sex ed. That new law also blocks abortion providers, such as Planned Parenthood, from providing sex ed in public schools.

The massive influx of money into Montana, combined with the state's tightening of its public school sex ed laws, means that more and more rich families can simply transfer their kids into private school if they think the public option isn't good enough. By virtue of their wealth, some people end up with more parental rights than others.

"The private schools are like, 'Yes, we can have conversations about supporting a friend who maybe identifies as part of an LGBTQ+ community!'" Armijo-Grover said. "'We should absolutely have long discussions about consent with them!'

"The haves have more and the have-nots have even less," she continued. "Now that they don't have information and don't know they can get services, they may or may not have an unintended pregnancy that they may or may not want."

About half of teen moms receive a high school diploma by twenty-two, and 10 percent graduate from a two- or four-year college program. Their children are more likely to drop out of high school and give birth as teenagers, too.[45]

Sex ed is a class issue. As attacks on it intensify, the rich can buy better sex ed, while the rest of us become poorer for it. They can also just buy their kids the books that are no longer allowed on library shelves. This is what Lynn, the Iowa sex ed teacher ambushed for showing a cartoon, is talking about when she speaks of the destruction of public education.

The irony of all these efforts is that sexual conservatives didn't need to go to such lengths to undermine sex ed for a generation, because the outbreak of the coronavirus already did it for them. Multiple interviewees told me they did not receive sex ed in school because of the pandemic.

Hugh, an eighteen-year-old from New Jersey, learned only about bodies, not how to have sex with them, in his middle school sex ed class. Then the pandemic broke out in 2020, during his freshman year of high school. By the time his school had cobbled together a Zoom curriculum, sex ed wasn't on it. "We really think that it was because they didn't want to have genitalia on the screens and parents be like, 'Oh, what's that?'" Hugh said.

Hugh was fifteen and not yet sexually active, so the lack of sex ed didn't initially bother him too much. Soon, though, he started to see how it impacted his friends. "I had friends testing positive for STIs and not even knowing that they had STIs. I can't even tell you how many pregnancy scares I've witnessed," Hugh said. He found himself going to CVS multiple times, sometimes with the same people, to pick up pregnancy tests, because they had never learned the basic mechanics of how sex leads to pregnancy. "That really could have all been solved with sex education," Hugh said.

Hugh, who is gay, realized he also had no one to whom he could turn for help. "For any member of the LGBTQ+ community, it is so much harder to get accurate sex education, especially from the peers around you, because there's significantly fewer members of LGBTQ+ community in general," he said. "It's not like my parents could just tell me, 'Oh, do this, do this,' because they're not gay or having gay sex."

Sex ed classes were shortened or canceled entirely during the pandemic for a multitude of reasons. Schools wanted to focus only on the core subjects because the switch to online teaching was so tumultuous; educators feared having their sex ed recorded and being taken out of context.[46] "They didn't want any negative heat from parents and to respect the students' learning space," a community and K-12 sex ed teacher told researchers in one study. "For example, if the student lives with an abuser, that class could be incredibly triggering."[47] It's galling: If you were trapped in a situation where you were in dire need of tools to talk about sex, that was a reason for you *not* to get them.

Sadly, sexual violence against young people seemed to surge during the pandemic, likely because so many were indeed trapped at home with family members who abused them. Between March and June 2020, for the first time ever, minors made up more than half of all callers to the National Sexual Assault Hotline.[48]

"KIDS KNOW WHAT THEY ARE DOING"

When Selena started having sex with her boyfriend at sixteen, she didn't know that women could orgasm during it. She wasn't really sure whether women were meant to enjoy sex at all.

Maybe I'm not supposed to get pleasure out of this, she thought. *I'm supposed to be submissive. . . . I don't have a say in what I want during sex.*

During her childhood in northeast Texas, Selena's only experience of school-based sex ed was a lecture about puberty, periods, and reproduction in her public middle school. She didn't receive any further sex ed in high school, and her deeply Catholic parents never talked to her about sex, other than to warn her against having it. No adult ever talked to her about consent; they certainly did not discuss pleasure. Sex was so special, so apart from everyday life, and so reserved for committed heterosexual relationships that it could not even be discussed.

Yet because the adults in her life acted as though sex could occur only in the context of love, Selena came to see sex as a transaction with her boyfriend. *Men need sex, and sex is the same as love,* her math went. *If I give my boyfriend sex, he loves me.*

It made her feel like sex was all she was good for. She wondered: *Am I just with him because he wants to have sex with me?*

In college, Selena met a classmate who was part of a campus group that gave sexual health presentations to students. She decided to attend a meeting. And another. And then another. They talked about rape culture, about hookup culture, about gender roles, about feminism, about—finally, for the first time in Selena's life—consent. It was there that she learned: "Do things for yourself and not for other people."

While the parental rights movement and sexual conservatism curtail what teachers and other authority figures can tell students, young people are sidestepping these restrictions altogether using a model of sex ed known as "peer-to-peer." Although it's not clear that peer-to-peer sex ed can change behavior, it can improve knowledge of sexually transmitted infections, contraception, and sexual violence, as well as lessen stigma around HIV and condoms.[49] In interviews, people told me they yearned for something like peer-to-peer sex ed. "Nobody wants to hear their seventy-year-old science teacher tell them not to post bikini pictures on the internet," said one eighteen-year-old from Washington state. "If we were able to bring more voices into sex ed, especially from people your own age, or hear from people who are a little bit older who have had those experiences and can look back and actually speak on them, that would be so much more impactful."

Young people talking to other young people about how to have sex is as old as sex itself, but formalized peer-to-peer sex ed emerges and evolves when institutions fail. The modern model of peer-to-peer sex ed can trace its roots back to New York City in the early 1970s, when a group of high school students grew fed up with their lackluster sex ed and decided to teach it to one another.[50] Dubbing themselves the Student Coalition for Relevant Sex Education, the students secured a major grant from the Ford Foundation to expand their work to roughly a dozen New York City schools.[51] And when I say major, I mean *major*.

"A reputable grant-giving institution gave the 2019 equivalent of $1.6 million to a bunch of teenagers, encouraging them to self-organize and then talk to their friends and fellow students about sex," historian Lisa M. F. Andersen wrote of the endeavor. "What previous generations of American educators had described as the problem that sex education would prevent—kids teaching other kids—was now being endorsed as a game-changing strategy."[52] (When the funding fell apart, though, so did the coalition.[53])

Then, in the 1980s, HIV/AIDS hit. Between 1981 and 1990, more than a hundred thousand people died from AIDS in the United States; it became the leading cause of death for young adult men in San Francisco, Los Angeles, and New York.[54] The depth of the crisis revealed that peer-to-peer sex ed might be more than game-changing. It could be lifesaving, too.

As federal, state, and local governments refused to devote the resources needed to combat the virus ravaging LGBTQ+ communities, gay men started organizing their own efforts to encourage one another to have sex safely.[55] It soon became clear that similar efforts were needed among the young. One in five American adolescents diagnosed with HIV/AIDS was a New Yorker, but the AIDS unit at the city's board of education operated on a pathetic budget of 8 cents per student.[56] The formidable AIDS Coalition to Unleash Power, better known as ACT UP, created a group that was dedicated to agitating board of education members into taking a stand on HIV/AIDS education, but the group also started organizing peer-to-peer sex ed.[57] "If young people are educated so that they can tell each other the facts, that cuts right through everything else," said one student member of the group, which was named Youth Education Life Line, or YELL.[58]

"When we hand condoms to kids, we encourage them to take their lives into their own hands and we acknowledge their decision-making autonomy," one gay activist wrote in a 1990 issue of the magazine *Out-Week*. "Kids know what they are doing. Letting them address their actions responsibly will not only save their lives, it will empower them. I have seen this student-generated approach work better than any paternalistic pedantry in the classroom. It rips the blinders off those who control the curriculum—those who, in Eric Epstein's words, 'see no evil, hear no evil, and pretty soon they'll have no kids.'"[59]

HIV/AIDS is no longer as much of a threat as it once was. But it is hard not to read those words and think of the mental health epidemic that now imperils the lives of all Gen Z-ers and late millennials, particularly those who are LGBTQ+.

Selena, the Texan who didn't know whether women should even enjoy sex, became an officer of the campus group that changed her life. When she leads workshops with her fellow students about sexual health, she asks people to raise their hands if they're from Texas. Most are.

82 | CARTER SHERMAN

Then she tells them: "We're equals in this room. And if you have anything to say, please, let's discuss." While most U.S. sex ed pathologizes youthful and premarital sex, Selena instead normalizes sex simply by being a young person willing to have an honest conversation about it.

"Some of these people—it's their first time ever talking about comprehensive sexual health or learning about STIs or talking about consent," Selena, who is now twenty-one, told me. "It makes me feel disappointed knowing that there are resources and that Texas just doesn't provide that."

It is noteworthy that the Student Coalition for Relevant Sex Education was originally named the High School Women's Coalition and that YELL arose due to a disease believed to primarily impact LGBTQ+ folks. There seems to be a dearth of straight cis men in American peer-to-peer sex ed; whenever I brought this issue up to sex educators, they would groan in recognition and agreement. This is unfortunate—not only because straight cis men make up the majority of people in power and because their sex lives seem to set the agenda for the rest of us, but also because I believe these men would gain so much from having open conversations with one another about sex. However, restrictive notions of masculinity don't exactly allow for wide-ranging, vulnerable conversations about sex and sexual health. And perhaps women and LGBTQ+ folks, forced to be far more aware of how the very idea of their sex lives can cause friction both personally and politically, are more inclined to try to investigate and improve them.

After graduation, Selena wants to become an intimacy coordinator for acting productions, helping performers navigate sex scenes safely and comfortably. She also has a new boyfriend.

"I feel comfortable to express what I like and what I don't like," she said. "I want to make sure I'm still having pleasurable sex."

FLORIDA RISING

Peer-to-peer sex ed alone cannot fix young people's sex lives. In Florida, the home base of the new parental rights movement and its onslaught on public education, activists are doing more than focusing solely on

THE SECOND COMING | 83

providing better sex ed for their peers. They're trying to influence the stakeholders who set sex ed policy in the first place.

In 2022, the same year it pioneered Don't Say Gay legislation, Florida implemented more than 350 book bans, second only to Texas.[60] The following year, Florida passed a law restricting material with "sexual conduct" in schools, leading one district to remove library copies of dictionaries, *The Guinness Book of World Records,* and *Ripley's Believe It or Not.*[61] It was off to the races: By the close of the 2023–2024 school year, Florida had instituted more than 4,000 book bans.[62]

Behind many of Florida's moves is the group Moms for Liberty, which launched in Florida in 2021 to combat Covid restrictions in schools and later spearheaded much of the parental rights movement, funded in part by influential conservative groups like the Heritage Foundation.[63] Over the next few years, at least 250 chapters of Moms for Liberty sprang up in forty-two states.[64] In Florida, they objected to fourth graders learning words like "isolation," "quarantine," and "spinal tap" because they were too "scary of words."[65] (No word on whether "crucifixion" was too scary.) In Tennessee, they found a children's book about seahorses to be too scandalous to teach.[66] An Oklahoma chapter called for the deplatforming of the Scholastic Book Fair, claiming the beloved literary tradition, which gives kids the chance to buy books at pop-ups, is "largely focused on indoctrinating youth with radical viewpoints and sexual ideologies."[67]

Moms for Liberty has also zeroed in on LGBTQ+ kids. Members have suggested that they should be put into specialized classrooms, asked whether the (cis male) mass shooter in Uvalde, Texas, was "an eighteen-year-old transgender boy trying to be a girl," and called gender dysphoria "a mental health disorder that is being normalized by predators."[68] (Broadly, gender dysphoria is the distress born from an incongruence between someone's assigned sex at birth and their gender identity.)

Moms for Liberty, which the Southern Poverty Law Center has designated an anti-government extremist group, are the ideological and tactical successors of Mel and Norma Gabler and Save Our Children founder Anita Bryant. All these activists make the same claim about their legitimacy and their aims: Their "innate" parental knowledge of what's good for their children is supposedly so total as to constitute ownership over not only their children's bodies and minds, but everybody else's, too. Given

84 | CARTER SHERMAN

that some of the people who are "normalizing" gender dysphoria are parents themselves—parents who take their LGBTQ+ children's questions and identities seriously—it is clear the parental rights movement does not encompass *all* parents' rights. Instead, the movement aims to establish rights only for particular kinds of families.

Organizations like Moms for Liberty can rise and fall. As of this writing, the group is struggling to shake off sexual assault allegations against one of its cofounders' husbands—and that cofounder's admission that she and her husband, the ex-chair of the Republican Party of Florida, had a threesome with a woman.[69] (The husband denied the sexual assault allegations and police ultimately declined to press charges.[70]) But even if Moms for Liberty stumbles off the national stage by the time this book comes out, their efforts will embolden future successors who will likely veer even farther to the right.

Young Floridians, however, have refused to give in to their state's sexual conservatism. Just as Moms for Liberty has led the parental rights movement, today's youth are trying to inspire a national movement, too.

"Millennials always had the internet too, but I think with Gen Z—we have even more access to information and a clearer picture of how completely fucked up the situation is and the status quo is in the United States," Cameron, the nineteen-year-old activist from Florida, told me. "Our secret weapon is the fact that we have millions and millions of young people who—especially Gen Z—are passionate about what's going on around them, who reject the idea that they shouldn't care, and that it's not their place to say something."

Over the course of summer 2022, in the months after the school walkout over Florida's Don't Say Gay bill, Cameron started an organization to oust two members of his local school board.[71] His organization partnered with the Florida Democratic Party and knocked on almost five thousand doors.[72] And although the odds were stacked against Cameron and his allies—Trump had won Cameron's home county by more than 20 percent in both the 2016 and 2020 elections—both school board members ended up losing their seats. Cameron has since launched a new organization called Youth Action Fund to help build a progressive youth movement within Florida.

American politicians and government officials have never embraced comprehensive sex ed, let alone sexual progressivism, but between 2000 and 2020, the United States took its support of abstinence-only-until-marriage sex ed to unparalleled heights as it forced countless late millennials and members of Gen Z to sit through inadequate, misleading, and bigoted sex ed classes—or deprived them of sex ed entirely. And yet the post-2020 debate over sex ed is so polarized, hateful, and uninterested in reality that, in retrospect, the 2000–2020 era seems almost benign.

While teachers are being driven out of their jobs, students are fleeing their home states. Some of Cameron's friends who helped organize the walkout have left Florida. One told *Inside Higher Ed* he was leaving not over safety concerns, but because he thought education in Florida was on the decline. "Given that Florida has initiated a takeover of our university system, I know my schooling would be hyper-politicized and often censored," he said.[73] He wasn't the only one to feel that way: A 2023 survey found that one in eight high school seniors in Florida won't attend a public college because of Governor Ron DeSantis's education policies.[74]

Their concerns are justified. In 2023, DeSantis banned public universities from teaching general education courses that "distort significant historical events," teach identity politics, or suggest that "systemic racism, sexism, oppression, and privilege are inherent in the institutions of the United States." In response, Florida universities pushed to cut hundreds of classes, such as "Introduction to LGBTQ+ Studies" and "Humanities Perspectives on Gender and Sexuality" from their general education curricula.[75]

Cameron, though, stayed. When we spoke, he was a student at the University of Florida. He got into this work, he said, "to reject this mindset that we should stay quiet and just ignore who we are. It's kind of the same thing, if I were to leave Florida.

"The last few years, I think, have been the greatest of my life. I've been able to be comfortable with who I am," he continued.

He has not started to date. "That's less about being scared to or anything, but I'm just focused on my work," Cameron said with a laugh. "I think I'd be a terrible boyfriend."

Although making young people feel unwanted or scared can delay some of their sexual urges, the parental rights movement will never be able to control everybody's sex drive. And when young people feel like they can't talk to trusted authority figures about their wants and desires, or when they can't talk to educated peers, they go looking for information and help elsewhere.

There is one glaringly obvious place to look.

4.

"THERE IS PORN OF IT. NO EXCEPTIONS."
Internet Porn, Romance Novels,
and the Legacy of *Fifty Shades of Grey*

A normal dictionary might describe how to use the word "sex" in a sentence. *Merriam-Webster*'s website, for instance, provides this example: "Her mom talked to her about sex."

But when Margaret was a preteen and using her Kindle's internet connection to surreptitiously look up the word "sex," she didn't go to *Merriam-Webster*'s website. She didn't talk to her mom, either. She went to Urban Dictionary—because on Urban Dictionary, users wrote smutty vignettes to demonstrate how to use "sex" in a sentence.

"It was a cold winter night when Tom had his girlfriend Shelia over," one such vignette begins. "Things were getting steamy. Shelia was still a virgin and tonight was the night she told Tom." The word "sex" appears only at the very end of the vignette, as in: "They laid next to each other that night remembering the wonderful sex."

"I would spend so long scrolling through all the entries," said Margaret, a nineteen-year-old from Kansas. "I don't think that I really knew what I was doing at the time, but looking back on it, I was doing it because it made me feel something inside. At the very least, it was titillating to read."

Various other sexual slang terms were woven into and highlighted throughout Urban Dictionary's vignettes, which allowed Margaret to "get deeper and deeper into this sex Urban Dictionary rabbit hole." One day, Margaret clicked through to the word "cum." The descriptions for that word were so graphic, so beyond her experience, that they instantly overwhelmed her. She quickly closed the page.

But she kept going back for more. There may be nothing that people love more than stuffing pornography into every nook and cranny of the internet, and nothing that young people love more than discovering it.

"I don't know why anyone was doing this on Urban Dictionary," Margaret said. "There's a whole world of places for you to do that, but whatever, that was a thing!" We both collapsed into laughter.

Failed by their sex ed for two decades, late millennials and Gen Z instead spent their formative years downloading an alternative sex ed curriculum from the internet. Often, people were savvy enough—even from a young age—to find their way to proven online resources like Planned Parenthood. Those resources were, however, almost always supplemented by sources that were *not* intended to be a replacement for school-based sex ed: video porn, fanfiction and written erotica, chat rooms, YouTube, Twitter (or X), Reddit, Tumblr, and, of course, Urban Dictionary. The education provided by these sources, whether straightforward or subliminal, is frequently an underrecognized form of sex ed, but it is just as impactful on young people's sex lives as information about condoms. And, importantly, the internet's sex ed curriculum is far more X-rated, communal, joyful, terrifying, interrogatory, and just flat-out weird than anything anyone would ever encounter in schools. It is often all of these things at once.

Porn is the most obvious form of internet sex ed, and its rise may be the greatest divide between growing up as a late millennial or Gen Z-er and growing up as a member of an older generation. Rather than encountering porn for the first time through stealing our fathers' *Playboys*, late millennials and Gen Z have always been just a few keystrokes away from it online. Three-quarters of young Americans have seen porn by their eighteenth birthdays, and 15 percent have seen it by age ten or younger. Most have seen it by accident, although just under half say they've sought it out intentionally.[1]

In addition, rather than being limited to whatever still photographs *Playboy* had on offer, the internet generation can easily find videos and written erotica of every possible proclivity. We learned early on how to taxonomize desire, to label individuals by the kind of sex they could offer. As I wrote this chapter, I opened up Pornhub, where I was greeted by categories of porn and people to get off to: "Japanese," "ebony," "MILF."

(Some of these categories are, clearly, sexist and racist.) After I went to Pornhub, I pulled up Archive of Our Own, the foremost source for online fanfiction, to check recent stories' bookmarks. I found "face-fucking," "femdom," and "human furniture," to name just a few options. My favorite was the bookmark that simply read "too many weird kinks."

There is an infamous idiom about the internet known as Rule 34. "There is porn of it," it declares. "No exceptions."

The very first time Ashton stumbled across sex online, it was in the form of a fanfiction based on the children's book series *Percy Jackson*. It featured one male character inserting his penis through the urethra of another character's penis.

"I was just sitting there, like, 'There's no way this can be how this works, right?'" said Ashton, who is twenty and hails from a Midwestern town that's home to just eight hundred people. Ashton, a trans man, received no sex ed after a deeply heteronormative lesson on puberty in elementary school. "Having fanfiction as my only source for that sort of education, for some reason—I wanted to read more out of pure, like, 'How does it actually work?'"

Hopefully, no one tried to stretch out their urethra because of that fanfiction. It's decidedly not a beginner move.

Learning about sex from porn is like learning how to drive by playing *Grand Theft Auto*, but people do so anyway. Sex educators repeatedly told me that students in elementary and middle school frequently ask questions that clearly stem from video porn: Is it normal to have pubic hair? When should I start getting waxed? Why do people moan so much during sex? Justine Ang Fonte, the sex educator who left her job at a Manhattan private school, put it simply: "If you don't teach sex ed, porn will."

These students' questions speak to a failure of U.S. sex ed policy, not of porn. If your sex ed teachers only tell you to *not* have sex, if they only focus on fear and threaten you with pregnancy, STIs, and death—well, they certainly can't acknowledge that sex feels good, much less how to give and receive consensual sexual pleasure. Even websites that are dedicated to sharing sexual health information frequently fail to talk about pleasure comprehensively. A study of a dozen top sexual health websites found that, of those that even covered pleasure, most touched only on masturbation and did not mention partnered pleasure.[2]

But porn does recognize sexual pleasure. (More than that: It induces it.) Sure, porn tends to skip right on over the things that lead to pleasure and actually make someone good at sex: safety, communication, a willingness to be open and awkward and unserious and self-deprecating. All that takes place off-screen, because the actors negotiate their boundaries ahead of filming or, in the case of written erotica, off-page, because they're fictional characters who magically intuit and execute their conquests' deepest desires. Porn depicts what may appear to be technically perfect sex, with screaming orgasms and cream pies and money shots.[*] It replaces intimacy with gymnastics and theatrics, letting the audience evade vulnerability by handing them total control and instant gratification. It also often depicts deeply gendered and racialized scripts about who likes what in sex. Usually, those scripts suggest that the people who already maintain power outside of the bedroom deserve to keep it inside, too.

And yet, because porn welcomes the existence of desire and is meant to depict, in extreme and evocative detail, what attraction and fulfillment look and feel like, young people can't shake the belief that porn can teach you how to be "good" at sex. Although less than a third of American teenagers think porn accurately represents sex, about three-quarters say they have learned what sexual behaviors are likely to feel pleasurable for themselves and for a partner from watching porn.[3]

In a world and a time when every U.S. institution can seem sexually conservative and dedicated to pathologizing youthful sex, porn can be an instrument of sexual progressivism that helps people realize they are not abnormal or alone. More than 90 percent of participants in a study about OnlyFans, a platform where creators can make porn for subscribers, said they tried new bedroom-related activities after watching OnlyFans. They learned they had foot fetishes; they learned about safe words; they said that they "learned that there are a lot of people who prefer my body type," that "the things I find quirky or weird about me, others will find sexy and be turned on," and "about the beauty of gay sex." The vast majority of their experiences were positive.[4]

---

[*] If you don't know what cream pies and money shots are, please take a page out of Margaret's Kindle and spend some time on Urban Dictionary before reading more of this chapter.

"The younger the participants were, the more they learned from their use of OnlyFans," researchers concluded.[5]

Is this a good thing? Should minors watch porn? Should porn serve as sex ed? I imagine most people would answer "no" to all of these questions; I personally don't endorse minors' use of porn and certainly wish they had elsewhere to turn for sex ed. But the fact remains that minors *do* watch porn and that the failures of school-based sex ed have left the internet, and in particular porn, as many minors' *only* source of sex ed. There is no easy or fast solution to this. When sexual conservatives have tried to limit access to porn, their fumbling efforts have endangered everybody's access to the internet as well as to free speech. So, rather than wringing our hands over our inability to stop minors from watching internet porn, it is better to recognize that we will never be free of it. Instead, let's focus on understanding its impacts and mitigating its downsides.

ARE WE WHAT WE WATCH?

Because horny humans invented the internet, our sexual desires—and our biases—will always seep through the pixels on our screens. It is not at all surprising, then, that the internet and porn were intertwined from the start.

A pair of California programmers first figured out how to send messages between computers in 1969,[6] the same year the Supreme Court loosened restrictions on pornography by ruling that people have the right to possess obscene materials in the privacy of their own homes. Four years later, computer engineers used a photo of a nude *Playboy* model named Lena Sjööblom to test out image processing, utilizing the porn we were already committing to ink and paper to develop the technology that would later enable us to create internet porn.[7] The so-called Lena image proved so popular that it remained in use throughout the industry for decades.

The picture is carefully cropped so that only Sjööblom's bare shoulders are visible. Still, as Sjööblom pouts at the camera over her shoulder, the "come hither" invitation is clear. "The Lena image is a picture of an attractive woman," the editor in chief of an industry journal wrote in a

1996 open letter. "It is not surprising that the (mostly male) image processing research community gravitated toward an image that they found attractive."[8] Meanwhile, the real Sjööblom was neither kept in the loop about her image's use nor well compensated for it.[9]

The World Wide Web, the foundational technology of the internet as we know it today, became available to the general public in 1993, right around the time of the birth of late millennials like myself. Even within those first few years of its existence, young people were using the internet to navigate their sexual awakenings. In a 2001 survey, about a fifth of teenagers said that they liked to "go online to find information that is hard to talk about with other people," including relationships, sex, and sexual health.[10] "It's less weird and cheaper than going to a doctor to ask," said one seventeen-year-old girl.[11] Because the government had not provided them with adequate and nonjudgmental access to education and health care, some teens were already relying on the internet more than on medical professionals.

Late millennials and Gen Z came of age during the 2000s emergence of Web 2.0, which the *New York Times* defined in 2008 as "those interactive websites where we, the public, supply the material."[12] (It was an early, far more optimistic version of that now-infamous internet cynicism: "If you're not paying for the product, you're the product.") As the saga of the Lena image showed, the development of the internet—and of internet porn—has been fueled by lust, entitlement, and an entrepreneurial willingness to harness both. Web 2.0 was no different.

When three male twentysomethings realized just how desperately people wanted to see footage of Justin Timberlake exposing Janet Jackson's breast at the 2004 Super Bowl halftime show,[13] they made a website where people could upload and share videos: YouTube,[14] one of the defining platforms of Web 2.0. A year later, YouPorn launched, modeling itself after YouTube and becoming the first-ever "tube" site for free porn.[15] In 2007, the year I entered seventh grade, Pornhub arrived. That tube site's name would eventually become synonymous with internet porn; its parent company, known as of this writing as Aylo, has built an oligopoly on video porn by buying up potential competitors by the dozens.[16]

Pornhub and other purveyors of video-based internet porn have faced the brunt of public scrutiny over the past two decades, so I'll focus on their kind of porn first. To distinguish between video porn and other forms of pornography available on the internet, I'll defer to convention and call video porn simply "porn," while using more specific terms for other forms of pornography.

Untold hours of research, countless dollars, and swimming pools of ink have been dumped into trying to ascertain porn's impact. Study after study has purported to discover that porn ruins relationships, that porn stimulates desire in relationships, that frequent porn viewing is linked to the objectification of women, that men are objectified just as often in porn. For seemingly every study that shows porn is dangerous, another seems to discover that porn is just fine. For every former sex worker who speaks out about abuse in the industry, another is ready to warmly reminisce.

So much research into porn is riddled with bias. Anti-porn scholars tout their results without acknowledging their baked-in assumptions about what constitutes "rough" sex or that certain acts—anal sex, money shots—are always degrading. The porn industry's reports on itself should also be viewed with a raised eyebrow. Many media outlets dutifully recycle Pornhub's annual reports into clickbait headlines, despite the fact that the reports cannot be independently verified[17] and that Pornhub wants to present the rosiest possible view of its own business.

Consider Pornhub's 2019 "Year in Review" report, which declared that users loved searching for porn of celebrities like Ariana Grande, Selena Gomez, and Miley Cyrus. "Coincidentally, the day that Miley allegedly split from Liam Hemsworth, her searches spiked by 102 percent—do Pornhub users love a single lady?" the report wondered cheekily.[18]

No, you have not missed a sudden left turn in Hannah Montana's career. Neither Cyrus nor any of those other celebrities have ever done porn. Instead, journalist Samantha Cole found that searching for their names surfaced AI-produced, or "deepfake," explicit imagery of these women that had been made without their consent. Such imagery is supposedly against Pornhub's own rules, but the videos were posted against ads on the site, indicating they made money for Pornhub.[19]

"That there still exists non-consensual pornography at the other end of those searches after the company has stated repeatedly it does not allow them, shows that it is unable to do anything about them," Cole wrote in *Vice*'s tech vertical, *Motherboard*. "Less generously, it shows that Pornhub doesn't care."[20] Does it also show that Pornhub's users—who are likely aware these former child stars have never done porn—don't care if these women are transmogrified, through AI, into sex toys without free will? Does Pornhub's refusal to stop it quietly teach these users that it's fine to treat women this way?

We will probably never be able to measure the impact of AI porn, or of internet porn overall, in a way that meets the highest standards of scientific rigor. In 2009, a researcher from the University of Montreal sparked laughter across the internet when he announced that he had launched an effort to study "the impact of pornography on the sexuality of men, and how it shapes their perception of men and women"—but couldn't find a control group because he couldn't find a single twentysomething man who had never seen porn.[21] As porn industry scholar Shira Tarrant once joked, "It's been said that the one thing porn is actually known to cause is masturbation."[22]

But in interview after interview, people told me they felt porn *had* deeply impacted their sex lives. Honestly, it feels foolish to claim that porn has zero impact on us; all media, particularly that which we consume as children, has some effect. I'm constantly astounded by the randomness of the material that triggers young people's sexual awakening. (And by the recurrent theme of dictionaries. One twenty-one-year-old gay man told me that, in elementary school, he masturbated to the words "penis," "vagina," and "sex" using his family's pocket dictionary.)

When Diego was eight years old, his male cousin came over for a sleepover. In the gleefully superior manner of older cousins, the cousin snagged Diego's PlayStation, used its browser function to go online, and summoned porn. *Wow*, Diego thought, *this is awesome.*

By the age of twelve, Diego was watching porn every day. He lost his virginity at fourteen, to a girl whom he admits he saw no future with; the relationship was built on physical attraction and a mutual interest in exploring sex. "All of our conversations were practically sexting," Diego said. He genuinely liked his next girlfriend, whom he started dating at sixteen, but he lost interest in her quickly. He kept her around only because he wanted easy access to sex, a compulsion he blames on porn.

"I just constantly wanted it, but I didn't care for it," said Diego, who grew up in Montana and is now twenty. "We'd be done, and I'd be like, 'Okay. When's the next time?'"

It was pleasureless consumption. It felt like gluttony. A sin.

Tom, a twenty-three-year-old from the South, can't remember how he first ran across porn, although he knows he must have been ten or eleven. "It so negatively influenced my view of women that there was a point where I was having a conversation with a female colleague of mine and I had to repeatedly say to myself, 'Tom, she's a human being. She's more than an opportunity for sex,'" he told me. "I essentially had to re-train myself to view women as human beings. I really want to convey the gravity of that to you.

"I feel like it's just drugged me down my whole life, frankly. I think it really just serves to cripple every virtuous or good aspect of men," Tom continued, referring to porn. "I was definitely a slave to it for a while. It makes me wish I was born before the internet."

Tom's use of the word "drugged" is something of a Freudian slip. Tom, like many other young men I talked to, believed that he had once been addicted to porn.

We don't really know whether porn can truly be "addictive." Before the advent of internet sex, even psychologists who believed in sex addiction—itself a disputed diagnosis—did not think porn itself was addictive. "It wasn't until internet-connected computers started appearing in family rec rooms in the late '90s did the idea of someone getting so hooked on internet porn that it could ruin their lives enter the mainstream," Samantha Cole wrote in her book *How Sex Changed the Internet and the Internet Changed Sex*.[23] Millennials and Gen Z are—again—a pioneering generation, the first to grow up with the specter of "porn addiction" hanging over our heads.

Porn addiction is not in the latest edition of the *Diagnostic and Statistical Manual of Mental Disorders*, and experts remain split on its legitimacy. Studies have found that people who describe themselves as addicted to porn or sex, or who have those labels placed upon them, may actually watch porn at normal rates. These so-called porn addicts feel more shame about their behavior due to religious or spiritual beliefs, or they belong to marginalized groups whose sexuality has always been more highly policed.[24] "I think the overrepresentation of homosexual men in sex addiction centers is strong evidence that the diagnosis is primarily used for social control of sexuality, rather than treating any actual disease that should affect all men equally," one neuroscientist told Cole.[25]

At the start of my interviews, I often asked people if they had a religious background or identity. Tom initially told me he did not. Then, at the end, he confessed that he had not quite told the truth: He is a Christian. "I didn't want my answers to be conflated with dogma or think that it comes from some sort of doctrine," Tom said. "I wanted to give you my own honest thoughts because they were my own honest thoughts."

I don't want to write off Tom's genuine anguish over pornography, which he went so far as to accuse of "crippling my entire country," although it was initially hard for me not to see his opinions on porn as part and parcel of a fairly conservative worldview. His opinion of pornography is in line with his approach to partnered sex—which he has had, although he is now celibate. Premarital sex is, in his opinion, "a crime to my future wife."

To my surprise, however, many of the left-leaning people I interviewed did not particularly like porn either. I would categorize these individuals as open to sexual progressivism; they were often familiar with the ideals of sex positivity and identified as such. Yet their views on porn hewed closer to the sex-negative side of the feminist sex wars. Men, women, and people outside that binary spoke of porn addiction as though it was an established fact; even those who supported sex work were suspicious of porn's labor practices. One individual, Phoebe, felt that porn might even be responsible for her body's rejection of penetrative sex.

Despite hailing from deep-blue Massachusetts, self-described "leftist" Phoebe did not receive in-depth sex ed in school. All she got were horror stories about penis-in-vagina sex. "I remember always hearing things like 'It's meant to hurt.' Everything was very centered around male pleasure," Phoebe said. "I was just bracing myself for pain."

When Phoebe checked out Pornhub, what they saw left them petrified. "It looked painful, because obviously all I really saw was heterosexual porn," recalled Phoebe, whose pronouns are she/they. "The noises that the women made felt so fake. Also, I had read stories about porn stars confessing about how terrible the industry is and how much pain they were in and stuff, and I think that scared me too."

Still, Phoebe wanted to try penetrative, penis-in-vagina sex.

"The first time I tried to have sex with my now-ex boyfriend in high school, it just did not fit. I was like, 'What is going on?'" Phoebe recalled. "I thought, 'Okay, maybe my hymen isn't broken.' We could eventually get it in, and it hurt really bad."

Eventually, after a few more painful attempts at penetrative vaginal sex, Phoebe went to the gynecologist for help. The gynecologist diagnosed Phoebe, then seventeen, with vaginismus, a disorder where someone's vaginal walls contract to the point that penetrative sex becomes painful or even impossible. It's often caused by anxiety and fear.

Phoebe was distraught. *Why can I not do something that billions and billions of other people with vaginas have been capable of doing for thousands of years?* she thought.

Phoebe blames their vaginismus on their lack of comprehensive sex ed coupled with their early exposure to porn, which effectively supplanted the sex ed Phoebe's school should have given them. By the time we spoke, two years' worth of intermittent physical therapy later, Phoebe was still struggling with vaginismus and had been able to have penetrative sex only once or twice without extreme pain. On bad days, Phoebe's terror of the future wells up: "I can't do this. Is anybody gonna want to be with me if I can't do this?"

Gen Z's reputation as sex-negative puriteens is perhaps most justified when it comes to porn: 46 percent of adult members of Gen Z believe porn is harmful, compared to 37 percent of millennials.[26]

"Porn really does re-create the structures of power that exists in life and, I think, really magnifies them and amplifies them and fetishizes them," said Vivian, a twenty-year-old from Texas, sounding astonishingly similar to the sex-negative feminists of the 1980s. "I think, when you're a young person and that's your only way to understand sex, you don't really have a choice but to accept the model of sex that's very much integrated in those social hierarchies of power."

A PORN OF OUR OWN

The first time Charlotte discovered porn, she was looking for hamsters.

Specifically, she was searching for hamsters.com, because she wanted to mail a hamster to her house in defiance of her parents' rules against the rodents. Instead, Charlotte found humpsters.com.

She was in second grade.

When Charlotte's dad found her scrolling through the porn site on the family computer, he immediately blocked the website. "That's a very adult site," he told Charlotte, who is from Ohio. "Those are things that adults look at and those are things adults do. Until you're older, we're never going to talk about this again. And you're still not getting a hamster."

The second time Charlotte discovered porn, she was in fourth grade. The boys in her class had started to talk about it, so at a sleepover, Charlotte and her female friends decided to Google "What is a blow job?"

Just typing in the query felt like breaking the law, but in a fun way. In the video she found, a man slapped his female partner across the face multiple times. *Okay, blow job: You suck a dick and you get slapped in the face,* Charlotte thought. *Got it.*

The feeling of joyful rebellion soon wore off. As Charlotte grew older, video porn started to make her feel queasy. Steeped in Catholicism, Charlotte felt guilty, even immoral, for viewing it. She was terrified her parents would one day discover her watching porn.

The third time Charlotte discovered porn, she was closer to fifth grade. This time, it wasn't video porn. It was fanfiction, and she loved it.

Unlike with video porn, no one had explicitly warned her that erotica was wrong, so she felt far less conflicted about its morality. (Plus, there were no errant moans to tip her parents off to the fact that she was reading pornography on her iPod Touch.) Within the wordy confines of fanfiction, Charlotte was free to imagine herself as former One Direction star Zayn Malik's girlfriend. During gym class, she and her friends would even swap recommendations for stories on Wattpad, a website for original fiction, and thus combine their fandom with their burgeoning sexual interests.

"I was a Zayn fan. The other girl was a Harry fan. My other friend was Niall. So we didn't have a lot of overlap in what we were reading," said Charlotte, referring to Harry Styles and Niall Horan, two other members of One Direction. "None of the things that we shared were ever probably the most explicit things we ever read, but there was also a little bit of a game to see who could push the boundary and shock the other girlies."

The emergence of Web 2.0 allowed late millennials' and Gen Z's adolescence to coincide not only with the birth of porn tube sites, but also with the rise of centralized fandom platforms across the internet, such as Tumblr and Wattpad. Like the rest of the internet, those platforms were in turn shaped by sex and squeamishness around it. But unlike porn tube sites, fandom platforms that have lasted have proven extremely welcoming to the sexual and romantic desires of women and LGBTQ+ folks.

In 2009, author Naomi Novik teamed up with other fanfiction lovers to start Archive of Our Own, or AO3, in part because the then-popular blogging platform LiveJournal got nervous about the legal ramifications of sexually explicit fanfiction and started deleting accounts.[27] Backed by the nonprofit the Organization for Transformative Works and free from corporate pearl-clutching, AO3 was committed to letting fans get freaky with their characters. After Fanfiction.com, one of AO3's chief competitors, purged itself of thousands of explicit stories in 2012,[28] AO3 and Wattpad became citadels of online fanfiction.

Compared to video porn, there's been far less attention paid to the impact of sexually explicit fanfiction, particularly on young women and LGBTQ+ people. Yet in numerous interviews, young people told me their first taste of sex online was not porn, but fanfiction. Even if they did somehow stumble across porn first, they did not develop a taste for media depicting explicit sex until they found fanfiction.

While video porn so often focuses on the perspective of straight white men, LGBTQ+ folks and those assigned female at birth found a mirror in written porn's depictions of their bodies and desires. "There are straight white men who write and read fanfiction," said Z, a twenty-seven-year-old who volunteers with the Organization for Transformative Works. "But it does tend toward being a lot of women, AFAB people, but also trans women, gay men, trans men, and nonbinary people."

I want to be very clear: Not all fanfiction features sex, but the fanfiction that is sexual can compete with Pornhub. (Just go look back at the AO3 tags at the beginning of this chapter.) For many young people, fanfiction was a gateway drug to original erotica and romance novels, whose sales are now spiking thanks to Gen Z.[29] For some, it also proved to be a vital form of sex ed.

Through written porn, Cyprus learned about the existence of the

G-spot. DeeDee, a twenty-five-year-old Texan, learned about the existence of vaginal, oral, and anal sex. (Yes, that's how terrible her sex ed was.) This medium also led people to realizations about the emotional, rather than mechanical, pleasures of sex. "It made me realize that I like romance, I like the yearning," said twenty-four-year-old Simone, who read sexual fanfiction practically every night in high school. "It made me realize that I really liked boys—that I really, *really* liked boys." She sighed. "It's just hard for me to deal with them."

By some metrics, the stories of power and pleasure embedded in written porn are more equitable than those usually found in video porn or, indeed, in real life. While 95 percent of heterosexual men say they usually orgasm during partnered sex, just 65 percent of heterosexual women say the same;[30] this gulf has long been known in sex research as "the orgasm gap." (This is not necessarily because orgasms can be more biologically elusive for AFAB bodies. Eighty-six percent of lesbian women say they usually orgasm during partnered sex.[31]) This enormous IRL orgasm gap yawns even wider in video porn. A 2017 study of the most-viewed straight porn videos on Pornhub found that 78 percent of the male performers were shown having orgasms, compared to only 18 percent of the female performers.[32] Meanwhile, in romance novels, female characters are more likely than male characters to be depicted having orgasms and to have multiple orgasms.[33] And while I wouldn't go so far as to describe the sex in romance novels as realistic, these books better capture the activities that really lead to female pleasure. Porn tends to show female performers orgasming from vaginal and anal sex,[34] but heroines in romance novels often come from oral and manual stimulation in addition to vaginal sex[35]—the kinds of sex that, in real life, are associated with higher frequency of female orgasm.[36]

Pornography of all types, and the modern internet it helped usher into being, can be an instrument and product of sexual progressivism, leading people to embrace their sexuality and scramble conventional sexual mores. (For as much as porn can portray fairly traditional, if not sexist, gender roles, it's certainly not aligned with the sexual conservatism movement's goal of married, heterosexual, and procreative sex.) But without sex ed that contextualizes video and written porn, people can forget that it is fictional, an inspirational jumping-off point—not necessarily *aspirational* and certainly not a step-by-step instruction manual.

Indeed, video and written porn may have, separately and together, normalized some deeply dangerous sexual practices.

CHOKE ME, DADDY

In 1989, the year before late millennials started being born, sadomasochistic art by the artist Robert Mapplethorpe triggered a national moral panic and a congressional proposal to ban federal funding of "indecent" art.[37] Today, one's adventures in BDSM can be casually discussed over brunch. Gen Z are more likely than any other living generation to report fantasizing about BDSM and most likely to say they've done it.[38]

The mainstreaming of BDSM—which can variously stand for "bondage and discipline," "dominance and submission," and "sadism and masochism"—can be attributed to fanfiction, since the BDSM behemoth *Fifty Shades of Grey* began life as an online *Twilight* fanfiction. Published between 2011 and 2012, the *Fifty Shades* trilogy became the bestselling books of the decade[39] and were later turned into a trio of respectably successful movies. One twenty-three-year-old woman from Florida told me she encountered the books in middle school, when her aunt loaned her a copy. "I didn't realize it was that spicy." She laughed. "That's how I got introduced to smut, and that just started to snowball."

There is no way to know for sure if BDSM-y behavior has spread since *Fifty Shades*, because there were no "national benchmarks" of the practice before the series took off;[40] scientists long regarded BDSM to be a deviancy that needed fixing rather than a valid sexual expression. *Fifty Shades* has, however, been linked to rising rope sales, sex toy sales, and "BDSM sex-toy injuries,"[41] while public acceptance of BDSM has soared. By the end of the 2010s, BDSM—and some other forms of kink—had become mainstream enough that *Buzzfeed* regularly published quizzes with titles like "Are You More Kinky, Vanilla, or Somewhere In Between" and "This Quiz Will Reveal What % Dominant and Submissive You Are During Sex." (That last quiz's URL read "punish me daddy.")

When it's well practiced, kink, including BDSM, is extremely concerned with boundaries, enjoyment, and providing aftercare for your partner(s). One long-standing rule within the kink community declares that kink should always be safe, sane, and consensual. "As a woman, it made me much more powerful in knowing what I wanted and asking for what I wanted from men, and actually doing a better job of ruling out men who would just use me to masturbate," one elder millennial woman who discovered kink in her twenties told me. "There's this idea that you're gonna meet your Disney prince and he's gonna know everything that you like in bed right away, and you're gonna have a million orgasms just from penetration. No. Sex is complicated. And I think kink allows you to talk about that a lot more openly and easily."

Ironically, the idea of instantly perfect sex with the perfect partner is exactly what so much of video and written porn sells to its audience. And despite the promise of kink, *Fifty Shades*'s portrayal of BDSM is nauseatingly inaccurate. Rather than depicting the communication skills and strong ethics needed to entwine pleasure with consensual pain, *Fifty Shades* is a melodrama about a middle-class woman being brainwashed into an abusive relationship with a preposterously wealthy man. (If Christian Grey weren't rich, would he still be sexy? Or just a stalker?) Like all kinds of media, written porn can advance regressive and damaging ideas about men's supposedly innate dominance over women.

"A lot of it—looking back, as an adult—was really, really, really, really graphic things," Charlotte, who is now twenty-three, said of the fanfiction she read. "Like orgies and really aggressive, gang-banging stuff that they just randomly throw in, or a lot of, like, dubious consent situations— which I didn't realize at all, because I had no kind of concept of terminology for any of these things. And I was just like, 'Yeah, this is cool.'"

Dubious consent, or "dubcon," refers to situations where it's unclear whether one party consents to sex. ("Noncon," in internet speak, refers to unmistakably nonconsensual sex, or rape.*) In real life, there's no such thing: If you don't have consent, you're committing sexual assault. But in fanfiction, the ambiguity can be papered over and eroticized. More than 160,000 works on AO3 have been appended with its "dubious consent" tag.

Personally, I was never all that interested in video porn—not growing up and not now. I'm keenly aware that I am not its target audience; if I

---

*This is *not* the same thing as "consensual non-consent," a sexual practice that involves people negotiating scenes in which they act out having nonconsensual sex.

want to watch porn, I'm probably going to spend several minutes swimming through content until I find something that doesn't feel totally foreign to my desires. But I also know that the reason porn feels foreign to me is not only because I'm outside its purview. It is also because I have far more experience with whitewashing the red flags found in written porn.

I don't remember how I first stumbled across erotica, but I know it happened by middle school. After school, I frequently parked myself in my parents' office, opened up the shared family computer, and spent hours wandering in the wilderness of sexy fanfiction and original smut. (Had my parents ever peered over my shoulder, they would have been appalled at the filth that their preteen daughter read with a straight face.) Dubcon and noncon initially revolted me, but the more I ran into stories with these themes, the more I struggled to summon disgust. There's no other way to say this: I got used to it. Today, fantasies featuring dubcon, noncon, and worse continue to litter the "dark romance" section of Amazon's Kindle Unlimited, the company's online, bizarro version of a library.

Matt described a similar relationship with video porn. For years, the twenty-eight-year-old from Pennsylvania would trawl Reddit for porn and let the stream of sex wash over him. "I think you can do damage to your brain, when all that is just being fed to you in between puppy videos and TikToks of people working on cars and shit like that," he said. "It's a desensitizing effect.

"I know for a fact it's taught a lot of guys poor behavior. And aggressive and felonious behavior," Matt said of porn. He believed that its "animalistic" sex sent a clear message to men: "Just take what you want."

As my interviews continued, a narrative started to emerge. In young people's telling, written porn's mainstreaming of a bastardized version of BDSM has worked in tandem with video porn to normalize "rough sex." This "rough sex" lacks BDSM's prioritizing of safe words and carefully negotiated scenes in favor of more stereotypical displays of dominance and submission, where men spank, choke, and pull the hair of women with little to no communication. Young women consume this sex through fanfiction. Young men consume it through tube sites. For many, particularly those who have heterosexual sex, the line between the categories of "rough sex" and "sex" collapses. To have sex means to have rough sex.

Choking, in particular, came up again and again in my interviews.

Young women told me that they felt their male partners' relentless interest in it, as well as women's acquiescence to it, was driven by porn, both video and written.

In high school, Anne and her friends called choking a "love squeeze." "All of us were having sex for the first time, but all of us were being choked," said Anne, a twenty-one-year-old from Wisconsin. "Some people are into it and that's great, but I just don't really believe that everybody was *that* into it."

Choking is something of a generational kink, since adults under forty are almost twice as likely to have been choked during sex.[42] One 2020 survey of college students found that 58 percent of women, 45 percent of gender-expansive students, and 26 percent of men have been choked during sex.[43]

As Anne said, if you enjoy rough sex and choking, more power to you. The problem is not that it occurs—it's that consent often does not. Of college students who have been choked, 32 percent said they had sometimes been asked for consent prior to being choked, while 21 percent said they had *never* been asked. "The person was behind me. . . . Yeah, I think I probably knew it was happening 'cause I, like, saw them [grabbing] for the belt," recalled one twenty-three-year-old woman in a 2022 study. "But it's not like we like sat down and was like, 'Hey, is it cool if I choke you with my belt?'"[44]

"I wish asking if something is okay during sex before doing it was more normalized," twenty-four-year-old Uzi Orji[45] posted on Twitter in 2022. "Why TF [the fuck] would you just assume that I like being choked. It freaks me out." Orji's post was liked more than 4,500 times. "The amount of men who just put their hands on my neck [without] asking is *alarming*," one user replied, adding that they had told men not to touch their neck at all, only for men to reply, "But your neck is so perfectly fitted to my hands."

Jessica, a twenty-one-year-old Virginia college student, once had a boyfriend choke her to the point that she almost passed out. "It was a new relationship and somebody doing something they saw in porn and they thought it was cool and it wasn't," she told me. Her words sped up as she spoke, but her voice remained even, as if deadened with distaste. Once she got her breath back, Jessica exploded at her partner: "Who the *fuck* do you think you are?"

For obvious reasons, choking—or strangulation—can be dangerous even in situations where someone has obtained consent. But most women in that 2022 study felt like choking was safe, although the majority had also never researched safe choking practices. Some women even seemed to expect male partners to choke them, or even think less of men who didn't—a potential side effect, researchers hypothesized, of the stereotype that to be masculine is to be dominating, to like rough sex.[46]

Asked where they learned about choking, many women in the study cited *Fifty Shades of Grey*, fanfiction, and porn.[47] (One even suspected she learned about it from One Direction fanfiction she read at twelve.[48]) "Face slapping, choking, gagging, and spitting [have] become the alpha and omega of any porn scene and not within a BDSM context," Erika Lust, a famous feminist pornographer, told the *Guardian* in 2019. "These are presented as standard ways to have sex when, in fact, they are niches."[49]

This normalization can have widespread legal consequences, said Susan Edwards, a British law professor. If choking seems normal, "it means that a woman whose partner chokes her might not report it—and if she does, it might go nowhere," Edwards told the *Guardian*. "It means that if a woman dies this way, judges and juries feel 'this is how people have sex now' and questions aren't always asked."[50] We Can't Consent to This, a United Kingdom–based advocacy group, has uncovered at least sixty cases of people in the U.K. who were killed by partners who claimed that rough sex had gotten out of hand.[51]

Has internet porn, whether in video or written form, actually caused nonconsensual choking and rough sex? As I said earlier, it is impossible to know for sure. (Can we ever definitively trace the source of any sexual desire or behavior?) Porn could be a scapegoat. Take Phoebe and her vaginismus: As much as porn scared her, her anxiety over sex also stemmed from the warnings she heard—in school, from peers—about sex prior to her first encounter with porn.

Yet many of the people I interviewed clearly feel immense grief over their relationship with porn. We have gotten so sidetracked by the question of whether porn is bad for us that we overlook the fact that we have already convinced much of Gen Z that it *is* bad—and that, as one of the first generations to grow up on an internet infested with degrading sex, they have been uniquely at risk and uniquely harmed.

As I've said, sex is a story we tell ourselves. We are telling young people a story about porn that leads them to believe they are stranded before the maw of a vast and dehumanizing internet. We are telling them this story while offering next to zero authoritative resources to deal with this internet, because their school-based sex ed pretends sexual pleasure and porn don't exist or dismisses them as shameful. Regardless of whether this story is true, the feeling of powerlessness that it engenders does not make for quality mental health or good sex.

Similarly, no matter the reason for its popularity, choking is now a common sexual behavior, and there is an urgent need for guidance on how to handle an interest in "rough sex" safely and respectfully. Lives could very well be at stake.

If young people weren't forced to turn to alternative resources like video porn and fanfiction for their sex ed—that is, if they had sex educators who could discuss topics like consent—they would be better able to grasp the importance of boundaries, know how to navigate conversations about them, and recognize when theirs have been violated. But rather than help them through sex ed, many states are set to drive minors into some of the internet's most frightening corners.

THE WAR ON PORN

Sexual conservatism has hijacked good-faith concerns about porn, combined them with old-fashioned prudery and whorephobia, and enacted sweeping anti-porn laws. We are in the midst of a crackdown on online sex and pleasure—one that can seem well-intentioned, even effective, if you don't look too closely at the machinations behind it. Sexualities that have been deemed "other" in some way are at extreme risk. In 2018, Apple banned Tumblr from its app store over its not-suitable-for-work nature. Tumblr then announced it would be outlawing "adult content"—which is to say, porn. Between 2018 and 2021, visits to the site's website and app plummeted by more than 40 percent,[52] leveling online communities that had been built around exploring female and LGBTQ+ sexuality.

But what happened on Tumblr pales in comparison to what's going on today.

"Pornography, manifested today in the omnipresent propagation of transgender ideology and sexualization of children, for instance, is not a political Gordian knot inextricably binding up disparate claims about free speech, property rights, sexual liberation, and child welfare," the Heritage Foundation, a conservative think tank, wrote in its Project 2025, a playbook of policy recommendations for a future conservative presidential organization. Former Donald Trump staffers and advisors penned many of Project 2025's policies, and the playbook as a whole was backed by more than a hundred conservative groups.[53]

Project 2025 continued of porn: "It has no claim to First Amendment protection. Its purveyors are child predators and misogynistic exploiters of women. Their product is as addictive as any illicit drug and as psychologically destructive as any crime. Pornography should be outlawed. The people who produce and distribute it should be imprisoned. Educators and public librarians who purvey it should be classed as registered sex offenders. And telecommunications and technology firms that facilitate its spread should be shuttered."

This all sounds suspiciously like the rants of hysterical parents at a school board meeting. And like those rants, it is no empty threat. Sexual conservatives across the country are already working to make good on it.

In 2018, the year Tumblr banned "adult content," Trump signed into law a pair of bills collectively known as SESTA-FOSTA. Ostensibly meant to curb online sex trafficking, SESTA-FOSTA punched a massive hole in the fundamental law of the internet, Section 230 of the 1996 Communications Decency Act. Section 230 broadly guarantees that platforms cannot be held responsible for the content of third-party creators and, as such, has long been regarded as an essential protection for online free speech. (For example, Section 230 allows platforms like Amazon to host one-star reviews without fear of liability. If Amazon could face liability, the company would likely remove one-star reviews and thus curtail its users' speech.) Under SESTA-FOSTA, however, if a third party posts ads for sex, including consensual sex work, on a platform, then the hosting platform could be held responsible.

Given the law's sweeping scope, platforms struggled to ascertain what sexual content crossed the line. Companies like Reddit, Microsoft, and Craigslist all cracked down on explicit content.[54] The result: a sanitized and shrinking internet, one where smaller platforms and freewheeling sexuality have far less ability to either sneak beneath or break through the cultural cacophony.

Before Trump signed SESTA-FOSTA, sex workers and their advocates warned that the law would endanger people who engage in consensual sex work, because they would be kicked off platforms they used to vet clients. They were right. More than a third of sex workers experienced increased violence after SESTA-FOSTA took effect.[55] Meanwhile, the law did not even work for its intended purpose. As of June 2021, the Justice Department had filed just one criminal case using SESTA-FOSTA.[56]

SESTA-FOSTA was, according to one sex worker, nothing more than "the government controlling what women do with their bodies in a failed attempt to clean up the internet by fearmongering."[57] It was also an early example of the phenomenon that, post-2020 and partially thanks to the parental rights movement, would become far more commonplace in school districts and national conversations: The specter of sexualization, sex abuse, and sex trafficking, especially around children, was invoked to restrict consensual sex writ large—with little effect on actual crimes but a severe impact on marginalized people. This is a key tactic of modern sexual conservatism.

In the years since the pandemic, states have taken up the battle against porn. Since 2022, lawmakers in at least twenty-eight states have introduced legislation requiring sites that host some degree of adult content to verify that their users are over the age of eighteen.[58] Even if most people can agree that porn is not meant to be viewed by minors, these laws come with a litany of issues.

First, it is impossible to stop minors from watching porn in the internet age. Encouraging them to avoid porn online is the equivalent of digital abstinence-only sex ed, because it refuses to engage with the basic reality that most people *want* to have sex—with themselves, with others—and will do so even if it makes them feel bad about themselves. (I'm going to assume that you have masturbated to porn before. Did you feel reflexive shame afterward? Did it stop you from doing it again?) (If you didn't feel shame afterward, please forward me your therapist's contact information.) If age-verification laws block minors from accessing the major tube sites, experts fear that minors will head to websites that are less obvious targets for enforcement, websites where deepfakes and image-based sexual abuse—explicit photos taken or disseminated without their subjects' approval, a practice that was once known as "revenge porn"—flourish with even less regulation than Pornhub.

Second, this legislation has slashed even adults' access to porn—which is perhaps its true intent anyway. As of this writing, Pornhub has blocked access to all users in at least seventeen states that have passed age-verification laws.[59] (All seventeen states are Republican-dominated.) In a blog post, Pornhub explained that the age-verification methods required by the new laws put their users' data at too much risk for identity theft. "Since age verification software requires users to hand over extremely sensitive information, it opens the door for the risk of data breaches," the company wrote. "Whether or not your intentions are good, governments have historically struggled to secure this data."

Third, this legislation can rope off entire sections of the internet. In 2024, Kansas passed a law implementing age-verification requirements on websites where 25 percent or more of the content viewed by visitors is "harmful to minors," which Kansas law defines as materials that feature "nudity, sexual conduct, sexual excitement or sadomasochistic abuse." This law goes on to clarify that "sexual conduct" includes "acts of masturbation, homosexuality." Hence, under the Kansas bill, minors could be blocked from viewing information about sexual orientation and gender identity, or even from seeing depictions of gay people. Sexual health and sex education websites could be in danger, too. Even mainstream social media sites like Tumblr, Reddit, and X might be impacted by age-verification legislation, since they all host some amount of porn.

Covenant Eyes, an app that purports to help shield internet users from porn and is popular among Christians, demonstrates how all-encompassing anti-porn censorship can be. After the far-right Speaker of the House Mike Johnson, a Republican from Louisiana, publicly praised Covenant Eyes, a *Guardian* writer downloaded the app—which proceeded to flag photos of a woman in a bikini and female soccer players as porn.[60]

"Broadly speaking, if a woman's midriff or upper chest is visible,

Covenant Eyes will not like it. It serves as a neat reflection of the evangelical world Covenant Eyes operates within," the writer Adam Gabbatt reflected. "Curiously, the app does not have a problem with the male form. When a friend sent a link to a New York City-based all-male strip club, Covenant Eyes didn't seem to care—even letting it slide when I clicked through to some photos of the oiled-up dancers."[61] Given Covenant Eyes' provenance, this oversight seems like less of an endorsement of homosexuality and more an indication that the app is laser-focused on policing the bodies of women, not men.

States' crackdown on porn also perpetuates the myth that porn is scientifically proven to be unhealthy. After Texas passed its age-verification law, *404 Media* found that Texan visitors to some video porn sites were greeted with the following pop-up[62]:

> TEXAS HEALTH AND HUMAN SERVICES WARNING: Pornography is potentially biologically addictive, is proven to harm human brain development, desensitizes brain reward circuits, increases conditioned responses, and weakens brain function. TEXAS HEALTH AND HUMAN SERVICES WARNING: Exposure to this content is associated with low self-esteem and body image, eating disorders, impaired brain development, and other emotional and mental illnesses. TEXAS HEALTH AND HUMAN SERVICES WARNING: Pornography increases the demand for prostitution, child exploitation, and child pornography.

Although this warning was attributed to a Texas health agency, a court found that the agency did not make those findings or the warning.

"One of the most beautiful things about the Wild West days of the internet is it showed us that *so much* is normal—that whatever it is, there's porn of it on the internet," Jessica Stoya, the millennial porn performer better known by the mononym Stoya and one of the most prominent sex workers of the twenty-first century, told *Document* in 2023. "All this censorship makes me think that the goal of the other side—and it does very much feel like the other side right now—is to erase all pleasure and all individuality from the internet."[63]

PORN LITERACY

Not everyone I spoke to detested internet porn. Some said porn was just another way to spend time online or to fulfill the biological function of masturbation. "Sometimes I'll be scrolling through TikTok or something and, if I see a video of an attractive woman, sometimes that will prompt me to want to masturbate," said Jimmy, a twenty-four-year-old straight man who lives in Alaska. "I feel like masturbating, I usually watch porn. And then when I'm done, I don't really think about it anymore."

But no one described their relationship to porn quite as thoughtfully as Nicole.

A New Yorker born to parents who immigrated from Colombia, Nicole has Gloria Steinem–style glasses, a canyon-wide smile, and a shatter-proof cheerfulness. Interviewees often laughed out of embarrassment, but during our two-hour-plus chat, Nicole laughed at sex with delight and marvel, like a scholar in the midst of surfacing career-making discoveries. That attitude, I found, was precisely because Nicole treated sex like she was a scholar of it.

Nicole's first foray into online sex was a Google search for "sexy ladies," but she really began to watch video porn in eighth grade, around the same time that she started masturbating. "There was not really a period of time where I was not masturbating with porn. Those were really interlinked for me. I remember trying to see if I could masturbate without porn and being like, 'Holy shit. I can't get wet,'" said Nicole, who prefers not to label her sexuality. "I didn't want to be dependent on it to experience pleasure."

Nicole, who is now twenty-one, wanted to know: *Can I masturbate and can I reach orgasm without porn?* She decided to start experimenting on herself.

For two and a half years, Nicole stopped watching video porn entirely. To wean herself off it, she replaced it with erotica. Then she stopped reading erotica, too. She even phased out using her vibrator because "it was so easy to orgasm and I was kind of dependent on it, or too impatient to do anything else."

Instead, Nicole said, "I would use my imagination." She graphed her orgasm in her journal, trying to chart out how arousal can build around a narrative. "There's one time where I distinctly remember not even touching myself and I had an orgasm. It was kind of life-changing."

When Nicole reconfigured her relationship with porn, she was embarking on what scholars Jennifer Hirsch and Shamus Khan have called a "sexual project," their shorthand for "the reasons why anyone might seek a particular sexual interaction or experience."[64] People can have a vast array of sexual projects, and they may have more than one: to lose their virginity, to get into a relationship, to have sex in a public place, to have children, to not have sex at all. Nicole, through her sexual project of examining and reclaiming her own pleasure, fortified her sense of what Hirsch and Khan call "sexual citizenship," or "a socially produced sense of enfranchisement and right to sexual agency."[65] Such citizenship may seem like a basic right—because it is!—but it is enormously difficult it to cultivate within U.S. society, in large part because of rampant aversion to sexual progressivism, the worsening state of our sex ed, and the alternatives that today's youth are forced to rely on.

Young people need social reinforcement of their sexual citizenship so that they can intrinsically feel it enough to assert it in sexual situations and to recognize one another's. But, as Hirsch and Khan wrote in their book *Sexual Citizens*, "All but the most progressive American sex education consistently denies young people's sexual citizenship—communicating, in the words of one of our mentors, the notion that 'sex is a dirty rotten nasty thing that you should only do to someone you love after you are married.'"[66]

Nicole was, in fact, the beneficiary of some of the nation's most progressive sex ed—which also happens to be among the nation's most expensive. (In case you needed further proof that sex ed is a class issue.) Although she was raised middle-class and attended public school through sixth grade, Nicole participated in a program that helps New Yorkers of color attend prestigious private schools. To my shock, Nicole revealed that her sex ed teacher was none other than Justine Ang Fonte, the educator who had been driven out of her job at a Manhattan private high school. And Nicole just so happened to learn about porn literacy from Fonte.

"Most of it was talking about self-esteem and safe sex practices in porn. The schtick was like: 'Porn is not a reflection of sexuality [that happens] not in front of the camera. This is an industry,'" Nicole said. "It was great that it was taught in a classroom."

Teaching porn literacy does not involve showing students porn. Instead, porn literacy is effectively an extension of media literacy, as it focuses on drawing a line between education and entertainment. In middle school, a porn literacy class may involve teaching young people not to commit nonconsensual image abuse by sharing pornographic images of their classmates as well as talking about how such images could follow you forever. A high school porn literacy class may dive deeper into what porn implies about body size or hair, emotional connection, pleasure, and even racial and gendered power dynamics.

"When students will want to ask about what ethical porn looks like, I answer those questions. And I say: 'Just like many things in any industry, some things are going to be produced ethically and some things are not going to be produced ethically.' Free, mainstream porn that is accessible to people at no cost—we have to wonder who's benefiting from this and who is marginalized by this," Fonte explained to me. "Those are things that some [high school] seniors are ready to tackle, but a lot of them aren't even thinking about it to that much depth, even though they might be asked to do that in their history classes, their AP English classes.

"This is what intersectional sex ed looks like, and it is just as academic as any other subject when it's done right," she added.

After taking a porn literacy course, Massachusetts youths were less likely to believe that porn is realistic, to want to try the actions shown in porn, or to consider it their only form of sex ed.[67] A longitudinal study of nearly two thousand Dutch people between the ages of thirteen and twenty-five also discovered that, the more people learned about porn literacy as part of school-based sex ed, the more they were able to consume sexually explicit materials without thinking of women as sex objects. (Researchers measured this by asking participants to gauge their level of agreement with statements like "An attractive woman should expect sexual advances.") This finding held true across genders and age, indicating that porn literacy has a lasting effect in mitigating the sexism that porn may unleash.[68]

Young people understand more than we think about porn and the stories it tells. In focus groups assembled to discuss porn, Canadian undergraduates were able to articulate its "explicit and implicit connections to larger issues of gender, race, sexuality, representation, power, deviance, impotence, labor, pleasure, desire, consumption, and consent." These undergraduates so enjoyed being able to speak openly about porn that one focus group wanted to start "a weekly Porn Club" to keep the discussion going.[69] Personally, I lost count of the number of times that interviewees told me that they had never spoken so openly about sex before our conversation, but that they had loved doing so. If given the space and tools to have nonjudgmental conversations about porn, young people can downgrade porn from a powerful source of sex ed into a form of media like any other.

Of course, in an age in which teachers are being attacked for the merest hint of sex and legislators are targeting internet porn, it is naïve to imagine that U.S. schools, so hostile to the very idea of sex among young people, would openly acknowledge that many of them consume porn—let alone set up classes to help them navigate the seething jungle of sex that is Pornhub. But it is also naïve, if not morally misguided, to attempt to eliminate porn. At the very least, schools should encourage students to understand that it is possible for them to adopt thoughtful sexual projects and that these projects can encompass more than marriage and babies. If we encouraged this understanding, young Americans might naturally treat their relationship with porn as a sexual project, analyzing it with critical distance and independent thought. It might also lead them to approach their interest in rough sex with the same care.

Porn literacy is far from a panacea. Nicole has been choked without her consent. But when that has happened, she has told her partners to stop or—less directly but still effectively—changed positions to feel more comfortable. She doesn't feel like porn obligates her to let people wrap their hands around her throat. And when a sexual partner has asked her to do something she recognizes from porn, Nicole felt enough freedom to make a joke of it.

Once, during a threesome with a man and another woman, the man asked Nicole and the other woman to arrange themselves "ass-up, face-down on the bed" while he got behind them, Nicole recalled. "I was laughing with the other girl. We were both like: 'This is from porn!'" Sure, the request jarred Nicole out of the moment, but the idea of re-creating porn didn't ruin the mood.

Nicole also wants to pass down what she learned in porn literacy class. In between her college classes, she's part of an organization that teaches sex ed to Connecticut students, including a lesson about porn, pleasure, and media literacy. Schools rarely let the group's educators teach that section, which saddens Nicole, but her organization still tries to braid the importance of power dynamics into every element of their sex ed.

"Power is everywhere. People have different power in different contexts and power isn't inherently bad, but power can be harmful," Nicole said. "It's about how you talk about it."

Although porn may dominate discussions about the internet's sex ed curriculum, it is far from young people's only online source of information about sex and power. And these sources have helped countless Americans—particularly those who have long been confined to the margins of U.S. society—recognize their *own* power.

5.

INTERNET SEXPLORERS
The Rise of Young LGBTQ+ Americans

Eli Erlick was a newly minted eighth grader, and she was incredibly nervous about sex ed.

It was rural California in 2008. Same-sex marriage still seemed like a pipe dream; Californians, who were supposedly living in one of the most progressive states in the country, were slugging it out in a vicious election over whether to allow it. (Anti-LGBTQ+ forces would win, eliminating same-sex marriage in California until a court ruling restored it in 2013.) Pop star Hilary Duff was urging the nation's youth to stop using the word "gay" as a slur. The word "transgender" was years away from entering the general public's vocabulary.

But Eli knew the word, because she had come out as trans in the third grade.

Her parents were generally supportive, but they had also been deeply influenced by a 1990s book that claimed almost all trans children will "just grow out of it." No other trans people lived in her hometown, and her school had denied her identity for years, refusing to let her classmates call her by the correct pronouns. So, whatever awaited Eli in sex ed, she was convinced that it would be inadequate, if not torturous.

The teacher split the class into boys and girls. As the conversation turned to sex, reproductive organs, and gender roles, one of Eli's classmates raised their hand and asked, "What about Eli?"

Eli got kicked out. Banished to the art classroom, she wasn't allowed to talk to any of her classmates about what they were learning.

At the time, it felt like the best-case scenario.

"I knew that if I went in with the boys or the girls, I would be mercilessly teased," Eli told me. "While it was still isolating and frankly humiliating to be sent to a separate classroom just for being trans, it was still my safer option." Still, she added, "I was singled out from the very beginning of the year, and that definitely had a lasting impact."

But as a late millennial, Eli had a secret weapon that past generations could have only dreamed of: She fired up her computer and went online.

As Web 2.0 took shape, it burned off the anonymity of the early internet in favor of crafting lasting identities on social media platforms like Facebook, Tumblr, Instagram, and Twitter (now known as X).Those platforms came to dominate our relationship with the internet and with ourselves, as our online identities both reflected and shaped who we were, who we wanted to be, and who we just *wanted*. Through roaming the open internet, Eli found websites with information about LGBTQ+ health and learned about other trans folks' experiences. By the tenth grade, she ended up running what she said was, at the time, probably the largest Facebook group for trans youth, with hundreds of members around the world. They could complain about being unable to find helpful doctors, discuss the intricacies of transitioning, and talk openly about the texture of being trans—experiences their teachers and parents were incapable of understanding.

"I was able to communicate my needs and not feel alone," Eli said. "I also think it helped me gain the confidence that I needed to demand transition, to realize that this was not something that was a privilege but a necessary part of being myself."

She laughed and added: "I felt a hell of a lot better."

About a quarter of Gen Z identify as LGBTQ+. That's almost twice the number of millennials, according to estimates by Gallup, one of the nation's most prominent polling groups.[1] The number of trans Americans is increasing, too, primarily among the young. As of 2022, 5 percent of people younger than thirty were trans or nonbinary, compared to 1.6 percent of people between the ages of thirty and forty-nine.[2] (People can also identify as both trans and nonbinary.)

This increase is not occurring only in big cities or in blue states, where it may be more socially acceptable to be out. Between 2014 and 2021, trans identification in states like Ohio, Wyoming, and Texas kept pace with that in California and New York.[3]

LGBTQ+ identities are also increasingly normalized among young heterosexual people. The Supreme Court's legalization of gay marriage in 2015 almost certainly played a role in this normalization; for the first time in U.S. history, a generation grew up knowing the nation's highest court recognized the validity of LGBTQ+ relationships. As of 2023, more than 80 percent of non-LGBTQ+ Americans supported equal rights for LGBTQ+ people.[4] (This is further proof that a vocal minority is behind Don't Say Gay bills and other attempts to restrict students' access to info about LGBTQ+ issues and people.) More than half of Gen Z believe there are more than two genders,[5] and even three in ten young Republicans think society needs to be more accepting of people outside the gender binary.[6] At a time when few very issues transcend party lines, acceptance for LGBTQ+ folks has.

Incensed by this sudden spike in out LGBTQ+ young people, sexual conservativism has scrambled to find a bogeyman to blame. *It must be comprehensive sex ed or the "groomers" behind it! We need Don't Say Gay bills to save our children from indoctrination!* But there's an obvious reason why so many young, LGBTQ+ Americans have suddenly become visible: It's the internet, stupid. It's not "turning" people gay; rather, the information it provides enables people to come out earlier in life by uplifting LGBTQ+ viewpoints, allowing LGBTQ+ folks to connect with one another, and expanding the idea of what it means to be somewhere outside of "straight."

The subsequent rise of out LGBTQ+ Americans marks one of the greatest generational changes in how young people do sex, sexuality, and gender. Crucially, while school-based sex ed has withered under the harsh glare of the spotlight, the sex ed found on the internet is often deeply and purposefully intertwined with politics, recognizing that the political intrudes on the personal in ways that schools cannot or will not acknowledge—and pushing young people toward sexual progressivism. Web 2.0 and social media made many late millennials and Gen Z fluent in the lingua franca of identity and social justice from their earliest stirrings of sexual hunger, long before they lost their virginities. It turned their bedrooms into an escape hatch not only into sex itself, but also into communities that could question, affirm, and broaden their approach to sex and gender. Those communities, in turn, led people into activism, as they realized how their institutions were failing them. Among Gen Z, identifying as LGBTQ+ is linked to increased participation in politics, according to political scientist Melissa Deckman.[7] That participation, she wrote in her book *The Politics of Gen Z*, can be traced to a sense of "direct threats to their rights"[8] as well as to "dissatisfaction with government."[9]

By the time we spoke, Eli was twenty-nine and had devoted her life to fighting for trans and queer rights. In 2011, she helped found a group called Trans Student Educational Resources, which is still the only national organization led by trans youth. The internet also continues to be a hub of her activism. In 2022, as a wave of states pushed legislation targeting trans minors, Eli posted online that she would help young people get hormones in states that ban them. A right-wing media personality soon discovered her efforts and blasted her online.

"I think the most offensive part of that is that he accused me of selling them," Eli said. "Of course I was giving them out for free."

"AM I GAY"

When Levi changed the pronouns in his Tumblr bio, an inner relief valve suddenly loosened. Those few keystrokes made him feel like the pressure inside his body at last matched that of the air around him, like he was no longer being crushed.

"When I first came out, that did come back to bite me, because my parents were like, 'Well, it's just because you're on the internet all the time that you're getting all of these warped ideas on what people are,'" said Levi, a twenty-year-old from Texas. "But if I look at my feelings, how I felt after my first testosterone injection, how I felt after top surgery, how I feel being called my sibling's 'brother,' how I feel being called 'son,' being a boyfriend—all of these things feel so much more right to me than anything ever could have."

And, he added, "If I had known more trans people near me, or if I had been in a community that made me feel—and it sounds harsh—but made me feel loved, I wouldn't have gone to strangers on the internet for that kind of support and community."

Compared to their straight peers, LGBTQ+ young people are twice as likely to turn to the internet for information about sex.[10] They're also far more likely to say that they did so because they had "no one to ask,"[11] which suggests they knew zero LGBTQ+ adults or were growing up in an environment that would quickly turn hostile if they came out. Between 2004 and 2023, searches for the phrases "am I gay," "am I lesbian," "am I trans," "how to come out," and "nonbinary" soared by more than 1,300 percent—especially in red states.[12]

In elementary school, Luke sometimes realized, *Oh, this other guy's kind of cute.* But, he told me, "I just assumed that's something everyone felt."

Luke, who is "mostly gay, a little bisexual," grew up in relatively small Midwestern towns. At twenty-two, he's not out to either of his parents. "My dad—he would fall into homophobic at one point. Now, his ideas of sexuality are 'antiquated,' I guess you could say. I think he's coming around to things," Luke said. His dad grew up in a small town; he coaches a sports team. "It's a very 'man's man' environment. It's less hatred and more just confusion."

His mom is another story. "She is very rooted in religion-based vitriol," Luke said. "She's got very specific qualms about gay people that she just can't reconcile."

While Luke felt like his parents wouldn't understand or accept him, YouTube did. The platform was the first place he checked when, in middle school, he decided to go hunting for information about sex. Coming-out videos were a balm. "If I didn't have YouTube videos, I probably wouldn't know much about non-heterosexual identities," Luke said. "It was very good that I had access to the internet, because even though it had some downsides, it showed me that I'm not a crazy person and that there's people out there like me."

Access to LGBTQ+ porn—video and written—helped, too. Growing up as a *Doctor Who* fan in New Jersey, Liz was intoxicated by fanfiction that featured gay sex. Little of it was realistic, but it felt educational. More importantly, it made sleeping with someone of your own gender seem normal. At the time, Liz, who is bisexual, didn't know anybody who was out IRL. "I was very online in spaces that were super gay-friendly," she said. "Even if it was in a weird, fetishizing way, I definitely felt like that was a way that I could be." (Later on, for more realistic information about sex, like instructions on how to go down on her high school girlfriend, Liz turned to YouTube.)

For years, there was one platform behind countless late millennials' and Gen Z's pornographic gay awakening: Tumblr. "Whereas Facebook aimed to bring everyone and their mother online, Tumblr was the opposite: an online underground, a place where your mother, in particular, would *never* see you," Kaitlyn Tiffany, a journalist who covers the internet and technology, wrote in *The Atlantic*. "The platform was optimized for secrets and for pseudonyms, which meant it was for art and confession and porn."[13] In other words, Tumblr was for the girls, gays, and theys. Naturally, its users made porn for the same.

Logging into Tumblr was like walking into a museum of sex, where visitors could stop and peer at small, looping exhibits of sex's best moments. Users surgically sliced mainstream video porn into GIFs, filtered out its lacerating lighting, and turned it into something approaching, if not art, then at least aesthetic: a fist tightening around long hair, teeth sinking into a lip, a few well-timed thrusts. These GIFs allowed people to plaster their own scripts onto preexisting media, stripping away the elements that don't rev their motors or the prejudices that douse their libidos. By transforming and curating porn to elevate the desires of LGBTQ+ (and female) communities who had never been deemed valuable enough by the mainstream porn industry, porn GIFs reclaimed the narrative of sexual desire from the cisgender and straight men by asserting that other kinds of people deserve to *want*, too. (And it doesn't have to be fancy—it can just be smash-bang smut.)

Izzy Ampil, a twenty-four-year-old journalist who grew up outside New York City, originally took to wikiHow to learn how kissing and oral sex "worked," as she put it when we talked. However, Ampil's "underbelly Tumblr sex education" was far more important. Ampil luxuriated in Tumblr re-blogs of "Italian black-and-white porn GIFs," which she found "more intimate" than straightforward video porn, and pored over discussions of slut-shaming and female masturbation.

"I remember seeing this quote being passed around, of this woman who was talking about discovering female masturbation," said Ampil, who tends to avoid labeling her sexuality and is "kind of agnostic" about pronouns. Ampil had known that boys masturbated since she was twelve, because male masturbation is a hallmark of middle school humor—but until Tumblr, Ampil had no idea that girls could do it, too. "When I think back to pivotal moments in my sex education, I'm like, 'Oh my God, yeah, the fact that I was explicitly given permission to experiment with my body in that way was hugely pivotal for my engagement with sexuality.'"

One of the least understood sexualities within the LGBTQ+ pantheon, asexuality, has especially benefited from the rise of internet-based sex ed. Asexual folks now make up about 0.1 percent of U.S. adults and 1.3 percent of LGBTQ+ adults, according to Gallup, which started tracking asexual identification in 2023.[14]

Blake, a nineteen-year-old from Illinois, had so little school-based sex ed that when she first got her period, she thought she had internal bleeding. But Blake has long known that she is not interested in sex. "I don't want to see it. I don't want to hear it," Blake explained. "But I know it exists and I'm fine hearing it exists. Say, in a movie, if it's on the screen, I'll cover my ears, turn away, or just take fifteen. It's not gonna ruin the whole thing for me. It's just something I don't do."

One day, a lesbian friend mentioned the concept of asexuality to Blake. The more Blake Googled about asexuality, the more convinced she was that she was on the "ace" spectrum. But when Blake tried presenting her findings to her mom, her mom replied, "Oh, no, honey, you're too young to know."

Blake was affronted. "I was a second-year in high school. I knew people who had been dating since first year of middle school," she told me. "It made no sense."

In discussions of the sex recession, asexuality and the internet are often portrayed as evil twins. Asexuality is dismissed as a fake sexuality made up by too-online young people to explain their lack of interest in sex; rather than being taken seriously, people on the ace spectrum are urged to get off their screens, go outside, meet people, pull up their bootstraps, pull down their pants, et cetera, et cetera. Asexuality is likely so misunderstood because it fundamentally challenges the societal conviction that all humans must crave sex, a conviction that asexuality scholars call "compulsory sexuality." Here's a brief Asexuality 101: Someone who is asexual does not feel sexual attraction. However, people on the ace spectrum can possess a broad range of desires and experiences. Some people are repulsed by the very idea of sex, while others may have it due to romantic interest, social pressure, or any of the many, many reasons why people have sex other than pure attraction. One survey famously identified no fewer than 237 reasons why people have sex, including curiosity, boredom, several different flavors of revenge, and "to get closer to God."[15]

For Blake, forums and Discord groups for ace folks make her feel less lonely. "It helps, having people like me," she said. "Sometimes not understanding the sex stuff can feel like a whole language I'm not understanding."

By normalizing being LGBTQ+, social media platforms like YouTube, Tumblr, and Discord can soothe young people's mental health struggles— which is critical to keeping them alive. More than 40 percent of LGBTQ+ people between the ages of thirteen and twenty-four, including asexual people, have seriously considered suicide in the past year.[16] (Almost one in three say their mental health is so poor because of anti-LGBTQ+ policies or legislation.[17]) Among LGBTQ+ youth between the ages of ten and twenty-four, social media use has been linked to decreased anxiety, paranoia, and depression.[18] "Real life isn't safe for LGBTQ people, but online there is more control where I can find people who have similar beliefs," one young person told researchers in a 2023 study.[19] Another added, "On social media, I am able to choose to be around the people that don't make me uncomfortable, that don't make me hate myself."[20]

The pandemic vividly demonstrated how social media can be a lifeline for LGBTQ+ youth. Within weeks of lockdown, use of the Trevor Project's 24/7 crisis services and of Q Chat Space, an online chat for LGBTQ+ folks, doubled.[21] "It's stressful, no one outside of this chat uses my name or pronouns," one teenager told the moderators at Q Chat Space. "I'm not [allowed] to dress femininely at all, I haven't slept in a whole day, I once again didn't eat anything today, and I'm slowly losing my mind."[22]

Social media can also save lives another way: Since school-based sex ed so routinely fails to provide young people with information about LGBTQ+ identities and activities, social media has proven key to spreading information about sexual health. "I relied on gay YouTubers to educate me on things like why you should use condoms, HIV, and all that," Luke told me, with a slight, rueful laugh. "That wasn't anything I learned at home or at school."

Late millennials and Gen Z are the first Americans in decades to be able to entertain the possibility of an adult sex life without HIV/AIDS. In 2012, the year I graduated high school, the FDA approved a drug called Truvada, a pre-exposure prophylaxis, or PrEP, that guards against HIV. Today, other PrEP drugs have been developed and HIV diagnoses in the United States are on the decline.[23] One study went so far as to call gay and bisexual men born in the 1990s the "Post-AIDS Generation."[24] For these young men, PrEP embodies hope and optimism, because it improved "gay men's sexual culture by reducing anxiety and increasing comfort with sex," the study's authors wrote.[25]

"I didn't have to look at a sexual partner [thinking], 'You could be the person that devastates my life,'" one twenty-six-year-old man in San Francisco, once considered the heart of the AIDS epidemic, told researchers in a 2017 study. "I never have to do that again."[26]

To be clear, PrEP remains hard to access. Luke isn't on it because he's worried about his dad, whose insurance he is still on, finding out. The people who are at risk of HIV and less likely to be on PrEP are also the people who are too often overlooked and underserved in the United States: people who live in rural areas and in the South, poor people, Black people, Latinx/e people.[27] But yet again, research shows that social media is a promising tool for spreading awareness of and access to PrEP.[28]

While Don't Say Gay bills do real harm, depriving kids of the chance to interact with LGBTQ+ authorities and teaching them that their identities are something to be ashamed of, the internet punches a fatal hole into the bills' bigoted attempt to curb access to LGBTQ+ education. As inundated as we are with dire warnings about the dangers of social media, Dan Delmonaco, a researcher who has studied how LGBTQ+ youth learn, believes social media is a "necessity" for LGBTQ+ young people.

"The adults in their lives have failed them by not having a system where they can get this information from family, health care providers, and school. There's really no other way for young people to get this information," Delmonaco said. When people worry about health misinformation online, Delmonaco wants to know: "Okay, you got any other better ideas? Because I don't know what else to do about this situation

126 | CARTER SHERMAN

that the people before us and our lawmakers and the powers that be have put us in."

THE INTERNET AND IDENTITY POLITICS

We often talk about "identity politics" as though it's a millennial invention (and addiction), but identity-driven political movements held strong sway among the youth of the 1960s as they rejected the white nuclear family ideal of the 1950s. "Only by becoming Black, or Chicano, or a liberated woman, or an out-of-the-closet homosexual—and only by showing solidarity with those similarly identified—could one hope to overcome the psychological barriers to liberation imposed by discriminatory cultural norms," Andrew Hartman wrote of the 1960s in his history of U.S. culture wars, *A War for the Soul of America*. "Becoming an identity— identifying as an oppressed minority—meant refusing to conform to mainstream standards of American identity."[29] These movements permanently pushed the nuclear family off its pedestal, to sexual conservatives' lasting outrage and attempts to remount it.

Sexual conservatism and progressivism are thus intertwined in a kind of double helix with identity politics. While modern-day sexual conservatism surges, promoting the supremacy of the family and parental rights, the internet and its sex ed curriculum have led to both sexual progressivism among the young *and* rising interest in identity politics. Many members of Gen Z started to think about the relationship between sex, identity, and power from an early age (rather than just assuming that having sex constitutes an identity and equals having power, as I did).

In 2018, Angeli Luz was reeling from a breakup with her first boyfriend. They had met on Tumblr, but the relationship, in Angeli's retelling, soon melted into a maelstrom of manipulation and abuse. It was all so traumatic that Angeli, then nineteen, decided to stop dating men altogether.

"It really allowed me to explore relationships with women and think about my identity outside of men. Who am I and who do I want to be in this world? It was very healing for me, I feel," said Angeli, who speaks in marshmallow-soft tones and has the doll-like looks to match, with a cur-

THE SECOND COMING | 127

tain of brown hair and rosebud lips. "I was like, 'Okay, I think I'm actually a lesbian.'"

Angeli had long known that she was attracted to women. Bullied and largely friendless in school, she joined Tumblr as a preteen and cultivated an active social life there. While the Floridian's high school sex ed did not discuss non-heteronormative identities and activities, on Tumblr Angeli encountered posts from women discussing their attraction to other women. It was permission to experiment: Angeli dabbled with the label of "asexual" before discarding it and realizing they were nonbinary. (Angeli's pronouns are she/they.)

"It did give me a sense of community. I think it did change my life for the better," Angeli said of Tumblr. "That's also how I was introduced to feminism, social justice. I was educated on a lot of things at a young age. These things that people are talking about now—diversity, inclusion, being socially aware—I know that it's really big in schools, businesses, and corporations. They're all giving them diversity training and social justice training. But I've known about this stuff since I was thirteen, fourteen, because I was educating myself through Tumblr."

As much as sex and porn GIFs thrived on Tumblr, so too did discourse around them. By the early 2010s, many users had grown fed up with the corporate waffling of the blogging platform LiveJournal,[30] which had a history of fostering conversations about social justice, and relocated to Tumblr. Those users took that interest in social justice with them, spreading it across Tumblr and to its younger users.[31]

Inspired by feminist and queer scholarship that framed gender as a social construct, Tumblr became the cradle of a sexually progressive politics that is deeply concerned with gender fluidity, disability, race, and other markers of identity. Pop feminism's explosive popularity in the 2010s, for example, can be partially credited to Tumblr. "While the roots of this whole political sensibility may be found in academia and activist culture, its emergence into the mainstream that led to Hillary [Clinton] using terms like 'check your privilege' and 'intersectionality' was the culmination of online development on Tumblr, in fan cultures, on previous platforms like LiveJournal and a mixture of social media," critic Angela Nagle wrote in her 2017 book *Kill All Normies*, which explores how internet subcultures have transformed mainstream politics.[32] "If the generation of college-going millennials that followed the rise of this online culture could be described, as they are today by the conservative press in particular, as 'generation snowflake,' Tumblr was their vanguard."[33]

When she decided to stop dating men, Angeli did what she had always done and went to Tumblr to do some research. As she looked up the key word "lesbian," a different phrase kept popping up: "compulsory heterosexuality."

In her classic 1980 essay "Compulsory Heterosexuality and the Lesbian Existence," the poet Adrienne Rich defines "compulsory heterosexuality" as the society-wide "enforcement of heterosexuality for women as a means of assuring male right of physical, economic, and emotional access."[34] This is accomplished, Rich wrote, in part by "the rendering invisible of the lesbian possibility."[35] Angeli was fascinated.

After devouring Rich's writing and Wikipedia entry, Angeli went back to Tumblr and read more opining about compulsory heterosexuality, which is often known as "comp het" in internet-speak. (Compulsory sexuality is a descendant of compulsory heterosexuality.) She compiled all of her research into a Google doc, listed credits for some lesbian and feminist Tumblr accounts, and added a title: "Am I a Lesbian?"

"I just poured out my heart," Angeli told me.

Posted to Tumblr in 2018, Angeli's Google doc soon became known as the "Lesbian Masterdoc." It's a rambling, thirty-one-page-long opus, rife with bullet-point lists and references to Tumblr-famous pop culture icons, like Shego from *Kim Possible*. It strives to make readers feel like their experiences are normal, that there's nothing wrong with them if they just can't summon up an interest in men. "Attraction is supposed to feel good," Angeli wrote. "If being in relationships with men isn't appealing to you, if you can't truly see yourself ending up happy in relationships with men, or if your attraction to men makes you uncomfortable, you may be a lesbian. Lesbian isn't a dirty word and being a lesbian is beautiful."

As they continued to sort out the detritus of the breakup, Angeli ended up deleting her blog and leaving the internet for several months. "I dated a lot of women," Angeli said. "I had a lot of fun. I was in long-term relationships with [women], short-term relationships, relationships of all kinds. I really explored my sexuality, my sexual orientation, my attraction to women."

Then they started getting emails: *Hey, I can't access the Lesbian Masterdoc.*

Angeli's creation had been converted into copies that lived on their own, its existence separate from Angeli—who is not credited by name on it—and even from Tumblr. It has been shared on Reddit, covered in news outlets, and passed between young LGBTQ+ people like a talisman; *Vice* dubbed it "internet canon."[36] Its popularity has repeatedly surged over the last several years, particularly during the pandemic—an era now credited with helping many people realize that they're LGBTQ+, as people spent more time on the internet and going down online rabbit holes like the Lesbian Masterdoc and lesbian TikTok. There is, in fact, a whole genre of TikTok videos where people reveal that the Masterdoc led them to question their entire lives. "I got divorced after I read the Masterdoc," one user commented on a 2022 TikTok about the document, to which the creator replied, "samez." In a 2023 video, another TikTok creator told the internet, "The Lesbian Masterdoc was such an important document when it came out at the time because there was nothing else as accessible and as intelligently written as the Masterdoc was."

The sex ed curriculum that began on Tumblr has now traveled far beyond it. Even more so than when Angela Nagle wrote *Kill All Normies*, the sexually progressive concepts that once flourished in Tumblr's countercultural spaces—such as comp het, but also sex positivity, gender fluidity, and rape culture—are now established in the mainstream, becoming fodder for heated debates on cable news and in legislative chambers. And thanks to the internet, a generation came of age perceiving even the most personal sexual actions within the prism of the political.

"What we're seeing with the younger generation is, it's a political statement. 'I reject the notion of masculinity and femininity as you understand them,'" said Justin Garcia, executive director of the Kinsey Institute. "It doesn't mean that there's not still a commitment, psychologically, to attraction to men or women or both, to their own masculinity or femininity. It's a generation that's saying, 'We're not going to be boxed in by your construct.'"

Sociologist Colby Fleming has encountered a similar sentiment. He's now at work on a study that has collected more than a hundred interviews of nonbinary people scattered across the United States. His interviewees, whose average age is twenty-seven, are mostly people assigned female at birth who spent their younger years chafing at sexism and misogyny. "They really did feel so trapped by feminine expectations, even if a lot of their interests in childhood were feminine. They usually had kind of a mix of like, 'Oh, I like to play video games, but I also liked my dolls,' and things like that. That category of 'woman' started to be so constraining, but they didn't want to be men, because now they see masculinity as something that's toxic," Fleming said. "They are just opting out entirely."

QUEER AMBIGUITY

One overcast day in early 2022, I sat in down in a patch of crispy park grass in Charlotte, North Carolina, and prepared to interview a nonbinary high school student. As my female cameraperson fiddled with our equipment, the student started telling us how beautiful we were. My colleague and I demurred, gently pointing out it was somewhat uncomfortable for us to be hit on while at work and by a minor. The student apologized, adding by way of explanation, "I'm gay—I just think all women are beautiful."

"Is that your girlfriend?" I asked, referring to another student who was patiently waiting on a nearby bench for the interview to end.

"No, we're just friends," they replied, then pointed to a young man who was also lingering near us. "That's my boyfriend."

After the interview, the three proceeded to snuggle.

As I eyed them, bemused by the prelapsarian possibilities of teenage romance, I had never felt more elderly and out of touch, even though I was scarcely more than a decade older than the cuddle puddle before me.

This feeling returned, more often than I'd like to admit, while I reported this book. Within the first few minutes of my interviews, I usually asked people to describe their sexual orientation and gender. They often struggled to come up with the words or even refused to. "If I had to put a label on it, I would describe it as 'queer,'" one nineteen-year-old told me. "But usually, I'm just open to whatever. I like who I like."

This attitude was more common among Gen Z, but it surfaced when I talked to late millennials, too. "If you could just use 'queer,' I like the ambiguity of it," a twenty-seven-year-old from Minnesota told me.

THE SECOND COMING | 131

"Great," I replied. "And how would you describe your gender identity?"

"Probably somewhere in the world of nonbinary . . . transmasculine . . . ish," they said. (Their pronouns are they/he.) They described their approach as: "My gender is your problem, not mine."

I laughed and said, "You're the second person I've interviewed today who's given me a very similar answer."

The fight for LGBTQ+ civil rights has long been rooted in an argument that LGBTQ+ identities are fixed, that people are "born this way." One's sexual orientation and gender identity were rooted in the body, located in some innate place that might be hard to reach—the way clouded by stigma—but that, once found, were immutable and true. LGBTQ+ advocates were somewhat boxed into this argument: Because sexual conservatives have claimed for decades that heterosexual desire is naturally ingrained in all of us, the default response is that LGBTQ+ identities are, too.

Some LGBTQ+ people do feel themselves to have a singular, immutable, true self. (Unlike sexual conservatives, I'm not here to tell anybody who they are or how to live.) But over the course of reporting this book, I came to feel that understandings of what it means to be LGBTQ+ are multiplying among young people, as they are increasingly willing to experiment with fluidity, language, and ambiguity. When you're coming of age, everything can feel like it's on the brink of collapse—but the discovery of a label that fits you, that makes you realize somebody else has already named the feelings you have been desperately trying to articulate, can provide much-needed stability. Thus, adolescence and young adulthood have always involved trying on newfangled labels, remixing them, and tossing them off. LGBTQ+ labels are now, finally, part of that iterative process.

"It is trendy to be complicated with regard to your gender identity," said one teacher at a secular, private New Jersey middle school. "About two years ago, when 'they/them' hit middle school life, I had a lot of students who wanted to be a 'them' and did not want anyone to assume their gender identity or their sexuality, which was really cool." (By the time we spoke, the teacher said, "I want to say half of them have reverted to the gender you would assume.")

Even Angeli Luz eventually realized she was open to dating men again—and to coming out, so to speak, as the creator of the Lesbian Masterdoc. In November 2020, they told me, they posted a TikTok video claiming credit for it. Angeli, who now hopes to become a therapist for LGBTQ+ folks, decided to come out for two main reasons: The timing seemed astrologically fortuitous, and they were annoyed by accusations that the document was biphobic. As Angeli revealed on TikTok, she also no longer identifies as a lesbian. She's bisexual and dating a man, whom she became friends with through Tumblr.

"Plot twist!" Angeli said.

Young Americans' fraught, even contradictory, relationship with categorization is deeply informed by the rest of their experiences online. Late millennials and Gen Z were raised on an internet where searching for the right hashtag could help them navigate to a greater understanding of themselves and of social justice, while using the wrong one could cast them off the cliff of cancellation. Thanks once to Tumblr and now to platforms like Instagram, that internet is also sliced into increasingly infinitesimal "aesthetics" where people identify objects and personalities as "dark academia" and "coquette" and whatever word got slapped with "-core" this week. (You're not "messy"; you're Sofia Coppola–core.) To be clear, being LGBTQ+ is not an aesthetic and attraction is not a mood board—yet the online pressure to find *exactly the right word* can lead people to be able to rattle off their sexual orientation like a laundry list. One twenty-eight-year-old Californian told me that she was a "biromantic demisexual, leaning AFAB and transmasc partners." (Someone who is biromantic feels romantic attraction to multiple genders; someone who is demisexual is on the ace spectrum.) Such atomizing of one's sexual orientation can help people find others like themselves, as well as challenge heteronormative ideals about identity and love.

It can also cause intense panic.

When Denis's mom told him that his older sibling liked girls and was genderqueer, Denis's reaction was: "Okay. I don't know what the fuck 'genderqueer' means."

Naturally, Denis, a nineteen-year-old who grew up in the Northeast, went online for answers. He didn't find many, but, he said, "that led me to start to follow a lot of queer information accounts on Instagram, when

I was in middle school, and then that led me to general feminism accounts." Throughout middle and high school, social media helped Denis learn not only about queerness and feminism, but also about political movements like anarchy.

Many of the accounts that Denis followed, he told me, were what he would now call "*Buzzfeed* feminism." "It's a lot of language policing, a lot of posts about, 'Here's why you shouldn't say the R-word! Here's why it's harmful and problematic!'" he recalled. "The description of language was really ingrained in my mind as: 'In order to be queer, you need to have a specific queer identity, but you need to specifically identify as a bisexual or aromantic or genderqueer or something.' I felt a primordial anxiety about labeling myself.

"I would flip-flop in between bisexual and straight for a long time," Denis went on. "My senior year of high school, I started hooking up with some of my friends who were not women and who were very, very proud and defined in their queer stance. I had this epiphany that labeling myself did not make me feel good—and so I stopped labeling."

Now, he said, "if I had to pick between the letters, bisexual would probably be most similar to my sexuality, but I identify as queer."

Many LGBTQ+ young people have begun to shirk labels entirely. They're making nonspecific words like "queer" more common while expanding the meaning of words like "gay" and "bisexual." One in six members of Gen Z say that they are bisexual, according to Gallup,[37] but that survey can't capture how the term "bisexual" is in flux. Depending on who you ask, "bisexual" may refer only to individuals who are attracted only to people on the gender binary, or it may be another synonym for "pansexual."

In a 2020 analysis of more than seventeen thousand LGBTQ+ thirteen-to-seventeen-year-olds, a quarter identified with what researchers dubbed "emerging labels," such as "queer," "pansexual," "asexual," or "questioning."[38] As the number of trans and nonbinary folks within our population rises, it's only logical that the prominence of "queer," with its lack of emphasis on gender, also rises.

To be sure, plenty of young people are still inside the closet, and, clearly, sexual conservatives are intent on bricking more in. To come out, let alone to be publicly ambiguous or flexible in one's gender and

134 | CARTER SHERMAN

sexuality, is a privilege that is undoubtedly more easily available to white people who come from money. It is also likely more available to AFAB folks, who are less battered by the homophobia embedded in so many stereotypes of masculinity; strikingly, while 31 percent of Gen Z women identify as LGBTQ, 18 percent of Gen Z men say the same.[39] Are people assigned male at birth really just more inclined to be cis and straight? Or are AMAB people more afraid of coming out? Because AMAB folks are so often pigeonholed as big strong cavemen who love rough sex, we are not as accepting of their sexual and gender diversity.

Critically, the word "queer" is more than a synonym for "LGBTQ+." In fact, it was long a slur for homosexual people. Then, in the 1990s, a group of activists grew fed up with the advocacy group ACT UP's focus on HIV/AIDS and formed a splinter organization called Queer Nation, which set out to reclaim "queer."[40] "We're here," the group's motto went. "We're queer. Get used to it."[41]

"Using a word that is so offensive is a way of showing your anger," one adherent of Queer Nation told the *New York Times* in 1991. Another added, "Queer signifies a rebirth of energy, the spirit of activism that happened in the '70s. This is a newer, hipper generation."[42] Queerness was linked to youth and a changing of the guard. It was a rallying cry for a kind of brash and radical politics, a politics that wanted more for LGBTQ+ folks than privacy, tolerance, and assimilation into a heteronormative society.

For a generation reared on an internet that constantly furthered the cause of sexual progressivism and regularly reminded them of the politicization of identity and sexuality, to be "queer" makes a whole lot of sense. Even if my interviewees didn't always know the history of queer theory and activism, I think they could hear the ring of politics in "queer," like a whistle too high for (straight) older ears to hear. Like sexual progressivism, queer politics prioritizes flexibility, change, and freedom.

"At the very heart of queer politics . . . is a fundamental challenge to the heteronormativity—the privilege, power, and normative status invested in heterosexuality—of the dominant society," Cathy J. Cohen wrote in her 1997 essay "Punks, Bulldaggers, and Welfare Queens: The Radical Potential of Queer Politics?"[43] Cohen, now a University of Chicago professor, did not consider herself a "'queer' activist or, for that matter, a 'queer' anything," she wrote.[44] Cohen thought the queer politics of the era lacked a much-needed focus on intersectionality, but she seemed to believe that intersectionality was possible. She wondered: "Who, we might ask, is truly on the outside of heteronormative power—maybe *most* of us?"[45]

Angeli might say that asking this question is challenging comp het. It is certainly challenging sexual conservatism.

When Denis got to college, he decided to download dating apps. The apps wanted to know: Whose profiles do you want to see? Men? Women? Everyone?

He clicked "everyone."

"It took me a long, long time to realize that my gender is just not that important to me in deciding who I'm gonna date or fuck or whatever," he told me.

Recently, Denis found himself talking to a friend who had recently come out as nonbinary and was mulling over whether it still made sense to call themselves "straight." "I was like, 'Dude, it doesn't matter,'" Denis said. "The labels that you use are supposed to be good for *you*. They're not imposed on you by society. You establish the labels for yourself, especially when it comes to sexuality."

Denis gave his friend a final bit of advice: "All you have to do is date hot people and be a hot person."

That well-intentioned advice, however, naturally raises another question: How do we know what's hot?

6.

THE FUCKABILITY TRAP
How Social Media Turns Us into Sex Objects

Of all the places to be struck with the lightning bolt of lust for the first time, it had to happen to me at Disneyland.

As a preteen, I was enthralled by the exotic species known as teenage girls. I felt like we were so alike and so alien to each other, all at once; whenever I encountered one in the wild, I studied her body for clues as to what mine would look like in a few short years. That day at Disneyland, as my family examined a park map, I found myself transfixed by a group of teen girls who had gathered in line for a ride. My eyes fastened on the cut of their pink, midriff-exposing shirts, which showcased how their plump stomachs curved out over their low-rise jeans. I thought their stomachs looked so beautiful. More than that: I thought they looked *sexy*. Dizzying heat scorched my head, my chest, my own belly. My blood carbonated with want.

Honestly, I couldn't tell you if I wanted to touch them or to be them. But I know that when I got home, I practiced hunching over in front of my bedroom mirror, trying to make my stomach look like theirs.

Shortly after that trip to Disneyland, I went out to a restaurant for brunch with my family. Our waitress's stomach and hips spilled out over the top of her pants, like those of the girls at Disneyland. "See that?" a male diner asked me. "That's what we call a 'muffin top.'"

He said it with a grin, like he was sharing a secret, but today I know it was an open one: Men—and, really, people of all kinds, including complete strangers—will mock you for the slightest hint of fat. Fat isn't supposed to be sexy but reviled, in others and yourself.

I sat in the sunny restaurant and picked at my toast, watching butter drip through the crags of the sourdough. Shame flared through me, just as searing and unforgettable as the lust at Disneyland had been.

Earlier, I wrote something of a eulogy to the politics of Tumblr. But I have to be honest. When I became a teenager, I did not go to Tumblr for a political education. I went to Tumblr to learn how to be thin.

Curled up in a window nook in my lilac-walled bedroom, half-submerged in pillows, I spent whole weekends scrolling through Tumblr photos of thin white girls. I lingered on how their skin seemed Saran-Wrapped over their skeletons: the hip bones that jutted as sharply as table corners, the thighs that gapped enough to fit a fist between them, the sternums and rib cages that had grown so prominent their grooves looked like subdermal spiderwebs.

When I was a freshman in high school and had to undergo a physical before playing on my school's lacrosse team, the school nurse informed me that I was "almost underweight." Her tone held no alarm, and she did not follow up her pronouncement with any health recommendations. Had I been deemed "almost overweight," I'm sure she would have given me advice on how to "fix" it. Instead, I felt like she was congratulating me. I practically skipped out of her office, delighted by the success of my morning routine of eating only a few bites of cereal and substituting coffee for lunch—a routine I just so happened to start around the same time that I began dating my first real boyfriend. The lack of nutrition, combined with the caffeine, left me rickety with anxiety every day, but I was *skinny* and a boy *liked* me. And, as my favorite Tumblr blogs reminded me, nothing tastes as good as skinny feels.

I discovered this mantra while browsing "thinspo" ("thin" plus "inspiration") as well as "pro-ana" (pro-anorexia) and "pro-mia" (pro-bulimia) content. These accounts post and praise images of bulging bones; they give encouragement and advice on how to best starve yourself, such as "MY LIST OF THINGS TO DO INSTEAD OF EATING: Watch Instagram edits." Frequently, thinspo accounts are also altars to photos of the shimmery tally marks of self-harm scars.

News outlets and social media sites had caught on to the dangers of thinspo and its sister "fitspo" by the time I graduated high school. In 2012, Tumblr declared that it would take down thinspo accounts and make public service announcements pop up whenever users searched

THE SECOND COMING | 139

terms like "purging." But social media sites have never been able to fully purge themselves of thinspo. Users evade filters with the clever use of fonts and accents—"thinspo" becomes "thïŋspo," for instance—or by turning to new names that take a while for moderators to catch on to, like #skinnycheck or #thighgapworkout. Those hashtags, which had respectively garnered one million and 2.6 million views on Instagram as of late 2021, have no doubt already been retired or subtly renamed.[1] But thinspo creators and consumers don't need to work that hard to stay online, because the apps don't seem to care that much. More than a month after an advocacy group flagged twenty-two hashtags that were being used as eating disorder fodder on Instagram, fourteen of those hashtags were still in use on TikTok.[2]

I thankfully never developed a full-tilt eating disorder, although I still struggle with disordered eating, like 65 percent of all American women between the ages of twenty-five and forty-five.[3] In a perverse stroke of luck, my overwhelming desire to be thin was always counterbalanced by my overwhelming fear of my hair falling out, which I knew to be a symptom of starvation. (I also gleaned that potentially lifesaving knowledge online. Thanks, WebMD.) My fear pushed me to eat just enough to stay on the right side of the line; being attractive to my high school boyfriend meant being skinny, but it also meant having hair. I never had sex with him, but I knew even then that I had to stay fuckable.

Social media taught me how to do that, too.

When we get horny (or bored, or lonely), young people turn to porn to understand how to feel, give, and receive sexual pleasure. But we look at social media—every day, all day, no matter our mood—to understand how to look sexy: sexy to peers and strangers, as sexy as celebrities, and sexier than everybody else. Ideally, this expands our conception of what "sexy" can be, given the diversity of sexualities and bodies that are accessible on social media. But more often, social media has compounded some of our society's deepest and darkest biases around sex appeal, who gets to have it, and what it says about our individual worth. This, too, is all part of the internet's sex education curriculum, and it does not need to be as explicit as thinspo.

Like the science on porn, the science on social media can be surprisingly murky. Clearly, it is indispensable to LGBTQ+ young people and other marginalized communities, as well as to furthering the cause of sexual progressivism. But we also know that mental health issues among adolescents, particularly teen girls, increased around 2010, around the time that I entered high school and that smartphone-enabled social media use became far more common. "Distress could be a function of screen time itself, of the kinds of thinking it generates (e.g., comparison, body insecurity), or what that screen time is displacing (such as face-to-face socializing, hobbies, or sleep)," Harvard University researchers Emily Weinstein and Carrie James wrote in their book *Behind Their Screens: What Teens Are Facing (and Adults Are Missing)*. "It could also be the result of broader social and cultural changes that have happened alongside radical connectivity."[4]

There is mounting evidence that social media threatens young people's mental health in at least one crucial way: It decays their self-esteem and body image. In doing so, it trains people—especially cisgender girls and women—to turn themselves into objects for sexual consumption, at the possible cost of their own sexual safety and happiness. Furthermore, as they self-objectify, social media reminds them that not all objects have equal value.

Philosopher Amia Srinivasan has a word for how this value is assigned: "fuckability."

Fuckability is not a measure of "some pre-political, innate desirability," Srinivasan explained in her book *The Right to Sex*. Instead, she wrote, fuckability is "desirability as constructed by our sexual politics, which enforces a racialized hierarchy that places the white woman above the brown or Black woman, the light-skinned brown or Black woman above the dark-skinned brown or Black woman, and so on."[5] The hierarchy of fuckability is not limited to race: Thinner bodies possess more fuckability than bigger ones, able bodies more than those with disabilities, and so on.

Fuckability courses through every aspect of our society, not just across our screens. But when we log on, refreshing again and again and again, social media turns the subtext of fuckability into literal, on-screen text—into likes and comments and dollar signs and matches on dating apps. Because, yes, dating apps are social media, and they run on fuckability.

The attitudes that fuel fuckability can fuel sexual conservatism, too. And because sexual progressivism is so invested in dismantling traditional modes of gender and sex, it can involve recognizing and interrogating the role that politics play in shaping desire. That's what young people are doing when they question the power dynamics of porn; it is also exactly what the Lesbian Masterdoc and other challenges to comp het do.

However, compared to the rest of the book, this chapter focuses less on the policy tug-of-war between sexual conservatism and progressivism, because our most powerful politicians have abdicated their responsibility to regulate social media. Or, rather, they are not regulating the ginormous companies that now control these platforms.

In 2023, U.S. Surgeon General Vivek Murthy issued an advisory about the emerging evidence of social media's negative effects on children and adolescents, especially for their mental health and especially for already-marginalized groups, such as adolescent girls, adolescent girls of color, and "sexual minority youth."[6] A year later, Murthy called for Congress to require a surgeon general's warning label on social media platforms, similar to the kind found on cigarettes. No such warning has surfaced as of this writing.

"Why is it that we have failed to respond to the harms of social media when they are no less urgent or widespread than those posed by unsafe cars, planes or food? These harms are not a failure of willpower and parenting; they are the consequence of unleashing powerful technology without adequate safety measures, transparency, or accountability," Murthy wrote in the *New York Times*. "The moral test of any society is how well it protects its children."[7]

Politicians across the ideological spectrum would agree. If anything, sexual conservatives would agree the fastest, given how the protection of children is one of their strongest post-Covid talking points. Yet they seem to act quickly only when it involves the opportunity to police online sex work. See: SESTA-FOSTA and bans on internet porn.

THIS IS YOUR BODY ON SOCIAL MEDIA

In high school, the boys would leer at Thalia's "fat ass."

The Black, working-class daughter of Caribbean immigrants, Thalia grew up in a predominantly white Pennsylvania suburb and went to a predominantly white Catholic high school. "There are some features of Black women that are fetishized, and I was fetishized in my high school," Thalia said. "I learned that I was good enough to be sexually objectified and I was good enough to maybe sleep around with, but not serious girlfriend material."

At sixteen, Thalia fell into an all-consuming, yearslong infatuation with a male classmate. When they first started fooling around, Thalia was less excited by the prospect of discovering sex itself than by the thrill and hope of one day discovering sex with him; she sent him nude photos of herself because, she told me, it was "a way for me to get closer to him." She resisted having intercourse with other people. "I was hoping he was going to be my first," Thalia said. "I was kind of saving myself for him, to be honest."

At the time, Instagram allowed people to see other users' likes. Thalia would open the app, which she got when she was eleven or twelve years old, and surreptitiously track whose photos earned a double tap from her crush. "It was always blonde girls. It was always white girls," Thalia said. And she always thought, *Wow, I don't look like them.*

Instagram eliminated the feature that let people see one another's likes in 2019. But you can still easily go to your crush's profile, thumb through their "following" list, and see if they follow white, blonde influencers who look nothing like you.

Body image scholars posit that parents, peers, and traditional media outlets all shape people's body image by persuading them to internalize culturally defined beauty ideals—being slender, having light skin and Eurocentric facial features—and to frequently compare their appearances with others'. (Like an unsuspecting waitress, to pick a totally random example.) People then feel shame when their bodies don't measure up.[8] These "appearance comparisons" play a role in what's called "social comparison," or the evaluation of one's overall status against others; coming up short in social comparisons once again leads people to feel shame and dissatisfaction about their bodies.[9] In *Behind Their Screens*, Weinstein and James dubbed this phenomenon "comparing and despairing."[10]

Body shame and dissatisfaction are also linked to what's known in scholarly parlance as "self-objectification" and "objectified bodily consciousness." This academese describes a basic reality: Girls and women, in particular, are taught to understand their bodies as objects separate from themselves. Rather than inhabiting their bodies and paying attention to how they feel—or valuing or acting on those feelings—they instead watch a kind of internal, continuous, and distorted surveillance tape of their own bodies that leaves them acutely aware of their appearances and sex appeal. That tape convinces them that they have more control over their bodies than they actually do, reinforcing a false belief that they can and must adjust their bodies to increase their sex appeal.

Patriarchy runs much more smoothly if the work of turning women into sex objects is delegated to the women themselves.

Studies conducted on young people across the planet have exposed the connections between self-objectification and eating disorders, symptoms of depression,[11] and even decreased cognitive function.[12] People start to spend more time focusing on how their bodies look rather than what their bodies and minds can do. Embarrassment over their bodies, as well as the emotional labor of staving that feeling off, literally leaves them too busy and dumb to think about achieving more.

Academic theories about self-objectification and parents, peers, and media outlets' influence over body image emerged long before social media became ubiquitous; the power dynamics and prejudices that inform shame-inducing beauty standards stretch back centuries, if not the whole of human history. When that male diner clued me into "muffin tops" and fatphobia, I had never heard the words "Myspace" or "Facebook." Thinspo blogs didn't dream up the slogan "Nothing tastes as good as skinny feels," but rather cribbed it from legacy women's magazines.

Today, however, social media platforms have a tentacular reach that surpasses that of parents, peers, and media outlets. As we scroll through our social media feeds, posts from ordinary people—parents, peers, strangers—pop up alongside posts by the rich and famous. We start to believe it is possible, recommended, or even mandatory for ordinary people to look like celebrities, despite our lack of glam teams and disposable income. "The people on TikTok are supposed to be 'everyday people.' Obviously, some of them are not, but you'll see somebody and they're in their sweatpants and their jeans, lying on their couch. So you're like, 'Wow, they're so normal,'" said Jo, a twenty-two-year-old from California. "You see someone on the cover of *Vogue*, you don't think that. They're a model."

Everybody raised in the era of social media has spent their whole adolescence, if not their childhood, juggling their persona and their self. They have learned how to craft and refine their digital persona, which they then monitor for proof that they look hot and happy—ideally, hotter and happier than their physical and interior self feels. Social media has literalized the metaphorical surveillance tape of self-objectification. We just call it by another name: It's our "digital footprint."

In high school, Riley felt obligated to post attractive bikini pictures of herself. She was constantly calculating: *What angles does [my body] look best at?* "That also obviously highlighted what angles it didn't look best at. It also brought me into a lot of weird situations with my friends. They would be trying to make me feel confident, but it would be like they were jealous of my body in a way," recalled Riley, who is twenty and was raised in Michigan. "When they were taking these pictures of me, they'd be like, 'I wish I had your boobs, I wish I had your stomach, I wish I had your legs, your shoulders, your whatever, your hips,' or something like that. I knew they meant it as a compliment, but I just didn't really like the idea that somebody was thinking about my body that much." Essentially, Riley's friends were running appearance and social comparisons against her.

"I think Instagram really taught me how to see my body as a marketable object. It basically was highlighting the ways in which my body was good and was what society wanted—and highlighting the ways in which it wasn't and asking me to fix those ways," Riley continued. "I don't even know who I wanted to see them. I posted them because I wanted somebody to see them and think I was attractive."

As Riley and I talked more, Riley realized that she *did* know whose eyes she was seeking out when she posted bikini pics. "It was never consciously, explicitly for men," she said. "But it was definitely for men." Riley, a white woman, was doing what she had been trained to do: look for proof of her fuckability.

It works.

"I'll meet someone, and then I'll see their Instagram is a bunch of pictures of them in a bikini, and it will open my mind to seeing them in that light," said Noah, an eighteen-year-old who graduated from his New York City high school a few weeks before we talked. "I don't think it goes immediately to fantasizing about them in a sexual context, but I guess it opens the door to the possibility of that, if that makes sense. Unfortunately, I feel like social media is so comparative. When a girl posts her body, the next post you'll see later is another girl's body. Your mind naturally will be like, 'Oh, but this girl's really great, as opposed to this girl.'"

Fuckability is another factor in social comparisons, because it is not merely a matter of being "fuckable" but rather a measure of the status someone receives from fucking a particular kind of body. "The bodies of brown and Black women—especially when they belong to women who are also poor, incarcerated, or undocumented—are in an important sense supremely fuckable, much more so than the bodies of white women," Srinivasan pointed out. "For these bodies can be violated with impunity and without consequence. Black women's bodies are coded as hypersexual, inviting, and demanding men's sexual attention, while conferring on the men who have access to them less social status than they gain by having access to the supposedly chaste and innocent bodies of white women."[13]

Research indicates that white girls and women particularly idealize being thin and are thus more susceptible to the dangers of thinspo, but we also simply know less about how girls and women of color feel and think about their bodies because so much of the research into body image has focused on white people.[14] Black female college students, one 2021 study found, feel pressured to meet both Black and white body image ideals, to have Eurocentric features and to be "slim thick," with "longer and straighter hair, lighter skin, bigger buttocks, bigger breasts, and generally an hourglass figure." These dual, conflicting pressures can leave Black women at greater risk of disordered eating.[15]

The fetishization of Black women and other women of color, the sexual attention publicly lavished on white women, the social status afforded to people with Eurocentric facial features—none of those dynamics can be blamed solely on the internet or social media. But the internet dials their visibility and pressure up to eleven, to ever-younger audiences.

At fourteen, Rian started stumbling across videos on social media where influencers would ask men: "What's the one race you wouldn't date?" "A lot of the times, it was Black women and then Indian women," recalled Rian, a twenty-two-year-old of Indian descent who was raised in Texas. "I already knew people in general date people that look like them or find people that look like them attractive. I did know that before I saw

146 | CARTER SHERMAN

those videos. But I never was confronted with, like, 'Oh, people think I'm *ugly*.'"

Critically, even people who may be believed to benefit from fuckability are harmed by it. When she was fifteen, Iris took a walk with her grandfather on a beach. She filmed the walk, including shots of her feet moving through the sand. She posted the video to TikTok, went to bed, and woke up to find that it had garnered ten thousand likes. Her social media accounts were flooded with direct messages. "All old men, asking for feet pics, asking how much it cost, asking how much I cost for one night," said Iris, a white woman who hails from the Northwest and is now eighteen. "I had one of my friends text me and be like, 'Hey, girl, just wanted to let you know that your feet are on a "prettiest girls with pretty feet" Reddit thread.'

"Things are posted on social media in the kind of guise of it being sexually liberating and being like, 'My body, my choice! I have control over what I post!'" Iris continued. "But what isn't talked about is, you can post whatever you want, but that doesn't change the way that people are going to prey on young women or the way that people are going to perceive the information or what they're going to do with it."

It's the hollow philosophy of 2010s pop feminism all over again: pretending that climbing to the top of the pyramid of fuckability is the same thing as defeating it, that being rewarded for your body on social media can replace enjoying the sensation of being in it. Fuckability, Srinivasan was careful to note, is "not some good that should be distributed more fairly. It isn't a good at all."[16]

Because cisgender girls and women are so specifically sexualized on social media at the expense of their sense of worth, this chapter focuses more on their experiences. However, cis men are not immune to the pressure to showcase bodies that conform to gender stereotypes. In interviews, they agreed that social media pushes men to look one way: jacked.

Throughout high school and the beginning of college, Sawyer tensed whenever the topic of partying and sex came up. A devout Catholic, Sawyer wanted to lose his virginity within the context of a committed relationship. He wanted sex to be "sacred." (In a classic case of sex ed fearmongering, Sawyer's freshman year health teacher also told him: "You absolutely never forget your first time. It's something that sticks with you for life. And a lot of people make the mistake of messing it up.") But while Sawyer prized his virginity, he knew most of his peers—particularly the male ones—wanted to shuck it as quickly as possible. When his classmates brought up their body counts, he would silently beg, *Please don't ask me about this.* The fear of not fitting in tore at him. *Do I lie? Do I tell them the truth?*

As Sawyer waited longer and longer to get naked with somebody, social media compounded his anxieties about his body. His bigger size and gynecomastia—a hormonal condition that leads to swollen breast tissue in people assigned male at birth—already made him insecure, but when Sawyer started going to the gym and looking up workouts online, the exercise influencers he encountered destroyed his confidence. "You see these people that are just absolutely massive with eight-packs. They have huge muscles and everything," he told me. "Granted, all those people either have been in the gym for over a decade or are on steroids, but you compare yourself to those people. It definitely creates a negative image."

Women on social media, Sawyer felt, constantly talked about what they wanted in a man. They valued features men can't control, like their height or penis size, or features they could change but not overnight, like the size of their chest and arm muscles. "There's a lot higher expectations for men to have their body in shape than for women," said Sawyer, who is now nineteen. (That said, social media is particularly linked to making adolescent girls internalize the idea that they should be "fit"[17]—which is the new word for being thin, just softened by the suggestion of athleticism.)

Sawyer grew terrified that the first time he took off his clothes in front of someone else, they would reject him over his body. He started going to the gym every day, no exceptions. "I knew I wanted a partner who enjoyed the way I look," he said. "It's not the biggest deal, but attractiveness was always a thing. I wanted to make sure that that was something that I wouldn't be [self-]conscious about in a relationship."

Dewayne grew up overweight and playing football; he tried to be under a certain weight every time Saturday morning rolled around. "As I've grown older, I realized how critical that made me around my body," said Dewayne, who is eighteen and from Florida. Dewayne felt like he had a voice in his head that constantly, even violently, hated on him; the voice grew stronger when combined with the cultural expectation that men should be good at securing and having sex—or, as Dewayne put it, "If you don't have good dick and money, you definitely are shit."

He started to dissociate during sex. "I would become hyperaware that I am a body and this other person is a body as well and also very hyperaware of my own performance," Dewayne said. "It was a lot of body dysmorphia and performance anxiety that was shaped by the standard of masculinity."

Research on how self-objectification impacts young people's sex lives suggests it worsens them. Female teenagers who score high on body objectification measures have been found to use condoms irregularly, feel more uneasy talking about sex, and feel more regret about having had it. "Because self-objectification entails thinking about and treating the body as an object for another's pleasure and use, adolescent girls, who are high in self-objectification, may be more likely to acquiesce to the sexual requests of boys and less likely to advocate for protecting their sexual health in sexual interactions," researchers wrote in one 2020 analysis.[18]

Alternatively, research on Belgian adolescents indicates that young people with high levels of self-objectification may avoid sex because they see it as yet another objectifying experience where they must overly focus on how their body looks.[19] Social media and its overwhelming self-objectification, then, may play a role in the spread of the sex recession: If you feel like you have to look perfect to get naked with somebody, you're unlikely to do it.

Now twenty-three, Thalia stayed in touch with her high school crush throughout college, but she didn't end up losing her virginity to him. She knew from an early age that, although she didn't want to wait till marriage for sex, she did want to have sex for the first time with the right person. Her crush never treated her well enough to make the grade.

"It's just been very clear to me that all I will ever be is—he'll use me as a sexual object," she said. "I noticed that I was being sexually objectified and I was like, 'Okay, I can't control that. But what I can control is when I start to have sex in a certain way and, at least theoretically, I can control who I'm going to have sex with.'"

It took Thalia a long time to find someone who treated her well enough. Thalia had sex for the first time at twenty-two, after she graduated college.

THE SECOND COMING | 149

INSTAGRAM FACE

A few weeks before we spoke, Jo, the twenty-two-year-old from California, had borrowed another user's filter to post a video to TikTok. At first, she thought the filter had only shifted the background of the video. "I put it on, I was like, 'Wow, I look really pretty.' And then I turned it off and I realized that that filter fully blurred my face and slimmed my face as well," Jo said. "That's so sad, to be disappointed when you see your own face. That's not how it should work."

Most of us know that these editing tools are out there, but we're not always good at recognizing them. A study of Dutch teenage girls found they could not consistently detect when bodies of other teenage girls had been edited in photos, such as to create a more wasplike waist. After viewing the photos, girls who were more likely to make social comparisons saw their own body image dip further.[20]

"Almost all my female friends that I know edit their bodies before they post on social media," Noah said. "How much of social media is really just showing off of editing skills?"

This isn't just a problem among girls and women, though. Later, I asked Noah: "Have you ever edited your body on social media?"

"Yeah, I did, actually," Noah replied. "My long-term girlfriend wanted to post a picture of us while I was shirtless in it. I made my shoulders look bigger."

Noah wouldn't have posted that photo unless he "met the criteria"— a phrase he used over and over. Young men and women, he said, must feel like their bodies "meet a certain criteria" or else they won't post images of them. "That's probably a source of a lot of pain."

Part of the "criteria," at least for women, is a look that millennial writer Jia Tolentino has popularized as "Instagram Face," a singular ideal of highly feminine beauty that is practically impossible to achieve IRL without plastic surgery. Think: plush lips, catlike eyes, and poreless cheeks that seem young yet also appear to have zero buccal fat, in the mode of Kylie Jenner and Bella Hadid.

In the *New Yorker* article where she discussed Instagram Face, Tolentino had a celebrity makeup artist give a globe-spanning tour of the face's most prized features. "We're talking an overly tan skin tone, a South Asian influence with the brows and eye shape, an African-American influence with the lips, a Caucasian influence with the nose, a cheek structure that is predominantly Native American and Middle Eastern," the artist explained. Despite this "We Are the World"–style approach to beauty, Instagram Face is not available to all. "It was as if the algorithmic tendency to flatten everything into a composite of greatest hits had resulted in a beauty ideal that favored white women capable of manufacturing a look of rootless exoticism," Tolentino reflected.[21]

Her use of the word "manufacturing" is key, because while no one naturally possesses Instagram Face, you can make it. There are, of course, apps for that: Filters and editing tools can whiten your teeth, smooth out your face, lengthen your eyelashes—to name just a few of the myriad tune-ups on offer. But social media may seduce people into more permanent solutions. Research on Dutch and Chinese adolescents has found links between social media use, selfie editing, and the desire for cosmetic surgery.[22]

"I think there used to be a kind of mysticism with plastic surgery. Now, people know what [the procedures are] called. They know the surgeons, they're on social media," Rian told me. "People go and get their face done and then they all look the same."

Rian got Instagram in sixth grade. By twelve, she started thinking about getting a nose job for her "kind of big" nose. "It feels like everyone is trying to project a very specific image about themselves. And I get it," Rian said. "But I don't want to see it. It makes me feel bad."

The FDA first approved the use of Botox in smoothing wrinkles in 2002. Many millennials and virtually all of Gen Z have lived their entire conscious lives under the promise that, with the prick of a relatively inexpensive and painless syringe, wrinkles could become optional. In 2022, more than twenty-five thousand people under the age of twenty subjected themselves to injections of wrinkle-treating chemicals, including Botox. That's an increase of 75 percent since 2019. Another eight thousand enjoyed injections of hyaluronic acid fillers, which can erase wrinkles and inflate lips. That also marked an increase, of 71 percent, since 2019. Such procedures soared by similar percentages among twentysomethings.[23]

You may wonder how such youthful people could possibly be worrying about wrinkles, but they are. In one TikTok that amassed more than

130,000 likes, a girl with braces and talon-like nails vamped into the camera as she confided in a perky voice-over: "Here's some things that I do to slow down the aging process as a fourteen-year-old. I started doing most of these things at twelve." She smeared sunscreen and retinol on her face, drank green tea as an "anti-inflammatory," and taped a sheaf of paper over her car window to block out the sun's damaging rays.

It is my job to not judge young people, but even I was taken aback by the implication that seeing the world is literally less important than the world liking what it sees in you. When I found this fourteen-year-old's Instagram account, I was unsurprised to discover that she had already mastered the art of transforming her own face into Instagram Face through expertly applied makeup and a tilt of the lips that never quite became a smile. After my initial horror faded, I remembered: She learned to do this somewhere.

Instagram Face maestros Kylie Jenner and Bella Hadid, born into famous families rich enough to fund the retooling of teenagers' faces and bodies, have admitted to undergoing plastic surgery. Jenner got lip fillers by seventeen[24] and her breasts augmented at nineteen,[25] while Hadid shaved down what she called "the nose of my ancestors" at fourteen.[26] (Hadid is of Palestinian descent.) Both women say they regret the procedures. "I was on this calorie-counting app, which was like the devil to me," Hadid told *Vogue* of high school. "I'd pack my little lunch with my three raspberries, my celery stick. . . . I can barely look in the mirror to this day because of that period in my life."[27]

If you're starting to feel like all roads lead back to eating disorders, you're not wrong. Between 2000 and 2018, as social media use exploded, the global prevalence of eating disorders more than doubled.[28] In 2020, trapped indoors by the coronavirus pandemic, Sriya took to scouring social media for workout regimes. She obsessively watched YouTube videos about how to shrink the circumference of her thighs and waist. "It was never about moving your body because you enjoyed it," Sriya recalled. "It was always because you wanted this one specific image or ideal."

She weighed herself every morning. "If the scales didn't go down, I thought something was wrong with me," she said.

As the pandemic wore on, Sriya stopped getting her period. Because she lived in sky-blue California, Sriya had relatively comprehensive sex ed compared to the rest of the country—but she had never learned that she could stop menstruating. Petrified, Sriya didn't tell her parents that her period had gone missing.

She was eleven years old. It was not until three years later, when Sriya was hospitalized for a running injury, that she learned the real reason for her period's disappearance: anorexia nervosa.

Out of all the major social media platforms, Instagram encourages some of the worst feelings of social comparison—and Meta, its parent company, has worked diligently to play down its own research into the matter. In a bombshell 2021 exposé, the *Wall Street Journal* discovered and published internal research from Facebook—as Meta was then known—showing that one in five American girls who use Instagram say it makes them feel worse about themselves. Of teenage users who have felt "unattractive" in the past month, 40 percent say that feeling started on Instagram.[29]

"Teens blame Instagram for increases in the rate of anxiety and depression," revealed another internal Facebook slide, according to the *Wall Street Journal*. "This reaction was unprompted and consistent across all groups." More specifically: Six percent of teens who reported suicidal thoughts traced those thoughts back to Instagram.[30]

Despite these findings, a former executive brushed off the idea of overhauling Instagram to deemphasize social comparisons, the *Wall Street Journal* reported. "People use Instagram because it's a competition," the executive said. "That's the fun part."[31]

Mark Zuckerberg, Meta's CEO, has tried to avoid the topic, too. Asked about mental health and young social media users in a 2021 congressional hearing, he told lawmakers that "the research that we've seen is that using social apps to connect with other people can have positive mental-health benefits."[32] (After the *Wall Street Journal* exposé broke, Zuckerberg said the newspaper had mischaracterized Instagram's effects.[33])

Congress's cluelessness about social media and internet culture can make it too easy for Meta and other social media giants to evade accountability. In 2021, Senator Richard Blumenthal, who was then seventy-five years old, asked a Facebook executive, "Will you commit to ending finsta?" The executive had to haltingly explain that the company does

THE SECOND COMING | 153

not "do" finsta and that "finsta" is slang for a private Instagram account where people dump the photos or thoughts they don't want preserved on their main account. This incident was only slightly less embarrassing than Senator Orrin Hatch's gaffe in 2018, when the octogenarian Utah Republican asked Zuckerberg how Facebook could afford to remain free. Zuckerberg blinked and, after a moment of dumbstruck silence, replied, "Senator, we run ads." (As I said earlier: If you're not paying for the product, you're the product.)

Blumenthal, at least, has not proven so hesitant or ignorant about social media that he hasn't made money off it. In 2020, the Connecticut Democrat and his wife made more than $1 million in capital gains from stock in Pinterest,[34] which, like every other social media site, has struggled to eradicate thinspo. (Yes, the social media site that's practically a shrine to domesticity can be toxic.) It's almost as if politicians weaponize incompetence and inaction to cover up conflicts of interest.

As we all try to ascertain and negotiate our positions in the politicized hierarchy of fuckability, social media not only reveals our position but reinforces it, as certain bodies continue to be ranked higher by both our peers and the mysterious workings of algorithms. By the time you read this book, platforms like Instagram or TikTok may have fallen out of favor or tweaked their algorithms. There will be new filters and new editing tools. But the overarching truth remains: An internet that emphasizes bodies and perfection is one that endangers young people, especially girls and women, and their ability to forge sexual relationships.

YES, DATING APPS ARE SOCIAL MEDIA

By college, Tatiana had only ever kissed somebody once, as a sophomore in high school. She had never dared hope for more. "Why would anybody want to date me? I was a chubby brown girl," Tatiana, who is of Bangladeshi descent, recalled thinking. "I found myself unattractive and assumed that other people found me unattractive."

But as an eighteen-year-old freshman at a Texas college, surrounded by friends who were in relationships, Tatiana was desperate to lose her virginity. She had started exercising more and losing weight. She felt ready for someone to see her naked. *I feel good about how I look,* she decided, *and I want somebody to want me.*

She also couldn't help but compare her own lack of sexual experience to all the funny or crazy Tinder stories that she saw posted on social media; in order to fit in, Tinder hookups started to feel obligatory. "You read the stories and people's experiences—it just reinforces that that's something I *should* do," Tatiana said.

So, she downloaded Tinder.

Like most of us, Tatiana might not necessarily think of dating apps as a form of social media, but of course they are: They're built to encourage online socializing, even if they are supposedly "designed to be deleted," as Hinge puts it. Furthermore, research indicates that dating apps may impact people's body image similarly to straightforward social media platforms. People who use Tinder, for example, tend to have poor body image, idealize being thin or athletic, and compare their appearances to others' more often.[35] These behaviors are all hallmarks of self-objectification—and, research has found, are (again!) linked to symptoms of eating disorders.[36]

After Tatiana matched with a twenty-two-year-old guy, they sent GIFs back and forth for a bit, until he sent a GIF of a person pulling down a bed's sheets and patting the mattress. The invitation was clear, but it didn't quite feel real yet. The silent, hypnotic movement of the sheets, receding and rising like waves, seemed impossible to reconcile with rapidly escalating interaction. Still, Tatiana replied, "I'm down."

"I'm down. You're cute," he shot back.

Oh shit, Tatiana finally realized. *People actually hook up off of this app. It's not just for jokes.*

She quickly consulted two friends about whether to go for it. The friends' verdict: "Fuck yeah."

Tatiana didn't tell her match that she had never had sex before. Instead, the pair hastily arranged to hook up in his car. When they met up, Tatiana stuck out her hand to shake his, but he hugged her instead and then opened the door to the back seat. "Why, thank you," she told him, and climbed inside.

Ultimately, Tatiana's Tinder match didn't see her naked; Tatiana kept her dress on and just took off her underwear. She also never again spoke to her match, who unmatched her on Tinder right afterward.

Before the spread of the internet, straight couples often met through places like college or church, while same-sex couples encountered one another through friends and restaurants.[37] Law professor Elizabeth Emens calls these meetings "intimate accidents"—the seemingly random intersections of timing and geography that end up determining "who meets whom, who interacts with whom, who has the chance to fall for whom." As Emens points out, these accidents are less incidental and more politicized than we may think. The government and politics play a role in building the physical spaces needed for such accidents—or in curbing those spaces to eliminate the possibility of diverse pairings, through policies like redlining, segregation, and the institutionalization of people with disabilities.[38]

In theory, the internet frees us from all that. Thanks to dating apps and social media, we can fall for—or at least bang—people whom we would otherwise never encounter, whose backgrounds may look nothing like ours. The sexual and romantic possibilities of the internet are utopian.

These possibilities, though, have largely failed to pan out. Instead, self-objectification and fuckability might be most pronounced on dating apps. "When you have a dating profile, you're very much *selling dating you*. It's so weird. What are the photos that are going to get someone to want to date you? What are the text blurbs that are going to get someone to want to date you? I don't really know the answer to that, so I do a lot of course-correcting," said Jo, the twenty-two-year-old from California. "I'm not trying to be inauthentic, but my goal isn't authenticity. My goal is selling myself as a person."

In a study of messages sent between straight, urban users of an unnamed "popular, free online dating service," researchers reveled in how online dating provides an "unprecedented opportunity" to "quantify the dating hierarchy"—that is, to lay fuckability bare. People, they found, usually try to date individuals who are about 25 percent more desirable than they are. (Researchers sketched out daters' relative desirability using multiple metrics, including how many messages they received.) Straight women and men, researchers concluded, "are aware of their own position in the hierarchy and adjust their behavior accordingly while, at the same time, competing modestly for more desirable mates."[39]

How do we all silently determine who is 25 percent more desirable than we are? We do so, it seems, based on some of the worst stereotypes about gender. Women were most pursued when they were just eighteen years old. Men's desirability did not peak until they hit fifty. Even after controlling for age, women's desirability decreased the more postgraduate education they accumulated, while more education only made men more attractive.[40]

This is a hierarchy of desire constructed by the sexism and politics we all swim in. This is fuckability.

Race especially demonstrates how stark a role fuckability plays in online dating. In 2014, OkCupid revealed that its female users tended to give the highest ratings to profiles of men of the same race.[41] Most of its male users felt the same—except for white men, who preferred Asian women over white women, and Black men, who preferred Asian and Latina women over Black women (and, out of all men, gave the lowest ratings to white women).[42] "When you're looking at how two American strangers behave in a romantic context, race is the ultimate confounding factor," Christian Rudder, OkCupid's co-founder and a data scientist, once remarked.[43]

Gay dating apps like Grindr have long tolerated a—shall we say—*overt* approach to racism and fuckability. One analysis of three hundred Grindr profiles found that 180 used racial slurs or instructed people of color not to reach out. The "About" section of one profile read, "I block more Asian[s] than the Great Wall of China."[44] This sexualized racism, predictably, corrodes people's mental health. Young, non-straight Black men are more likely to experience symptoms of depression when they run into profiles from white people who reject people based on race or when they feel fetishized by white people due to their race.[45]

Intriguingly, research suggests that young men who use dating apps feel just as bad as young women do about their bodies[46]—or even worse.[47] "I can be on there for weeks and maybe get a few people who message me first, and I feel like that's not usually how it goes in the real world," said Jacob, a twenty-six-year-old white man who lives in Nebraska and called himself "as straight as it gets." "I look very different in pictures than I see myself. The visual aspect is quite scary.

"Outside of dating apps, I've been lucky in that I've never really had to pursue anybody," he continued. "It was very different on a dating app. I felt like a lot of people who would like me in person were passing me by. It's just not great for your self-esteem when you don't feel that desired by people."

Just like everybody else, young men who get on dating apps are putting themselves out there to be judged. Unlike everybody else, these men are also operating under the weight of crushing stereotypes that insist that "real" men are good at procuring sex.

Given all this, it is perhaps unsurprising that Gen Z is thought to be in the midst of a generation-wide defection from dating apps. "Not enough young people are willing to pay for subscriptions to dating apps—partly because younger daters are increasingly looking to platforms like Snapchat and TikTok to make connections—and it's not clear what will change that," the *New York Times* fretted in 2024.[48] (The mentions of Snapchat and TikTok reveal just how much the line has blurred between traditional social media platforms and dating apps.) Between 2021 and 2024, the market value of the dating behemoths Bumble and Match Group—which owns Tinder, OkCupid, and a suite of other dating apps, giving Match a near-oligopoly on virtual love—tumbled by more than $40 billion.[49]

Elle, a twenty-two-year-old from Texas, is burned out on dating apps. When she first got Tinder at sixteen, Elle would be bombarded by messages from older men about "things that they would do to me," as she put it. (Tinder requires its users to be adults, but many interviewees said they started using dating apps when they were underage.) "I was being objectified and sexualized," said Elle, who is of Asian descent. "It was the first time that I, like, really understood what the male gaze meant. That's really when it all set in. I was like, 'Well, now I can't unsee it.'"

Elle still has an account, but she's turned off notifications. "The constant availability of people, just at your fingertips, and the ability for you to just swipe them away at first glance really desensitizes people and dehumanizes people," she said. "You're constantly scrolling and judging people, and the small talk—it's draining. I don't really care to see it anymore."

Tatiana, who first had sex in a car with her Tinder date, has never regretted how she lost her virginity. But now that she's twenty-five, Tatiana believes dating apps enable too much callousness toward sex and other people. "They're a cesspool," she said bluntly.

DEMANDING MORE

Although it can feel like one, social media isn't a total hellscape for body image all the time. There is no doubt that it showcases more body diversity than traditional media outlets—which played such a role in shaping our body images pre–social media—and that social media has pressured both outlets and brands into platforming more individuals who are not thin, white, and generically "sexy." For young people desperate to find a shard of a mirror in pop culture, social media is often their best option.

Born with a neuromuscular disability, Jo has used a wheelchair since the fifth grade, but as a child she didn't know anybody else who used one. She felt like an outsider, even inside her family. "Every day I would go on Instagram and whenever I felt bad myself, I could see people who either looked like me, or didn't look like me, but also were disabled," Jo said. "And that's really important when you literally go to school and go home and don't see anybody that actually looks like you."

Her sixth-grade hero was Chelsie Hill, a twentysomething influencer who leads a dance troupe filled with women who use wheelchairs and occasionally poses in lingerie in her wheelchair. Jo would scroll through Hill's photos and marvel: *She's living independently. She dresses well, she's pretty, she's cool.* Sure, sometimes Jo's chest caught fire with that thrashing feeling named *I want to be her.* But often, Jo said, "it was more for me, like, 'I *can* be her.'"

"Being disabled, I definitely struggle with my sense of desirability and feeling desired by others," she explained. "It's very helpful for me to see other disabled people, because that makes me feel more normal. . . . Maybe they get into relationships. Whether they are successful or not, that makes me feel not only happy for them—these people that I don't know—but also makes me feel hopeful for myself and more desirable as a person."

Tatiana credits social media with helping her feel more confident in her bigger body. "I'm even coming around to that little belly pooch that we all have," she said. "I found that attractive on other women a lot before, but I never thought it was okay on myself. I didn't understand why, because I would look at a woman with a bigger pooch and I'd be like, 'She looks so fucking good.' But I see myself in an outfit where my pooch shows and I'm like, 'That's disgusting.'"

THE SECOND COMING | 159

Her words bit with familiarity, because I had come to feel the same way about the girls at Disneyland. Although Tatiana grew up two thousand miles away from me, our body images lived in the exact same place.

"I'm working on rewiring that thought process and I've made some progress on it, but social media has definitely played a part," Tatiana went on. "Seeing women whom I find attractive with those features helps me rewire and be like, 'No, that's what it looks like for me too.'"

Australian researchers have found that when young women viewed Instagram content that boosted body positivity—sometimes known as "bopo," like a Cinderella to the evil stepsisters of thinspo and fitspo—their mood and satisfaction with their bodies improved.[50] However, body-positive content that features women who wear little clothing or are posed suggestively is still linked to increased self-objectification. It's depressing, but it makes sense. Even if those women are trying to expand ideals about beauty and sexiness, scrolling through photos of bigger bodies still includes breaking bodies down into slopes and shades. It's still watching, pausing, and rewinding an internal surveillance tape. It's still looking rather than being.

A few years ago, a survival instinct led me to cut all celebrities, influencers, and fitness accounts out of my social media diet. I thus evaded learning about the online disdain for "hip dips," or the indents that can appear where women's thighs meet their waists, until multiple interviewees brought them up. "It made me feel bad, because I have them," Rian, the Texan who considered a nose job, said of talk of hip dips. "I started going on YouTube and looking up 'hip dip workouts' to fix it. Then I did a little more research, and it was like, 'That's your bone structure and the only way to change it is to break your bones.'"

Objectively, I knew hip dips were another passing fad; every few months, somebody on social media declares that a random body part is suddenly hot or objectionable. But despite this knowledge—and the wisdom that supposedly comes with aging—I once again found myself contorting my body in my mirror and attempting to ascertain whether my body possessed yet another flaw. After a few minutes of searching, I realized that I had previously noticed the waveform of other women's hip dips before. But I had originally found those nearly secret curves to be sexy—just as I'd felt about the girls' stomachs at Disneyland.

What features would we admire, in ourselves and in others, if no one told us we were supposed to find them ugly? Who would we care for if no one told us that their bodies were beneath us? Would we take better care of ourselves? This is part of what Amia Srinivasan was wrestling with when she coined the term "fuckability": Is there such a thing as desire untouched by politics and prejudice?

Sexually progressive young people want to answer this question; that's clear from their interest in analyzing porn, comp het, and all kinds of sexual and gendered mores. But unless we enter some golden age of sexual progressivism, where millions of people commit themselves to unlearning the stereotypes that surround gender and race and every other category of personhood, we will probably never know. (Such an age is, to say the least, unlikely in the current American political environment.) But I do know this: When unchecked technological advances encourage young people to devalue themselves and one another, it doesn't end at poor self-esteem, bad body image, and flawed relationships. It ends in violence.

7.

"OF COURSE HE'S GONNA SEND YOU DICK PICS"
Nudes and the Manosphere in a Post-#MeToo World

Zoe was twelve years old the first time she took a photo of her naked body and sent it to a stranger on the internet.

They had met on Kik, an anonymous messaging app that, at its height in the mid-2010s, was used by 40 percent of American teenagers.[1] Zoe had gotten Kik because so many of her friends were on it, but she had begun to feel alienated from them—not because of anything they had done, but because the world had already started to treat her as a sex object. Zoe got her period at nine and started developing breasts soon afterward. By the time she was eleven, her mom forbade her to wear leggings to the mall because she "didn't want old men staring at me," Zoe recalled.

Around that time, a group of teenage boys accosted Zoe while she was hanging out in a park. They began to grope her; when she tried to resist, they hit her in the face with a stick. The boys scampered only after a nearby woman spotted what was going on and threatened to call the cops.

Zoe was terrified to tell an adult about the sexual assault. She imagined she would be plunged into an episode of *Law & Order: SVU*, complete with angry, demanding police and courts. When her family asked her about the scratches on her face, Zoe lied and said she had collided with a tree.

Zoe was still trying to wrap her head around the assault when she met a man on Kik. "I was just really looking for a safe place to talk about that with. You know how grooming goes: That makes you the perfect candidate for a relationship like that to flourish," she said. "My mentality was like: 'Well, I'm already kind of tainted. What else is there?'"

Zoe thought she was in a long-distance relationship with the man from Kik. He told her he loved her, that she should send him nudes, that the nudes would be safe with him.

Still, "I knew that something felt wrong with it," Zoe said. Adopted into an evangelical household in the Midwest, Zoe felt "icky" and ashamed, like she wanted to rush off and ask Google: "Am I going to hell for this?" She knew she wasn't ready and recognized, dimly, that she was being pressured. But, she thought, *I want this person to know that I love and care.*

Zoe sent the photos. "I felt like I had to."

As far as Zoe knows, this man kept his promise and didn't share her nudes. But two years later, when she was fourteen, Zoe sent photos of her naked body from the neck down to a different man, with whom she was in a "digital situationship." This time, her nudes ended up splashed across Ask.fm, another anonymous social network.

The comments poured in. "You're fat." "Slut." "I will put my mouth on your body." "Kill yourself."

"I had never really been called a slut or anything like that before," Zoe said. "I was like, 'Oh, is this not what people wanted?'" Bewilderment curled her words into a question.

Harassment, especially of the sexualized variety, is the elevator music of the internet: an ambient hum that you may not notice or can ignore—right up until it drives you mad. More than 60 percent of Americans between the ages of eighteen and thirty say they have been harassed online, and 48 percent say the harassment was sustained over a period of time or included stalking, physical threats, or sexual harassment.[2] That's far more than any other age demographic.

A gender gap emerges early. About half of all U.S. minor teenagers have been bullied or harassed online in some way, but girls are more likely to face this behavior and to experience multiple forms of it.[3] One in five young American women say they've been sexually harassed online, compared to one in ten men.[4] On dating apps, young female users are roughly twice as likely as male users to be contacted by people after they say they're not interested, to be sent explicit images they didn't ask for, and to be physically threatened.[5]

"There's an expectation among a lot of the men that there will be some sort of sex involved," one female college student remarked of dating apps in a 2020 study. "If that isn't present, then the harassment begins."[6] Given its gendered nature, scholar Danielle Citron believes this harassment is more accurately understood as "cyber gender abuse."[7]

The forces of sexual conservatism are pushing to dominate, even dismantle, public education, leading young Americans to receive little to no accurate education from authorities about how to have safe, respectful, and pleasurable sex. Then young people fire up their phones and computers, where they can find this sex ed on their own—but where they also encounter a deluge of porn, messages about fuckability and how to be sexy, harassers, predators, and other assorted hateful bullshit. While we tend to recognize that social media and smartphones enable people to hurt one another in unprecedented ways, we often treat this as justification for a moral panic over sexual progressivism and the Big Bad Internet rather than seeing it as a call to introspection or action over our approach to sex ed or sexual misconduct.

The real problem is that we live in a culture where sexual misconduct is ordinary, even expected, including when it is directed against the youngest among us. This rape culture expects victims to prevent sexual misconduct and blames them if they do not. Forget about holding actual perpetrators responsible.

If I sound bitter, consider that one in four American women has been the victim of an attempted or completed rape. More than 80 percent of female rape victims were first raped before they turned twenty-five, and almost half were minors. One in twenty-five American men have been penetrated against their will and one in nine have been made to penetrate someone* else.[8] Of the men forced to penetrate someone else, more than 80 percent were also younger than twenty-five when it first happened. Again, almost half were minors.[9]

Now consider the fact that, out of every one thousand sexual assaults committed in the United States, only 310 are reported to police, according to the Rape, Abuse, and Incest National Network (RAINN), the nation's leading anti–sexual assault organization. There's little incentive to

---

*To be clear, I believe both of these circumstances constitute rape. The CDC draws a distinction in its data collection.

report, anyway: Just twenty-five reports result in the incarceration of the perpetrator—and incarceration is not necessarily the same thing as justice.

If this is how we react to *offline* sexual misconduct, to the physical violation of people's bodies, it's no surprise that online sexual misconduct is rarely taken seriously.

When authorities shrug at such harassment, its victims learn to do so, too. Many young women write it off as the cost of being female online. "It's like, 'Oh, well, you're on Tinder. What did you expect? Of course he's gonna send you dick pics. If you're gonna have Tinder, you'd better accept it,'" one female college student said in a 2020 study.[10]

"I just think going into the internet, we should understand that anything is gonna happen and anything will happen," said a female philosophy major in the same study. Yet another woman went even further, declaring harassment part of "how the internet is supposed to be."[11] In other words, the mere act of going online—something all of us do every day, all day—is *asking for it.*

As much as the internet can be sexually progressive and help young people decipher their sexuality, it is also the perfect breeding ground for some of the core beliefs that animate rape culture: namely, that cisgender men are entitled to sex and that, when denied sex, misogyny is an appropriate response. This attitude can be bred through everyday activities like sending nudes and through extremist spaces like the manosphere.

I know, I know: #NotAllMen. Clearly, not all cis boys and men harbor this entitlement to sex or act on it. Obviously, cis men can be victims of sexual abuse and rape culture. Certainly, people who are not assigned male at birth can perpetuate this culture and sexually abuse people. These complexities are why the popular interpretation of misogyny, as a hatred of women, is wrong. Kate Manne, a philosophy professor at Cornell University, has offered a different, more useful interpretation: Misogyny—and all the attacks that flow from it, including sexual harassment and assault—is sexism's law enforcement branch. Misogyny polices the sexist status quo, such as the expectation that it is a woman's job to be sexually available to men and that all men should always want sex from women, by retaliating with violence whenever people dare to disobey.

"I think of misogyny as being a bit like the shock collar worn by a dog to keep them behind one of those invisible fences that proliferate in suburbia," Manne wrote in her book *Entitled: How Male Privilege Hurts Women*. "Misogyny is capable of causing pain, to be sure, and it often does. But even when it isn't actively hurting anyone, it tends to discourage girls and women from venturing out of bounds. If we stray, or err, we know what we are in for."[12]

After her nudes were shared and she was both sexualized and slut-shamed online, Zoe "just hated looking at myself.

"I was mad that I risked a part of myself for someone else and for someone who betrayed me. I really struggled to cope with that," Zoe told me. She barely blamed the man who had shared her nudes because she was so consumed with raging at herself. For days, she couldn't even bring herself to eat. "I felt dirty. I felt fat. And I felt like I . . ." Zoe flailed for a way to describe it. "I felt very disconnected from my body."

She felt like she had been sexually assaulted again.

Sexual conservatism uses the supposed sexualization of children as a rallying cry, but its fiercest advocates are not devoting themselves to demanding more rights and resources for young victims of sexual misconduct. Rather, they are fighting efforts to expand sex ed that would help prevent it and even rolling back laws meant to help survivors. The beneficiaries of sexual conservatism who sit on the Supreme Court have literally laughed at efforts to curb cyber gender abuse. And whether the movement wants to recognize it or not, sexual conservatism stands to politically profit from the thriving online communities that coax young men into believing that, actually, men *should* be able to rape frigid bitches.

SEND NUDES, SLUT

If there is a single activity that demonstrates how online rape culture develops and the threat it poses to young people's physical and mental safety, it is sending nudes. While it can be a fun act of sexual exploration, it sours into image-based sexual abuse and slut-shaming at alarming rates.

Like sex itself, sending nudes is not inherently right or wrong. It can be just another component of twenty-first-century rituals of flirting, dating, and relationships. A fifth of youths have sent sexts, including explicit images and videos,* while upward of a third have received them.[13] Sexting gets more common as people age, with more than a third of people between the ages of eighteen and twenty-nine having both sent and received sexts.[14]

As Rue, Zendaya's character in the TV show *Euphoria*, declared: "Unless you're Amish, nudes are the currency of love."

Yet because the practice of texting nudes is new and lewd, there has long been an assumption that it is bad for us, even when it occurs among consenting adults. Researchers have looked for links between sexting and unprotected sex, sexually transmitted illnesses, poor mental health, "delinquency," substance use, and the use of porn, to name just a few of the "risk behaviors" that have been examined. A 2019 analysis of a decade's worth of sexting research found that teenagers who sexted were more than three times more likely to have experienced sexual activity.[15] (This wording of the study seemed to discount the fact that sexting *is* sexual activity.) They were also more likely to use drugs and alcohol, experience anxiety and depression, and avoid contraception.[16]

This analysis, however, didn't differentiate between sexting that happened in relationships compared to sexting that happened between single people. More importantly, it did not dive into the differences between nonconsensual or unwanted sexting—like the kind that Zoe engaged in at twelve—and consensual, wanted sexting. The latter kind can help strengthen relationships—particularly of the long-distance variety—improve body image, and boost sexual satisfaction.[17] Just like sex ed that stigmatizes all young sex, stigmatizing sexting makes it harder for young people to recognize or seek help when something goes wrong.

And sexting does go wrong. A lot.

Girls and women frequently report feeling pressured, harassed, or threatened into sexting, as well as feeling worse about themselves afterward.[18] One young woman told me that, after the Covid pandemic forced her to isolate away from her high school boyfriend, he begged for

---

*Scientific studies tend to lump the practices of sharing explicit images and explicit messages together under the banner of "sexting," even though laypeople tend to think of sexting as sending explicit text messages. I'm mirroring studies' choice of language in order to accurately reflect their findings, but these studies *are* examining the practice of sending nudes even when they call it "sexting."

nudes. She didn't really want to send them—but she also didn't want to fight. Covid had shuttered her school and locked the world down; her social circle had shrunk to the size of a snow globe, leaving her incredibly dependent on her few remaining relationships. She didn't want to jeopardize the most important one.

She gave in and sent the nudes. By the time we spoke, years later, shame still sizzled through her.

Refusing to sext can get girls labeled prudes—or worse. "When boys get rejected, they turn into the most hostile, violent people you've ever known. I've known girls who will get bottles thrown at their heads for rejecting somebody," one teenager reported in the book *Behind Their Screens*. "[Boys] feel so entitled that it's like: 'How dare you say no to me?' And so oftentimes, I feel like it's nothing but violence and verbal assault that comes after that."[19]

Boys and men, meanwhile, can feel pressured by their male peers to request sexts.[20] Particularly among straight, cisgender boys and men, sharing tales of sexual escapades—*conquests*—can be a way to cement their bonds with one another, even if it's at the cost of the girls and women in their lives. Nudes, then, are holy-grail proof that they got some.

Hegemonic masculinity, or the stereotype that men are ultra-tough dominants who love to fuck around, is at work here. Not only are boys and men made to feel like they should shame themselves and one another for being virgins, but they are also made to feel like they're not "real men" if they don't carve some fantastical number of notches into their bedposts.

"The standard of masculinity set is that you make money, you have good sex, and you provide. That's the extent of what you do in a household," said Dewayne, who appeared in the last chapter. "Whether that is implicitly or explicitly stated, it is very true and underlying. It is what ultimately brings a lot of folks to either have an overcompensating orientation toward masculinity or a very resentful relationship with masculinity, because it's like, 'This is not all I am, and I don't feel like I have access to express who I am.'"

It's such an impossible standard that boys and men sometimes feel like they can't turn down sexual activity, including sending nudes, looking at others' nudes, or sharing them. In one study of Boston teenagers, researchers encountered a stunningly blithe eighteen-year-old who said he and his friends share videos of themselves having sex and even watch them on the subway together.[21] "All you hear is the girl moaning," the eighteen-year-old said. "We watch it and, like, nobody's ashamed of it."[22] Researchers did not know if the girl in the video was underage, or if she had consented to being filmed having sex or to having the video shared.[23]

As a student at an all-boys high school in the Northeast, Isaiah rarely interacted with girls, but it was common for his classmates to show off their collections of nudes. "For guys then, it was kind of like a trophy," said Isaiah, who is now twenty-one. "'Hey, I did this. Hey, I managed to get nudes from a bunch of different people.' Like showing off their prowess."

Once, a close male friend of Isaiah shared the "My Eyes Only" section of his Snapchat with Isaiah. As he scrolled through it, Isaiah saw "a bunch of nudes from various women our ages." Stunned, Isaiah didn't tell his friend off. He summed up his reaction: "Didn't really get involved with it."

About one in seven youths and young adults have forwarded sexts without consent.[24] This practice used to be called "revenge porn," but today experts use terms like "image-based sexual abuse" and "nonconsensual intimate images." (Depending on the ages of those involved, image-based sexual abuse can also involve what is now called "child sexual abuse imagery."*) These terms make clear that this practice is not porn but a form of sexual misconduct and intimate partner violence. Research is mixed on whether young men or women experience image-based sexual abuse more frequently, but men seem more likely to perpetuate it.[25] The impact of image-based sexual abuse is also more devastating for women, who are more likely to say their perpetrator made them fear for their safety and reputations.[26]

Lesbian, gay, and bisexual people are more likely than straight people to deal with image-based sexual abuse, but again, LGB+ women are more

---

*More commonly referred to as "child porn." Just as experts now recommend that people do not use the term "revenge porn," they also do not want people to use the term "child porn" because the word "porn" implies the imagery was produced through consensual means and should be considered sexually pleasurable.

likely to be worse off afterward.[27] Regrettably, there is little research that solely examines the experiences of transgender, nonbinary, and otherwise gender-diverse individuals, but a study of Belgian non-cis youth found that, while they are just as likely as their cis peers to sext, they are much likelier to feel pressured into it.[28]

Hegemonic masculinity conditions people to believe that men gain through having sex while women lose. Similarly, girls risk their reputations if they send nudes (or if they refuse to), while boys can get off scot-free or even improve their reputations. If a man's nudes leaked, the only thing he might face blowback from would be his "own appearance, if anything," according to Isaiah. Translation: He would get teased if he had a small penis.

When Camilla learned that her high school's football team had a group chat where they secretly exchanged nudes of girls, the eighteen-year-old said she reported it to her school in the Northwest. A counselor tried to convince her it wasn't a big deal. "But the girls really sent these nudes, right?" the counselor said, according to Camilla. "It's not like the guys set up cameras in their locker room or anything, because that'd be a whole different thing. These were willingly shared images."

"There was definitely always the feeling that if a girl's nudes got leaked, or if a girl's nudes got spread, she shouldn't have sent them in the first place," Camilla explained. "That culture of exchanging nudes and that culture of guys doing things like that was so normalized that, when my parents figured out that I'd reported it, they were angry at *me*."

Young Americans watched Donald Trump brush off the "grab 'em by the pussy" *Access Hollywood* tape as mere "locker room talk"—a stunningly bald acknowledgment that men degrade women behind closed doors. Camilla, meanwhile, ended up so ostracized for trying to report that kind of behavior that she switched schools.

Sharing a partner's nudes without permission is a form of intimate partner violence and, as always, what happens online bleeds into our offline lives and vice versa. Exploitative sexting, such as pressuring someone into doing it, has been linked to IRL dating violence among Italian teenagers.[29]

The good news is that as boys leave high school and enter college, they tend to realize this kind of behavior is wrong. The bad news is

170 | CARTER SHERMAN

that they don't necessarily take responsibility for it. In focus groups of eighteen-to-twenty-two-year-old Australian men, participants stressed that it was other, less-experienced men who shared nudes and that they had moved past seeing nudes as "kind of like a trophy."[30] Isaiah, raised on the other side of the planet from these men, used the *same exact language* to describe the act of scoring nudes.

The focus group moderators were skeptical. "This has the effect of writing off their earlier, potentially problematic practices as the deeds of naïve novices who simply did not know better," they wrote in a preprint paper, "thereby diminishing, and even somewhat legitimizing, these practices as a sort of rite of passage."[31]

Tellingly, the men in the focus groups emphasized that, while it was wrong to share nudes of girlfriends, hookups could still be fair game. "If they're going to be doing that, and they're not your girlfriend? They're a slut," one man said. Another agreed, "Well, they wouldn't care anyway."[32]

These men zip-lined to two conclusions: First, they decided that single women who share nudes with men are "sluts"; second, they decided that these sluts don't deserve privacy. This is a perfect, if inadvertent, demonstration of how slut-shaming undermines scholars Jennifer Hirsch and Shamus Khan's concept of sexual citizenship, or the "acknowledgement of one's own right to sexual self-determination and . . . that right in others."[33] Because slut-shaming is a refusal to respect others' right to sexual choice, it legitimizes abuses against them—which is a fancy way of saying it leads people to victim-blame. In the United States, customs around sending nudes, when combined with our society-wide nonchalance toward online rape culture, work together to foment slut-shaming and victim-blaming. In a survey of more than 3,600 U.S. youths, about 60 percent agreed that "if someone sends a naked picture to someone else, it's their own fault if the picture ends up getting shared with other people."[34]

Take this thinking even further and you can end up justifying all kinds of behaviors, including rape. It's no coincidence that, until second-wave feminists took action in the 1970s, rape victims' sexual history could be brought up in court proceedings, as if "sluts" can't be raped. It is also no coincidence that the right to privacy, what these Australian men sought to strip from "slutty" girls who send nudes, once provided the legal foundation for *Roe v. Wade* as well as for the Supreme Court cases that gave Americans the right to same-sex intimacy, contraception, and interracial marriage. Without respect for privacy, without respect for others' control over their own sexual and romantic lives, sexual citizenship is impossible—as is respect for others' agency writ large.

Technically, most states ban the nonconsensual sharing of intimate images.[35] But there is no federal law against image-based sexual abuse, and the differences between state statutes can strand victims "at the mercy of a confusing patchwork of laws," according to the Cyber Civil Rights Initiative.[36] Some states legally recognize that minors can consensually send nudes, but others leave them vulnerable to being charged with creating or sending child sexual abuse imagery.[37] Most importantly, enforcement of these laws is scattershot, as police frequently fail to take abuse or its consequences seriously, according to Danielle Citron, originator of the term "cyber gender abuse." In New York, Citron found, one cop told a victim she should "feel good about appearing on 'cum tribute' sites that showed videos of men masturbating to [the victim]."[38]

The photos of Zoe's fourteen-year-old body were ultimately wiped from Ask.fm. At least, she thinks so. After that catastrophe, she decided to send nudes only to people she was dating.

"All my friends were doing it," Zoe said. "It was almost expected, honestly."

On one occasion, during sex, her high school boyfriend pulled out his phone and started filming them, Zoe said. "I didn't consent in the act, but I felt like I was killing the mood if I was like, 'What are you doing?'" Zoe recalled. "My face was definitely in that."

Zoe obtained a copy of the video, which also included shots of her boyfriend's face, to deter him from sharing it. It was a kind of mutually assured destruction. But mostly, Zoe just refused to think about the possibility that her boyfriend would leak her nudes. *He would never do that,* she tried to reassure herself.

He did do that.

After about a year of dating, when Zoe was seventeen, she tried to break up with her boyfriend. He issued an ultimatum: If she didn't keep dating him, he would send her nudes to his friends. This was "sextortion," a type of blackmail where people threaten to spread explicit photos unless they get what they want, which is often more photos, money, or sex. Five percent of middle and high school students have been victims of sextortion, while 3 percent of students admit to carrying it out.[39]

When Zoe didn't back down, her ex followed through on his threat. Photos of her naked body ended up on a spam Instagram account, or a finsta, a "fake Instagram."

"In the present of it, I think I was really desensitized to it. Unfortunately, I wasn't surprised," Zoe said. *His stinky friends can do whatever they want,* she told herself. *I'm gonna move the fuck on.* Her friends reported the Instagram account, and luckily it was soon deleted.

But once your nudes hit the internet, you can never be sure that they're gone for good.

THE RISE AND FALL OF #METOO

Wasn't the #MeToo movement supposed to fix this? Wasn't it supposed to teach young people how to better respect one another's boundaries, drive them to hold each other accountable, refuse to accept unequal treatment and rape culture? Alternatively: Weren't #MeToo, social media, and the specter of "cancel culture" supposed to make people *too* nervous to cross someone's boundaries? Could "cancel culture" be the reason for the sex recession?

Not quite.

Originally started in 2006 by activist Tarana Burke, #MeToo took over social media in the fall of 2017, after the *New York Times* published an exposé of Harvey Weinstein's sexual predations and the actress Alyssa Milano urged people to tweet "me too" if they had been sexually harassed or assaulted.* Going public with sexual harassment or assault on social media is a modern-day form of what second-wave feminists called "consciousness raising," a practice of sharing stories to demonstrate that what may seem like unique and private problems are in reality common and

---

*The Me Too movement, as started by Burke, is connected to but distinct from the social media uprising of #MeToo in 2017. To differentiate between the two, I use the term #MeToo to refer to the uprising.

structural ones. Consciousness raising makes people realize that the personal is political, the essential first step in taking action to fix it.

When I asked interviewees to name political or cultural events that shaped their approach to sex, many cited #MeToo. Although they had been raised on an internet where feminism and queer activism flourished, it was not until #MeToo that they got the chance to watch a singular social justice movement dominate that internet. Many of the Gen Z-ers I interviewed understood, much earlier than I had, that it was unfair they were left haunted by their early sexual experiences. Through #MeToo, they had learned to tell themselves a new story about their sex lives, one that was closer to the truth and that recognized the political dimensions of sex.

In high school, Simone's boyfriend penetrated her with his fingers without her consent. She broke up with him, but he coaxed her back into a relationship by telling her, "I talked to a ton of female friends, and they say stuff like this happens all the time and it's okay."

"I felt like I was like betraying him because I didn't like what he did to me," Simone recalled. He ended up breaking up with her.

After she watched #MeToo sweep across social media, Simone, who is now twenty-four, began to understand what happened to her as "gray-area rape."* She decided to share her own #MeToo story. "It's disheartening to see girls that were a part of feminist clubs in high school hang out with somebody that basically raped me when we were dating," Simone tweeted.

In the year after Milano first tweeted "me too," the hashtag #MeToo appeared more than nineteen million times on Twitter alone.[40] But by the end of 2018, the limits of #MeToo and consciousness raising were made clear.

In fall 2018, Christine Blasey Ford testified that Brett Kavanaugh, whom Trump had recently nominated to the Supreme Court, had sexually assaulted her in high school. Seated before the Senate Judiciary Committee, with the eyes of the entire United States on her, Blasey Ford

---

*The legal meaning of "rape" can vary across jurisdictions, but the FBI defines it as "penetration, no matter how slight, of the vagina or anus with any body part or object, or oral penetration by a sex organ of another person, without the consent of the victim."

shared her account of how a drunk, teenage Kavanaugh, urged on by a male friend, had pinned her to a bed and ground his hips into her.[41] "Indelible in the hippocampus is the laughter," she told senators. "The uproarious laughter between the two, and their having fun at my expense." They were, apparently, just two boys cementing their bond to one another through sexual conquest. Like the boys and men who pass around leaked nudes.

While Blasey Ford was measured and calm throughout her testimony, Kavanaugh shouted and cried. He brandished calendars and rattled off names of female friends, as if it is impossible to hurt one woman because you like others. The allegation, Kavanaugh raved, was nothing more than a "calculated and orchestrated political hit, fueled with apparent pent-up anger about President Trump and the 2016 election, fear that has been unfairly stoked about my judicial record, revenge on behalf of the Clintons." (In case it's unclear, Kavanaugh denied all wrongdoing.)

In hindsight, the Senate hearings over Blasey Ford's allegations marked #MeToo's crest. Kavanaugh was confirmed to the Supreme Court. Four years later, in 2022, Kavanaugh joined the rest of the court's conservative supermajority—including Justice Clarence Thomas, another man accused of sexual misconduct—in overturning *Roe*.

Social media and #MeToo led public awareness and support of feminist aims to soar to perhaps their highest point in decades. When #MeToo crash-landed back on earth, brought down by powerful individuals and institutions, it carved a crater so deep that it obliterated *Roe*, one of the biggest victories of 1970s second-wave feminism. For many late millennials and members of Gen Z, then somewhere between their twenties and grade school, this arc exposed the deep societal indifference, even hostility, toward survivors of sexual misconduct and those who seek to change the status quo. Young people can see evidence of this hostility every time they go online.

At the height of #MeToo, Jane scrolled through the hashtagged confessions of sexual trauma on Twitter. What she remembered most was not the confessors' vulnerability and strength, but the fact that so many faced vitriol, hate, and accusations that "you're just accusing him because he's successful."

"It made me realize that a lot of people, even if they're nice, won't necessarily support you in your time of need or believe you," said Jane, who is twenty and from Kansas. "After that, I became more hesitant to talk about those kinds of things. Even after I was assaulted, I didn't really tell anyone what had happened until months, *months* after. I didn't know what they would do, because he was the friend of some of my friends. I didn't want to face that kind of backlash that people got."

Rather than affirming her ability to speak up, #MeToo had the opposite effect on Jane. This is how cyber gender abuse becomes normalized.

After Simone tweeted about her ex, she got word that his mom wanted to sue her for libel, even though she had not named him. This was a potent threat, since defamation lawsuits against accusers quietly mounted in the years after #MeToo. Between 2018 and 2023, almost 20 percent of the legal cases supported by the Time's Up Legal Defense Fund—started in the wake of #MeToo to help people who faced sexual misconduct at work—involved cases where victims had been sued for defamation.[42] Consciousness raising, it turns out, can be a legal liability.

Terrified, Simone took down her tweet.

"I felt failed by other women and women who attended the Women's March," Simone said, her voice breaking. "Because people knew! People knew after we broke up. People knew and they still hung out with him."

Yes, Weinstein and Bill Cosby were convicted of sexual assault after #MeToo. But #MeToo led to few permanent legal reforms beyond reshaping workplace nondisclosure agreements. (Not exactly helpful for the young people who don't work.) Plus, many so-called canceled men rebounded. Weinstein's New York conviction was overturned, while Cosby was released from prison on a technicality. #MeToo did not even lead to the inclusion of more information about how to prevent sexual misconduct in sex ed. If anything, the very concept of consent has become more demonized.

Like several other Gen Z interviewees who were on the younger side, eighteen-year-old Noah has no memory of #MeToo. (Noah popped up in chapter six.) Sharing someone's nudes, Noah said, would be "pretty frowned upon" among his friends. "It was more middle school that that was a big deal," he said. "Now, it's kind of kicked to the side."

But it was still common for his male high school classmates to draw up fantasy football–style drafts that ranked girls' hotness and to call them words like "bop" and "ran through" if they were perceived as having had too many sexual partners. Most guys his age, Noah said, just don't see the connection between the importance of asking for consent and, as he put it, "needing to see a person's personhood, a girl's personhood" when she's not around.

"You're talking about #MeToo, which is about consent stuff, but you're also just talking about how women should be treated and seen," Noah told me. "But I think, now, those are kind of split apart."

They shouldn't be. People ask for consent because they recognize their partners' sexual citizenship and thus their personhood. Nobody asks vibrators or Fleshlights how they feel about getting fucked.

In 2023, five years after Blasey Ford testified that Kavanaugh's laughter was seared into her brain, laughter rang out in the halls of the Supreme Court, where Kavanaugh now sat. The nation's highest court was hearing a case about the stalking conviction of a man who, court records show, had sent hundreds of Facebook messages to a singer-songwriter he had never met.

"Fuck off permanently," he told her.

"Staying in cyber life is going to kill you," he told her.

"You're not being good for human relations," he told her. "Die."

The singer repeatedly blocked the man, only to have him contact her through a new account. Some of his messages seemed to suggest that he knew where she was. She stopped sleeping and walking alone, canceled social engagements and performances. She lost out on chances to further her career, to add her voice to public life. Finally, she called Colorado law enforcement, who convicted the man and sentenced him to four years behind bars.

The man appealed, arguing that the state law he had been convicted under violated the First Amendment. When his case reached the Supreme Court, the justices seemed skeptical that online interactions could really be that bad.

"'Staying in cyber life is going to kill you,'" read Chief Justice John Roberts, a conservative. He quipped: "I can't promise I haven't said that."

As the room erupted with laughter and Colorado's lawyer tried to argue that the line needed to be put into context, Roberts interrupted. "I think that might sound solicitous of the person's development," he said.

In a 7–2 decision written by the liberal Justice Elena Kagan and joined by both Roberts and Kavanaugh, the Supreme Court vacated the man's conviction. "The majority made clear that the speech that mattered was that of people who might self-censor for fear that their words would be construed as a threat," Danielle Citron wrote. "The court said *nothing* about the speech interests of victims."[43] (The emphasis is hers.) It seemed not to occur to the majority that victims and would-be victims might self-censor, too.

The internet is our modern public square, far more so than any physical space, especially in a post-pandemic world where we live so much of our lives online. But more than 40 percent of American women between the ages of fifteen and twenty-nine—more than any other age group—say they censor themselves online to avoid harassment.[44] Lesbian, gay, and bisexual people are also more likely to self-censor for this reason.[45] This is how the misogyny of cyber gender abuse successfully upholds sexist norms: When people are ridiculed or punished for speaking up, or witness others' punishment for doing so, they are pushed out of arenas where they can make a difference. This is also how activism, including that in support of sexual progressivism, is silenced.

After more than a decade of trying to strengthen protections against cyber gender abuse, including image-based sexual abuse, Citron concluded in 2023 that it remains legally invisible, thanks to attitudes like Chief Justice Roberts's—attitudes that dismiss online rape culture as unserious and unworthy of institutional intervention. "And an even more insidious message is sent to perpetrators: Cyber gender abuse is unlikely to cost them anything even as it costs victims everything," Citron wrote.[46]

"RAPE-WORTHY"

Rian, the twenty-two-year-old Texan from chapter six, has not had sex. She used to chalk her celibacy up to the demands of school, the difficulty of building a relationship, her own laziness. But now, Rian has realized, it has a far more concerning cause: "a mix of fear and disgust toward men." Although she's straight, she's repulsed by the behavior of men online.

"I think men are treating women even worse now than usual," she told me. This, she indicated, is another potential factor in the sex recession.

Rian continued: "A lot of women are just not having relationships with men anymore, and I cannot blame them. I'm one of them."

Rian believes the ideology of incels, an online subculture of men who claim women have denied them sex and forced them into "involuntary celibacy," has infiltrated the internet and, with it, the wider theater of gender relations. Born out of an online community for lonely romantics established in the 1990s, modern-day incels believe that Western society is organized according to a looks-based sexual hierarchy and that incels are consigned to the bottom rung. Their forums seethe with self-hate, but incels don't believe they're to blame for their sexlessness. Instead, incel lore dictates that incels exist because women have the freedom to choose their partners, to be such *sluts*. As one incel forum user put it: "Women should have never been given any rights."[47]

Incels think feminism has corrupted society's natural order, an order in which men are entitled to sexual relationships with women. This kind of entitlement is the core belief behind rape culture—and incels are the worst-case outcome of online rape culture. While more marginalized people censor themselves online out of a fear of cyber gender abuse, incels are so emboldened by online rape culture that they feel comfortable posting comments that not only excuse sexual assault but retcon it out of being a crime at all. "Rape is the alpha method of pleasure and procreation and foids know this, that's why they prefer to get raped," wrote a user of an incel forum. He added, "I wouldn't feel like a real man if I had consensual sex."[48] ("Foid" is an incel slur for women, fashioned through the dehumanizing combination of "female" and "humanoid" or "android.")

There's no way to gauge how many men identify as incels, but research indicates they are concentrated in North America and Western Europe. They tend to be around twenty-four years old, middle-class, and more racially and ethnically diverse than is often assumed. Still, they idolize whiteness and can be jaw-droppingly racist. For example, they call Asian women "noodlewhores."[49]

Incels believe the rise of online dating and social media is also responsible for the concurrent rise of the incel subculture. It's not that incels have a problem with dating platforms and social media's exposure and reinforcement of fuckability; indeed, their worldview very comfortably accommodates the existence of fuckability—a concept that Amia

Srinivasan devised in part because of incels and their obsession with wringing status out of women's bodies. "I was often attracted to ugly girls around my looksmatch but every one of them rejected me because they could find better using Tinder and shit like that," one user posted on an incel forum, using the incel term "looksmatch" to describe a partner of comparable attractiveness (or, perhaps, fuckability). "I was called 'ugly' even by girls WAY MORE ugly than me. Like 2/10 obese roasties."[50] ("Roastie" is yet another incel slur for women they deem promiscuous. They think women who've had a lot of sex develop labia that look like slices of roast beef.)

Rather, incels are upset with dating apps and more conventional forms of social media, like Instagram, because they think these platforms reveal how modern society has handed far too much sexual power to women while stripping it from men. "Every woman is a celebrity with Instagram," one user of an incel forum complained. "Basically, a 2/10 foid gets much more sexual interest in her than a 10/10 did from the 1990s."[51]

"A guy might not be involuntarily celibate, but he'll believe some of the stuff these guys are saying," Rian explained. "Online dating is very visual and so people—men, especially—who are not as conventionally attractive are having trouble. They're like, 'Oh, it's because I'm ugly,' which is the beginning of the incel rabbit hole."

Consider Jacob, the twenty-six-year-old straight Nebraskan man who also showed up in chapter six and who is absolutely not an incel. Not only does he have a girlfriend, but while incels cling to hegemonic masculinity and its notions of sex, Jacob has questioned them. ("I was on my third or fourth sexual partner before I realized that it was desirable for me to make noise of my own during sex," he said. "Men don't make noise in porn, unless they're degrading the women.") Growing up, Jacob steered clear of Reddit and 4chan—websites where incels have long flourished—relying instead on Tumblr for his sex ed and porn. It felt "less exploitative," more considerate of women. "Hearing women talk about these things, I think, was a big help," Jacob said of Tumblr. "There have been a few posts where people were like, 'People do not know how to choke other people. Here is a guide.' I was like, 'Oh, I've been doing that wrong. I'm gonna remember that for later.'"

Yet even Jacob, already insecure about how he looked in photos, was convinced women on dating apps were in far more demand compared to men. He resented the inequality. "I think they're quite stressful and not good for self-esteem, at least on the male side of things," he said of the apps. "I also didn't like the imbalance, I guess—the power imbalance that shows up right away. Right from the get-go, I know that she has a lot of other options. Lots of people are messaging her."

Jacob isn't totally off base. Women on dating platforms do receive more messages than men and are more likely to get replies to their messages.[52] But as much as these statistics enrage incels, women's surfeit of messages reveals less about their supposed power in the "sexual marketplace" and more about how men and women are socialized to approach one another. Namely, men are still expected to make the first move. Women on dating platforms initiate far fewer exchanges then men.[53]

What is destabilizing, for both incels and the "very, very liberal" Jacob, is women having the greater choice of sexual partners. The key difference between Jacob and an incel is that, unlike an incel, Jacob blamed dating apps for making him feel at a disadvantage, rather than condemning women as sluts or feeling like he was entitled to sex with them. It is also striking to me that Jacob grew up perusing Tumblr. How might he have reacted if he had instead mainlined Reddit and 4chan? Online rape culture makes it all too easy to run into misogyny and to regurgitate it.

The sex recession, unfortunately, may be both a symptom and cause of incels' spread. Almost half of adult Americans who are under thirty are single—but that number masks an extraordinary gender gap. While 63 percent of men in that age group are single, only 34 percent of their female peers say the same.[54] Who are these women dating? Older men they meet on dating apps? Other women? (Gen Z women are far likelier than Gen Z men to identify as LGBTQ+.) No matter the reason, many young men are desperately lonely and dealing with a mental health crisis that has sent rates of male suicide skyrocketing.[55] When they go online to hunt for guidance on handling these very real issues, they can find it in incel ideology.

Incels' fundamental issue is that they feel deserving of sex by virtue of being men—but somehow, they are not having it. Hegemonic masculinity so stigmatizes male virginity, demanding that men hype up their sexual history through supposed proof like nudes, that it really is toxic.

THE SECOND COMING | 181

In a 2020 study, Australian researchers asked male adolescents whether they agreed with statements like, "I think it is important for a guy to act like he is sexually active even if he is not," "In a good dating relationship, the guy gets his way most of the time," and "I would be friends with a guy who is gay."[56] The more these adolescents endorsed the values of hegemonic masculinity—that men aren't allowed to have complex feelings about sex, that men should direct relationships, that it's okay to be homophobic—the less likely they were to seek mental health help.[57] And rather than encouraging men to do the hard work of challenging stereotypes that make them sick, incels offer them a way out: *Actually, the problem isn't the airless, impossible expectations placed on men. The problem is women.*

On May 23, 2014, a twenty-two-year-old California college student named Elliot Rodger stabbed his three roommates to death. Then he bought a triple vanilla latté at Starbucks, uploaded a video titled "Retribution" to YouTube, and emailed a 137-page manifesto to family members and acquaintances. "I don't know why you girls aren't attracted to me, but I will punish you all for it," Rodger warned.[58] He wanted to wage "a war on women."[59]

His plan was to "attack the very girls who represent everything I hate in the female gender: the hottest sorority" at his college.[60] But when he pounded on the sorority's door, no one let Rodger in. Enraged, he started shooting and driving at people on the street, killing three people and injuring fourteen more. The massacre ended only after Rodger shot himself in the head.

Police and journalists soon discovered that Rodger was a virgin and spent extensive time skulking in incels' online underworld. In the years since his deadly spree, incels have canonized Rodger as a kind of patron saint; they call his attack "going ER."[61] In 2018, a twenty-five-year-old named Alek Minassian posted on Facebook, "The Incel Rebellion has already begun! . . . All hail the Supreme Gentleman Elliot Rodger!" He then plowed a van into a Toronto sidewalk. Ten people died; more than dozen were injured.[62]

If misogyny serves as the law enforcement arm of sexism, terrifying people into obeying sexist norms, then incels are SEAL Team Six. And, terrifyingly, incels are not as fringe as we may like to think.

Incels have long lurked in the "manosphere," a "loose confederacy"[63] of websites, blogs, and forums where individuals gather to spew the ideology of "male supremacy." In 2018, the Southern Poverty Law Center started tracking this ideology on its map of hate groups,[64] in an indication of just how much the advent of the internet had helped misogynists connect, organize, and radicalize more followers. Bodybuilding forums—you know, those websites that help young men get jacked and feel good about displaying their bodies on social media—are particularly fertile "recruitment ground for male supremacist and white supremacist extremists, calculatedly targeting young men," according to *Men Who Hate Women*, Laura Bates's book-length tour of the manosphere.[65]

Another entryway into the manosphere may be through leaking nudes, thanks to websites devoted to sharing explicit images obtained through nonconsensual means—or, as the United Kingdom–based Revenge Porn Helpline calls them, "collector sites." Remember how Isaiah and the focus groups of Australian men said that men see nudes "kind of like a trophy"? These sites are what happens when men turn pro.

"The sole purpose of these sites is to categorize women by their location and trade their nude images like a dystopian version of Pokémon," the Revenge Porn Helpline explained in a 2020 report. "Men discuss women as if they are less-than, mocking how 'they could look their [victim's] boyfriend in the eye knowing they had seen their missus naked,' and that women in the images are 'asking for it,' or 'rape-worthy.'"[66]

In 2013, there were forty collector sites. By 2023, there were more than 9,500.[67]

As AI and deepfakes become sophisticated and common, incels and other members of the manosphere have used them to abuse women through nonconsensual intimate images. In 2024, 4chan users used AI to craft explicit images of Taylor Swift as part of a sick game to test the limits of AI content moderation.[68] Those images soon sloshed out of 4chan and were viewed millions of times,[69] leading even the White House to call their rapid spread "alarming." (Not alarming enough to take strong action, though.)

It is increasingly easy for young men to stumble across the tools to make these kinds of images. In 2022, the firm Graphika uncovered about 1,280 comments and posts on X and Reddit that directed people to services that can make deepfake intimate images.[70] In 2023, they found more than thirty-two thousand.[71] Male middle and high school students in states like Washington,[72] California, and New Jersey have started using AI to generate deepfake intimate images of their underage classmates, sharing the images in group chats, on the school bus, and in their school lunchrooms.[73]

We have spent decades taking little to no action to address rape culture and cyber gender abuse; our institutions have yet to curb the entitlement, slut-shaming, and dehumanization that surround image-based sexual abuse. Is it really any surprise that, when given a tool that enables the literal dehumanization of their peers, young men feel entitled to use it?

Once I started hunting for evidence of incels' influence, I found it everywhere online. For example, incels have spent years quietly popularizing the practice of "mewing," which claims people can use muscle exercises to redefine their jawline. Today, mewing has been mentioned more than one billion times on TikTok.[74] (The American Association of Orthodontists does not recommend mewing and has said that the "scientific evidence supporting mewing's jawline-sculpting claims is as thin as dental floss."[75]) Mewing is also part of incels' broader interest in what's called "looksmaxxing," a self-improvement regimen that combines a Silicon Valley–style optimization obsession with incels' pseudoscientific conviction that women only want to sleep with "Chads." (Chads are tall, muscular men with jawlines so square you could use them to level a picture frame. Think Chris Hemsworth.) The day I started writing this chapter, I tried to procrastinate by opening up the *New York Times*, only to find the paper of record innocuously using the term "smellmaxxing" to describe teenage boys' social media–fueled obsession with cologne.

Some scholars believe we are now in the "normie-fication" phrase of incel-dom and the manosphere, where male supremacist vocabulary and ideas will become more common on social media platforms, then in news outlets, until they finally seem not only common but normal. In a 2023 study, researchers discovered that two incel-linked TikTok accounts had garnered more than two million views.[76] Commenters frequently "trivialized sexual violence by claiming that women incite and deserve to be subjected to such acts."[77]

184 | CARTER SHERMAN

The bulldozing of sex ed, free expression, and public education plays a fundamental but underacknowledged role in this normie-fication. When teachers, schools, and libraries are censored, students lose out on opportunities to learn the context and critical thinking skills that they need to counter online misogyny.

"You have young men who are like, 'I want to get to get fit and healthy,' so they're like, 'Let me go follow this gym bro'—who then also on the side talks about how women shouldn't have rights," Zach, a twenty-four-year-old who hails from Indiana, explained to me. "Two years down the road, they're like, 'I'm pumped and women shouldn't have rights.' People are like, 'Where did that come from?' Well, we didn't teach them to have critical thinking skills, and then we put them in front of media, so it's not really surprising."

THE RAPE-CULTURE-TO-REPUBLICAN PIPELINE

Incels and other denizens of the manosphere are somewhat strange bedfellows for the sexual conservatism now commandeering our classrooms, legislatures, and courthouses. Sure, both groups lament the Sexual Revolution of the 1970s, but forums like 4chan—as well as the rest of the internet—really owe their existence to the sexual permissiveness that it ushered in, as Angela Nagle noted in her book *Kill All Normies.* "From the start it was teeming with weird hardcore pornographic images and discussions—gay, straight, transgender, and everything in between—and a culture of relish transgressing any and all moral codes when it comes to sexuality," Nagle wrote of 4chan.[78] While sexual conservatism wants to elevate married and procreative sex, much of the manosphere wants sex on their terms, up to and including rape, rather than to get married.

Yet incels, the manosphere, and sexual conservatives are all reactionaries raging against the same thing: sexual progressivism, or the fact that people who are not straight white cisgender men are openly advocating for their right to have sex when and how they choose. JD Vance, Donald Trump's second vice president and one of the United States' most powerful skeptics of the Sexual Revolution,[79] has suggested that people who don't have kids should have fewer votes than those who do; although he later tried to walk back his suggestion as a "thought experiment,"[80] he has made numerous other remarks accusing childfree *women*, not childfree men, of ruining the United States. In aggregate, these kinds of comments start to sound a whole lot like the incel complaint that "women should have never been given any rights."

It's predictable, then, that the manospheric anti-feminist, anti-women sentiment now spreading among Gen Z men can turn into political support for sexual conservatism.

The greatest political and cultural upheavals of Gen Z's lives— Trump's victory in the 2016 presidential election, the Women's March, #MeToo, the overturning of *Roe*—have mainly centered women and LGBTQ+ people, helping turn Gen Z women into one of the most progressive and politically energized cohorts ever measured in U.S. history. But Gen Z men, unsure of their place in these struggles or even resentful of them, have stunned political scientists by drifting to the right. While feminism has made extraordinary gains among millennials and Gen Z women, Gen Z men are less likely to identify as feminists compared to their millennial older brothers;[81] roughly half of men under thirty believe that "feminism is about favoring women over men."[82] More than half of men in that age group think "things are generally better when men bring in money and women take care of the home and kids."[83]

"I agree a lot with what the #MeToo movement was talking about, but it was very anti–cis male," said Davan'te, a twenty-seven-year-old man who lives in Georgia. "A lot of men felt attacked and felt like, 'Wow, I'm a man, so I'm the reason for all the problems in the world.'" The manosphere and misogyny peddlers like Andrew Tate, a muscle-bound British-born influencer who loves to talk about his wealth and how he dominates an apparently endless parade of women, seized the moment. Davan'te explained: "All of a sudden you got this charismatic, good-looking, wealthy person being like, 'No, masculinity's not bad! Actually, being ultra-masculine looks like *this*, and it's a good thing.'"

"This" is a deeply hateful view of women, especially those who dare to have sex. Tate has said that women who've slept with more than three men are "vile,"[84] that he prefers to sleep with eighteen- and nineteen-year-olds because they've "been through less dick,"[85] and that women who've been sexually assaulted "bear some responsibility."[86] "He even appeared to endorse sexual slavery, once insisting on the Dave Portnoy podcast that a woman in a relationship 'belongs' to the man, 'and the intimate parts of her body belong to him,'" journalist Lisa Miller wrote in a 2023 *New York* magazine investigation into Tate's disturbing popularity among boys and young men.[87] Again: Slut-shaming invalidates individuals' personhood, including to the point that they can be deemed literal property.

As of this writing, Tate is battling criminal charges of rape, human trafficking, and forming a criminal gang to sexually exploit women in Romania,[88] where he reportedly moved in 2016.[89] Two British women have also told the BBC that Tate strangled and raped them.[90] Tate has denied all wrongdoing.

Davan'te is no fan of Tate or of the kinds of traditional gender roles hawked by the manosphere, but he understands how young men get swept up in it. In his early twenties, Davan'te struggled to maintain relationships and an income. *Am I hardcore enough? Am I tough enough?* he thought at the time. *Maybe I'm being too nice of a person, and me being too caring is hurting me in life.*

"Now that I'm getting my feet up under myself and understanding myself, I totally know that's BS," Davan'te said. "You can still be strong, a protector, a provider, all those things, and still *feel* emotionally. That's fine, bro. That doesn't make you weaker or any less of a man."

Davan'te is now passionate about Democratic politics and serves as a reproductive justice activist. Because he focuses on helping men get more involved in the fight for abortion rights, masculinity and misogyny come up all the time in his advocacy. Recently, Davan'te recalled, an anti-abortion man suggested that there was a simple solution to this whole debate: "Women should keep their legs closed."

Support for hegemonic masculinity and traditional gender roles ultimately translates to votes for people and parties that are all too happy to advance the cause of sexual conservatism. When asked whether they agree with statements like "Women seek to gain power by getting control over men," Republicans are twice as likely as Democrats to show signs of hostile sexism, or negative views of people—especially women—who break with traditional gender roles.[91] People who agree with the statement that U.S. society is "too soft and feminine" are also highly likely to have voted for Trump in 2016.[92] In 2022, 49 percent of Gen Z men agreed with the statement that U.S. society is "too soft and feminine"; by 2023, 60 percent agreed with that statement. In fact, the more people—both men and women—generally believe that stereotypes of hegemonic masculinity are true, the more likely they were to vote for Trump in both 2016 and 2020.[93] Buying into these stereotypes also leads men and women to have a more positive opinion of Brett Kavanaugh and a more negative view of the women who accused him of sexual misconduct.[94]

I doubt that anybody has ever shown Trump these studies. But his 2024 presidential campaign revealed that he knew where his audience's sympathies lay, as Trump spent its final weeks palling around with fratty YouTubers and podcasters like the Nelk Boys and Joe Rogan, whose audiences are primarily male and whose work evinces little to no interest in the interior lives of women. On Election Day, one nineteen-year-old Arizona voter in a scarlet "Make America Great Again" hat told me that he considered Trump, a convicted felon who'd also been found liable for sexual abuse, to be a "good man."

He added: "I couldn't complain about any of his stuff."

This may sound jarring—even plenty of Trump voters complain about Trump—but according to the rubric of hegemonic masculinity, Trump *is* a "good man." He's dominant, loudly sexual, and emotionally one-note. Because hegemonic masculinity also tells men that they must provide for their families as breadwinners, Trump's gold-plated wealth further strengthens his status as a "good man." This is also, by the way, why anxiety around "the economy" is inextricable from anxiety around masculinity—especially in an age where Instagram frequently makes teens feel like they don't have enough money[95]—and helps explain why young voters whose top issue was the economy also broke for Trump.

Ultimately, in 2024, 56 percent of male voters between the ages of eighteen and twenty-nine, including 63 percent of young white men, cast their ballots for Trump.[96] "The Manosphere Won," a *Wired* headline announced bluntly.

The depth of the manosphere's victory became devastatingly clear in the first few days after the election. On November 5, 2024, when Trump's victory was all but declared, white nationalist and self-described "proud incel"[97] Nick Fuentes gloated on X, "Your body, my choice. Forever." Within days, the Gen Z-er's post had been viewed more than thirty-five million times—and mentions of the phrases "get back in the kitchen" and "your body, my choice" had surged on X by 4,600 percent.[98] Now that online sexual harassment has become normalized and the manosphere normie-fied, even this kind of hate can go mainstream.

With both online rape culture and sexual conservatism in ascension, the relationship between the two must be scrutinized. Because sexual conservatives are far more skilled than sexual progressives at taking cultural anxieties around gender and sex and cementing them into policy, the questions that most concern the manosphere are set to rise to the top of the national agenda: *Who gets to have sex? Under what terms? Who sets those terms?* Obviously, Fuentes—who, notably, once dined with Trump at his Mar-a-Lago club[99]—has one answer to these questions. And it's a horrifying one.

As influential as the internet is in all of our lives, we can't overlook how IRL institutions also affect how young Americans answer these questions. U.S. schools are failing to provide comprehensive sex ed, but they have offered late millennials and Gen Z another kind of instruction: a crash course in how institutions regularly and severely fail survivors of sexual assault. Arguments over the terms of sex have become more pressing and divisive since Barack Obama was in office—and in that division, sexual conservatism saw an opening to remake federal policy. The repercussions still reverberate today.

8.

A DISTURBING RITE OF PASSAGE
Sexual Violence and the Destruction of Title IX

By the time the Charlotte-Mecklenburg Board of Education finally opened up their March 8, 2022, meeting for public comment, officials had spent more than two hours lecturing before a packed auditorium. They had talked about the difficulty of hiring more administrators and teachers. The catastrophic impact of the coronavirus pandemic on students' education. The merits of clear backpacks, whose unspoken purpose was, presumably, to catch students who brought guns to class.[1]

Nikki Wombwell and Serena Evans waited nervously, furiously through it all. As she sat in the back of the auditorium, Serena twisted her curly dark hair between her fingers and checked the meeting schedule on her phone to see when she and Nikki would be allowed to speak. ("Now we're down [at] the end," Serena whispered to her mom, who sat beside her. "They moved you guys later so people wouldn't listen," her mom whispered back.[2]) Nikki's hands trembled as she held her speech, which the twenty-two-year-old had carefully typed and printed out. She had done everything carefully that day: dressed in a charcoal blazer and dark blue button-down, put on her professional-looking cat-eye glasses, smoothed her bleached blonde hair into a low ponytail.

Nikki wanted people to take her seriously, because she and Serena had already spent too long feeling ignored. This was their moment. They were going to try to publicly shame Charlotte-Mecklenburg Schools, a North Carolina school district that oversees more than 141,000 students and nearly two hundred schools, into reckoning with campus sexual assault.

Eight years before that board meeting, on an afternoon in October

2014, Nikki was raped by an ex-boyfriend in the woods that line the campus of Myers Park High School, a school within Charlotte-Mecklenburg Schools, according to a lawsuit Nikki later filed. At the time, Nikki was fifteen. So was the ex-boyfriend whom she accused of raping her.

I should note now that the defendants named in Nikki's lawsuit, including officials at Charlotte-Mecklenburg Schools and the Charlotte-Mecklenburg Police Department, have all denied wrongdoing. No criminal charges were ever filed in connection to Nikki's case. What follows is Nikki's account, pieced together from court documents and interviews given to reporters—including me—over the course of several years.

At the time of the rape, Nikki's ex had trapped her in what her lawsuit called an "ongoing pattern of dating violence and sexual harassment." When Nikki tried to cut off contact with him, he threatened to hurt himself. He used similar threats to pressure her into performing oral sex on him and sending him nudes, which he disseminated at least once.

"He was very pushy the entire time we were together," Nikki told me. "It was, 'Oh, like, you let me kiss you, can I touch your breasts?' Or like, 'Oh, you know, it doesn't count if you're wearing underwear.' And then it was, 'Oh, we already did it with your underwear on. What's the difference?' And then it was, 'Oh, I did it to you. You have to do it to me.' And it just kept escalating and escalating.[3]

"I don't think I have had a single first, sexually, that was completely consensual," she added.[4]

That day in October, Nikki's ex texted her to say he had a gun in his backpack and that if she didn't meet him after school, he would shoot himself in the head. Nikki was terrified. She felt like she had no choice but to meet him on the campus quad.

From there, Nikki's ex walked her into the woods, where, she said, he raped her. She only escaped after she said she had theater practice and that people would look for her if she was late.

"I was in shock. I didn't know what had just happened. I was—I was scared," Nikki told lawyers later. The ex, she said, "started texting me immediately afterward being angry that he hadn't finished, or whatever you want to call it, and that we were going to have to do that again because it wasn't fair that I left before he was done."

Nikki had never had intercourse before.

THE SECOND COMING | 191

Nikki first reported the rape to a Myers Park official the following day, but all they seemed to do was contact her ex's family, which led to more threatening texts from the ex. Weeks later, in December 2014, Nikki tried to report what had happened again. She spoke with the principal, who she said offered to meet with Nikki's ex to discuss the "proper way to treat a lady"—a phrase she could still recall years later. Nikki said the principal also warned her: If her story didn't hold up, she could be suspended for having sex on campus.

Humiliated, confused, and afraid for her academic future, Nikki declined to make a formal report. Afterward, she frequently missed school, suffering mental breakdowns and flashbacks. She couldn't bring herself to talk to another adult about what had happened. "I was scared and embarrassed and fifteen years old," Nikki said in a legal deposition. "And something horrible had happened, and I wanted to—I didn't know how to talk about it. It was, like, the hardest thing for me to talk about in the world."

In college, Nikki told me, she was sexually assaulted again.[5] (Women who are raped as minors are more than twice as likely to be raped as adults.[6]) She dropped out of her dream school and tried to die of suicide.[7]

Nikki had no idea that there is a federal civil rights law that could have helped her. It's called Title IX.

Many young Americans have never heard the words "Title IX," but their parents may remember that it has something to do with school sports. Signed into law by President Richard Nixon in 1972, Title IX bans discrimination "on the basis of sex" in the tens of thousands of school districts, postsecondary educational institutions, and charter schools that receive federal funding. Because Title IX blocks schools from, say, refusing to give female student athletes uniforms while splurging on the men's, the number of girls participating in school sports has shot up since the 1970s.

Yet Title IX's mandate stretches far beyond sports, as it is also supposed to compel educational institutions to stand against sexual harassment and assault. If schools are leaving students mired in an environment so polluted with unchecked sexual misconduct that it threatens their ability to get an education, those students are being discriminated against "on the basis of sex."

For American teens, particularly those assigned female at birth, being sexually assaulted is so common as to be a rite of passage. K-12 schools reported almost fourteen thousand incidents of sexual violence to the federal government during the 2017–18 school year, the most recent year as of this writing for which the Department of Education had data.[8] That's a 43 percent increase from the 2015–16 school year,[9] a finding that could be the result of better reporting of sexual violence in the wake of #MeToo in 2017, an actual rise in sexual violence, or a combination of both. In 2021, when the CDC conducted its biennial Youth Risk Behavior Survey, 14 percent of female high school students told the CDC they had been "forced into sex." Four percent of male students said the same.[*10]

"If you think about every ten teen girls that you know, at least one and possibly more has been raped, and that is the highest level we've ever seen," a CDC official told the *Washington Post*. "We are really alarmed."[11]

The statistics on college sexual assault aren't much better. Roughly one in four undergraduate female college students and gender-expansive students has reported "nonconsensual sexual contact by physical force or inability to consent," which is sexual assault; those reports rose by about 3 percent among undergraduate women between 2015 and 2019.[12] About 7 percent of male undergraduates have also reported nonconsensual sexual contact,[13] which may sound relatively small until you consider that these men face unique risk. Male college students between the ages of eighteen and twenty-four are 78 percent more likely to be sexually assaulted than their peers who aren't in college, according to the anti–sexual assault group RAINN.

As the United States struggles to solve the mental health crisis among young people, it's worth remembering that people who have been sexually abused are more likely to be diagnosed with anxiety, depression, eating disorders, and post-traumatic stress disorder.[14] Sexual abuse is also linked to an increased risk of suicide attempts,[15] which have become more common among millennials and Gen Z.

Survivors of sexual violence tend to see their sex lives suffer afterward, since they can struggle to become aroused or have orgasms.[16] They are also likely to start having more sexual partners, to use condoms less

---

*The survey's results, released in 2023, did not break down the data beyond the gender binary.

frequently, and to use drugs and alcohol during sex.[17] Activists who believe "consent" should be stricken from young people's sex education are potentially setting them up to have more sex that is less safe.

In 2020, when she was seventeen, Diana was having sex with someone when she realized that she wanted to stop. When she tried to tell him, he complained, "But I'm so close."

"I was like, 'Okay, fine. We'll keep doing it,'" said Diana, who grew up in Kansas. "I was so mad at my younger self for doing that."

As we spoke, Diana used all kinds of words to describe what happened to her: "skeevy," "a red flag," "predatorial," "fuckery." She insisted she did not consider it sexual "assault." It was, at most, "harassment." Still, she tried to tell another guy that the experience had left her feeling "really strange" and "violated."

"Well, that's not rape, that's not sexual assault," he told her, as she recalled it. "You shouldn't tell anybody that that happened, because that's not that big of a deal."

Maybe to you, she thought, *but not to me.*

Months later, Diana found herself having uncomfortable, if not outright humiliating, sex—the kind of sex where your body shuts down, leaden with the knowledge that you're just an object for another person to use to get off. Her partner pulled her hair to the point of pain and choked her while pressing down on her with his entire body weight. Because his bed was lofted, Diana's head thumped against the ceiling. It got so bad that she started wondering: *Are you getting off on the fact that I'm uncomfortable?*

I just want to leave, she thought. *I don't want to continue having sex.*

But this time, she didn't say anything.

"That would happen to me a lot, where I would want to stop but I would just wait until he finished because he would get mad at me," Diana told me. "Men can't handle rejection, you know? I was scared that, for the men who can't handle rejection, they would hurt me. That's a fear that I think a lot of women deal with."

My throat felt clogged with burning charcoal. It may have been a minor slip of the tongue, but I was struck by the difference in those two sentences. Diana initially implied that *all* men can't handle rejection, then suggested that only a subset of men can't handle it. The problem, of course, is that you don't know if a man can handle rejection until you reject him. It's simply safer to treat all men like they can't.

Diana is right: This is a fear that a lot of women deal with. I know it intimately. One summer in college, I told a hookup that I didn't want to have intercourse—and he didn't listen. What had been a clumsy, drunken roll in my bed suddenly slipped into a struggle as he kept shoving his hand inside my jean shorts and I kept trying to push him off me. Finally, he declared that he wasn't leaving without a blow job. I don't exactly remember how I got him out of my apartment without submitting, but I know I got lucky, because he was far drunker than I was. He couldn't get a good grip on the situation or my body.

I never tried my luck again. The next time a man asked me for sex I did not want, I smiled through gritted teeth and, like Diana in Kansas, agreed. I was afraid he'd feel rejected. What if he couldn't "handle" it? Would it happen again? Would it be worse? Better not to find out.

This ritual of fear, entitlement, and acquiescence is ghastly, but it is nothing new. What is new for young people today is that rough sex has been normalized to the point where many don't feel like they even have to ask their partners before they perform a painful or even dangerous sexual maneuver, like choking. ("I feel like this guy was trying to emulate something that he's seen in porn," Diana said of the man who pulled her hair and choked her.) As more and more young people try out rough sex, what options do they have if the worst happens?

The #MeToo movement is also a new addition to young people's sex lives. While that movement raised their consciousness around sexual violence, it did not lead to large-scale institutional changes and tools that could rectify that violence. Instead, it left young Americans more aware than ever of the gulf between how sexual misconduct should be handled and how it actually is. "It's not a straightforwardly good thing that victims can recognize they've been victimized if they're not in a position to do anything to get safe," explained Nicole Bedera, a sexual violence researcher. "One of the reasons why, psychologically, survivors will blame themselves or struggle with labeling something 'sexual assault' is because it isn't really safe to grapple with living in a society [in which] this kind of violence is happening all the time and nobody's doing anything. That's a horrible reality to be aware of. Our minds will just try to convince us

THE SECOND COMING | 195

that we're actually a little bit safer than we are, which ironically puts us in more danger, because we're not aware of scenarios that are unsafe."

While I have previously covered the need to improve school-based sex ed to prevent sexual harassment and assault from occurring, this chapter focuses on what happens after it's too late to stop it—when people have been hurt and are looking to trusted institutions for help. Title IX could have been that help. But the federal government has transformed Title IX into a political football in the culture wars—a football that will likely be punted across the field every four to eight years as Republicans and Democrats win and lose elections and write and rewrite the rules of the game. So far, one side is winning. And it's the side made up of players with deep ties to sexual conservatism.

As long as Title IX is volleyed back and forth, young people will always lose. And they never won that much to begin with.

"A SHOT ACROSS THE BOW"

Perhaps because the smell of school gymnasiums clung to Title IX, its power to address sexual misconduct went underused and underenforced for years. Between 1998 and 2008, the Department of Education's Office of Civil Rights, which oversees schools' compliance with Title IX, ruled against a mere five universities out of twenty-four resolved complaints, according to a 2010 investigation by NPR and the Center for Public Integrity.[18]

The other major federal law used to hold schools accountable for sexual assault, the Clery Act of 1990, was also rarely enforced. Named after Jeanne Clery, a nineteen-year-old freshman who was raped, tortured, and strangled by another student,[19] the Clery Act requires universities to report all campus crimes or face fines. But by 2010, only six fines had ever been levied under the Clery Act; the largest was just $350,000.[20] Eastern Michigan University had to pay that princely sum after administrators were accused of spending months assuring a student's parents that their daughter—whose body had been found naked from the waist down, with semen on her leg and a pillow over her face—did not die of foul play.[21]

In 2011, the Obama administration issued guidance, now known in some circles as the "Dear Colleague" letter, that let schools know they had an obligation under Title IX to take "immediate action to eliminate [sexual] harassment, prevent its recurrence, and address its effects." Although the administration—which also issued a 2014 supplement to the 2011 "Dear Colleague" letter—did not create a blanket policy outlining how schools should handle Title IX cases, the letter did lay out some recommendations and requirements, such as notifying schools that accusations should be evaluated based on whether they are more likely than not to be true, a standard of evidence known as "preponderance of evidence." Put simply, schools were supposed to find perpetrators responsible in Title IX cases if officials were 51 percent convinced that Title IX had been violated. Civil proceedings commonly use the "preponderance of evidence" standard; many colleges used it in their Title IX cases, too, even before the 2011 "Dear Colleague" letter.[22]

The letter was a "a shot across the bow," Catherine E. Lhamon, then the assistant education secretary for civil rights, told the *Washington Post* in 2014. "It was the first time any administration had called out sexual violence as a civil rights issue."[23]

Complaints flooded the Department of Education in the wake of the Obama administration's new Title IX guidance. Over the course of six months in 2014, the Office of Civil Rights received about four times as many sexual violence–related complaints as the office received in the entirety of fiscal year 2010.[24] The administration also stepped up public pressure around Title IX. In 2014, it released a list of fifty-five colleges that were under investigation over their handling of sexual misconduct complaints. By including schools like Harvard and Princeton on that list, the Obama administration humiliated some of the United States' most august institutions.[25]

This increased attention to campus sexual assault, as well as the growing public understanding that pervasive sexual misconduct is a form of gender discrimination, helped pave the way for what would erupt on social media as #MeToo a few years later, in late 2017. Some high-profile cases also contributed. In 2014, a Columbia University student named Emma Sulkowicz became the face of the fight over campus sexual assault when she vowed to carry a fifty-pound mattress until the man she said raped her was expelled.[26] Then, in 2016, *Buzzfeed News* published an extraordinarily powerful letter by a woman who had been sexually assaulted by Brock Turner, a Stanford University student sentenced to just six months in jail for the crime. (The judge feared that a long sentence would have a "severe impact" on Turner.[27]) Thanks to the internet's ability to amplify long-silenced voices, the letter, whose author was later identified as Chanel Miller, amassed eleven million views in four days.[28] In a rare show of bipartisan unity, Democratic and Republican members of Congress even read it aloud on the House floor.[29]

Predictably, however, the Obama administration's Title IX guidance triggered a backlash from both the left and the right. Critics, including some feminists, worried that it trampled over students' right to due process of law. I'm certainly not saying the changes were above reproach—but less officially, much of the backlash was laced with a striking supposition: that men were being targeted by women who regretted having consensual sex. Or, put more baldly, that women were lying.

Sexual conservativism has succeeded in large part by making parents fear for their children, especially when it comes to their sex lives. The Title IX backlash tapped into this fear, as parents worried their male children could be falsely accused of sexual assault and left without legal recourse. According to a headline in the libertarian magazine *Reason*, the Obama administration had made "all sex unsafe on campus." The magazine's implication was clear: Wily women could change their minds and cry rape!

Confusingly, these complaints—that the government was penalizing male students amid an epidemic of false rape accusations—were taking place right as many media outlets and moralists were panicking over "hookup culture" and accusing this culture of leading to a real increase in sexual assault. These narratives were in open conflict. Should people be concerned about a rise in casual sex and sexual assault? Or should people worry about rising false accusations and *attacks* on casual sex?

Either way: While false accusations of sexual assault happen, all available evidence suggests these accusations are vanishingly rare. Men are more likely to be sexually assaulted than they are to be falsely accused of it.[30]

Perhaps a better explanation for why male college students may have wrongly thought their partners consented to sex is that their bar for consent was so low as to be in hell. In 2015, Nicole Bedera led a study examining how male students knew their partners wanted to have sex. Of the signals they relied on in recent sexual encounters, "explicit conversations about sexual expectations" made up only 13 percent. Instead, they often cited physical, nonsexual actions as proof of consent, like eye contact. "When pressed for further details, most participants struggled to explain what differentiated ordinary eye contact—like the eye contact we made during our interviews—from sexualized eye contact that indicated consent," Bedera wrote. "Many made no such distinction at all.

"It is possible that men are the only ones who consider an interaction sexualized, allowing them greater control over sexual activity that may occur, despite attributing sexual initiation to their partners," Bedera continued. "These findings have practical implications for those adjudicating sexual assault complaints, as those accused commonly claim the event in question was consensual or even initiated by the complainant."[31]

Ultimately, just as rising awareness of campus sexual assault in the early 2010s helped lead to the breakout of #MeToo, the backlash to the Obama administration's Title IX guidance would end up feeding into the eventual backlash against #MeToo. Really, it's all one backlash, predicated on the same argument: *It's a witch hunt!*

As it turned out, those who sympathized with the backlash were far more skilled at implementing institutional change. As #MeToo became breaking news, the Trump administration was breaking Title IX.

HELLO, BETSY DEVOS

After Donald Trump took over the White House in 2017, he nominated Betsy DeVos to lead the Department of Education. As secretary, DeVos would spearhead a transformation of Title IX so total that the law became, in Bedera's words, "completely unusable for survivors."

DeVos was the walking, talking personification of the links between the demolition of Title IX and sexual conservatism. Before she took a job leading the nation's public education, DeVos had little experience running a large bureaucracy but had spent plenty of time fighting to divert government dollars to private schools, including religious institutions. DeVos also belonged to a "GOP royalty"[32] family that is worth billions.[33] Her kin have spent years giving hundreds of millions of dollars to powerhouse conservative organizations like the Heritage Foundation, the Federalist Society—an influential network of conservative lawyers dedicated to defeating "orthodox liberal ideology"—and the Christian legal group Alliance Defending Freedom (ADF).[34] This group has, over the past decade, become the right-wing answer to the ACLU, as it has masterminded the conservative legal attack on LGBTQ+ rights and abortion access.

The DeVos family has also long supported anti-abortion crisis pregnancy centers, facilities that aim to convince people to continue their pregnancies (and that have taught sex ed).[35] The DeVos Family Foundation is even one of the "major donors" behind attacks on comprehensive sex ed, according to SIECUS, the United States' leading comprehensive sex ed advocacy organization.[36]

DeVos dollars have, in short, remade young Americans' sex lives. To follow the money even further: The Federalist Society and ADF are directly responsible for the demise of *Roe v. Wade*. ADF helped craft a Mississippi abortion ban to provoke a legal challenge to *Roe*, then carefully shepherded that challenge up to the Supreme Court, where it became the case that overturned *Roe*.[37] Top members of the Federalist Society advised Trump on all three of his Supreme Court picks,[38] including Brett Kavanaugh, all of whom (of course) then voted to destroy *Roe*.

As I wrote earlier, if there's a moneyed conspiracy tilting the field of sex education—and, really, the state of sexual freedoms overall—it's not on the left. And if there's a "deep state," its enemies are not conservative presidents like Trump.

Soon after assuming office, DeVos tapped activist Candice Jackson to temporarily head the Department of Education's Office of Civil Rights. Jackson and DeVos quickly zeroed in on Title IX. In July 2017, Jackson told the *New York Times* that Title IX "accusations—90 percent of them—fall into the category of 'we were both drunk,' 'we broke up, and six months later I found myself under a Title IX investigation because she just decided that our last sleeping together was not quite right.'"[39] (Jackson, herself a rape survivor,[40] later clarified that her stance was based on feedback on accused students' cases and that "all sexual harassment and sexual assault must be taken seriously."[41])

That same month, Jackson and DeVos met with three men's rights organizations that claimed male college students were being plagued by false rape accusations,[42] including one group that has been designated as a key site in the manosphere by the Southern Poverty Law Center and has lobbied against the Violence Against Women Act, which it compared to Jim Crow. Representatives from the men's rights organizations ended up playing an integral role in retooling Title IX as they emailed, offered legal advice, and met with Department of Education staffers, according to *The Nation*. "In public and in e-mails with DOE employees, members of these organizations have demeaned the credibility of young women, ridiculed sexual assault survivors, and pushed junk science on campus rape," the outlet reported.[43]

Extremist ideas from the manosphere fringe had infiltrated the highest level of government, with consequences for millions of young Americans. And as manosphere-influenced young men increasingly vote conservative, it makes sense for the conservatives they vote into power to take meetings—and cues—from them. This reciprocal relationship seems likely to only deepen.

In September 2017, DeVos rescinded the Obama administration's guidance around Title IX.[44] Rather than requiring schools to use the "preponderance of evidence" legal standard, the Department of Education allowed them to adopt a stricter, "clear and convincing evidence" standard.[45] Schools were also no longer urged to complete Title IX investigations within sixty days.[46] They needed to do so only within a "reasonably prompt" time frame.[47]

That's pretty much bureaucracy-speak for "never."

Over the next few years, DeVos embarked on the lengthy, intensive process of officially rewriting the rules of Title IX. Unlike the "Dear Colleague" letter, the DeVos rules, which were officially adopted in 2020, could not be easily rolled back by a new administration. Thanks to the slow grind of federal bureaucracy, changing them would take much more time and effort.

The DeVos rules narrowed the Obama administration's definition of sexual harassment and required colleges to hold live hearings where accusers and the accused could be cross-examined; it also blocked schools from using Title IX to regulate most off-campus conduct, such as an assault at an apartment or during a party or study abroad program.[48] If a school was reported to the Department of Education for violating Title IX, that school would face repercussions only if it was proven to be "deliberately indifferent" to its obligations under Title IX.[49]

"There are so many more barriers to reporting than there used to be," Bedera said. "Reports mean less than they used to. A lot of the protections that used to just be for survivors are now given to perpetrators too. And that makes reporting a really risky thing to do for a survivor."

"ANTI-MALE BIAS"

While DeVos upended Title IX, some of the highest courts in the country were buying into an interpretation of the law that also subverted its original mission. This interpretation revived the idea that the Obama administration's Title IX guidance had been a pitched attack on men.

In the latter half of the 2010s, a spate of lawsuits claimed the guidance had engendered "anti-male bias" to the point that it violated the Title IX rights of men *accused* of sexual misconduct.[50] In effect, these lawsuits took an anti–sex discrimination law that protects against sexual misconduct and, in a kind of Uno-reverse, said people accused of such misconduct were the real victims of sex discrimination.

It worked.

These lawsuits survived motions that would have derailed other anti-discrimination lawsuits at "surprising rates," lawyers Dana Bolger, Alexandra Brodsky, and Sejal Singh wrote in a law article analyzing anti-male bias lawsuits.[51] While still a federal circuit court judge, future Supreme Court Justice Amy Coney Barrett ruled that young man disciplined for sexual assault under Title IX had plausibly been a victim of anti-male bias. In another case, a federal court suggested that a young man had been the victim of anti-male bias because when his school ruled on Title IX cases, "most if not all the [accused] were male," and all were deemed "responsible (i.e., guilty)."

Sure, maybe this is evidence of bias. Or maybe it's a reflection of the fact that men make up the overwhelming majority of culprits in sexual misconduct cases. In fiscal year 2022, 94 percent of the people sentenced for federal sex abuse crimes in the United States were men.[52]

202 | CARTER SHERMAN

"The case law that has developed from Title IX suits filed by students accused of sexual harassment threatens to set up an alarming regime: Anti-discrimination law will primarily serve members of dominant groups accused of discrimination, rather than members of historically oppressed groups usually subject to that discrimination," Bolger, Brodsky, and Singh wrote. "Title IX has become a more powerful tool for men accused of sexual harassment than for victims and other members of marginalized groups."[53]

On the surface, stripping back the Obama-era Title IX guidance may seem unrelated to sexual conservatism's endgame of enforcing hetero-sexual, married, and potentially procreative sex. Wouldn't its operatives cheer on the Obama administration making, in the words of *Reason* magazine, "all sex unsafe on campus"?

Well, no, because the sexual conservatism movement keeps power in the hands of already-powerful groups. When they dictate the terms of sex, sexual conservatives foster a 1950s-esque societal order wherein men and women are married with babies. The Obama administration's efforts to hold people accountable for sexual misconduct threatened that order by empowering women, LGBTQ+ folks, and people of color (given that they are all disproportionately likely to face sexual violence). Stamping out those efforts, then, serves sexual conservatism's overarching aim.

In the last chapter, I established that a core belief of rape culture is that cis men are entitled to sex. The backlash to the Obama-era guidance and the emergence of the DeVos rules and anti-male bias lawsuits all reinforced that belief: They suggested that men are *so* entitled to sex that challenging their acquisition of sex, such as by claiming it was illegally obtained through rape, is an affront. The darkest version of this belief is, of course, that men are so entitled to sex that obtaining it through rape should be legal—as incels, the manosphere, and cries of "your body, my choice" so vividly demonstrate.

"I CAN'T START OVER"

The irony of this entire backlash is that, when it comes to sexual misconduct, Title IX has never been enforced all that well—not even under

Barack Obama. It is simply untrue that Title IX enabled universities to ruin scores of men's lives.

Between 2014 and 2020, only one in five students who had been found responsible for sexual misconduct was expelled, according to a colossal *USA Today* investigation into dozens of public universities. Just one in three was suspended. More typically, when students were found responsible for violating Title IX, they received lighter punishments that did not disrupt their education.[54]

One Georgia State University student was accused of masturbating while strangling a woman in a student center stairwell, groping a second woman at a party, and raping a third on two separate occasions, *USA Today* reported. He received probation for the first two cases, was suspended for a summer semester for the third, and graduated with a degree in political science and government.[55]

Meanwhile, a survey of more than one hundred people who reported sexual violence to their schools between 2002 and 2020 found that 39 percent took a leave of absence from school, transferred, or dropped out altogether. "When I started having severe panic attacks because of his presence on campus, they forced me to drop all my classes," one survivor said. "I tried to reenroll for the next semester but couldn't do it and left for good over spring break. Because of my federal loan status, I can't start over at another school. I'll never get the degree I spent years working toward."[56]

Staffers at the Department of Education's Office of Civil Rights, tasked with holding schools accountable when they fail to uphold Title IX and other civil rights laws, were barely keeping their heads above water. Between fiscal years 2010 and 2016, as the Obama administration publicly championed Title IX, the number of complaints filed to the office nearly doubled.[57] What did not double was the Office of Civil Rights' budget, which remained relatively flat amid staffers' exploding workload.[58] Justice suffered accordingly. In 2010, the office took an average of 289 days to wrap up a sexual violence investigation; by 2017, that average had swelled to 963 days.[59] The office just did not have the money to fulfill its mandate, leaving both students and schools in the lurch.

When DeVos arrived, she took this backlog of complaints and essentially put them through a wood chipper. By June 2018, ProPublica had discovered that the Office of Civil Rights had "scuttled" more than twelve hundred civil rights investigations started under the Obama administration.[60] The office also eliminated an appeals process, reserved the right to drop cases that seemed like too much work,[61] and became more lax. Under Obama, it substantiated 41 percent of complaints involving allegations of sexual harassment and violence; under DeVos, it substantiated 31 percent.[62] The office also stopped substantiating as many complaints involving discrimination over disabilities and racial harassment.[63]

Once you start to unravel enforcement of Title IX, it's easier to start rolling back the enforcement of other civil rights laws that are intertwined with Title IX—like Title VI, the clause of the 1964 Civil Rights Act that prohibits racial discrimination in schools. Protections like those enshrined in Titles IX and VI are essential to young people's ability to safely enjoy the benefits of public education. Undermining their enforcement contributes to the long project of dismantling public education overall.

Although the culture wars' debate over Title IX has heavily focused on colleges and universities, enforcement of Title IX is even spottier among K-12 schools, which usually have far fewer resources devote to staffing and running effective Title IX offices. Between 2018 and 2020, at least 330 lawsuits were filed across the United States accusing K-12 schools of failing to protect students from sexual misconduct or mishandling reports of it, an *NBC News* investigation found.[64] In one lawsuit uncovered by the outlet *K-12 Dive* and settled in 2019, a California school district had a school resource officer—a campus police officer who is not typically trained in Title IX procedures—step in to question a minor girl who had reported being drugged and gang-raped. "The first thing he asked me was whether I was a virgin or not," she said.[65] Later, he asked: "Do you *really* feel like you were raped?"[66]

One expert estimated to *K-12 Dive* that at least 60 percent of school districts are semi- or noncompliant with Title IX.[67]

"People do a lot of stuff to avoid having to face the reality of it," Nikki, the young woman who said she was raped in Charlotte, said of sexual violence. "They question stories so that they can make the number smaller in their head. They want to pretend it doesn't happen to people younger than a certain age and if it does, it's this rare thing—but it's not. They think that we need to protect our children from this and that the way to protect them is to not tell them about it, because it's upsetting for them.

But they're actually putting those children in danger by not teaching them the resources."

As states weaken young people's ability to learn about sex and gender in schools, they are simultaneously making it harder to learn what's going on in these young people's sex lives in the first place—and thus obscuring the impact of sexually conservative policies. Some of the states that have banned books or passed laws limiting schools' ability to discuss LGBTQ+ issues have also left or announced their plan to leave the CDC's Youth Risk Behavior Survey, the source for those harrowing statistics about forced sex in high schools;[68] after Donald Trump returned to the White House in 2025, his CDC temporarily wiped the decades-old survey from its website. The attacks on this survey will have an outsize impact on LGBTQ+ students, since one in five told the CDC that they had been forced into sex.[69]

When Florida dropped out of the Youth Risk Behavior Survey in 2022, shortly after the state passed its Don't Say Gay bill, officials didn't give much explanation for their actions other than to say that the state would develop its own version of the survey.[70] But a year later, when Florida's education commissioner learned that a school district was still participating in the CDC survey, he sent a letter expressing his "grave concerns."[71]

"The CDC survey asks leading questions phrased in such a way that may actually introduce risky behaviors to students, prompting them to engage in potentially detrimental activities," the commissioner wrote. "Such an inflammatory and sexualized survey is not in the best interest of Florida students."[72]

It was a regurgitation of the same logic that has so long bolstered abstinence-only sex ed and torpedoed efforts to implement comprehensive sex ed: that, by neutrally acknowledging the mere existence of sex, institutions will tempt students into trying it out. This has always been a ridiculous idea, but it's extra silly in the age of the internet. Just look at the last several chapters of this book.

Full disclosure: I have filed a Title IX complaint. Not about being sexually assaulted by my classmate—I always believed I had no hope of proving *that*, because it would be my word against his. Instead, toward the end of my senior year of college, I alleged to my school's Title IX office that a professor had sexually harassed me by commenting in front of my entire class that I could win a mentor in journalism by wearing "a tight black skirt," then laughed it off as his "little joke." My complaint was deemed unsubstantiated by the Title IX office, a fact I learned from a single terse email sent after months of silence.

To be honest, I had kept my expectations low. The comment had occurred in my sophomore year of college, but I didn't file a complaint until much later because I didn't realize Title IX existed. (I may have been told about it during my college orientation, as many students are. But in the rush of those heady, alcohol-fueled first days away from home, it's easy to forget some arcane-sounding rules from the 1970s.) By the time I went to the Title IX office, many of the people who were in the classroom when the comment occurred had since graduated. I didn't know how to contact them; I don't know if the office tried. Still, I went forward with the complaint. Professors shouldn't be allowed to demean students with a "little joke."

By the time the email hit my inbox a few months later, I had left my college campus to pursue an internship at a women's fashion magazine in New York City. My new office had floor-to-ceiling windows that over-looked Central Park, rows of gleaming white desks stacked with books and past issues, and coworkers so charismatic they could flirt with a toaster. Even fetching coffee felt glamorous; I saw everything as evidence that I really could hard-work my dreams into reality. But as I sat in my desk chair and stared at that email, something inside me iced over. It has never thawed.

Although I had intellectually accepted that my complaint would be hard to substantiate, I had still hoped. That email reminded me that I would never be able to hard-work everything into working out, that I would never be enough to get what I was owed—not for the harassment and not for the assault. Like so many other survivors, I would just have to learn to operate at a loss for the rest of my life.

JOE BIDEN AND TITLE IX

During his 2020 presidential campaign, Joe Biden called the DeVos Title IX rules "a green light to ignore sexual violence and strip survivors of their rights." But the wheels of his administration turned slowly. It did not officially roll back the DeVos rules until summer 2024, months before the presidential election.[73]

These regulations were immediately drawn into the culture wars over LGBTQ+ students' rights. The Biden administration believed that Title IX prohibits discrimination on the basis of sexual orientation and gender identity; Christian and conservative advocacy groups, unsurprisingly, rejected that view. More than twenty Republican-led states promptly sued to block the Biden Title IX rules. ADF sued, as did Moms for Liberty.

Federal judges soon halted the Biden Title IX rules from taking effect in several states,[74] creating a system where people in one state had more federal rights than those in another and casting the entire future of Title IX into doubt. Donald Trump deepened that doubt in 2025, when—after another federal judge tossed the Biden Title IX rules completely—his administration announced it would revert to enforcing the DeVos rules. What is certain, however, is that sexual conservatives are willing to hold Title IX hostage as they pursue their agenda. While they talk about their (unfounded) fear that transgender students will sexually assault cisgender ones in bathrooms, they curtail students' ability to seek justice for real assaults.

It is worth noting that the Biden administration deployed the Clery Act, the other major federal law regulating campus sexual assault, to record effect. In March 2024, the Department of Education fined Liberty University $14 million for a slew of yearslong Clery Act violations. A Christian school cofounded by the famed evangelical pastor Jerry Falwell Sr., who created the Moral Majority in 1979 and helped articulate the sexual conservatism movement, Liberty University had an extensive honor code that took its cues from sexual conservatism. It banned students from "sexual relations outside a biblically ordained marriage, romantic displays of affection with a member of the same sex (e.g., hand-holding, kissing, dating, etc.), and actions confirming denial of biological birth sex (e.g., asking to be referred to by pronouns inconsistent with one's birth sex, using restrooms and changing facilities reserved for persons other than one's birth sex, etc.)." In practice, the Department of Education found, this honor code contributed to a "culture of silence" around sexual misconduct, as Liberty University penalized sexual assault victims for breaking the honor code while allowing assailants to evade punishment.[75] If this isn't evidence that stigmatizing premarital and LGBTQ+ sex will not only fail to prevent sexual misconduct but may even worsen it, I don't know what is.

Still, Biden wasn't exactly a champion for LGBTQ+ students, as his administration hammered a massive crack into their Title IX rights that is sure to widen under conservative administrations. After LGBTQ+ students filed Title IX discrimination complaints against Baylor University,[76] Biden's Department of Education agreed that the Christian university, which believes that "sexual relations of any kind outside of marriage between a man and a woman are not in keeping with the teaching of Scripture," was exempt from Title IX "to the extent that they are inconsistent with the university's religious tenets."[77] Baylor, by the way, has settled claims by more than a dozen women who said they were sexually assaulted at the school.[78] Some claimed the school's sexually conservative honor code, like that at Liberty University, was used to pressure them to keep silent.[79]

"The Biden administration is taking this public victory lap, saying that they have done more than any other administration to protect LGBT students," Bedera said. "But if you look at the fine print, that's not true. In fact, they're denying LGBT students Title IX rights that were commonplace during the Obama administration."

FIGHTING BACK

In 2018, Nikki came across a news story about a twenty-year-old woman, known in court papers as Jane Doe, who had filed a lawsuit accusing Charlotte-Mecklenburg Schools of violating her Title IX rights. Doe said that, in 2015, she had been raped in the woods around Myers Park High School and that officials at the school had brushed off her report. Doe's story was so similar to Nikki's that Nikki decided to reach out to Doe's lawyer and offer to help. *Wow, I'm not alone,* she realized. *I need to do something about this so it doesn't happen again.*

The following year, Nikki filed her own lawsuit.

"There's going to be dozens of women in the future who go to the police and go to the school and go to [Charlotte-Mecklenburg Schools] and expect to be helped," she said in a deposition. "If I could do something to make sure that they actually are helped instead of being silenced like I was, then I think that's the most meaningful thing I can do."

The lawsuit was grueling. In her deposition, Nikki was asked deeply personal questions, like whether she'd ever had an abortion and when she first had sex with her then-fiancé. Her mental health frayed, particularly as she came to realize her lawsuit wasn't going to result in the substantive changes she craved. "It was made pretty clear to me throughout the process that I wasn't going to get policy change through the legal system and that only the Board of Education had the power to make that legal change," she told me.[80]

In 2021, Nikki settled her lawsuit for $50,000. She did it over Zoom, because she had checked into a mental health facility.[81]

After news of Nikki's and Jane Doe's lawsuits went public, Serena Evans came forward and alleged that another student had raped her in a Myers Park High School bathroom in 2016, when Evans was just fifteen. Like Nikki and Doe, when Serena tried to report what had happened, an official warned Serena that if her story didn't check out, "you'll be suspended and this will damage your chances of getting into college," according to a Title IX lawsuit Serena filed. (In court papers, Charlotte-Mecklenburg Schools denied wrongdoing and said that the student Serena accused of raping her had denied it.)

Story after story started coming out about Charlotte-Mecklenburg Schools. In late 2021, a sixteen-year-old student charged with a felony sex crime was allowed to play a high school football game—while wearing an ankle monitor.[82] After students held a walkout in protest, two female members of the school's volleyball squad were benched for taking part.[83] "Honestly, I'm just disgusted that they let a football player who has sexual assault allegations against him play with an ankle monitor," one player told the *Charlotte Observer*. "But because I speak out for feeling unsafe, I get punished and not allowed to play in a game."[84]

A few weeks after that, a student at yet another high school told a local news outlet that when she told school officials that a male classmate had sexually assaulted her, the officials accused her of making a false report, suspended her, and mandated she attend a class called "Sexual Harassment Is Preventable."[85] (After a media outcry, the student didn't have to endure the suspension or the class.[86]) Charlotte police, meanwhile, reportedly pressed charges against the classmate.[87]

These protests and reports were part of a national, sexually progressive movement over frustration with schools' handling of Title IX. In the years after the coronavirus pandemic broke out, hundreds of K-12 students in states like California, Texas, and Massachusetts protested or walked out of their schools over what they saw as failures to enforce Title IX and stop sexual assault.[88] This movement was in part made possible by young people's post-#MeToo awareness of sexual misconduct, but the pandemic was also instrumental. After it drove much of student life online and Black Lives Matter protests over George Floyd's 2020 murder erupted, students started using anonymous social media accounts to call out racism in their schools and communities—and similar accounts devoted to exposing sexual misconduct sprang up, too.[89] Like #MeToo, these accounts spotlighted the sheer scale of sexual violence. Unlike #MeToo, though, the accounts were localized. They made the fight feel personal.

"The mentality was always like, 'Oh, that happens to other people, but it doesn't happen to us,'" said Emily, a seventeen-year-old who stumbled onto an Instagram account that collected sexual misconduct allegations from her California community in her freshman year of high school, around the time the pandemic broke out. "I didn't really realize how much of a problem it was in my district." Emily had heard of Title IX before, vaguely, but the account helped convince her to join her school's new Title IX club. Social media, Emily said, "helped not only with the knowledge of Title IX and the knowledge of all these other social movements, but it's also helped us create changes. Because without working together, I don't think the new Title IX rules could have been passed."

By the night of the Charlotte-Mecklenburg Board of Education meeting, in 2022, Nikki and Serena had joined forces to advocate against sexual assault and for change within their old school district. They led protests and talked to numerous local and national reporters, including me, about their pain and their hopes. And like so many other members of their generation, they used the internet to solicit anonymized accounts of sexual misconduct at Charlotte-Mecklenburg Schools, which they planned to share at the board of education meeting.

THE SECOND COMING | 211

Before they could speak, though, they had to watch as the meeting temporarily transformed into a textbook example of frenzied post-2020 school board fights. Parents took to the podium to convince the board to ban books that had already been targeted in other school districts, including by Moms for Liberty,[90] for mentioning "fingering," sexual assault, curse words, and suicide. As the United States battles over the future of sex, this exact juxtaposition is now playing out in communities across the country. While sexually progressive activists work to better and protect these communities—including their mental health—a small sexually conservative minority stands just feet away, raving about made-up sex monsters and refusing to confront the complexity of reality.

Finally, Nikki and Serena were able to take the podium. "It really amazes me that some of the administrators who are shoving our rapes and assaults under the rug have children of their own, and more specifically, daughters," Serena told the board of education. In her own speech, Nikki added, "When you delay accountability or meaningful change, it sends a clear message: You don't care."[91]

Nikki and Serena's allies also shared the anonymized accounts. One recited testimony from a Charlotte-Mecklenburg Schools student who said she was repeatedly groped by an older classmate. ("I told my teacher, who asked me if I was sure that it happened and if I was willing to take the risk of making an accusation, which made me doubt myself completely.") Another read the words of a graduate who said they had reported a fellow student to the school for rape. ("They did nothing for me, regardless of me saying I felt unsafe on campus.") After a few people spoke, a board staffer quietly informed Elyse Dashew, the dark-haired and bespectacled chair of the board of education, that there was a policy against letting statements be read by somebody who was not signed up to speak.

A bearded young man, another ally of Nikki and Serena's, took the podium. "This is another story from the CMS—" he started to say.

"Oh, yeah, I'm sorry. We really do—people sign up to speak for themselves," Dashew interrupted. "So anybody else who has their own testimonial or feedback to share—"

In the back of the room, Serena yanked off her face mask. "How do you expect a rape survivor to stand in front of the people that threatened them with suspension?" she cried out. "Are you serious?"

212 | CARTER SHERMAN

People started to clap and shout. "Everybody's story matters!" someone yelled. "Every single one of them!"

"Absolutely. Absolutely," Dashew said. "Is anyone else here to speak for themselves?"

"May I continue?" the young man at the podium asked.

"No, no. We do have rules that we kind of have to follow here," Dashew told him. As people started yelling again—"He did sign up!" "He did it!"—Dashew gave up.

"Okay. Alright," she said. She sounded like she could barely keep the annoyance out of her voice. "We'll break all the rules tonight."[92]

Nikki burst into tears. She collapsed into Serena's outstretched arms, and they sobbed together as the board meeting went on.[93] If Charlotte-Mecklenburg Schools officials refused to even *listen* to survivors' stories, if they were seemingly willing to smack survivors down in public, how could Nikki and Serena ever hope that they would change for the better?

"I was betrayed by the school system. I had an extremely traumatizing experience with the legal system. I was completely dismissed and ignored by the police system," Nikki told me years later. "I did every single path of what a survivor is supposed to do to get justice and on every single path I was met with, at best, indifference. At worst, active antagonism."

Throughout the sexual assault scandal engulfing Charlotte-Mecklenburg Schools, the district and officials have denied wrongdoing and said they followed district policy and the law.[94] In 2023, a jury decided Charlotte-Mecklenburg Schools did not violate Jane Doe's Title IX rights because its officials did not approach her case with "deliberate indifference."[95] A federal circuit court later affirmed the jury's finding. Serena ended up dropping her lawsuit,[96] while Nikki's settlement prevents her from suing again.

Not that she'd want to.

Although the Charlotte-Mecklenburg Board of Education later fired the district's superintendent—reportedly for a number of reasons[97]—and the district beefed up its Title IX team,[98] that board meeting convinced Nikki that she could not trust Charlotte-Mecklenburg Schools to fix itself. Her mental health struggles metastasized. In 2023, Nikki checked into a mental health facility again. By 2024, she had moved out of Charlotte and stepped back from activism.

THE SECOND COMING | 213

"Sometimes I feel like it's selfish for me to stop or take care of myself because I had a platform. Some people never get a platform like I did. It feels like—how am I choosing my own life over potentially hundreds or thousands of other people's lives?" said Nikki, who is now twenty-five. But, she continued, "if it's something that is as damaging to my mental health and my life as it was becoming, then maybe I need to find a different way to contribute to making society more fair and just."

Title IX is not the only avenue available to sexual assault survivors who want justice. Restorative justice, a philosophy and process where victims, perpetrators, and the community come together to talk through conflicts and make reparations, is becoming more popular on some campuses. Theoretically, the police are an option, too. However, the criminal justice system very rarely results in incarceration in sexual assault cases—and the entire process can be yearslong, prejudiced, and degrading. As their cases drag on, victims may be forced to stay in dorms or classes alongside the people who sexually assaulted them. Furthermore, people of color and other groups who so often face police brutality may be less than interested in involving the cops.

Regardless of whether a survivor wants to use Title IX, the decade-plus-long battle over the law has sent a message to survivors and their advocates: Some of the nation's most important politicians and institutions don't care enough about traumatized students who are just trying to get an education. Rather, these students have been sacrificed to political games.

Throughout this book, I've shared stories of people who are taking their sex educations and lives into their own hands as well as standing up to what they see as injustices in their community. It's admirable, but how much of themselves are they sacrificing in the process? Are we grinding a generation down? At the very least, we have forced them to take on immense risks, if not actual harms. This is true today more than ever—especially now that *Roe v. Wade* is gone.

9.

ROE V. YOUR SEX LIFE
Sex and Abortion After *Roe v. Wade*

On June 24, 2022, the day the Supreme Court overturned *Roe v. Wade* and erased the constitutional right to choose abortion, Sophie was driving through Utah, on her way to her parents' new place in Arizona. On June 25, Sophie was sitting in her dad's car when she suddenly threw up.

Two pink lines confirmed what she immediately suspected: She was pregnant. And she did not want to be.

On June 26, Sophie sent me a direct message over social media.

"All of the abortion clinics near me have shut down their services," she wrote. "If I order pills online and take them at my parents' house, I am sure to be kicked out, should they find out. . . . Even scrolling through Twitter and seeing so many people in the same position that I am in adds to the panic that we [are] all in the worst possible position in our lives right now and we are being punished in the most public and humiliating way for simply having sex."

She was twenty-three years old.

In the immediate aftermath of *Roe*'s demise, abortion providers in Arizona were in disarray. No one knew for sure whether an 1864 total abortion ban—passed before Arizona was even a state—was now in effect, although Republican state legislators rushed to declare that it was. Out of an abundance of caution, abortion providers stopped offering the procedure.

There is no question that the case that toppled *Roe*, *Dobbs v. Jackson Women's Health Organization*, sets the sexual and reproductive lives of young Americans apart from older generations—perhaps more than anything else in this book. A right that was guaranteed for half a century evaporated one June morning, enabling more than a dozen states to ban almost all abortions over the next few years. Tens of millions of women of reproductive age live in those states, but that statistic gives us only a baseline guess at the number of individuals who have now lost the right to end a pregnancy, because people who are not women can also get pregnant. By the time the dust from *Roe*'s collapse settles, a process that may take many more years, more than half of states are expected to enact abortion bans. A federal ban may even be in effect by the time you pick up this book.

These bans disproportionately impact young people: More than 65 percent of abortion patients are under thirty.[1]

Sophie frantically rushed to find some way, any way, to end her pregnancy, without her ultraconservative parents finding out. She roped in her ex-boyfriend, who lived states away. She called local abortion clinics, an abortion fund—which helps pay for abortions—and even, by accident, a crisis pregnancy center. Finally, one of the people she called told her, "I'm not supposed to say this, but your best option is ordering online."[2]

When *Roe* fell, protesters took to the streets holding up signs emblazoned with images of coat hangers and chanting, "We won't go back!" But we were never going to go back to the days of abortions in darkened back alleys, because we have the internet.

In the years since the FDA first approved the drug mifepristone for use in abortions in 2000, a gray market for abortion pills has blossomed online. Experts widely agree that it is medically safe for people to take doses of mifepristone and a second drug, misoprostol, to induce or "self-manage" their own abortion in the first trimester of pregnancy. (People can also induce an abortion by taking misoprostol on its own, although it's less effective and may lead to more complications.) This does not mean, however, that people who induce their own abortions are totally safe, because self-managed abortion is legally fraught.

American abortion bans typically make it illegal for people to either perform abortions or help others undergo them, rather than penalizing abortion patients themselves. As of this writing, just one state—Nevada—bans people from inducing their own abortions. (This ban also applies only when a pregnancy has progressed beyond twenty-four weeks.)

However, abortion rights advocates have long warned that if a prosecutor wants to punish someone for a self-managed abortion, they'll find a statute pliable enough to do it. Between 2000 and 2020, U.S. law enforcement criminally investigated or arrested at least sixty-one people for allegedly ending their own pregnancies or helping someone else do so.[3] Many did not face abortion-related charges but were instead charged with child abuse, practicing medicine without a license, or even homicide and murder.[4]

These numbers are set to climb, given the United States' ballooning surveillance state as well as the growing influence of far-right anti-abortion activists who want abortion patients to be treated like murderers. Women and LGBTQ+ people of color, like Sophie, are the most likely to be criminalized for abortions in this post-*Roe* country.

But people will never stop having abortions. Providers performed over one million abortions in 2023—more than they had performed in a single year in more a decade.[5] The enormity of this number masked a deep geographical divide in the United States: As the number of abortions performed in states with bans plummeted, the nation's remaining abortion clinics had to absorb the overflow and then some. Many clinics were so overrun with people fleeing abortion bans that local patients could no longer get appointments, forcing even individuals who live in abortion-tolerant states to travel for the procedure or to self-manage their own. Experts estimate that in the six months after *Dobbs*, about twenty-six thousand more Americans used pills to self-induce abortions than would have done so if *Dobbs* had never happened.[6] The average age of someone attempting to self-manage an abortion for the first time is just twenty-one years old.[7]

Unfortunately, many people have used methods that are far less safe than abortion pills. Roughly a fifth of people who've tried to cause their own abortion hit themselves in the stomach. Almost one in five experienced a complication that was so severe, they saw a doctor or nurse.[8]

Rather than eliminating abortions, what *Dobbs* has done is create a generation—and, likely, multiple future generations—who will spend their adolescence and young adulthood evading the law to get abortions, no matter the risks.

Five days and a lifetime after Sophie and her ex-boyfriend ordered

218 | CARTER SHERMAN

the abortion pills, they finally arrived. Because self-managed abortions can take hours, if not days, Sophie and her ex holed up at a Hampton Inn over the Fourth of July weekend.[9]

Sophie's mood ricocheted. The pills—the tan wafer of mifepristone, the white tablets of misoprostol—made her feel nauseous and crazed. She cried while watching a show about the history of candy bars; she cried when she flushed bloody clots down the toilet. But Sophie never doubted her choice to get an abortion. She wanted to go back to college. She was thinking of designing aesthetics for small businesses, or maybe becoming a sex educator.[10]

"If I had chosen not to go through with this and put myself through all of these very dramatic situations, I would never be independent again," she told me. "My life would never be mine, and the thought of that is more terrifying than anything I'm doing right now. Future me will be so proud and thankful that I did this, even though it sucks right now. I can't stop. I can't give up, for her."[11]

But even if sexual conservatives hadn't stopped Sophie from getting an abortion, they may have succeeded in another way: The experience left her afraid to have sex.

"I cannot find myself in another situation with an ex-partner in a hotel room having an abortion," she said.[12]

THE NEW STAKES OF SEX— AND HOW WE SLEEPWALKED INTO THEM

There is no question that *Dobbs* has changed young people's sex lives, because—if you'll allow me to state the obvious—abortion is almost always preceded by sex or sexual assault.* As I wrote in the introduction, nearly 90 percent of Americans who are single and younger than fifty say *Dobbs* has affected their approach to sex and dating, according to Match Group's 2023 "Singles in America" study. Eleven percent of single millennials and 13 percent of single Gen Z-ers say it has led them to have less

---

*If you're scratching your head at "almost always," people also get abortions after getting pregnant through in vitro fertilization or other kinds of reproductive technologies.

sex and to feel more anxious when they do. Sixteen percent of Gen Z are now more nervous to date, period.

"It has become a litmus test for people that it's too much trouble to date," said one respondent in the study, which was co-conducted with the Kinsey Institute. Another added: "I'm bisexual, so it makes me think I should strictly date women."[13]

When I asked interviewees about political or cultural events that shaped their approach to sex, they frequently named #MeToo—but *Dobbs* came up just as often, if not more. "I was very angry. I'm still angry about it," said Jared, a twenty-two-year-old from Indiana, where abortion is banned. When his girlfriend missed her period after *Dobbs*, he wrestled with anxiety until it finally arrived a few days late. "Because of that decision, we have to be more careful than we otherwise would have."

Nineteen-year-old Ava lives in Tennessee, a state that has outlawed abortions. She has the socioeconomic resources and activist know-how to get an abortion if she really wants one, but *Dobbs* makes her worry about having sex. A lot. "It does give sex even more stakes, when it's not guaranteed that you're able to get an abortion or you're able to get any other sort of reproductive health care," she said. "Is this worth the potential consequences?"

Some people, Ava added, don't have the resources to flee Tennessee if they need an abortion. What does that mean for their sex lives? Are we consigning them to worse sex?

It's an open question—one that we are now forcing people to answer through high-stakes trial and error. Before *Roe* fell, we knew shockingly little about how access to abortion impacted individuals' approach to sex. As of June 2021, there were just two academic reviews of the relationship between abortions and sexuality among Americans; both reviews had been published around 2000 and focused exclusively on how individuals approached sex after having an abortion.[14] When researchers tried to unearth more publications that examined both abortion and sexuality in the United States, searching across books and health research and psychiatry journals and law articles, they found just seven publications.[15]

Seven. In the entirety of academia.

The reason for this lack of knowledge is, in retrospect, so obvious it feels boring to even write it: The publications considered abortion a "standalone event" in somebody's life,[16] as though abortion was as sudden and unexpected as immaculate conception (if you will). This attitude, as bewildering as it may sound, mirrored the general public's attitude toward abortion throughout the *Roe* era. Americans spent decades stigmatizing abortion and siloing it off from the rest of medicine, ignoring statistics that showed that one in four women got abortions. Most people didn't think all that much about how access to abortion, or lack thereof, could shape their sex lives.

I know, because I asked them. By June 2021, I—like many people who worked in and around reproductive health, on both sides of the abortion debate—knew that *Roe* was not long for this world. The Supreme Court, dominated 6–3 by conservatives following Justice Ruth Bader Ginsburg's death in September 2020, had publicly agreed in May 2021 to take up *Dobbs*, which dealt with the legality of a fifteen-week abortion ban out of Mississippi. The justices would consider whether states could ban abortion prior to fetal viability, or the point at which a fetus can survive outside the womb, a benchmark that generally occurs around twenty-four weeks into pregnancy. Under the *Roe* line of jurisprudence, states could not enact pre-viability bans. In challenging the viability standard, Mississippi's fifteen-week ban struck at the heart of *Roe*. Alliance Defending Freedom and its sexually conservative allies had engineered the ban exactly for this purpose.

So, that summer, I reported on how the then-impending fall of *Roe* was impacting people's sex lives. The answer? Not much. Even though states had enacted more than six hundred abortion restrictions between 2010 and 2022,[17] the American public did not seem to truly believe the federal right to abortion could disappear. This was especially true of people in the North, who have long written off the South as a backward place where sexism, homophobia, and racism naturally thrive—a place at whose policies and people they sneer, rather than take seriously. One New York sex therapist bluntly summarized her clients' feelings on abortion restrictions. "We're two countries," she told me, "and that's happening more in the other one."[18]

Only a handful of college students living in _that_ other country felt differently. One nineteen-year-old Texan desperately wanted to take her birth control implant out of her arm, because she was afraid it was making her already-awful depression worse, but she was terrified that Texas would soon ban abortion. If Texas outlawed the procedure while she was off hormonal birth control, she was pretty sure she and her boyfriend would just stop having sex.[19]

"If the possibility of pregnancy does happen," she said, "I kind of feel like my life would be over."[20]

In September 2021, weeks after we talked, Texas enacted a novel abortion ban that allowed Texans to sue one another for helping people get abortions past six weeks of pregnancy. This ban effectively outlawed abortions earlier than viability and flew in the face of *Roe*, but was allowed to stand because ordinary people, rather than the state, were deputized to enforce the ban. It was an ingenious sleight of hand, and in May 2022, Oklahoma used a similar mechanism to ban all abortions.[21] A few weeks after that, the Supreme Court issued its ruling in *Dobbs* and, well, you know the rest of that story.

Young people now have no choice but to move forward into a future about which we know very little. And as abortion further recedes into the shadows of American life, due to restrictions and the stigma that those restrictions engender, we will likely know less and less about how access to this procedure impacts young people's sex lives—or, indeed, the rest of their lives. Denying somebody an abortion reshapes their entire trajectory.

In the year after *Dobbs*, births rose in every state that enacted an abortion ban.[22] Almost a quarter of women who would have had abortions instead carried their pregnancies to term; births increased disproportionately among Black and Hispanic women, as well as among women in their twenties.[23] Additionally, in the eighteen months following *Dobbs*, rape led to an estimated fifty-nine thousand pregnancies in states with abortion bans that do not permit the procedure in cases of rape.[24]

If being forced to stay pregnant with your rapist's baby is hell, then it is a ring of hell that can hold unique horrors for LGBTQ+ people. Nineteen-year-old Connor was working at a hardware store in small-town Kansas when he saw the news that *Roe* had fallen. Connor immediately knew that *Dobbs* would do more than change transmasculine people's lives. It would end them.

Although some transmasculine people do choose pregnancy, the

222 | CARTER SHERMAN

changes that it induces in one's body can lead to intense gender dysphoria. As a trans man, Connor had already spoken to other transmasculine folks about how to handle a pregnancy. "Everyone I talked to was like, 'Yeah, I would just punch myself repeatedly until I miscarried or something.' That was their plan," Connor recalled.

Even if a trans man took every precaution against getting pregnant, there's no surefire way to prevent rape. More than half of all trans men and nonbinary people have been sexually assaulted.[25]

"I just knew a lot of people would die and I was mourning that all day," Connor said. "Meanwhile, I was surrounded by all these conservative old white men who I knew were probably happy about that verdict."

"THERE'S NO ANALOGUE FOR DOING THIS TO ADULTS"

When states first erected juvenile courts in the early years of the twentieth century, states frequently used them not to treat youthful offenders with more leniency but to create new categories of crimes that adults would *like* to prosecute, including crimes that targeted sexual activity. "Behaviors that were not illegal but that offended middle-class sensibilities—hanging out on street corners or at dance halls, gambling, engaging in sexual activity, showing 'carelessness about the rights of others,' even exhibiting 'lack of ambition to become something worthy'— became evidence of delinquency," Stephanie Coontz wrote in *The Way We Never Were*, her history of U.S. families and the policies that have shaped them.[26] The charges most often levied against girls were "violations of the gender order, usually designated 'sex offenses,'" Coontz found. Being convicted of "improper" sexual behavior could lengthen a young person's sentence in a reformatory or lead them to be institutionalized again.[27]

When you're using the law to enforce sexual norms, the young make for easier targets. (For a modern example, see: bans that try to restrict minors' access to internet porn.) The anti-abortion movement, which has grasped this perhaps better than any other strain of sexual conservatism, has spent decades transmuting adult unease with minors' sex lives into legal barriers and repercussions. Their arguments have long been draped in the language of "parental rights," but the resurgence of the parental rights movement in schools has lent new dimensions and new power to abortion opponents' rhetoric. Anti-abortion activists have been so successful in this effort that many states that otherwise embrace abortion rights still restrict minors' access to the procedure.

Some of the very first *Roe*-era abortion restrictions—the initial cracks in *Roe*'s firewall—were imposed on minors. In the 1979 case *Bellotti v. Baird*, the Supreme Court was asked to decide: Could states force minors to involve their parents in their decision to get an abortion? The justices decided that, no, they could not—but suggested that if states wanted to have a "parental involvement" law, they had to devise some kind of "alternative procedure" for the minors who would not or could not talk to their parents about abortion. Over time, states formalized this "alternative procedure" into what is known as a "judicial bypass." If a minor wanted an abortion but lived in a state with a parental involvement law, they had to go to court and convince a judge they should be allowed to get one on their own.

Even after *Roe*, parental involvement laws may be the most common abortion restriction in the country. Of the states that permit the procedure, more than a dozen have some form of parental involvement law on the books. Some of the bluest states in the country, like Maryland and Colorado, mandate that minors tell their parents before they get an abortion; Michigan, a state that passed a post-*Roe* ballot measure to enshrine abortion rights into its state constitution, still requires minors to get a parent's consent. If minors flee to those states in pursuit of abortions without their parents' knowledge or consent, they still have to secure judicial bypasses.

Judicial bypasses are relatively uncommon, since about 85 to 90 percent of minors do involve their parents when deciding whether to get an abortion.[28] But beyond that, we know very little about how the processes work or the kinds of minors who get them. This is by design. If their unredacted court records could be surfaced, minors' anonymity could be compromised.

However, lawyers involved in judicial bypasses say their clients are often among the most disenfranchised children. They live in abusive homes, have parents with intense religious or political beliefs, or have been

224 | CARTER SHERMAN

separated from their parents through the criminal justice system, the foster care system, or the immigration system. One Texas lawyer told *Mother Jones* she once represented a minor whose parents ran a meth ring. "She had split because she had the distinct impression they were going to start pimping her out," the lawyer recalled.[29]

Stephanie Loraine Piñeiro obtained a judicial bypass in the late 2000s, when she was seventeen and living in Jacksonville, Florida. A condom had broken during sex with her boyfriend, but Piñeiro was too young to legally buy emergency contraception, which is also known as the morning-after pill or Plan B. (A pharmacist also refused to sell it to her boyfriend, even though he was eighteen.) By the time Piñeiro realized she was pregnant, she already knew two important facts. She knew that, under Florida law, she had to inform her parents she wanted an abortion. And Piñeiro knew she absolutely could not do that.

The year before, Piñeiro had become pregnant through rape. Because she had to bring her father to the clinic to prove that he knew about the abortion, Piñeiro was effectively forced to get her father's consent—not just his knowledge—to undergo the procedure. Piñeiro's parents gave her a warning: "If you get pregnant again, you're going to be forced to remain pregnant, because you're gonna go to hell if you get another abortion."

Piñeiro's dad also threw her birth control out a window, she told me. She tried to get birth control from her pediatrician, as her dad hovered in the waiting room, but the Catholic male doctor refused to prescribe it.

Pregnant again and desperate, Piñeiro resorted to searching Yahoo! Answers for a shred of a solution. The forums buzzed with people sharing supposed tips on how to induce your own abortion, such as by taking thousands of milligrams of vitamin C. "Frankly, I was too scared to do that," Piñeiro said. "There was not any information about self-managed abortion in a way that was safe."

Finally, Piñeiro stumbled onto the number of a hotline she could call for help in getting a judicial bypass.

"I called for a few days until I finally got ahold of somebody who gave me the phone number of a lawyer who would accept my case," Piñeiro recalled. She went to the lawyer's office multiple times, obtained an ultrasound from an abortion clinic, and gathered documents to make her case. At her hearing to petition a judge for an abortion, she showed the judge her résumé, a transcript, an essay, and police records of the domestic abuse Piñeiro had survived at home.

"I remember sitting in the waiting room at the courthouse and seeing a friend of mine from middle school who was also clearly waiting for the same thing as I was," Piñeiro told me. "From the beginning to end, from the time I found out I was pregnant to the time I actually got my abortion, it was about three weeks." Although abortion is extremely safe, it becomes riskier and more expensive as pregnancy progresses.

As drawn-out and paperwork-heavy as Piñeiro's judicial bypass was, she was lucky to win it. When records of judicial bypasses do become public, it's frequently because a minor has lost her petition and had to appeal it to a higher court. These records reveal a system pockmarked with arbitrary decision-making. In recent years, Florida judges appeared to deny one teenager an abortion because she was too "soft spoken and shy" while denying another because she was too "curt."[30] One judge denied a seventeen-year-old's petition for an abortion because her GPA was too low and because she "has never had responsibility to care for younger family members." As an appeals court later pointed out, it would have been impossible for the seventeen-year-old to care for younger family members, because she didn't have any.

Minors can seemingly be judged both too responsible and too irresponsible for an abortion. Florida courts denied the petition of a seventeen-year-old who was already a single mom who worked full-time and had been disowned by her parents, just as they denied the petition of a fourteen-year-old whom one judge described as "a very young, immature woman."[31] The seventeen-year-old ultimately got an abortion, but activists don't know what became of the fourteen-year-old.[32] These denials raise a confounding question: How can someone be too immature for an abortion but mature enough to be forced into parenthood?

"There's no analogue for doing this to adults," said Kyriaki Council, a Colorado lawyer who represents minors in judicial bypass cases pro bono. "We don't make adults—almost in any circumstance—go under oath and disclose details of their sex lives."

In Council's view, the system aims to shame teenagers out of having sex. "We convince ourselves that it'll be a deterrent," Council said. "Because we're very uncomfortable with the idea of teenagers having sex.

But I promise you that no teenager is thinking about going to court. . . . If they have any idea that the law exists, they're not thinking about it when they're super horny in the middle of the night, sneaking out of their home."

"It didn't make me want to stop having sex," Piñeiro said of her judicial bypass, as she gave a knowing laugh. "I'll give you that."

If you oppose abortion and earnestly want to make it less common, you are likely better off helping teenagers avoid getting pregnant at all. You can do that through comprehensive sex ed, birth control, and, sadly, sexual assault prevention. A study of adolescents who sought financial help for abortions found that roughly 61 percent said they needed an abortion because they had zero birth control. About one in six adolescents said they had gotten pregnant through rape.[33]

But rather than provide minors with tools for pregnancy prevention or safe sex, sexual conservatism aims to prevent them from having sex, which—if it isn't already clear—is almost impossible. There is little evidence that teens stop having intercourse due to parental involvement laws. Instead, researchers have estimated that, between 1992 and 2015, parental involvement laws led to about 108,000 additional teen births.[34]

Because of the dearth of publicly available court records, it is unclear how *Dobbs* has impacted judicial bypasses. But Council suspects that Colorado's judicial bypass cases may have doubled or even tripled since *Roe* fell. She's seen cases from states like Nebraska, Kansas, Wyoming—even as far away as Georgia. Some of those states permit abortions, but as I mentioned earlier, their clinics are overwhelmed with patients.

Parental involvement laws can have deadly consequences. On September 16, 1988, seventeen-year-old Becky Bell died from pneumonia and an infection following a suspected illegal abortion.[35] Becky had been too afraid to tell her parents that she was pregnant but, under Indiana law, could not get one on her own.[36] After she died, Becky's parents campaigned against parental involvement laws for years,[37] to little avail. "Every time I think that my little girl died because of a law I probably would have voted for, I know I must never be quiet about this again," Becky's mother told the *New York Times* in 1991.[38]

Because people are so willing to curtail young people's access to abortion, the history of judicial bypasses offers a unique window into how the anti-abortion movement has successfully used young people to tee up future restrictions. In Alabama's very first judicial bypass case, in 1987, the minor's attorney was instructed to represent the fetus, not her seventeen-year-old client.[39] (She refused.) In the 1990s and 2000s, one Alabama judge appointed a local anti-abortion lawyer to represent a fetus in dozens of bypass hearings, leaving minors with no choice but to go to court against their own fetuses. In one case, the lawyer took the liberty of naming a teenager's seven-week-old fetus "Baby Ashley." He thundered at her: "You say that you are aware that God instructed you not to kill your own baby, but you want to do it anyway?"[40]

Other Alabama judges soon took up the practice,[41] and, in 2014, the state amended its judicial bypass law to officially let judges appoint lawyers for fetuses. Challenged in court and put on hold, the law was permanently struck down in 2021—just in time for *Roe* to crumble, enabling Alabama to ban almost all abortions.

Still, the practice and the law lent credence to a doctrine known as "fetal personhood," or the belief that embryos and fetuses should be endowed with legal rights and protections, such as representation in court. This doctrine is already on the books in every state—yes, even blue ones—in some form, but if fully enacted, fetal personhood would rewrite vast swaths of U.S. law. Do fetuses count as an extra person if you drive in a carpool lane? Can you claim fetuses as tax dependents? Or, more concerningly: If a pregnant woman crosses state lines without her partner's consent, is that considered kidnapping? Can he trap her within a state? Abortion is certainly off the table, but so is in vitro fertilization (at least as it is currently practiced). Alabama discovered this in 2024, when a state supreme court decision declaring embryos to be "extrauterine children" led many Alabama IVF providers to halt their work. In one unsettling example of fetal personhood being tested out on minors, Missouri men convicted of child molestation and statutory rape have attempted to argue that because the state has broad fetal personhood language on its books, Missouri courts should base victims' ages on their date of conception, not their date of birth. That math would make these men's underage victims nine months older.

Ultimately, fetal personhood pits the rights of an embryo or fetus against the rights of the person carrying it. And when the pregnant person

228 | CARTER SHERMAN

loses, they can face criminal consequences. In the first year after *Dobbs*, at least two hundred people were prosecuted for conduct connected to their pregnancies—the highest number ever recorded in a single year.[42] One researcher warned me: "I think we're scratching the surface of what is happening."[43]

PARENTAL RIGHTS, REDUX

After years of apathy at the ballot box, *Dobbs* compelled abortion rights supporters to finally vote like they cared about it. Republicans faltered in the 2022 midterms; voters in GOP strongholds like Ohio, Kentucky, and Kansas all voted to preserve abortion rights, while blue-state legislatures enacted laws to shield abortion providers and patients from prosecution. Democrats started to campaign on a cause they had long overlooked, while Republicans downplayed their decades-long marriage to the anti-abortion movement and how it led the United States into the post-*Roe* morass. In spring 2024, Arizona state legislators even struck down the 1864 ban that had blocked Sophie from getting an abortion at a clinic.

Yet, despite all this outrage and change, not a single state fully repealed its parental involvement law in the first few years after *Dobbs*. One activist in blue Minnesota told *Politico* that some Democratic legislators dodged her attempts to even discuss the topic. "We have been somewhat shut down in attempting to have these conversations," she admitted.[44]

Well aware they are losing ground, anti-abortion advocates have attempted to capitalize on the popularity of parental involvement laws and the parental rights movement. In 2022, Kyriaki Council had to repeatedly counter Republicans' false claims that a Colorado bill to enshrine abortion rights into state law would "gut" the state's parental involvement law.[45] Those claims leveled up in 2023, when Ohio voters were considering a ballot measure to add abortion rights into their state constitution. In the run-up to the vote, an anti-abortion group called Protect Women Ohio poured $5 million into an ad campaign[46] that claimed the ballot measure would not only nullify Ohio's parental involvement law but also allow minors to get gender-affirming health care without their parents' knowledge. "Your daughter's young. Vulnerable. Online," a female narrator intoned in one ad, as sepia-toned images of anguished women and children played. "You fear the worst. Pushed to change her sex or to get an abortion. You have some right to help her through this. But activists want to take all that away."

Legal experts rejected the idea that the ballot measure had anything to do with Ohio's parental involvement law or state regulations around gender-affirming care.[47] But in suggesting that the internet is undermining parents' control over their kids and that LGBTQ+ people are somehow to blame, Protect Women Ohio's ad tapped into the fears that had already been stoked, to great success, by the modern parental rights movement and its work in schools. It also recalled earlier iterations of the parental rights movement, as the ad's use of the word "pushed" evoked Anita Bryant's 1970s Save Our Children campaign and her infamous announcement that "homosexuals cannot reproduce, so they must recruit." With most Americans now in support of same-sex marriage,[48] Protect Women Ohio updated Bryant's pitch to align with the fight against gender-affirming care—a far trendier cause. Between 2021 and 2024, half of all states passed laws limiting youths' access to such care.[49] Ohio was one of them.

The battle against abortion rights is linked to the battle against gender-affirming care, as I'll discuss later. But in blending the school-based parental rights movement with LGBTQ+ issues and abortion, the ad created a miasmic suggestion that all this *sex stuff* was victimizing women and girls. (All the women and girls in the ad, by the way, appeared to be white.) If you're wondering how Protect Women Ohio got the millions to fund its ad campaign, the organization's pockets were lined by groups linked to a man named Leonard Leo, a top member of the Federalist Society who helped Donald Trump pick his Supreme Court nominees.[50] Because sexual conservatism does indeed see all this sex stuff as a single beast to defeat, its advocates' strategy is structured accordingly.

Despite Protect Women Ohio's best efforts, Ohio voted decisively in favor of the ballot measure to enshrine abortion rights into its state constitution. That vote prevented a six-week abortion ban from taking effect in Ohio. Had Protect Women Ohio succeeded, they would have successfully used fears, rhetoric, and tactics popularized by the parental rights movement to curb everybody's access to abortion—not just minors'.

Anti-abortion activists did not give up. In 2024, when ten states voted on abortion-related ballot measures, activists claimed that many of those measures would secretly green-light gender-affirming care for minors. They've also used a parental rights–based approach to test out undercutting interstate travel and free speech.

Days after *Dobbs*, national anti-abortion groups were already strategizing about how to restrict people's ability to cross state lines for abortions[51]—never mind that it's a right protected in the U.S. Constitution. (Abortion was, too, at one point.) To go straight for adults' right to travel, though, would be political suicide. Instead, when state legislators in ruby-red Idaho—home to one of the strictest abortion bans in the country—became the first in the country to pass a law criminalizing abortion-related travel, they focused on minors.

In April 2023, Idaho invented the crime of "abortion trafficking," which it defined as "recruiting, harboring, or transporting" a minor for an abortion without parental consent. Under the ban, people who help minors leave Idaho for legal abortions—or help them obtain abortion pills—could spend up to five years behind bars. Free speech advocates also worried that, because the word "recruiting" can have a wide range of meanings, even giving minors information about abortion could be considered criminal.

In a state legislative committee hearing, the law's Republican sponsors repeatedly insisted the abortion trafficking ban was about "parental rights." An anti-abortion lobbyist also assured legislators that it would help protect kids from trafficking and sex abuse, because predators would be banned from taking pregnant victims across state lines. (Like most states with abortion bans, Idaho does not allow abortions in cases of rape or incest.) The branding of "trafficking" harkened back to the parental rights movement's pandemic-era and post-pandemic attacks on sex ed, which have been electrified by conspiracy theories around child sex abuse and trafficking, as well as by the sex-trafficking fears that led to the online censorship of SESTA-FOSTA. Clearly, this branding works for sexual conservatives. It makes sense for anti-abortion activists to co-opt it.

A federal judge, however, was less convinced. In November 2023, U.S. Magistrate Judge Debora Grasham froze Idaho's travel ban. "The state can, and Idaho does, criminalize certain conduct occurring in its own borders such as abortion, kidnapping, and human trafficking,"

Grasham wrote in her ruling. "What the state cannot do is craft a statute muzzling the speech and expressive activities of a particular viewpoint with which the state disagrees under the guise of parental rights."

It was a victory for abortion rights supporters. A year later, however, a federal circuit court largely revived the law, as judges allowed Idaho's ban on "transporting" and "harboring" minors for out-of-state abortions to take effect. (The judges kept the "recruiting" provision on ice, deeming it a potential threat to Idahoans' First Amendment rights.) By that time, lawmakers in four other states had introduced bills to ban abortion trafficking. One, in Tennessee, had become law.

Conspicuously, both the Idaho and Tennessee laws resembled a "model" abortion trafficking ban written by National Right to Life, a major anti-abortion group. Anti-abortion activists routinely supply state legislators with pre-written bills; between 2010 and 2018, legislators across forty-one states introduced more than four hundred anti-abortion bills that had been based off model legislation and written by special interest groups.[52] Sixty-nine became law.[53]

If one state successfully passes an abortion restriction, others tend to follow with nearly identical laws. And if a court blocks one state's restriction, other states will tweak their own versions until they craft one that courts will accept. In all likelihood, bans on abortion trafficking are just getting started.

HOLY WAR

"Abortion hurts women!" twenty-two-year-old John yelled, shaking his gloved first.

"Women deserve better!" the throng of young people yelled back.

"One more time," John hollered. "Abortion hurts women!"

"Women deserve better!"

"Woo!"

"Woo!" everybody else repeated.

The snow had stopped falling in Washington, D.C., but the thousands of young people who had gathered in the nation's capital were still bitterly cold as they trudged off the National Mall and toward the block where the U.S. Capitol and the Supreme Court face one another. They carried signs that declared "WE ARE THE PRO-LIFE GENERATION," featured ultrasounds of fetuses above labels like "FUTURE DOCTOR" and "FUTURE WIFE," and read "ABORTION IS FAILED MANHOOD." (The messaging around masculinity really is one hell of a drug.) The temperature didn't matter. They had a message to send.

"I feel proud to be serving a movement and a position that I know is fighting for, frankly, the most important issue in American politics today," John told me. "You can't call yourself a man if you won't stand up [against] injustice."

One young woman went even further. "Abortion is the greatest injustice to ever happen to women in all of human history," she insisted.[54]

Welcome to the March for Life.

Well, welcome to the world of young anti-abortion activists. If you're not from that world, you can spend your entire life in the United States and never set foot inside it. But I've made the pilgrimage so many times I've lost track.

The March for Life is the anti-abortion movement's annual show of force. Every year, thousands of people travel to the National Mall, where they become a sea of sign-waving, cheering, praying anti-abortion activists. Their numbers and youth are a sign to the nation that the anti-abortion movement is already raising up its next generation of warriors.

Many have been ferried there by their Christian schools. Hannah, a twenty-year-old from Indiana, told me at the 2024 march that she had ridden a bus overnight to get to Washington, D.C., arrived the day before the march, and planned to get right back on the bus for another overnight drive home. She is so strongly opposed to abortion that she wants to ban it even in cases of rape and incest. It's a position most Americans— including most Republicans—disagree with,[55] but a pretty standard one within the anti-abortion movement.

"I believe that all people are created equally," Hannah said. "The situation surrounding someone's conception does not define their human dignity or their right to life."

The March for Life began in 1974, a year after the Supreme Court decided *Roe*. It was also around the same time that Christians were beginning to organize themselves against porn, sex ed, and other causes that offended their beliefs about the towering importance and supposed immutability of the (white) nuclear family. As I mentioned in chapter one, the famed evangelical pastor—and Liberty University founder—Jerry Falwell Sr. attempted to harness this activist energy by creating the Moral Majority, a turning point in the development of the religious right and the sexual conservatism movement.

In recent years, the March for Life has been followed, a day later, by the National Pro-Life Summit, the event where I first heard the Heritage Foundation's Roger Severino urge young people to "do your part" by getting married and having kids. ("Lots of them.") The National Pro-Life Summit is geared toward young people and organized by the influential Students for Life of America, which is one of the biggest anti-abortion organizations in the world and has more than fourteen hundred student groups on middle, high school, and university campuses. In 2023, the year I heard Severino speak, I stopped by another talk being held at the summit. It was called "Dating with Dignity."

Every talk I attended that day was packed, but this was on another level. With every seat occupied, people took to sitting on the floors; when the floor space ran out, they huddled against the walls. Early on in the talk, one of the two speakers cried, "Give it up for chastity!" The crowd erupted into applause and cheers so loud, it was as if Harry Styles had walked in and agreed to wear a promise ring.

On the off chance you haven't already guessed, the way to date with dignity is to do it without, well, doing *it*. "Chastity is not the same thing as abstinence. Abstinence just means no sex. It focuses on what we aren't doing," one of the speakers, a man, said. "Chastity, on the other hand, is about what we say yes to. We're saying yes to real love. . . . Saying: 'If you want to have me in my body, in sex, you've got to give me all of yourself in a marriage, because that's how much I am worth, and that's how much you are worth.'"

That worth, he added, is "God-given."

The other "Dating with Dignity" speaker, a woman, repeatedly referenced some amorphous, dominant, and decidedly ungodly "culture." "Saving sex for marriage is so difficult and it's countercultural, just like being pro-life in 2023 is countercultural," she told the (mostly white) crowd. At another point, she repeated a missive that she said a nun had once given her: "You want to do something radical for the Lord? Get married and stay married in this culture and raise a holy family in this culture."

Yet again, the crowd burst into raucous applause, complete with a wolf whistle.

Over and over again at the National Pro-Life Summit, young people heard that their religion, their purity, their approach to sex and families and personhood itself were under attack from insidious forces. They were urged to hold the line against those forces not only by adhering to religion and sexual conservatism in their personal lives, but by fighting for these causes in legislatures, courtrooms, and protest lines. Everybody at the conference, from its most senior leaders to its youngest attendees, seemed fixated on the feeling that they were victims, even martyrs—even though the anti-abortion movement had, just months before the summit, defeated *Roe*.

Whether or not the National Pro-Life Summit intended to cultivate this sense of victimhood, it served a tactical purpose. A bunker mentality had kept the troops energized and united during *Roe*'s lifetime. Why should they dispense with it post-*Roe*, when there are so many other battles to fight?

These battles, the "Dating with Dignity" talk made clear, were not limited to abortion, as the talk touched on many of the issues that most concern modern-day sexual conservatives. In addition to abortion and abstinence—sorry, but "chastity" is rebranded abstinence, just like "sexual risk avoidance"—the speakers brought up the evils of porn, with a pitch for the anti-porn app Covenant Eyes. They also called themselves "fans" of Jordan Peterson, the Canadian psychologist turned masculinity guru who once said he believes in enforced monogamy—a redistribution of sex whereby women are bound to men to ensure that men never fail to procreate.[56] (Failing to procreate is, according to Peterson, failing at life.) It all sounds eerily like something an incel would say; although Peterson has tried to distance himself from it, he has found an audience in the manosphere and right-wing communities that traffic in anxiety around sex and masculinity. The alliance between sexual conservativism and the manosphere remains strong.

Likely raised on abstinence-only sex ed, the "Dating with Dignity"

THE SECOND COMING | 235

talk attendees seemed to have a limited ability to even ask questions about sex. But if they ever do have questions, answers can always be found within the closed ecosystem of sexual conservatism, an ideological terrarium of Bible verses and "counterculture" warriors and political conventions. As a totalizing worldview, sexual conservatism teaches that there is a single, right way to do sex and relationships—just as there is a single, right way to do life. If you commit to sexual conservatism, people of all ages are promised, you never need feel uncertainty or purposeless pain around sex.

Growing up homeschooled in North Carolina, twenty-year-old Katie Rose Geer learned from a curriculum that followed what is known as the "success sequence." Reportedly coined in 2006 and embraced by right-wing think tanks in the years since,[57] the sequence offers an appealingly straightforward recipe for financial security: Graduate high school, get a full-time job, and get married before you have babies. Critics say the sequence ignores structural inequalities, but conservatives see it as proof that personal behavior can help people stay out of poverty and as a rationale for government policies that incentivize marriage.[58] It's sexual conservatism as told by the prosperity gospel.

"That's determined, in a sense, how I view sexuality," Katie Rose told me of the success sequence. "Because I don't want to have children before I'm married—I want be married before I have kids—then that is going to determine—I'm not going to have sex before I get married."

But as a young person growing up in the age of the internet, Katie Rose was guaranteed to encounter porn sooner or later. She ended up finding it at twelve. Katie Rose said she started watching porn four or five times a week; she felt, like so many others I've talked to, "addicted" to it. "I think the biggest thing that it impacted was my sense of self," she said. "I began to identify with someone who was dirty, someone who was not worthy of respect. Someone who was just bad overall. . . . For a year, I tried to stop. I tried to quit myself and I couldn't. Every day it was, 'I'm not going to do this again.' And every day, I fell."

At fourteen, Katie Rose came clean to her mom. Together, they set up internet blockers, including Covenant Eyes.

Porn has tormented the generations who have grown up on the internet, leaving people who might otherwise be sympathetic to sexual progressivism conflicted. Sexual conservatism acknowledges this pain and, as it does for so many other issues, responds with a saint-simple solution: Just say no. Katie Rose has since developed her own peer-to-peer sex ed program, taught in three states, which emphasizes the success sequence and sexual risk avoidance (as Katie Rose calls abstinence). The curriculum, as Katie Rose tells it, also addresses many of the issues that have plagued other young people in this book, such as social media–induced comparisons and mental health.

In high school, during the pandemic, Katie Rose found herself scrolling through social media for hours. "My mental health was severely affected by the amount of time spent online," said Katie Rose, who ended up attending Liberty University. "Everyone else has friend groups, and you're here in your room by yourself alone, and everyone else is out partying." That loneliness, for her, "morphed into feeling hopeless and down and sad." Her curriculum, accordingly, urges students not to base their worth on looking like celebrities or their follower count. It's good advice.

She may not use this language, but Katie Rose is a member of the next generation of sexual conservatism. She's now on the front line of the movement: In addition to developing her sex ed program, Katie Rose has become an anti-abortion activist. Through Katie Rose and others like her, the face and cause of sexual conservatism are evolving to incorporate the new and valid challenges facing young people, and to respond to their modern questions with the enduring answer of sexual conservatism.

THE POWER AND PERILS OF ELECTIONS

In 2019, as Aaliyah was preparing to travel to Florida to tour colleges, she suddenly had a realization. "I think I missed my period," the nineteen-year-old Louisiana native told her then-husband.

"Do you want to take a pregnancy test?" he asked.

She thought about it. "Let's wait till we get to Florida," she decided.

Sure enough, when they got to Florida and Aaliyah took the test, it was positive. Two thoughts seized her. First: Black women in the United States are almost three times more likely to die of pregnancy and birth complications than white women.[59] (And white women's maternal mortality rates are already exceedingly high for a rich country like the United States.) Second: Having a baby could tank her chances of securing student housing. Losing housing would jeopardize her educational career—and Aaliyah was determined to be the first in her family to obtain a bachelor's degree.

"People say, 'Oh, well, your family could have helped you and you have a supportive partner who will take care of you and a kid.' But let's be honest, everything is put on the mom," said Aaliyah, who is Black and the daughter of a woman who had her first child at seventeen. "On top of that, as well, the world is not nice to young Black moms. It's really not."

If Aaliyah had taken that pregnancy test in Louisiana, before she left for her trip, she might have canceled it. Although both Louisiana and Florida allowed abortion at the time, Aaliyah isn't sure whether she would have been able to end her pregnancy in Louisiana, given its rampant hostility to abortion. Looking back, Aaliyah has no idea why she decided to wait. But she's sure of one thing: "God had my back."

Within a week of her pregnancy test, while still in Florida, Aaliyah got her abortion. As she left the clinic, she took the business card of a Planned Parenthood volunteer with her. *As soon as I move out here, to Florida,* Aaliyah thought, *I'm going to help people.*

In the years since moving to Florida in 2020, Aaliyah has become a reproductive justice organizer and abortion storyteller, working to lessen the stigma around abortion by sharing her story of getting one. After Florida state legislators introduced the six-week abortion ban in 2023, Aaliyah spent every spare moment advocating against it. She was committed: "I'm gonna keep speaking. Y'all are gonna hear me."

Florida passed the six-week ban anyway. Aaliyah cried, hurt and defeated and scared. And then she got back to work and started collecting signatures for a ballot initiative to add abortion rights to the state's constitution.

Young people have been at the forefront of the state-by-state fight to protect reproductive rights post-*Roe.* Despite some young men's shift to the right on questions of gender roles and sex, more than 60 percent of Americans between the ages of eighteen and twenty-nine still believe abortion should be legal in all or most cases.[60] Shockingly, 42 percent of Republicans in that age range think that "abortion should always be allowed." (Just 27 percent of Republicans over thirty say the same.[61]) Young women, and especially young women of color, are exceptionally fervent about abortion rights. Even before *Dobbs*, 62 percent of all Gen Z women supported making abortion legal in *all* cases—more than women of any other generation.[62] It's a stunning show of sexual progressivism.

"Generation Z has been socialized politically in an environment in which a renewed women's movement has taken shape in response to Trump's election and the Me Too cause," political scientist Melissa Deckman wrote in her book *The Politics of Gen Z*.[63] "Evidence suggests that Gen Z women, as a generation, may be unique in their overwhelming support for abortion rights."[64]

They've taken that support right to the ballot box. In August 2022, more than 130,000 eighteen-to-twenty-nine-year-old voters—that is, the last of the late millennials and the oldest of Gen Z—showed up to vote on a Kansas ballot measure to protect abortion rights.[65] It was the highest level of youth voter primary turnout in recent Kansas history,[66] and it sent shock waves across the nation. Before that vote, Kansas was best known as the site of some of the most horrific anti-abortion violence in U.S. history, including the 2009 murder of the abortion provider George Tiller in his Wichita church. Afterward, Kansas became the turning point in the popular narrative around abortion politics. Suddenly, abortion could win elections.

It kept on winning elections, thanks in enormous part to young voters. Outrage over *Dobbs* is credited with halting Republicans' much-promised "red wave" in the 2022 midterms. More eighteen-to-twenty-nine-year-olds voted in that election in record numbers, and their top issue was, without question, abortion.[67]

On Election Day 2023, the day that Ohioans voted on the ballot measure to enshrine abortion rights into the state constitution, I tagged along as twenty-three-year-old Chelsea canvassed a Columbus neighborhood in support of the measure. The November day was unseasonably warm, but amber leaves crunched satisfyingly beneath our feet as Chelsea knocked on front door after front door. If no one answered, she tucked a brochure into their door; if someone was home, she gently urged them to vote for abortion rights. "Hi there!" she trilled. "We're talking to voters today about Issue 1. The election is today."

Chelsea had been passionate about politics since she was a teenager, so she always paid close attention to abortion rights. She was devastated when Ohio passed a six-week abortion ban in 2019. Although *Roe* blocked it from taking effect, "you just felt like a part of your rights was being taken away," Chelsea said. Still, abortion was not her main issue until *Dobbs*. She saw the ballot measure—Issue 1—as a battle for Ohio's future and its youngest residents.

"This isn't a space friendly to young people," she said. Although Chelsea had not had sex, *Dobbs* left her afraid of even trying it. "If I did become pregnant, it would be a lot harder for me to get an abortion."

The youth vote helped buoy the Ohio ballot measure to victory, with 77 percent of voters between the ages of eighteen and twenty-nine voting for it.[68] "At least I now know I have a little bit more safety if I do want to have sex," Chelsea told me weeks after the vote. "But still, our government's not great. It's just constantly a battle."

Another seven states passed ballot measures to protect abortion rights in the 2024 election, including at least four states that Donald Trump won; in states where data on the youth vote is available, voters between the ages of eighteen and twenty-nine favored these measures by margins as wide as 60 points. But although abortion remained a top issue among young voters in 2024—and was more important to them than to older demographics—it paled in comparison to their economic concerns.[69] In choosing Trump over Kamala Harris, American voters revealed the limits of their support for abortion rights—and, it seems, their inability to grasp the consequences of reelecting the guy who made the overturning of *Roe* possible and who maintains strong ties to sexual conservatism.

The fact is, citizen-led ballot measures can only go so far. Many Republican-controlled states do not permit such measures, and their state legislatures are unlikely to roll back abortion bans anytime soon. Moreover, federal limits on abortion access can override state-level protections.

Even if Kamala Harris had won, having the right to an abortion does not mean you have access to one. After undergoing her judicial bypass at seventeen, Stephanie Loraine Piñeiro was determined to help people who, like her, had grown up in poverty. Today, she runs Florida Access Network, an abortion fund that helps people pay for the procedure and the many costs that can come with it, such as travel, lodging, and childcare. She's up front about the fact that abortion funds, never exactly flush with cash, started running out of money after *Dobbs*.

Because more people have to go out of state, more people need help from abortion funds, and each abortion costs more. Before *Dobbs*, the Chicago Abortion Fund, one of the biggest abortion funds in the Midwest, spent an average of $174 on each abortion. After *Dobbs*, it spent $425. It also covered costs like travel and childcare for more than 3,100 people in the year after *Dobbs*—a sevenfold increase from the fund's pre-*Dobbs* numbers.

"It's never gonna be enough. It doesn't put a dent in what is an abortion access crisis," Piñeiro said. "The reality is that with any abortion restrictions, people who are most marginalized, people who have less resources, are not going to get access to an abortion. The people who can afford to travel are going to travel, and the people who can't are going to be forced to continue pregnancies that may be unwanted or unsafe."

"Ever since I had my abortion, I have helped other people get theirs," said Aaliyah, her voice starting to shake. "It gets harder and harder every time."

As access to abortion dwindles, preventing pregnancy in the first place will only become more important to young people. But the ability to do that, too, is under assault.

10.

THE *DOBBS* DOMINO EFFECT
The Rights Now Under Threat

Dobbs v. Jackson Women's Health Organization, Isobel said, "scared the shit out of me."

Isobel grew up in a rural, deeply Christian town of five thousand people in New Hampshire. It's the kind of place where, as Isobel put it, "you get married in high school or right out of high school, you have kids, you settle down, and you're there."

That wasn't what Isobel wanted for her life, so she left her hometown for college. But in the fall of her sophomore year, she sank into a chasmic depression—one she only started to claw her way out of after being diagnosed with bipolar disorder and starting new medications. "Within two weeks, I felt so much better," said Isobel, who is twenty. But, she added, "these medications aren't something you can really be on when you're pregnant."

Isobel has no plans to get pregnant anytime soon. As she sorted through her diagnosis and what it means for her life, Isobel realized she will need extensive support systems in place if she ever goes off her medications in order to have a baby. "I would have to be with a partner," she said. "Chances are, I wouldn't be able to function properly if I weren't on this medication."

Although Isobel's hometown is conservative, her mom is a liberal who supports abortion rights. (Their family has a list of anti-abortion states pinned to their fridge. It doubles as a list of states they're not allowed to visit.) So, Isobel said, "my mother and I sat down the day after *Roe* was overturned and I made an appointment to get an IUD."

Isobel was one of innumerable Americans who rushed to obtain contraception amid the chaos of *Roe*'s collapse. After a draft Supreme Court opinion overturning *Roe* leaked in May 2022, a company that ships emergency contraception reported a 300 percent increase in demand.[1] When the official *Dobbs* decision came down in June 2022, demand grew by 1,000 percent.[2] In the three weeks after *Dobbs*, Planned Parenthood reported a 21 percent spike in appointments for birth control, including a 41 percent increase for IUDs.[3]

Others sought more permanent solutions. Between June 2022 and September 2023, tubal ligations doubled among eighteen-to-thirty-year-olds, while vasectomies among that age group tripled.[4] The rate of tubal ligations was still on the rise well into 2023.[5]

By stockpiling morning-after pills, sterilizing themselves, or seeking out IUDs—which can last a decade, longer than any conservative presidential administration—young people were not only protecting themselves against an imminent pregnancy. They were also preparing for the possibility that, with the right to abortion gone, the right to contraception would be next.

Both of these rights are (or were) premised on the right to privacy. Although the right to privacy is not explicitly spelled out in the U.S. Constitution, Supreme Court justices have triangulated its existence in the Fourteenth Amendment, which guarantees our rights to due process and equal protection. Over the past sixty years, the right to privacy has become the legal foundation of Americans' intimate rights and, through broadening those rights, has changed our cultural understanding of sex. It lies at the center of Supreme Court cases like *Obergefell v. Hodges*, which legalized same-sex marriage nationwide in 2015; *Lawrence v. Texas*, which struck down sodomy bans in 2003; *Eisenstadt v. Baird*, which in 1972 established that single people have the right to contraception; and *Griswold v. Connecticut*, which established that right for married people in 1965. According to the majority opinion in *Planned Parenthood v. Casey*, which reaffirmed *Roe* in 1992, sex is woven into "the right to define one's own concept of existence, of meaning, of the universe, and of the mystery of human life." Sex was no longer something only married people should do to make babies. It could be a declaration of independence.

THE SECOND COMING | 243

These Supreme Court cases form a kind of Jenga tower of legal reasoning—they could all tumble if one case, like *Roe*, gets pulled out. In his concurring opinion in *Dobbs*, the ultraconservative Justice Clarence Thomas suggested the Supreme Court do exactly that. *Obergefell*, *Lawrence*, and *Griswold*, he announced, are "demonstrably erroneous."

Thomas, who is Black and married to a white woman, conspicuously did not mention the 1967 Supreme Court case *Loving v. Virginia*, which struck down laws against interracial marriage. But his line of reasoning also threatens that case, because *Loving* is another block in the Jenga tower that is the right to privacy.

Loving was one of the first things Sophie, the young woman who self-managed her abortion, thought of when she saw the news of *Roe*'s demise, because her parents are in an interracial marriage. "That seems so far-fetched when you say it out loud, but I don't know . . ." she said, her voice trailing off. She suddenly sounded even younger than her twenty-three years. "They're policing everything, so why would they not police race and love?"

She feared for her bodily autonomy. "Now what else will they take away from us?" she asked. "Now what else will I not have a say in?"

Anti-abortion activists spent five decades honing a playbook that, in the 2010s and 2020s, led to innumerable victories. They relied on model legislation to pass hundreds of abortion restrictions that hacked away at access to the procedure and created opportunities for courts to take up challenges to *Roe*. Alliance Defending Freedom represented the movement's aims in court, while the Federalist Society and Donald Trump helped install judges who would look favorably on anti-abortion legislation, including on the Supreme Court. They bet that liberals would be too arrogant or too distracted to pay attention until it was too late, and they were right. *Roe* crumbled slowly, and then all at once.

It was such an effective playbook that, as soon as *Roe* fell, sexual conservatives started to rerun parts of it—not only on the vestiges of abortion access, but also on the movement's myriad other causes. *Roe*'s demise has made sex riskier and more likely to be procreative, but the movement is nowhere near done.

HOW TO LOSE CONTRACEPTION

As jarring as many found Thomas's words in *Dobbs*, this was far from the first salvo in sexual conservatism's attack on contraception. The barrage had begun years before.

In a 2014 Supreme Court case called *Burwell v. Hobby Lobby*, the Christian owners of the Hobby Lobby craft-store chain argued that the Affordable Care Act, in commanding employers to cover employees' contraception, infringed on their religious beliefs. Specifically, Hobby Lobby's owners did not want to cover IUDs and emergency contraception, because the owners claimed they blocked fertilized eggs from implanting in the uterine wall. In the owners' eyes, this constituted a kind of abortion.

Please bear with me for a quick primer on birth control and pregnancy, because this belief glosses over some scientific nuance. Emergency contraception and IUDs, including the hormonal kind, primarily prevent pregnancy by altering ovulation or stopping sperm from ever reaching an egg. (They don't interfere with implanted eggs.) Moreover, although anti-abortion activists tend to believe pregnancy begins when a sperm fertilizes an egg, that's far from a settled fact. Since 1965, the American College of Obstetricians and Gynecologists has said that pregnancy begins when an embryo implants in the uterine wall.[6] Even if IUDs and emergency contraception blocked implantation—and, again, that's not how they usually work—they are not ending a pregnancy, because the pregnancy never started.

Nevertheless, the Supreme Court ruled that because Hobby Lobby's owners *believe* that IUDs and emergency contraception cause abortions, Hobby Lobby did not have to cover them. Under the court's reasoning, the mere belief that contraception causes abortions is legally meaningful.

Anti-abortion groups have since taken this reasoning and run with it. Students for Life of America opposes virtually all forms of hormonal birth control and claims they cause abortions. (They do not.)

Abortion rights advocates and legal experts sounded the alarm: If belief is enough to legally redefine contraception as abortion-inducing drugs, what is to stop states from claiming that their existing abortion bans outlaw contraception? But others insisted they were being Chicken

THE SECOND COMING | 245

Littles. When Senate Republicans blocked a bill that would have guaranteed a federal right to contraception in 2024, they claimed the bill was unnecessary because no one was seriously threatening birth control; Iowa Senator Joni Ernst accused Democrats of "fear-mongering in the name of politics."[7] Ignoring warnings from activists and experts, however, is what led to *Dobbs*.

You know what else led to *Dobbs*? Ignoring things because they happen to someone else, particularly marginalized someone elses. By the time the Supreme Court overturned *Roe*, millions of young people—many of them low-income and people of color—had already spent years without access to birth control due to policies put into place by Donald Trump.

When the Trump administration swept into the White House in 2017, prepared to pour money into abstinence-only sex ed and roll back the Obama administration's interpretation of Title IX, its officials also set out to rewrite the nation's only federal family planning program. First enacted in 1970 after research showed that unexpected childbearing—especially among teenagers—increased poverty and diminished women's ability to get an education or a job,[8] this family planning program is known as Title X of the Public Health Service Act. (No relation to Title IX, other than the U.S. government's annoying tendency of referring to laws using similar shorthand.) Thousands of clinics receive money through Title X, which they use to provide cheap or even free family planning services like birth control and STI tests. More than half of Title X users are under thirty; that's some 1.5 million people.[9]

Critically, Title X permits minors to get contraception without involving their parents. About one in five fifteen-to-seventeen-year-olds say they would not get sexual or reproductive health care if their parents could find out.[10]

What Title X does not do is pay for abortions. This is not unusual. Since 1977, a rule known as the Hyde Amendment has banned the use of federal funds to pay for abortions except in cases of rape, incest, or life-threatening emergencies (which means that low-income people who rely on federal Medicaid can't use it to terminate their pregnancies). For decades, however, clinics could use Title X dollars to counsel people about abortions or refer them for the procedure; clinics could also provide abortions so long as Title X dollars were not involved.

Then, in 2019, the Trump administration banned Title X providers from so much as mentioning the possibility of abortion to patients, even if patients asked about it. The administration also required Title X providers to physically and financially separate any services that involve abortions from those that don't.

Many Title X clinics refused to comply with the Trump administration's demands. Providers argued that the bans amounted to a "gag rule" and undermined the fundamental medical ethic of "informed consent," which dictates that patients should know all their options and all their risks. Many of the Title X clinics that offered abortion also could not afford to relocate their abortion patients to a totally separate facility and hire separate personnel to treat them. By decreeing that abortion had to be physically separate from other forms of health care, the Trump administration was literally sequestering abortion off on its own, where it could be more easily overlooked, stigmatized, and curtailed. It was what anti-abortion activists and the American public had done for years—but taken to new heights.

After the "gag rule" took effect, Title X lost more than 1,200 clinics.[11] In 2018, Title X helped nearly four million people, but by 2020, that number dropped to 1.5 million.[12] The mass exodus was catastrophic for minors. More than 1.8 million fifteen-to-seventeen-year-olds ended up living in areas where they could not access confidential contraceptive services.[13] Many likely went without.

In the summer of 2019, as sexual health experts went to war with the Trump administration over the so-called gag rule, I spent a few days at clinics that were leaving the Title X network. These clinics were in the northernmost corner of Maine, in a remote and rural place known as Aroostook County. Larger than Connecticut and Rhode Island combined, Aroostook is home to fewer than seventy thousand people, 95 percent of whom are white. The median household income hovers around $50,000, about $30,000 less than the national median. Given that Trump flipped Aroostook in 2016, after Barack Obama won it twice, I wanted to know how the people of Aroostook felt about Trump's attacks on the few clinics where they could afford health care.

On my second day in the clinics, I met eighteen-year-old Calleena, a recent high school graduate who aspired to help deaf kids and elders get cochlear implants. She wanted to get a Nexplanon implant, a knuckle-size rod that lives beneath the skin of the upper arm and is more than 99 percent effective at preventing pregnancy. But she was uninsured, and that tiny little rod—even with the Title X–facilitated sliding scale offered by the clinic—cost $283.50. (Without the sliding scale, it cost upward of $1,000.) A baby would have cost much more, but a baby was a theoretical expense. The Nexplanon was not.[14]

The clinic's nurse practitioner walked Calleena through her birth control options so gently and thoroughly that even I started taking notes on the pros and cons of each method. Calleena ended up getting the birth control shot for $16.20.[15]

"I honestly don't know what I would have done if I couldn't have come here," Calleena told me. "At least with my circle of friends, there's a lot of lower-income families. This is where we get our free birth control and our free condoms, and stuff like that. The stuff we need. I mean, in a perfect world, we'd all abstain from sex, whatever. But that's not gonna happen."[16]

Trump, by the way, won Aroostook again in the 2020 and 2024 presidential elections. If the people of Aroostook wanted Trump because of his economic policies, they evidently overlooked Trump's gutting of Title X, a program set up to better women's economic prospects by preventing unplanned pregnancies. Men, it is worth noting, also economically benefit when they're not forced into parenthood. One in five men has impregnated somebody who went on to have an abortion.[17] Compared to male teenagers whose partners get pregnant and give birth, those with partners who undergo abortions are more likely to graduate from college and make more money.[18]

Trump's administration made Title X history in yet another way: In 2019, it gave $1.7 million in Title X dollars to a chain of anti-abortion crisis pregnancy centers that does not offer contraception. Rather, the chain promotes "fertility awareness," which suggests people avoid sex when they're at the most fertile part of their menstrual cycle. (It is typically about 75 percent effective in preventing pregnancy.) In short, government money that had been designated for family planning went to a group that refused to engage with the majority of modern family planning methods—the methods that anti-abortion groups have falsely accused of causing abortions.

248 | CARTER SHERMAN

Historically, Title X isn't all that controversial. It passed the Senate unanimously and was signed into law by Richard Nixon, a Republican. But now, Title X has been transformed into a political football—much like Title IX. While liberals and conservatives toss these critical policies back and forth, young people suffer.

After Joe Biden won the presidency in 2020, his administration reversed the Title X "gag rule." So many clinics rejoined Title X that by May 2023 there were more participating clinics than there had been before Trump.[19] However, Title X remained flat-funded under Biden.[20] Thanks to soaring inflation, its budget effectively declines every year.

Conservative operatives also picked up the assault on Title X where the Trump administration left off. In 2020, a Texan father of three daughters named Alexander Deanda sued the federal government over Title X. By allowing minors to get contraception without parental knowledge or consent, Deanda argued, Title X was in violation of Texas law that gives parents rights over their child's medical care. "He is raising each of his daughters in accordance with Christian teaching on matters of sexuality, which requires unmarried children to practice abstinence and refrain from sexual intercourse until marriage," the lawsuit noted of Deanda. Prescription contraception and family planning services, it continued, "facilitate sexual promiscuity and premarital sex."

Deanda did not claim that his daughters even used Title X or tried to get birth control without his consent. He was just worried that they *could*.

Deanda was represented by an attorney named Jonathan Mitchell, the legal mastermind behind the 2021 Texas six-week abortion ban that let people sue one another over suspected abortions and that effectively broke *Roe* months before the Supreme Court overturned it. Mitchell filed the lawsuit in a federal court in Amarillo, a city in the Texas panhandle that is home to a federal judge named Matthew Kacsmaryk. Appointed to the bench by Trump, Kacsmaryk has criticized no-fault divorce laws,[21] opposed same-sex marriage,[22] called being transgender "a delusion,"[23] and once wrote that the Sexual Revolution "was more like the French Revolution, seeking to destroy rather than restore."[24] This is sexual conservatism par excellence. And by filing in Amarillo, Mitchell guaranteed that Deanda's lawsuit would be heard by a judge likely to agree with his cause.

In a 2022 ruling that referenced the medieval Christian theologian

THE SECOND COMING | 249

Thomas Aquinas, the eighteenth-century jurist William Blackstone (who believed women should basically lose their legal rights after getting married), and *Dobbs*, Kacsmaryk ruled that Title X infringed on Deanda's parental rights. With the stamp of a court clerk, the seven million–plus minors who call Texas home lost their right to confidential birth control.

Kacsmaryk's name might sound familiar. That's because in 2022, a group of anti-abortion activists, who were represented by ADF, filed a lawsuit in Amarillo and asked Kacsmaryk to overturn the FDA's approval of the abortion pill mifepristone. Kacsmaryk ruled to yank mifepristone from the market—an unprecedented rewriting of FDA regulations that would have devastated abortion access across the country, including in states that protect abortion rights. After the Supreme Court struck down that order in 2024, ruling 9–0 that the activists did not have the legal right to sue, Kacsmaryk agreed to let the Republican attorneys general of Idaho, Kansas, and Missouri resurrect the lawsuit. The Republicans' arguments were openly pronatalist and vehemently opposed to letting teens have non-procreative sex: Because mifepristone lowered "birth rates for teenaged mothers," they said, its availability threatened to leave states with a smaller population, "diminishment of political representation, and loss of federal funds."

In 2024, after the notoriously conservative U.S. Fifth Circuit Court of Appeals upheld much of Kacsmaryk's ruling in the Title X case, Mitchell joined forces with the State of Texas to launch another lawsuit against the federal government over Title X and its provision of birth control to minors. The lawsuit, filed on behalf of another pro-abstinence Christian parent, repeated the claim that "prescription contraception or other family planning services . . . [facilitate] sexual promiscuity and premarital sex." It was also filed in Kacsmaryk's court.

"This suit is likely a preview of where the Texas GOP—and national Republicans—stand on attacking contraception access," Mary Ziegler, a law professor who studies the legal history of reproduction, told the *Guardian* after the lawsuit was filed. "While Republicans say they don't want to take aim at contraception, this is another sign that this is actually where we're headed."[25]

Given the track record of everybody involved—Mitchell, Kacsmaryk, Texas itself—it is hard to imagine that the assault on Title X will stop with

250 | CARTER SHERMAN

eviscerating minors' access to it. Project 2025, a playbook for future conservative administrations written by the Heritage Foundation, suggests that Title X be "reframed with a focus on better education around fertility awareness and holistic family planning." In fact, Project 2025 wants to devote the entire Department of Health and Human Services, which oversees Title X, to what the playbook calls a "family agenda," promoting "marriage, work, motherhood, fatherhood, and nuclear families." Premarital and recreational sex—and the birth control that supposedly enables them—have no place in the United States that Project 2025 and its backers envision. Neither does homosexual sex.

So often, young people are canaries in the coal mine. When minors' rights are taken away, adults' may soon follow.

THE ATTACK ON GENDER-AFFIRMING CARE

Because sexual conservatives see the heterosexual and married family as the basic unit of civilization, they believe that a rejection of the fetters of traditional gender roles—roles that dictate women should be mothers and men should be fathers, without any recognition of genders beyond that binary—is an existential threat to the United States. So, naturally, they are now taking the political and legal maneuvers that were so successful in overturning *Roe* and retrofitting them to address this supposed threat, pushing for laws that would medically force young people back into strict gender roles.

I'm talking about bans on gender-affirming health care.[*] Like abortion restrictions, these laws seek to reshape people's medical decisions.

---

[*]This book will not delve too deeply into the battle between those who support gender-affirming care and those who worry—sometimes in good faith and frequently in bad—that children are being pushed into it, because, frankly, that's a book in and of itself. The provision of gender-affirming care to minors can be controversial, and medical providers around the world are still evaluating their approach to it. However, every major medical group in the United States, including the American Academy of Pediatrics, has said this care can be evidence-based and medically necessary. Moreover, these groups oppose political bans on gender-affirming care. The American Medical Association put its policy plainly: "Medical decisions should be made by patients, their relatives, and health care providers, not politicians."

In 2021, Arkansas became the first state in the nation to ban minors from accessing gender-affirming care—which can include a range of treatments, including help with transitioning pronouns, puberty blockers, and hormones—regardless of whether their parents approved of the care and against the advice of major medical groups. By 2024, half of the country had passed similar bans. At least twenty-five states also passed laws that block trans students from playing on sports teams that match their gender identity.[26]

Advocates for these bans have one particular talking point: that gender-affirming care "sterilizes" kids. When an Idaho Republican supported a bill to ban this care in 2022, he urged the state legislature, "The ability to procreate is a fundamental right that must be protected for these children. Leave their bodies alone."[27] "I see this conversation as an extension of the pro-life argument," another Idaho Republican said. "We are not talking about the life of the child, but we are talking about the potential to give life to another generation."[28] In a 2022 opinion to a state legislator, Texas Attorney General Ken Paxton designated gender-affirming care as child abuse because it "could permanently deprive minor children of their constitutional right to procreate, or impair their ability to procreate." It's difficult not to read these comments and recall sexually conservative fears over the decline of the U.S. birth rate, particularly among white women.

Gender-affirming care can impact somebody's future fertility, but it is possible to take steps to preserve it. Moreover, dying of suicide also deprives children of the chance to one day procreate. Roughly half of trans, nonbinary, and genderqueer people between the ages of thirteen and twenty-four have considered suicide in the past year.[29]

Alliance Defending Freedom, the group that was so instrumental in the overturning of *Roe*, has been behind many of the bans on gender-affirming care as well as the lawsuits to defend them. (An ADF-linked lawyer also helped write Florida's Don't Say Gay law.) Founded in 1994 with the goal of overturning both *Roe* and a Supreme Court case that forbids the "excessive entanglement" of government with religion, ADF is appalled by government attempts to "create or impose a new orthodoxy in human sexuality and sexual ethics," as ADF president Kristen Waggoner told the *New Yorker*. Fighting this "orthodoxy" means fighting against LGBTQ+ and abortion rights, and fighting for the central place of heterosexual marriage and children in American life. (An ADF staffer can be fired if they get divorced.) It also means fighting for enshrining parental rights in constitutional law. "I do think the court could say, 'Parental rights are fundamental rights,'" Waggoner said.[30]

Bans on gender-affirming care, however, do not respect parental rights. These bans prevent children from getting gender-affirming care even if their parents consent to it—and many, many parents do. So what's the difference? If parents should have a say when it comes to a medical procedure like abortion, why do they not get a say when it comes to medications like puberty blockers or hormones?

Levi, a trans man, lives in Texas, the biggest state to ban gender-affirming care for minors. "Before I had fully come out, when I thought I wasn't going to be accepted, I had a suicide plan and everything. Because I decided if I wasn't going to live as myself, I wasn't going to live," Levi said. As he watched Texas enact its ban, "I felt like I was watching children being murdered. I've had people talk to me like, 'Oh, that feels like an exaggeration.' No, it isn't. Testosterone is the only reason why I have made it to twenty. Top surgery is the only reason why I've made it to twenty."

On Yik Yak, an app that functions as a kind of localized and anonymous Reddit, Levi told me that he'd started to see posts like "I wish queer kids—especially trans people—would shut the fuck up on campus" or "Trans people think we're going to indulge their delusions."

"They've basically given people the go-ahead to hate us," Levi said, referring to legislators who push bans on gender-affirming care. "I think that if I were killed in Texas, the killer would get off. Or that I would just be one of many and it would make no difference."

In December 2024, the Supreme Court heard arguments in a case involving Tennessee's ban on gender-affirming health care for minors. In an indication of just how much legal firepower the *Dobbs* decision and its reasoning has lent to sexual conservatism, Tennessee cited *Dobbs* no fewer than ten times in the briefing it submitted to the Supreme Court ahead of arguments. Regardless of how the justices rule in 2025, the fact that bans on gender-affirming care are rising to the nation's highest court reveals just how important this issue is to sexual conservatives. Within weeks of starting his second term in 2025, Trump fired off a series of executive orders targeting trans and nonbinary people; one order—which may have taken its cue from the anti-abortion Hyde Amendment—banned the use of federal funds to pay for gender-affirming care for anyone under nineteen.

The president of one organization that lobbies for bans on youth gender-affirming care told the *New York Times* that, ultimately, his organization wants to ban the care entirely.[31] They're only starting off with minors because, he said, they're "going where the consensus is."[32] Just like the anti-abortion movement did.

ACCESS, NOT RIGHTS

The video that changed Sriha Srinivasan's life is set to a propulsive remix of *The Fairly OddParents* theme song. In the fourteen-second video, Sriha dances furiously, clapping her hands, shimmying her shoulders, rolling her fists and hips. At the beginning, she's smiling; by the end, as every part of her body shakes in time with the beat, Sriha's face can only be described as a mean mug.

To be fair, she is dancing for a serious subject: sexually transmitted infections.

"How often should you get tested for STIs?" reads black-and-white text posted over Sriha's body. "REMEMBER: most STIs present w/ NO SYMPTOMS!"

If you haven't already guessed, this video was posted to TikTok, where it garnered more than thirty-six thousand likes. It was the first sign that Sriha's senior project, a TikTok account about sex ed called @sexedu, would work.

Sriha hadn't planned to start @sexedu. The California native's original plan for her senior project was to teach sex ed in her parents' hometown in India; she'd already spent one summer doing that, inspired by her own mother's lack of sex education. But when the pandemic shut down the planet, there was no way she was going to India. Hence: TikTok. And as Sriha watched the likes roll in on her video, she thought: *Whoa. This is something I can keep doing.*

"Of course, the pandemic kept going, and so that summer, I had nothing better to do," Sriha recalled. "Just kept posting, kept posting, kept posting." By the time we spoke, in 2024, Sriha had more than 180,000 followers on @sexedu.

A year after she started @sexedu, an organization called Free the Pill reached out to ask if Sriha would showcase their work. Sriha ended up doing more than that: She joined the organization's campaign for nationwide over-the-counter birth control and even testified to the FDA in support of Opill, a nonprescription birth control pill. "I went to UCLA—blue-state public school, pretty liberal. It still was $747 a quarter—so three times a year—to get on student health insurance. I couldn't afford that," she told me. Without student health insurance, she had to find an outside gynecologist. "I called in January. And the first appointment they had for me was June, during finals week."

The night after she testified, Sriha got an image of a birth control pack tattooed on her hip. ("Definitely a leap of faith," she remarked.)

More than half of teens and young adults have faced at least one barrier to birth control pills that led them to go without.[33] Of those people, 20 percent dealt with an unplanned pregnancy and 16 percent sought an abortion.[34] This is exactly what happened to Stephanie Loraine Piñeiro.

In the summer of 2023, a year after *Dobbs*, the FDA approved Opill for use among people of any age. Sriha cried when she heard the news. She was impossibly happy.

Terrified, too.

"I've met so many people in real life who were there and fought for *Roe v. Wade*. I'm sure when *Roe v. Wade* passed, they were like, 'This is amazing. My children, my daughters, my granddaughters, my great-granddaughters, all of them—I'm sure they will have access to reproductive rights,'" said Sriha, who is now twenty-one. "I'm sure that they never imagined that nearly fifty years later it was gonna get taken down."

Sriha does not share that optimism. "I don't have the reassurance that fifty years from now, we will still have over-the-counter birth control. I hope and I pray and I fight for it," she continued. "The fall of *Roe v. Wade* was a massive win for anti-choice individuals, and they're definitely not done yet. I do think contraception is the next frontier."

In the wake of *Roe*'s demise, young people across the country leaped into expanding cheap and discreet access to birth control and emergency contraception. Thanks largely to student advocates, dozens of universities—including in states that have banned abortion—installed vending machines to dispense emergency contraception and pregnancy tests.[35] Janey, a twenty-one-year-old student at a college on the Illinois-Iowa border, started running a delivery service from her dorm room, supplying her classmates with condoms and emergency contraception.

"They're trying to get rid of everything—everything that's supposed to be protecting women, and that's super scary," Janey said. "People are still gonna have sex, whether or not you educate them on it."

Janey's delivery service got so popular that she gave away more than four hundred condoms in a single year. She ended up bringing on a whole team of people to help her and to build a sustainable operation.

Student advocacy went even further in some of the country's most liberal states, as they pushed colleges to offer abortion pills to students. As of 2023, at least three states—California, Massachusetts, and New York—passed laws requiring public universities ensure that students have access to abortion pills.[36] After a petition, Connecticut's private Wesleyan College agreed to cover emergency contraception and to pay for students' abortions, including the cost of the procedure and transportation.[37]

When Yamalí Rodas Figueroa started handing out Plan B on the campus of their Minnesota school, they were stunned to realize how often people needed it. Minnesota is a blue state, but Yamalí's college resisted attempts to add medication abortion as an on-campus service. According to Yamalí, college officials insisted there aren't enough people in need to justify it. "Well, I see them every day," Yamalí retorted.

Yamalí's mom gave birth to them at fourteen, then to Yamalí's brother a year later. Growing up in Guatemala, Yamalí's mom had zero sex ed and zero access to abortion. "My mom loves me and all that, but I know she holds a little resentment in terms of like, well, she didn't really have a choice to have us," Yamalí said. "She always said that she wished she had all the information she needs. And now, post-*Roe*, a lot of people are feeling that way in 2024." Yamalí doesn't understand it: How can the United States, the supposed land of the free and home of the brave, now be so similar to the Guatemala of two decades ago?

"I just imagine other people like my mom," Yamalí said, "suffering through."

"IT'S NOT OKAY"

On April 30, 2024, the day before Florida's six-week abortion ban took effect, I watched as a young woman slipped a pill under her tongue to start a medication abortion, then took a delicate sip of water from a small paper cup. Really, everything about her seemed delicate. She had luminous black eyes and held her pixie-thin legs, dotted with doodles of tattoos, with the tensed poise of a ballerina about to dance. An oversize T-shirt, emblazoned with the logo for a heavy metal band, engulfed the rest of her body. Thick, goth makeup made it hard to tell her age, but I guessed that she was maybe in her early twenties.

We sat down to talk in the back warren of an abortion clinic, in a cozy and dimly lit room decorated with butterfly collages. Married with two kids, the woman seemed dazed with gratefulness, like she still could not believe that she had made it to the clinic. She was six weeks and four days into her pregnancy. Had she made it to the clinic a day later, Florida's ban would have been in effect and she would have been unable to get an abortion in her home state. The woman's husband had just started a new job, but they had lived for a while with her mom because they couldn't afford anything else; she doubted that she would have had the money to go out of state for the procedure.

"If financially I wasn't able to do that, I would have to carry a pregnancy that I don't want to carry," she told me. "It would just be a very big financial, physical, emotional strain. I don't feel like that's something I can personally handle right now, and it would definitely have a very big effect on my life."

It was something in the way that she talked about the future—like there was just so much of it—that made me realize I had miscalculated her age. "Do you mind if I ask how old you are?" I asked.

"I'm nineteen. That's also part of it."

"How so?"

"I want to go to school and I'm just starting to try to find jobs," she said. "I want to be a tattoo artist and I'm trying to find an apprenticeship. A lot of my teenage years have been spent pregnant."

The first time she got pregnant, at sixteen, she had wanted an abortion, but her mom had refused to let her get one, she told me. When the woman gave birth, at seventeen, a birth injury left her son with disabilities.

"I was a seventeen-year-old kid taking care of a heavily disabled child. Any child is a lot of work, but he had doctor's appointments constantly and so many things that I had to worry about," she said. "I do love my son, but that definitely wasn't a smart decision at my age."

She told the story quickly and crisply. There were no "likes" or "you knows" or even "ums." It happened. This was her life now. No regrets. She had given birth to a second child, whom she had planned, with her husband. Now, pregnant yet again, she was making the kind of decision she had once been denied.

But when the young woman mentioned her mother, her words pulsed with anger. "It's not okay to force somebody to do that with their body," she said, adding, "When you're that young, you can barely take care of yourself. Either they don't care or they're just not thinking about it or probably both."

"There is a process in Florida where you can go to court to get an abortion when you're a minor," I started to say. "I don't know if you thought about that at all. . . ."

I trailed off. I couldn't read her face; I was suddenly paralyzed. What if no one had ever told her about judicial bypasses? What if, by cluing her in, I'd hurt her somehow? What if she realized just how different her life could have turned out, if not for that parental involvement law—and resented it?

I had wanted to ask this woman what she thought of the double whammy of Florida's six-week ban and its parental involvement law, but I swallowed my question down. Under a six-week ban, people likely have a mere two weeks to realize they've missed a period, decide to get an abortion, and obtain the procedure. Given that people who go through judicial bypasses see their abortions delayed by, on average, fifteen days,[38] Florida minors have next to zero chance of getting one in time.

Instead, I asked her what went through her head when she realized she had come so close to missing Florida's cutoff.

"As soon as I got here and I knew I was getting the care that I need, I was just so relieved," she said. "I knew that either I would need to go through a really difficult process to be able to get it—if I didn't get it here, today—or I wouldn't be able to."

258 | CARTER SHERMAN

Out of all the people I interviewed over the course of writing this book, I think about this woman the most. Maybe I'm just getting old, but she seemed so profoundly young to me. Because of a parental involvement law and a lack of access to knowledge about her rights, she had been forced into parenthood herself, taking on an indescribably serious obligation before she had the chance to explore what she wanted from her own life. At nineteen, she was married with kids. In theory, she was a sexual conservative's dream—and yet her government was still pressuring her into more. If she had been forced, while still a teenager, to have a third child, her chances of a fulfilling career could have been delayed, if not destroyed. And if that had come to pass, other young people's lives could have also been forever changed. What would have happened to her husband, her children?

Control over sex and its outcomes is tantamount to control over people. In this fight for the future of sex, it's people like this nineteen-year-old who have the most to lose.

CONCLUSION

The first major abortion-related story that I ever reported on was about judicial bypasses. It was the fall of 2016, and I was living in Houston, where abortion providers had just won a Supreme Court case over a law that had shut down roughly half the state's abortion clinics. Hillary Clinton and Donald Trump were locked in a battle for the White House, and all signs seemed to indicate that Clinton would win. Among abortion providers and their supporters, there was a cautious sense of optimism: Yes, Republicans had chipped away at access to the procedure through hundreds of state-level abortion restrictions—just like the one the Supreme Court had just struck down—but maybe the tide was turning. Maybe they would be able to save *Roe v. Wade* after all.

Texas, however, had already passed another law to limit minors' access to abortion, as the law threw up new bureaucratic obstacles that made the judicial bypass process far more difficult. One day, I left Houston and drove ninety minutes to a Starbucks, where I sat down with a young college student who had successfully obtained a judicial bypass and an abortion before the new law took effect.

We made sure to sit outside, at a wrought iron table, where no one would hear us talk. Had the new law been in place when she sought a judicial bypass, the student told me, she would never have been able to end her pregnancy or go to college. "I know that if I were to keep the baby and become a mom, any dreams I had—they're going to go out the window because I'm going to devote myself to being a mother," she said.

A few weeks after that interview, Trump stunned the United States by winning the presidency. The rest is history. But what stands out to me now, in thinking about that interview, is that Texan sexual conservatives *did not give up*. Dealt a staggering blow by the nation's highest court, they already had another anti-abortion law—one that targeted minors—in the offing. I didn't understand it in 2016, but now I know: What happens to young people is a precursor to what happens to everybody else. Despite abortion providers' victory at the Supreme Court, abortion rights were still in grave danger. Obviously.

Over the course of reporting this book, I have relearned this lesson again and again. Advocacy for abstinence-only sex ed has evolved into restrictions on free speech, LGBTQ+ rights, and the entirety of public education. Bans on minors' access to internet porn can end up cutting off everybody's access to it. Our tacit acceptance of fuckability and online rape culture among young people has mutated into fungal misogyny, which has in turn contributed to sexual conservatism's political power. Minors, once among the first groups of people to lose access to abortion rights, have become test subjects for restrictions on contraception and gender-affirming care. While I already knew that the overturning of *Roe* was and remains a blueprint for undermining access to sexual and gendered freedoms, I came to understand that *all* these seemingly disparate developments are connected by the sexual conservatism movement and its campaign to make it dangerous to have queer, unmarried, or recreational sex.

What I truly did not expect is the extent to which young people are now organizing in favor of sexual progressivism. Yes, my interview pool was biased toward activists, but not everybody had experience with picket signs. And no matter their background, I was consistently struck by my interviewees' thoughtfulness and curiosity. Raised in an era of unprecedented social change and connection, at the epicenter of the battle between sexual conservative and progressivism, they were not satisfied with the status quo. They were making connections between the personal and the political in ways that I simply did not at seventeen, when I was busy convincing myself that I would be a virgin forever. That I wasn't forced to make those connections speaks to my own privilege—I was a white girl raised in an upper-middle-class enclave of Seattle, after all—but this kind of ignorance is a luxury until it becomes a liability. You don't realize what you've lost until it's too late. I didn't realize, for instance, that I was growing up in the midst of a nationwide assault on sex ed, let alone that I could have found activists who could have given me a more inclusive and comprehensive sex education. Maybe if I had, I would have known about Title IX sooner and been able to seek better justice for myself.

So many young people today are simply more informed and engaged than I was. In interviews, they told me that they wanted accountability for sexual violence. They wanted to understand how social media had warped their body image, to question it, and to do better. Many weren't having sex, but they knew they deserved better than what the U.S. government had offered them.

* * *

I rode out the final days of the 2024 election in Phoenix, reporting on activists who were corralling voters in favor of a ballot measure to enshrine abortion rights into the state constitution. On election night, the activists held a watch party at an outdoor bar. They were jubilant; the measure was on track to pass—and it did, with an astounding 60-plus percent of the vote. As the sun sank beneath the desert horizon, the activists started to give celebratory speeches and I started to shake with cold. I couldn't stop staring at a woman who was watching MSNBC, where presenter Steve Kornacki was gesturing at a red-tinged map. Her face creased with the effort of holding back tears.

This woman and I were in the midst of the same revelation: If Donald Trump became president and implemented a federal abortion ban, none of these state-level laws would matter.

Sometimes, generational change and years of grassroots activism are not enough. Sometimes, you lose. And sometimes, that loss is so gaping that it feels like it swallows everything that came before it. As if all of it—the work, the faith, the suffering—was meaningless. As if you're meaningless.

The watch party wrapped up around nine o'clock. By that point, I was so cold that I kept shaking even after I drove home and burrowed into my hotel bed. Huddled under the covers, I started thinking about another woman—one I wrote about a few chapters ago, whom I called Zoe. When you lose entire institutions, it helps to think about the individual. Namely: that change happens one person at a time.

At fourteen, Zoe watched helplessly as her nudes were leaked on an anonymous social media network; in high school, her boyfriend had followed through with a threat to post her nudes to social media. Once she got to college, Zoe joined a peer-to-peer sex ed group, imagining that the group would focus on preventing sexual harassment and assault—topics that, for obvious reasons, she felt passionate about. But it soon became so much more. Rather than just reducing violence, the group focused on what Zoe calls "pleasure advocacy." This advocacy is rooted in sexually progressive principles shared by many of the other sex educators I've mentioned in this book: Everybody deserves information about sex, everybody should be allowed to talk about sex, and the more sex-related knowledge and resources people have, the better they are at having sex that is not only safe but *good*.

"I felt super empowered in this work. I felt really good about creating sex-positive spaces and not being bothered by slut-shaming," Zoe said. "The impact is so cool to see even on a small scale."

When she decided to get back on dating apps, Zoe refused to be pressured into anything she didn't feel comfortable with. "If I didn't like the vibe, right away I would be like, 'No, sorry,'" she said. She just wanted no-strings-attached hookups. "I went through my little Hot Girl Phase. I absolutely felt like I was reclaiming my sexuality and everything after sexual violence. I was loving it. I was Tinder's number one customer."

Then one day she met up with a guy whom she had found on Bumble. They went for a walk, then sat down by a lake for so long that they watched the sunrise together. The hookup never materialized. "The first time I've ever not done that!" Zoe said. "He's wonderful. Wonderful."

When her now-boyfriend first asked if she would be comfortable sending nudes, Zoe said no. But seven months into the relationship, she started to reconsider. "My 'no' was so respected that, over time, I was like, 'You know what, I want to do this,'" she said. "It felt very different from feeling like I was forced to."

There's always a risk that, one day, the boyfriend she thought was so wonderful will break her trust and share her nudes with the world. But Zoe's comfortable with that risk. Using the knowledge gained through her pleasure advocacy, Zoe made an informed choice to be vulnerable, rather than being forced into that position.

Although young people increasingly recognize that the personal is political, it's easy to forget that happy relationships carry political import, too. Alice Evans, a scholar who studies how societies around the world achieve gender equality, believes we overlook how powerful a tool romantic love can be. "Where love is mutual, and both parties deeply care about the other's happiness, they listen and learn," Evans has written. "When she says certain language makes her uncomfortable, he quickly takes note—rather than getting angry and lashing out. Eager for her to thrive, he shares the care-work, supports her career progression, and celebrates her wins."[1]

Of the many activities and attitudes that I've covered in this book, I barely talked about romantic love—but many of my interviewees spoke of their partners with affection and amazement, unable to believe they had gotten so lucky. Zoe's relationship has helped her heal the claw marks left by rape culture, take back a sex act that was stolen from her, and try to help others do the same. Now twenty-three, Zoe is at work trying to turn her college sex ed group into a national organization. "I see myself marrying this person and having a life with this person," Zoe said of her boyfriend. "Being able to also give a piece of myself that used to be so vulnerable and so scary, and know that it feels so much safer now, is nice and fulfilling."

Sawyer, the young man who went to the gym every day because he was terrified of having a partner see him naked, is in love too. Five months into his relationship with his new girlfriend, he broke down in front of her. All of his insecurities poured out of him. Sawyer wanted so desperately to be smaller, and he just couldn't make it happen.

His girlfriend told him: "I think you are perfect just the way you are. If I put my head on your chest, it's like a pillow. It's so comfy."

"She looked at the positive outlooks of everything, as well as the fact that she knows I'm always trying to improve myself," Sawyer said. His relief was oceanic. "She made me feel like what I was doing was enough."

I bring this up not because I want you to know that Zoe, Sawyer, and many of the other people I've written about in this book are doing okay. (Although to be clear: They are alright.) I bring it up as a reminder: When the rapid shifts in politics, education, and the internet start to feel overwhelming, showing people that you love them makes a difference. That you trust them to make choices, be vulnerable, and handle the consequences. That you believe they deserve dignity.

Throughout reporting this book, I saw this principle at work even among people who were not *in* love. At the end of my interviews, I liked to ask: What makes for good sex?

Being in a close relationship, whether romantic or friendly, one told me. Feeling safe and secure, another said. Trust, a third said.

DeeDee, the twenty-five-year-old from Texas who learned about sex's existence from fanfiction, perhaps put it the most succinctly. "It's a mutual respect and caring for each other," she said.

These are all synonyms for equality.

Good sex is impossible without equality. Sexually conservative policy can make it difficult for young people to approach each other on equal footing, such as through saddling one with pregnancy or making it impossible for another to seek recourse after a sexual assault. But when individuals wanted their partners to prosper—whether those partnerships lasted for a night or years—people walked away from their sexual and romantic encounters feeling respected and empowered. Treated with dignity in one area of their lives, they realized that they deserved dignity in all areas. That realization was at times so powerful it led them to fight for the dignity of others, too. It led them to imagine a better future, for themselves and their peers.

At its core, sexual conservatism is a failure of imagination. It's a failure to imagine a better future, to think that we can move beyond our history or that people may know more than those who have been in charge in the past. Sexual conservatives pretend that depriving young people of access to sex ed, abortion, birth control, and other sex-related resources will lead people to be uninterested in premarital sex and incapable of using sex to cause harm. Sexual conservativism also pretends that, when starved of resources, young people will revert to *its* version of good sex: sex that is heterosexual, married, and very possibly procreative. This belief is so silly as to border on stupid. Never, in all of history, have humans restricted themselves to heterosexual, married, procreative sex. And they're certainly not doing it now, when the internet offers up every kind of sex imaginable and then some.

Even when it seems like sexual conservatism is in control, people will find a way to live out their desires. Frankly, too many humans love sex too much to give in.

And yes, young people may make sexual choices that we disagree with. (There were multiple interviews where I wanted to howl, "Just dump them already!") But I have come to believe that they deserve to have the freedom to do so—not because making choices is part of growing up, but because making choices is part of being a person. Some choices may lead to regret, loss, or accountability, but nobody ever ages out of feeling uncertainty and pain, or out of obligations. You can't shield yourself through marriage or babies or trying to embody antiquated stereotypes of manhood and womanhood.

We can, however, treat the people in our lives as equals and push institutions to do the same. What if we held young people to a high standard while also giving them the tools and space to do better, to even exceed expectations? What if we accepted that—for lack of a better phrase—fucking around and fucking up are a part of fucking?

In the last few days of reporting this book, a few of the individuals who appear in these pages happened to update me on their lives. One had had sex for the first time. (An escapee from the sex recession!) Another had gotten engaged. Yet another had a baby. Gen Z will soon pass into the next stages of life and age out of their sex lives being a national obsession, just as millennials did before them. Generation Alpha is growing up. Soon enough, another generation will be on the front lines of the war between sexual conservatism and progressivism. The question is: Where will the rest of us be?

NOTES ON INTERVIEWS AND SOURCES

Writing a book takes time, so all of my interviewees have aged since our conversations. I cited the age of each as the age they were when we spoke, in order to best reflect their thinking at that particular point in their life. I also tended to delete "like," "you know," and other verbal throat-clearing from sentences. I occasionally edited quotes for clarity or to conceal names, such as in cases when someone mentioned a name but had asked for anonymity.

A very limited number of interviewees appear in these pages multiple times but under different names. These individuals were typically survivors of sexual violence; they may have felt comfortable with some elements of their stories appearing under their own first names but asked that other information be attributed to a pseudonym. I did not alter any details beyond their names.

ACKNOWLEDGMENTS

Thank you, first and foremost, to my agent, Jenna Land Free, who took a chance on me, championed my vision—even when it was decidedly cloudy—and served me delicious chocolates on the beautiful lake that we both call home. I couldn't have imagined a better shepherd for my first book.

Thank you to my editor, Molly Gregory, who grabbed onto this book with both hands, always encouraged me to think bigger and sharper, and remained extraordinarily patient and sunny even when I took ages to reply to emails. Your encouragement and edits were invaluable.

Thank you to Suzy, who told me from the very beginning that I was ready to take this on. None of this would have happened without you.

Thank you to Amanda, Dan, and Eden, who graciously reviewed these pages and offered their thoughts. Thank you to Taylor Swift (because Amanda asked to be thanked in the same line as Taylor Swift).

Thank you to Minerva and Mercury. You'll never read this, because you are cats, but you were essential to the writing process.

Thank you to Todd and Coco, who have somehow managed to be extremely proud of the fact that their daughter writes about sex and its by-products for a living. You are the best parents. (And Coop, I love you too.)

Thank you to everybody I interviewed. Many of you shared very personal stories about private and stigmatized topics, and I am so grateful for your trust.

Finally, thank you to Liam, who proposed just hours after I got an offer for this book, married me in the middle of writing it, and supported me through all the breakdowns, hunger-induced rage, and self-righteous rants that followed. When I was seventeen and despairing over the prospect of being a virgin forever, I never imagined that I would meet someone who loves me as well as you do.

GLOSSARY

Asexuality: A sexual orientation, sometimes shortened to "ace," wherein someone experiences lowered or zero romantic or sexual attraction to others. Asexuality exists on a spectrum and can manifest in many ways. For example, people may identify as asexual but experience romantic attraction to one or both genders; they thus may identify as "heteroromantic," "homoromantic," or "biromantic." Individuals who feel conditional romantic or sexual attraction may identify as "demisexual" or "demiromantic." (This is in no way a comprehensive list of ace labels.)

Assigned female at birth/assigned male at birth: The sex or gender—usually "male" or "female"—that an infant is socially perceived to be, thanks to their bodies and/or societal norms at their birth. This assignation may not align with their gender identity.

Biphobia: Prejudice against bisexual people.

Bisexuality: A sexual orientation wherein someone may be attracted to more than one gender. The definition of this term is somewhat in flux, as people may say it refers to an attraction only to people on the gender binary—that is, to men and women (who may be cis or trans)—or consider it a synonym for "pansexuality," which refers to attraction to people of any gender.

Cisgender: An adjective describing someone whose assigned sex or gender at birth matches their gender identity.

Gender-affirming care: Health care that is designed to "support and affirm individuals' gender identity," according to the World Health

272 | GLOSSARY

Organization. It can encompass a range of social, psychological, and medical services and treatments, including therapy, helping people transition their pronouns, puberty blockers, hormones, and surgery. Can also be called "trans health care."

Gender binary: A socially constructed system in which gender is broken down into two distinct categories: male and female. In this system, people are assigned these labels at birth and expected to act in accordance with traditional gender roles.

Gender identity: An individual's internal sense of their own gender. It is independent from both someone's assigned sex or gender at birth as well as independent from their sexual orientation.

Gender-expansive: An umbrella term used to refer to people who do not fit into binary notions of "male" and "female," such as folks who may identify as transgender, nonbinary, genderqueer, gender-fluid, etc.

Nonbinary: An umbrella adjective describing someone whose gender identity is outside the gender binary. Nonbinary individuals may also identify as transgender.

Pansexuality: A sexual orientation wherein someone may be attracted to people of any gender. It can sometimes be used interchangeably with "bisexuality." See *bisexuality*.

Sexual orientation: An individual's romantic or sexual attraction to others. It is independent from that individual's gender identity.

Transgender: An umbrella adjective that describes someone whose assigned sex or gender at birth does not match their gender identity or expression. Because "transgender" refers to someone's gender identity, it does not describe their sexual orientation; trans people can be straight, gay, lesbian, etc. Trans individuals may also identify as nonbinary.

Transfeminine/transmasculine: An adjective describing people who are not cisgender and whose gender identity leans toward the feminine or masculine spectrum.

This glossary was informed by resources compiled by groups such as the Association of American Medical Colleges, the Asexual Visibility and Education Network, the Human Rights Campaign, the Trevor Project, and the World Health Organization.

NOTES

INTRODUCTION

1. Peggy Orenstein, *Girls and Sex: Navigating the Complicated New Landscape* (Harper, 2016), 118.
2. Jeffrey M. Jones, "LGBTQ+ Identification in U.S. Now at 7.6%," Gallup, March 13, 2024, https://news.gallup.com/poll/611864/lgbtq-identification.aspx.
3. PR Newswire, "Singles in America: Match Releases Largest Study on US Single Population for 12th Year," news release, November 15, 2022, https://www.prnewswire.com/news-releases/singles-in-america-match-releases-largest-study-on-us-single-population-for-12th-year-301678813.html.
4. Carter Sherman, "US Single People Under 50 Having Less Sex Since Roe Overturned, Study Finds," *The Guardian*, January 24, 2024, https://www.theguardian.com/us-news/2024/jan/24/singles-sex-study-match-roe-v-wade.
5. Audre Lorde, *Sister Outsider: Essays and Speeches* (Crossing Press, 2007), 56.
6. Lorde, *Sister Outsider*, 58.
7. Lulu Garcia-Navarro, "Inside the Heritage Foundation's Plans for 'Institutionalizing Trumpism,'" *New York Times Magazine*, January 21, 2024, https://www.nytimes.com/2024/01/21/magazine/heritage-foundation-kevin-roberts.html.
8. Zack Beauchamp, "The European Country Where 'Replacement Theory' Reigns Supreme," *Vox*, May 19, 2022, https://www.vox.com/2022/5/19/23123050/hungary-cpac-2022-replacement-theory.

276 | NOTES

9. Garcia-Navarro, "Inside the Heritage Foundation's Plans for 'Institutionalizing Trumpism.'"

10. *Changing Partisan Coalitions in a Politically Divided Nation*, Pew Research Center, April 9, 2024, https://www.pewresearch.org/politics/2024/04/09/changing-partisan-coalitions-in-a-politically-divided-nation/.

11. Jones, "LGBTQ+ Identification in U.S. Now at 7.6%"; *A Political and Cultural Glimpse Into America's Future* (PRRI, 2024), 10, https://www.prri.org/wp-content/uploads/2024/01/PRRI-Jan-2024-Gen-Z-Draft.pdf.

12. *PRRI Generation Z Fact Sheet* (PRRI, 2024), https://www.prri.org/wp-content/uploads/2024/04/PRRI-Apr-2024-GenZ-Fact-Sheet-Final.pdf.

13. Daniel A. Cox and Kelsey Eyre Hammond, "Young Women Are Leaving Church in Unprecedented Numbers," Survey Center on American Life, American Enterprise Institute, April 4, 2024, https://www.americansurveycenter.org/newsletter/young-women-are-leaving-church-in-unprecedented-numbers/.

14. Lydia Saad et al., "Exploring Young Women's Leftward Expansion," Gallup, September 12, 2024, https://news.gallup.com/poll/649826/exploring-young-women-leftward-expansion.aspx.

15. *Overall Youth Turnout Down From 2020 But Strong in Battleground States* (Center for Information & Research on Civic Learning and Engagement, Tufts University, 2024), https://circle.tufts.edu/latest-research/overall-youth-turnout-down-2020-strong-battleground-states.

16. Saad, "Exploring Young Women's Leftward Expansion."

17. *Half of Youth Voted in 2020, An 11-Point Increase from 2016* (Center for Information & Research on Civic Learning and Engagement, Tufts University, 2021), https://circle.tufts.edu/latest-research/half-youth-voted-2020-11-point-increase-2016.

18. *The Youth Vote in 2022* (Center for Information & Research on Civic Learning and Engagement, Tufts University, 2022), https://circle.tufts.edu/2022-election-center#youth-turnout-second-highest-in-last-three-decades.

19. *The Youth Vote in 2022.*

I. A NATION OF VIRGINS

1. Lauren Kern and Noreen Malone, "Heirs to the Sexual Revolution," *New York*, October 18, 2015, https://www.thecut.com/2015/10/sex-lives-of-college-students.html.

2. "Chilling Facts About 'College Hookup Culture,'" *The View*, posted November 10, 2015, by ABC News, 6:41, https://abcnews.go.com/US/video/chilling-facts-college-hookup-culture-35108852.

3. *Youth Risk Behavior Surveillance—United States, 2011* (CDC, 2012), 24, https://www.cdc.gov/mmwr/pdf/ss/ss6104.pdf.

4. Elizabeth A. Armstrong et al., "Accounting for Women's Orgasm and Sexual Enjoyment in College Hookups and Relationships," *American Sociological Review* 77, no. 3 (2012), https://doi.org/10.1177/0003122412445802.

5. Kern and Malone, "Heirs to the Sexual Revolution."

6. Chris Reiber and Justin R. Garcia, "Hooking up: Gender Differences, Evolution, and Pluralistic Ignorance," *Evolutionary Psychology* 8, no. 3 (2010), https://doi.org/10.1177/147470491000800307.

7. Jean M. Twenge et al., "Sexual Inactivity During Young Adulthood Is More Common Among U.S. Millennials and iGen: Age, Period, and Cohort Effects on Having No Sexual Partners After Age 18," *Archives of Sexual Behavior* 46, no. 2 (2016), https://doi.org/10.1007/s10508-016-0798-z.

8. Peter Ueda et al., "Trends in Frequency of Sexual Activity and Number of Sexual Partners Among Adults Aged 18 to 44 Years in the US, 2000–2018," *JAMA Network Open* 3, no. 6 (2020), https://doi.org/10.1001/jamanetworkopen.2020.3833.

9. Ueda, "Trends in Frequency of Sexual Activity."

10. Scott J. South and Lei Lei, "Why Are Fewer Young Adults Having Casual Sex?" *Socius* 7 (March 2021), https://doi.org/10.1177/2378023121996854.

11. South and Lei, "Why Are Fewer Young Adults Having Casual Sex?"

12. Gisele Galoustian, "Think Millennials Are the 'Hookup Generation?'" Florida Atlantic University News Desk, August 2, 2016, https://www.fau.edu/newsdesk/articles/millennials-sex-study.php.

13. Amanda Barroso et al., "As Millennials Near 40, They're Approaching

278 | NOTES

Family Life Differently Than Previous Generations," Pew Research Center, May 27, 2020, https://www.pewresearch.org/social-trends/2020/05/27/as-millennials-near-40-theyre-approaching-family-life-differently-than-previous-generations/.

14. Andrew Reiner, "Love, Actually," *New York Times*, February 7, 2014, https://www.nytimes.com/2014/02/09/education/edlife/teaching-generation-y-the-basics-of-a-strong-relationship.html.

15. *Youth Risk Behavior Survey Data Summary & Trends Report: 2011–2021* (CDC, 2023), 13, https://www.cdc.gov/yrbs/dstr/pdf/YRBS_Data-Summary-Trends_Report2023_508.pdf.

16. Justin Lehmiller, "Gen Z Aren't Having the Sex You Think: Here's Why," Lovehoney blog, June 26, 2002, https://www.lovehoney.com/blog/gen-z-are-having-less-sex-here-is-why.html.

17. Debby Herbenick et al., "Changes in Penile-Vaginal Intercourse Frequency and Sexual Repertoire from 2009 to 2018: Findings from the National Survey of Sexual Health and Behavior," *Archives of Sexual Behavior* 51, no. 3 (2022), https://doi.org/10.1007/s10508-021-02125-2.

18. Herbenick, "Changes In Penile-Vaginal Intercourse."

19. Maddie Holden, "Gen Z Are 'Puriteens,' But Not for the Reasons You Think," *GQ*, July 30, 2021, https://www.gq.com/story/gen-z-puriteens.

20. Mari Yamaguchi, "Japan Had the Fewest Babies It Has Ever Recorded Last Year. Marriages Dropped Steeply, Too," Associated Press, February 27, 2024, https://apnews.com/article/japan-births-aging-population-7b0639bda2f2f8982fbb19789eb1f1a0.

21. Adriana Gomez Licon, "JD Vance Has Long Been on a Quest to Encourage More Births in the United States," Associated Press, August 16, 2024, https://apnews.com/article/jd-vance-childless-cat-ladies-birth-rates-555c0f78ef8dd4c13c88b9e8d5f0024a.

22. Andrew Kaczynski and Em Steck, "It's Not Just 'Cat Ladies': JD Vance Has a History of Disparaging People Without Kids," *CNN*, July 30, 2024, https://www.cnn.com/2024/07/30/politics/kfile-jd-vance-history-disparaging-people-without-kids/index.html.

23. Melina M. Bersamin et al., "Defining Virginity and Abstinence: Adolescents' Interpretation of Sexual Behaviors," *Journal of Adoles-*

cent *Health* 41, no. 2 (2007), https://doi.org/10.1016/j.jadohealth
.2007.03.011; Michael D. Barnett et al., "Sexual Semantics: The
Meanings of Sex, Virginity, and Abstinence for University Students,"
Personality and Individual Differences 106 (2017), https://doi.org
/10.1016/j.paid.2016.11.008.

24. Hanne Blank, *Virgin: The Untouched History* (Bloomsburg, 2007), 76.

25. Amanda Gesselman et al., "Has Virginity Lost Its Virtue?," *Journal of Sex Research* 54, no. 2 (2016), doi: 10.1080/00224499.2016.1144042.

26. Stephanie Coontz, *Marriage, a History: How Love Conquered Marriage* (Penguin Books, 2006), 254.

27. Laura Kaplan, *The Story of Jane: The Legendary Underground Feminist Abortion Service* (University of Chicago Press, 2019), 280.

28. *Median Age at First Age of Marriage, 2014* (National Center for Family & Marriage Research, Bowling Green State University, 2016), https://www.bgsu.edu/content/dam/BGSU/college-of-arts-and-sciences/NCFMR/documents/FP/anderson-payne-median-age-first-marriage-fp-16-07.pdf.

29. John D'Emilio and Estelle B. Freedman, *Intimate Matters: A History of Sexuality in America*, 3rd ed. (University of Chicago Press, 2012), 233.

30. Frances FitzGerald, *The Evangelicals: The Struggle to Shape America* (Simon & Schuster, 2017), 294–300.

31. Gail Sheehy, "Hers," *New York Times*, January 24, 1980, https://www.nytimes.com/1980/01/24/archives/hers.html.

32. FitzGerald, *The Evangelicals*, 291.

33. FitzGerald, *The Evangelicals*, 308.

34. Lawrence B. Finer, "Trends in Premarital Sex in the United States, 1954–2003," *Public Health Reports* 122, no. 1 (2007), https://doi.org/10.1177/003335490712200110.

35. "Decennial Censuses, 1890 to 1940, and Current Population Survey, Annual Social and Economic Supplements, 1947 to 2023," U.S. Census Bureau, 2023, https://www.census.gov/content/dam/Census/library/visualizations/time-series/demo/families-and-households/ms-2.pdf.

36. Francesca A. Marino, *Age Variation in Cohabitation, 2022* (National Center for Family & Marriage Research, 2022), https://doi.org/10.25035/ncfmr/fp-22-28.

280 | NOTES

37. Risa Gelles-Watnick, "For Valentine's Day, 5 Facts About Single Americans," Pew Research Center, February 8, 2023, https://www.pewresearch.org/short-reads/2023/02/08/for-valentines-day-5-facts-about-single-americans/.

38. Mark Greif, "Afternoon of the Sex Children," *N+1*, Spring 2006, https://www.nplusonemag.com/issue-4/essays/afternoon-of-the-sex-children/.

39. Greif, "Afternoon of the Sex Children."

40. Lorna N. Bracewell, *Why We Lost the Sex Wars* (University of Minnesota Press), 41.

41. Bracewell, *Why We Lost the Sex Wars*, 17.

42. Hermione Hoby, "Taylor Swift: 'Sexy? Not on My Radar,'" *The Guardian*, August 23, 2014, https://www.theguardian.com/music/2014/aug/23/taylor-swift-shake-it-off.

43. Armstrong, "Accounting for Women's Orgasm."

44. Armstrong, "Accounting for Women's Orgasm."

45. Rebecca Traister, "Why Sex That's Consensual Can Still Be Bad. And Why We're Not Talking About It," *New York*, October 20, 2015, https://www.thecut.com/2015/10/why-consensual-sex-can-still-be-bad.html.

46. Debby Herbenick, "Americans Are Having Less Sex. And That's Just Fine," *Washington Post*, March 16, 2017, https://www.washingtonpost.com/posteverything/wp/2017/03/16/americans-are-having-less-sex-and-thats-just-fine/.

47. Justin J. Lehmiller, "Is Voluntary Celibacy on the Rise?," *Psychology Today*, July 23, 2024, https://www.psychologytoday.com/us/blog/the-myths-of-sex/202407/is-voluntary-celibacy-on-the-rise.

48. Kelsey Osgood, "A Summer Without Sex," *The Cut*, June 22, 2024, https://www.thecut.com/article/women-celibate-dating-sex.html.

49. Cox and Eyre Hammond, "Young Women Are Leaving Church in Unprecedented Numbers."

50. Lou Cannon, "The Enduring Republican Grip on State Legislatures," *RealClearPolitics*, November 16, 2021, https://www.realclearpolitics.com/articles/2021/11/16/the_enduring_republican_grip_on_state_legislatures_146738.html.

51. Cannon, "The Enduring Republican Grip."

52. *The 334 Abortion Restrictions Enacted by States from 2011 to July 2016 Account for 30% of All Abortion Restrictions Since Roe v. Wade* (Guttmacher Institute, 2016), https://www.guttmacher.org/infographic /2016/334-abortion-restrictions-enacted-states-2011-july-2016-ac count-30-all-abortion.

53. *Youth Risk Behavior Survey Data Summary & Trends Report: 2011–2021* (CDC), 60.

54. *Youth Risk Behavior Survey Data Summary & Trends Report: 2011–2021* (CDC), 67.

55. Richard Weissbourd et al., *On Edge: Understanding and Preventing Young Adults' Mental Health Challenges* (Making Caring Common Project, Harvard Graduate School of Education, 2023), https://mcc .gse.harvard.edu/reports/on-edge.

56. Catherine E. Shoichet, "Does Gen Z Struggle More with Mental Health Than Millennials? New Polling Shows Signs of a Shift," *CNN*, September 14, 2023, https://www.cnn.com/2023/09/14 /health/gen-z-mental-health-gallup-wellness-cec/index.html.

57. *Pain in the Nation: Building a National Resilience Strategy* (Trust for America's Health, Well Being Trust, 2019), https://wellbeingtrust .org/wp-content/uploads/2019/06/TFAH-2019-YoundAdult-Pain -Brief-FnlRv.pdf.

58. *A Political and Cultural Glimpse Into America's Future* (PRRI, 2024), https://www.prri.org/wp-content/uploads/2024/01/PRRI-Jan-2024 -Gen-Z-Draft.pdf.

59. Weissbourd, *On Edge*.

60. Zack Hrynowski and Stephanie Marken, "Gen Z Voices Lackluster Trust in Major U.S. Institutions," Gallup, September 14, 2023, https://news.gallup.com/opinion/gallup/510395/gen-voices-lacklus ter-trust-major-institutions.aspx.

61. Jeffrey M. Jones, "LGBTQ+ Identification in U.S. Now at 7.6%," Gallup, March 13, 2024, https://news.gallup.com/poll/611864 /lgbtq-identification.aspx; *A Political and Cultural Glimpse into America's Future*, 10.

62. Paige Averett et al., "Virginity Definitions and Meaning Among the LGBT Community," *Journal of Gay & Lesbian Social Services* 26, no. 3 (2014), https://doi.org/10.1080/10538720.2014.924802.

282 | NOTES

63. Avarett, "Virginity Definitions."
64. Avarett, "Virginity Definitions."
65. Barnett, "Sexual Semantics."
66. Barnett, "Sexual Semantics."

2. GENERATION GUINEA PIG

1. Alexandra M. Lord, *Condom Nation: The U.S. Government's Sex Education Campaign from World War I to the Internet* (Johns Hopkins University Press, 2010), 28.
2. Laura Duberstein Lindberg et al., "Changes in Adolescents' Receipt of Sex Education, 2006–2013," *Journal of Adolescent Health* 58, no. 6 (2016), https://doi.org/10.1016/j.jadohealth.2016.02.004.
3. Lauren Bialystok and Lisa M. F. Anderson, *Touchy Subject* (University of Chicago Press, 2022), 90.
4. *CDC's 2022 School Health Profiles* (CDC, 2022), https://www.cdc.gov/healthyyouth/data/profiles/index.htm.
5. Amy Bleakley et al., "Public Opinion on Sex Education in US Schools," *JAMA Pediatrics* 160, no. 11 (2006), https://doi.org/10.1001/archpedi.160.11.1151.
6. *CDC's 2022 School Health Profiles* (CDC).
7. *CDC's 2022 School Health Profiles* (CDC).
8. Richard Carelli, "Court to Review Law Promoting Teen Chastity," *Washington Post*, November 9, 1987, https://www.washingtonpost.com/archive/politics/1987/11/10/court-to-review-law-promoting-teen-chastity/2adc4118-48ad-454c-89fc-354e4c42ce72/.
9. Rebekah Saul, "Whatever Happened to the Adolescent Family Life Act?," *Guttmacher Policy Review*, April 1998, https://www.guttmacher.org/gpr/1998/04/whatever-happened-adolescent-family-life-act.
10. Lord, *Condom Nation*, 167.
11. "Supreme Court Roundup; Justices Say They Will Rule on Teen-Ager Chastity Law," Associated Press, November 10, 1987, https://www.nytimes.com/1987/11/10/us/supreme-court-roundup-justices-say-they-will-rule-on-teen-ager-chastity-law.html.
12 *A History of AOUM Funding* (SIECUS, 2019), https://siecus

.org/wp-content/uploads/2019/05/AOUM-Funding-History-Re
port-5.2019.pdf.

13. Hanne Blank, *Virgin: The Untouched History* (Bloomsburg, 2007), 244.

14. *A History of AOUM Funding* (SIECUS); United States House of
Representatives Committee on Government Reform—Minority
Staff, *The Content of Federally Funded Abstinence-Only Sex Educa-
tion Programs*, December 2004, 1, https://spot.colorado.edu/~tooley
/HenryWaxman.pdf.

15. Ed Pilkington, "$1Bn 'Don't Have Sex' Campaign a Flop as Research
Shows Teenagers Ignore Lessons," *The Guardian*, April 16, 2007,
https://www.theguardian.com/world/2007/apr/16/schoolsworld
wide.usa.

16. John S. Santelli et al., "Abstinence-Only-Until Marriage: An Updated Review of U.S. Policies and Programs and Their Impact," *Journal of Adolescent Health* 61, no. 3 (2017), https://doi.org/10.1016
/j.jadohealth.2017.05.031.

17. Mathematica Policy Research, Inc., *Impacts of Four Title V, Section
510 Abstinence Education Programs* (U.S. Department of Health and
Human Services, 2007), https://files.eric.ed.gov/fulltext/ED496286
.pdf.

18. Mathematica Policy Research, Inc., *Impacts of Four Title V.*

19. Laura Duberstein Lindberg and Isaac Maddow-Zimet, "Consequences of Sex Education on Teen and Young Adult Sexual Behaviors and Outcomes," *Journal of Adolescent Health* 51, no. 4 (2012),
https://doi.org/10.1016/j.jadohealth.2011.12.028.

20. Sharon E. Hoefer and Richard Hoefer, "Worth the Wait? Consequences of Abstinence-Only Sex Education for Marginalized Students," *American Journal of Sexuality Education* 12, no. 3 (2017),
https://psycnet.apa.org/doi/10.1080/15546128.2017.1359802.

21. U.S. House of Representatives Committee on Government Reform—
Minority Staff, *The Content of Federally Funded Abstinence-Only
Sex Education Programs*, i.

22. U.S. House of Representatives Committee on Government Reform—
Minority Staff, *The Content of Federally Funded Abstinence-Only
Sex Education Programs*, i.

23. U.S. House of Representatives Committee on Government Reform—

284 | NOTES

Minority Staff, *The Content of Federally Funded Abstinence-Only Sex Education Programs*, i.

24. U.S. House of Representatives Committee on Government Reform—Minority Staff, *The Content of Federally Funded Abstinence-Only Sex Education Programs*, ii.

25. U.S. House of Representatives Committee on Government Reform—Minority Staff, *The Content of Federally Funded Abstinence-Only Sex Education Programs*, 17.

26. U.S. House of Representatives Committee on Government Reform—Minority Staff, *The Content of Federally Funded Abstinence-Only Sex Education Programs*, 17–18.

27. U.S. Government Accountability Office, *Abstinence Education: Efforts to Assess the Accuracy and Effectiveness of Federally Funded Programs*, October 2006, https://files.eric.ed.gov/fulltext/ED494026.pdf.

28. *A History of AOUM Funding* (SIECUS).

29. *A History of AOUM Funding* (SIECUS).

30. Bialystok and Andersen, *Touchy Subject*, 75.

31. *Comprehensive Sex Education: Research and Results* (Advocates for Youth, 2009), https://www.advocatesforyouth.org/wp-content/uploads/storage/advfy/documents/fscse.pdf.

32. Eva S. Goldfarb and Lisa D. Lieberman, "Three Decades of Research: The Case for Comprehensive Sex Education," *Journal of Adolescent Health* 68, no. 1 (2021), https://doi.org/10.1016/j.jadohealth.2020.07.036.

33. *Comprehensive Sex Education: Research and Results* (Advocates for Youth).

34. *Results from the OAH Teen Pregnancy Prevention Program*, Office of Adolescent Health, 2020, https://opa.hhs.gov/sites/default/files/2020-07/tpp-results-factsheet.pdf.

35. *Teen Birth Rates for Urban and Rural Areas in the United States, 2007–2015*, CDC, November 2016, https://www.jahonline.org/article/S1054-139X(16)30172-0/pdf.

36. Laura Lindberg et al., "Understanding the Decline in Adolescent Fertility in the United States, 2007–2012," *Journal of Adolescent Health* 59, no. 5 (2016), https://doi.org/10.1016/j.jadohealth.2016.06.024.

37. Jane Kay, "Trump Administration Suddenly Pulls Plug on Teen Pregnancy Prevention Programs," *Reveal*, July 14, 2017, https://revealnews.org/article/trump-administration-suddenly-pulls-plug-on-teen-pregnancy-programs/#:~:text=The%20Trump%20administration%20has%20quietly,Angeles%20and%20Johns%20Hopkins%20University.

38. Jessica Boyer, "New Name, Same Harm: Rebranding of Federal Abstinence-Only Programs," *Guttmacher Policy Review*, 2018, https://www.guttmacher.org/gpr/2018/02/new-name-same-harm-rebranding-federal-abstinence-only-programs.

39. *Federally Funded Abstinence-Only Programs: Harmful and Ineffective*, Guttmacher Institute, May 2021, https://www.guttmacher.org/fact-sheet/abstinence-only-programs.

40. Ema O'Connor, "In Closed-Door U.N. Meetings, Trump Administration Officials Pushed Abstinence for International Women's Health Programs," *Buzzfeed News*, April 17, 2018, https://www.buzzfeednews.com/article/emaoconnor/un-meeting-trump-administration-abstinence#.kw8ln711a.

41. Blank, *Virgin*, 244.

42. *Federal Funding Overview: Fiscal Year 2023* (SIECUS, 2023), 3, https://siecus.org/wp-content/uploads/2022/05/FY22-Federal-Funding-Overview.pdf.

43. *Federal Funding Overview: Fiscal Year 2023* (SIECUS), 3.

44. *Teen Birth Trends: In Brief*, Congressional Research Service, August 28, 2024, https://crsreports.congress.gov/product/pdf/R/R45184.

45. Apoorva Mandavilli, "Syphilis Is Soaring in the U.S.," *New York Times*, January 30, 2024, https://www.nytimes.com/2024/01/30/health/syphilis-cdc.html#:~:text=The%20rates%20soared%20in%20every,51%20infant%20deaths%20in%202022.

46. Tressie McMillan Cottom, "Why I Keep My Eyes—and My Mind—on the South," *New York Times*, April 11, 2023, https://www.nytimes.com/2023/04/11/opinion/columnists/tennessee-house-nashville-shooting.html.

47. Amanda Jean Stevenson et al., "Effect of Removal of Planned Parenthood from Texas Women's Health Program," *New England Journal of Medicine* 374, no. 9 (2016), https://doi.org/10.1056

286 | NOTES

/NEJMsa1511902; Eleanor Klibanoff, "Even After Planned Parenthood Stopped Performing Abortions, Texas Is Still Trying to Shut It Down," *Texas Tribune*, August 15, 2023, https://www.texastribune.org/2023/08/15/texas-abortion-planned-parenthood-lawsuit/#:~:text=Finally%2C%20in%20March%202021%2C%20the,Parenthood%20from%20the%20Medicaid%20program.

48. Alexa Ura et al., "Here Are the Texas Abortion Clinics That Have Closed Since 2013," *Texas Tribune*, June 28, 2016, https://www.texastribune.org/2016/06/28/texas-abortion-clinics-have-closed-hb2-passed-2013/.

49. Suzanne O. Bell et al., "Texas' 2021 Ban on Abortion in Early Pregnancy and Changes in Live Births," *JAMA* 330, no. 3 (2023), https://doi.org/10.1001/jama.2023.12034.

50. Eleanor Klibanoff, "Nearly 10,000 More Babies Born in Nine Months Under Texas' Restrictive Abortion Law, Study Finds," *Texas Tribune*, June 30, 2023, https://www.texastribune.org/2023/06/30/texas-abortion-johns-hopkins-study/#:~:text=Texas%20Right%20to%20Life%2C%20the,to%20Life%20president%20John%20Seago.

51. *Teen Birth Rate Data* (Healthy Futures of Texas, 2023), https://hftx.org/resources/teen-birth-in-texas/.

52. *Title V State Sexual Risk Avoidance Education (SRAE) Grantees FY2020 & FY2021*, Family and Youth Services Bureau, August 2, 2021, https://www.acf.hhs.gov/fysb/title-v-state-sexual-risk-avoidance-education-srae-grantees-fy2020-fy2021.

53. Lawrence Wright, "America's Future Is Texas," *New Yorker*, July 3, 2017, https://www.newyorker.com/magazine/2017/07/10/americas-future-is-texas.

54. William Martin, "The Guardians Who Slumbereth Not," *Texas Monthly*, November 1982, https://www.texasmonthly.com/news-politics/the-guardians-who-slumbereth-not/.

55. Douglas Martin, "Norma Gabler, Leader of Crusade on Textbooks, Dies at 84," *New York Times*, August 1, 2007, https://www.nytimes.com/2007/08/01/education/01gabler.html.

56. Martin, "The Guardians Who Slumbereth Not."

57. Andrew Hartman, *A War for the Soul of America: A History of the Culture Wars*, 2nd ed. (University of Chicago Press, 2019), 77.

NOTES | 287

58. Dena Kleiman, "Influential Couple Scrutinize Books for 'Anti-Americanism,'" *New York Times*, July 14, 1981, https://www.nytimes.com/1981/07/14/science/education.html.

59. Kleiman, "Influential Couple Scrutinize Books for 'Anti-Americanism.'"

60. Martin, "The Guardians Who Slumbereth Not."

61. Martin, "The Guardians Who Slumbereth Not."

62. Martin, "Norma Gabler, Leader of Crusade on Textbooks, Dies at 84."

63. Martin, "The Guardians Who Slumbereth Not."

64. Associated Press, "Health Class No Longer Required In Texas High Schools," *HuffPost*, August 8, 2009, https://www.huffpost.com/entry/health-class-no-longer-re_n_227805.

65. Pooja Salhotra and Sneha Dey, "For Teens in Deep East Texas, Accessing Sex Education and Contraception Is Next to Impossible," *Texas Tribune*, January 4, 2023, https://www.texastribune.org/2023/01/04/east-texas-teen-pregnancy-sex-education/#:~:text=For%20teens%20in%20Deep%20East,birth%20rates%20in%20the%20state.

66. *Conspiracy of Silence: Sexuality Education in Texas Public Schools in 2015–16* (Texas Freedom Network Education Fund, 2017), https://tfn.org/sex-ed/Sex%20Ed%20Executive%20Summary.pdf.

67. CDC, *Youth Risk Behavior Survey: Texas 2021 and United States 2021 Results*, 2023, https://nccd.cdc.gov/Youthonline/App/Results.aspx?TT=G&OUT=0&SID=HS&QID=QQ&LID=TX&YID=2021&LID2=XX&YID2=2021&COL=T&ROW1=N&ROW2=N&HT=QQ&LCT=LL&FS=S1&FR=R1&FG=G1&FA=A1&FI=I1&FP=P1&FSL=S1&FRL=R1&FGL=G1&FAL=A1&FIL=I1&FPL=P1&PV=&TST=True&C1=TX2021&C2=XX2021&QP=G&DP=1&VA=CI&CS=Y&SYID=&EYID=&SC=DEFAULT&SO=ASC&PF=1.

68. Anthony Paik et al., "Broken Promises: Abstinence Pledging and Sexual and Reproductive Health," *Journal of Marriage and Family* 78, no. 2 (2016), https://doi.org/10.1111/jomf.12279.

69. Paik, "Broken Promises," 13.

70. Janet Elise Rosenbaum, "Patient Teenagers? A Comparison of the Sexual Behavior of Virginity Pledgers and Matched Nonpledgers," *Pediatrics* 123, no. 1 (2009), https://doi.org/10.1542%2Fpeds.2008-0407.

71. Elena Rivera, "Texas Got a Sex Education Update Two Years Ago.

288 | NOTES

Advocates Say There Are Still Gaps," *KERA News*, February 21, 2024, https://www.keranews.org/health-wellness/2024-02-21/health-edu cation-std-texas.

72. *Evaluation of the Opt-In Sexual Health and Abuse Prevention Education Policy in Texas* (The University of Texas Health Science Center at Houston, Healthy Futures Texas, 2023), https://hftx.org/wp-content /uploads/2023/05/Opt_in_Eval_Report_FINAL-compressed.pdf.

73. *Evaluation of the Opt-In Sexual Health* (The University of Texas Health Science Center at Houston, Healthy Futures Texas).

74. Shannon Najmabadi and Carla Astudillo, "An Anti-Abortion Program Will Receive $100 Million in the Next Texas Budget, but There's Little Data on What's Being Done with the Money," *Texas Tribune*, June 8, 2021, https://www.texastribune.org/2021/06/08 /texas-abortion-budget/.

75. Najmabadi and Astudillo, "An Anti-Abortion Program Will Receive $100 Million."

76. Carter Sherman, "States to Award Anti-Abortion Centers Roughly $250m in Post-*Roe* Surge," *The Guardian*, December 28, 2023, https://www.theguardian.com/world/2023/dec/28/anti-abortion -pregnancy-crisis-centers-taxpayer-money-roe.

77. Sarah Butrymowicz and Caroline Preston, "'They Just Tried to Scare Us': Anti-Abortion Centers Teach Sex Ed Inside Some Texas Public Schools," Hechinger Report, October 2, 2023, https://hechinger report.org/they-just-tried-to-scare-us-how-anti-abortion-centers -teach-sex-ed-inside-public-schools/.

78. Butrymowicz and Preston, "'They Just Tried to Scare Us.'"

79. *Hope for a New Generation* (Charlotte Lozier Institute, 2022), https://lozierinstitute.org/wp-content/uploads/2023/12/Pregnancy -Center-Update_2022.pdf.

80. Sherman, "States to Award Anti-Abortion Centers."

3. CLASSROOM CULTURE WARS

1. *Public Poll Opinion Results* (The Texas Campaign to Prevent Teen Pregnancy, 2020), https://www.texasisready.org/_files/ugd /fae15f_24a607bc07df4f149d8f1cd6cad7dce6.pdf.

NOTES | 289

2. "Texas Education Agency, Committee of the Full Board, Tuesday, November 17, 2020, 9:00 a.m.," Austin, Texas, online video, https://www.adminmonitor.com/tx/tea/committee_of_the_full_board/20201117/.
3. "Texas Education Agency, Committee of the Full Board, Tuesday, November 17, 2020, 9:00 a.m."
4. *School Climate for LGBTQ+ Students in Texas* (GLSEN, 2021), https://maps.glsen.org/wp-content/uploads/2023/02/GLSEN_2021 _NSCS_State_Snapshots_TX.pdf.
5. *School Climate for LGBTQ+ Students in Texas* (GLSEN).
6. *2023 U.S. National Survey on the Mental Health of LGBTQ Young People* (The Trevor Project, 2023), https://www.thetrevorproject.org /survey-2023/assets/static/05_TREVOR05_2023survey.pdf.
7. *The Impact of Stigma and Discrimination Against LGBT People in Texas* (The Williams Institute, University of California, Los Angeles School of Law, 2017), https://williamsinstitute.law.ucla.edu/publi cations/impact-lgbt-discrimination-tx/.
8. "State Board of Education, Austin, Texas, September 11, 2020, 9:00 a.m.," William B. Travis Building, Room 1-104, 1701 N. Congress Avenue, online video, https://www.adminmonitor.com/tx/tea/general _meeting/202009112/2/.
9. Nicole Carr and Lucas Waldron, "How School Board Meetings Became Flashpoints for Anger and Chaos Across the Country," ProPublica, July 19, 2023, https://projects.propublica.org/school -board-meetings-flashpoints-for-anger-chaos/.
10. "Texas Education Agency, Committee of the Full Board, Tuesday, November 17, 2020, 9:00 a.m."
11. *America's Censored Classrooms* (PEN America, 2023), https://pen .org/report/americas-censored-classrooms-2023/.
12. *Educational Intimidation* (PEN America, 2023), https://pen.org/re port/educational-intimidation/.
13. *Missouri Book Bans in Response to SB 775* (PEN America, 2022), https://docs.google.com/spreadsheets/d/1AVW8q-B4uSZIJ3mLqc 5tY8DZyojI1KLIVBQzSCb7lbg/edit?gid=0#gid=0.
14. Erica Hellerstein, "Missouri Librarians Are Risking Jail Time—for Doing Their Jobs," Coda, March 30, 2023, https://www.codastory .com/rewriting-history/missouri-libraries-book-ban/.

15. *Educational Intimidation* (PEN America).
16. *Banned in the USA: The Mounting Pressure to Censor* (PEN America, 2023), https://pen.org/report/book-bans-pressure-to-censor/.
17. *Banned in the USA: The Mounting Pressure to Censor* (PEN America).
18. *Banned in the USA: State Laws Supercharge Book Suppression in Schools* (PEN America, 2023), https://pen.org/report/banned-in-the-usa-state-laws-supercharge-book-suppression-in-schools/.
19. Elizabeth A. Harris, "Utah Bans 13 Books from All Public Schools," *New York Times*, August 6, 2024, https://www.nytimes.com/2024/08/06/books/utah-public-school-book-ban.html.
20. Annette Choi, "State Lawmakers Have Targeted Restricting Sex Education Since the Dobbs Ruling, Especially in States Banning Abortion," *CNN*, May 16, 2024, https://www.cnn.com/2024/05/16/politics/sex-education-bills-united-states-dg/index.html.
21. *America's Censored Classrooms* (PEN America).
22. *School Climate for LGBTQ+ Students in Florida* (GLSEN, 2021), https://maps.glsen.org/wp-content/uploads/2023/02/GLSEN_2021_NSCS_State_Snapshots_FL.pdf.
23. Nikki Ross, "Student Organizer of FL's 'Don't Say Gay' School Walkout Suspended from Flagler School," *Daytona Beach News-Journal*, March 3, 2022, https://www.news-journalonline.com/story/news/education/2022/03/03/dont-say-gay-flagler-palm-coast-high-school-walkout-organizer-jack-petocz-suspended-indefinitely/9344494002/.
24. Ross, "Student Organizer of FL's 'Don't Say Gay' School Walkout Suspended from Flagler School."
25. Grace Abels, "Can You 'Say Gay' in Florida Schools? Explaining New Settlement over LGBTQ+ 'Instruction," *PolitiFact*, March 15, 2024, https://www.politifact.com/article/2024/mar/14/can-you-say-gay-in-florida-schools-explaining-new/.
26. *Digital Hate: Social Media's Role in Amplifying Dangerous Lies About LGBTQ+ People* (Center for Countering Digital Hate, Human Rights Campaign, 2022), https://hrc-prod-requests.s3-us-west-2.amazonaws.com/CCDH-HRC-Digital-Hate-Report-2022-single-pages.pdf.
27. *Digital Hate* (Center for Countering Digital Hate, Human Rights Campaign).
28. Jillian Eugenios, "How 1970s Christian Crusader Anita Bryant Helped

Spawn Florida's LGBTQ Culture War," *NBC News*, April 13, 2022, https://www.nbcnews.com/nbc-out/out-news/1970s-christian-cru sader-anita-bryant-helped-spawn-floridas-lgbtq-cult-rcna24215.

29. *Digital Hate* (Center for Countering Digital Hate, Human Rights Campaign).

30. *Digital Hate* (Center for Countering Digital Hate, Human Rights Campaign).

31. *Equality Maps: LGBTQ Curricular Laws* (Movement Advancement Project, 2024), https://www.lgbtmap.org/img/maps/citations-curric ular-laws.pdf.

32. Edward Larsen, "Crusading for Parental Rights May Cloak Other Motives," *Washington Post*, September 19, 2022, https://www .washingtonpost.com/made-by-history/2022/09/19/crusading-paren tal-rights-may-cloak-other-motives/.

33. Kristin Kobes Du Mez, *Jesus and John Wayne* (Liveright, 2020), 39.

34. Kobes Du Mez, *Jesus and John Wayne*, 39.

35. Andrew Hartman, *A War for the Soul of America: A History of the Culture Wars*, 2nd ed. (University of Chicago Press, 2019), 77.

36. American Library Association (ALA), "American Library Associa-tion Releases Preliminary Data on 2023 Book Challenges," news re-lease, September 19, 2023, https://www.ala.org/news/press-releases /2023/09/american-library-association-releases-preliminary-data -2023-book-challenges.

37. ALA, "American Library Association Releases Preliminary Data."

38. Arleigh Rodgers, "Misconceptions About Its Sex and Gender Re-search Cost Kinsey Institute Public Funds," Associated Press, May 23, 2023, https://www.latimes.com/lifestyle/story/2023-05-22/kinsey -institute-experts-study-sex-gender-as-misconceptions-block-state -dollars.

39. Hannah Natanson and Moriah Balingit, "Caught in the Culture Wars, Teachers Are Being Forced from Their Jobs," *Washington Post*, June 16, 2022, https://www.washingtonpost.com/education/2022 /06/16/teacher-resignations-firings-culture-wars/.

40. Natanson and Balingit, "Caught in the Culture Wars."

41. Dana Kennedy, "Dalton Parents Enraged over 'Masturbation' Videos for First-Graders," *New York Post*, May 29, 2021, https://nypost.com

292 | NOTES

/2021/05/29/dalton-parents-enraged-over-masturbation-videos-for-1st-graders/.

42. Valeriya Safronova, "A Private-School Sex Educator Defends Her Methods," *New York Times*, July 7, 2021, https://www.nytimes.com /2021/07/07/style/sex-educator-methods-defense.html.

43. Lorena Mongelli and Jackie Salo, "Billboards Outside NYC Schools Call for 'Diversity not Indoctrination,'" *New York Post*, https://nypost .com/2021/06/07/billboards-outside-nyc-schools-diversity-not-in doctrination/.

44. "Home," Prep School Accountability, archived March 30, 2023, https://web.archive.org/web/20230330042851/https://www.prep schoolaccountability.com/.

45. "The Adverse Effects of Teen Pregnancy," Youth.gov, archived November 27, 2024, https://web.archive.org/web/20241127182155 /https://youth.gov/youth-topics/pregnancy-prevention/adverse-ef fects-teen-pregnancy.

46. Lori A. Rolleri Insignares, Tanya M. Bass, and Bill Taverner, "Sex Ed Lessons from COVID-19," *American Journal of Sexuality Education* 16, no. 4 (2021), https://doi.org/10.1080/15546128.2021.1975592; Lauren K. Cahalan and Megan A. Carpenter, "Sexuality Education During the COVID-19 Pandemic: A Qualitative Analysis of the Challenges and Changes Experienced by Sexuality Educators," *American Journal of Sexuality Education* 18, no. 4 (2023), https:// doi.org/10.1080/15546128.2023.2174235.

47. Cahalan and Carpenter, "Sexuality Education During the COVID-19 Pandemic."

48. RAINN, "COVID Update: Hotline Continues to Hear from Children, Those Concerned for Their Safety," news release, June 19, 2020, https://www.rainn.org/news/covid-update-hotline-continues -hear-children-those-concerned-their-safety.

49. Wai Han Sun et al., "Assessing Participation and Effectiveness of the Peer-Led Approach in Youth Sexual Health Education: Systematic Review and Meta-Analysis in More Developed Countries," *Journal of Sex Research* 55, no. 1 (2018), https://doi.org/10.1080 /00224499.2016.1247779.

50. Lisa M. F. Andersen, "'Kids Know What They Are Doing': Peer-Led

Sex Education in New York City," *History of Education Quarterly* 59, no. 4 (2019), 502, https://doi.org/10.1017/heq.2019.41.

51. Andersen, "'Kids Know What They Are Doing'"; Lauren Bialystok and Lisa M. F. Anderson, *Touchy Subject* (University of Chicago Press, 2022), 61–62.

52. Andersen, "'Kids Know What They Are Doing,'" 501.

53. Andersen, "'Kids Know What They Are Doing,'" 503.

54. *Current Trends Mortality Attributable to HIV Infection/AIDS—United States, 1981–1990,* CDC, January 25, 1991, https://www.cdc.gov /mmwr/preview/mmwrhtml/00001880.htm#:~:text=From%20 1981%20through%201990%2C%20100%2C777,deaths%20 were%20reported%20during%201990.

55. Randy Shilts, *And the Band Played On: Politics, People, and the AIDS Epidemic, 20th-Anniversary Edition* (Macmillan, 2007), 134.

56. Andersen, "'Kids Know What They Are Doing.'"

57. Andersen, "'Kids Know What They Are Doing.'"

58. Andersen, "'Kids Know What They Are Doing.'"

59. Jeffrey Fennelly, "Writing on the Wall of Plato's Cave," *OutWeek*, June 27, 1990, http://www.outweek.net/pdfs/ow_52.pdf.

60. *Banned in the USA: The Mounting Pressure to Censor* (PEN America).

61. Gloria Oladipo, "Florida School District Pulls Dictionaries for 'Sexual Conduct' Descriptions," *The Guardian*, January 11, 2024, https:// www.theguardian.com/us-news/2024/jan/11/florida-schools-ron-de santis-ban-books-sexual-content.

62. *Banned in the USA: Beyond the Shelves* (PEN America, 2024), https://pen.org/report/beyond-the-shelves/.

63. Ali Swenson, "Far-right Group Moms for Liberty Reports More than $2 Million in Revenue in 2022," Associated Press, November 17, 2023, https://www.pbs.org/newshour/education/far-right-group-moms -for-liberty-reports-more-than-2-million-in-revenue-in-2022#:~:text =The%20conservative%20Heritage%20Foundation's%202022,ann ual%20Salvatori%20Prize%20for%20Citizenship.

64. Elizabeth A. Harris and Alexandra Alter, "A Fast-Growing Network of Conservative Groups Is Fueling a Surge in Book Bans," *New York Times*, December 12, 2022, https://www.nytimes.com/2022/12/12 /books/book-bans-libraries.html.

294 | NOTES

65. Tim Craig, "Moms for Liberty Has Turned 'Parental Rights' into a Rallying Cry for Conservative Parents," *Washington Post*, October 15, 2021, https://www.washingtonpost.com/national/moms-for-liberty-parents -rights/2021/10/14/bf3d9ccc-286a-11ec-8831-a31e7b3de188_story .html.

66. Mary Papenfuss, "Hugging Sea Horse Book Is Too Racy For Schools, Tennessee Moms Group Says," *HuffPost*, September 25, 2021, https:// www.yahoo.com/now/hugging-sea-horse-book-too-122530595.html.

67. Katrina vanden Heuvel, "The Moms for Liberty Platform Is Extreme—and Most Voters Are Loudly Rejecting It," *The Guardian*, November 21, 2023, https://www.theguardian.com/commentisfree /2023/nov/21/moms-for-liberty-school-board-elections.

68. "Moms for Liberty," Southern Poverty Law Center, https://www.splcen ter.org/fighting-hate/extremist-files/group/moms-liberty?gclid=CjwK CAiA75itBhA6EiwAkho9e1nO1pHe0ZhffWD6Yw8Qs25HEKoffR JP0TPZD2H2uFykWTEURpSEtBoCpyAQAvD_BwE.

69. C. A. Bridges, "Who Is Christian Ziegler? Former Florida GOP Leader's Fall from Grace After Accusations," *Herald-Tribune*, May 17, 2024, https://www.heraldtribune.com/story/news/politics/2024 /05/17/christian-ziegler-republican-party-gop-florida-police-investi gation/73736365007/.

70. Bridges, "Who Is Christian Ziegler?"

71. Christopher Kane, "Youth Activists Organize 'Recall Flagler County School Board' & Campaign," *Los Angeles Blade*, August 4, 2022, https://www.losangelesblade.com/2022/08/04/youth-activists-orga nize-recall-flagler-county-school-board-campaign/.

72. Christopher Kane, "Fla. Student Activists Oust Anti-LGBTQ School Board Members," *Washington Blade*, August 26, 2022, https://www .washingtonblade.com/2022/08/26/fla-student-activists-oust-anti -lgbtq-school-board-members/.

73. Johanna Alonso, "Florida's LGBTQ+ College Students Face a Tough Choice: Stay or Go?" *Inside Higher Ed*, August 8, 2023, https://www .insidehighered.com/news/students/diversity/2023/08/08/floridas -lgbtq-college-students-debate-whether-stay-or-go.

74. Intelligent.com, "1 in 8 Incoming Freshmen Won't Attend Florida State Schools Due to DeSantis Policies," news release, March 23,

2023, https://www.intelligent.com/1-in-8-incoming-freshman-wont
-attend-florida-state-school-due-to-desantis-policies/.

75. Andrew Atterbury, "Florida Universities Are Culling Hundreds of General Education Courses," *Politico*, October 14, 2024, https://www.politico.com/news/2024/10/14/florida-university-classes-ron -desantis-00183453.

4. "THERE IS PORN OF IT. NO EXCEPTIONS."

1. *Teens and Pornography* (Commonsense Media, 2022), https://www .commonsensemedia.org/sites/default/files/research/report/2022 -teens-and-pornography-final-web.pdf.

2. Amelia M. Holstrom, "Sexuality Education Goes Viral: What We Know About Online Sexual Health Information," *American Journal of Sexuality Education* 10, no. 3 (2015), https://doi.org/10.1080 /15546128.2015.1040569.

3. *Teens and Pornography* (Commonsense Media).

4. Marie Lippmann et al., "Learning on OnlyFans: User Perspectives on Knowledge and Skills Acquired on the Platform," *Sexuality and Culture* 27 (January 2023), https://doi.org/10.1007/s12119-022 -10060-0.

5. Lippmann, "Learning on OnlyFans."

6. Samantha Cole, *How Sex Changed the Internet and the Internet Changed Sex: An Unexpected History* (Workman Publishing Company, 2022), 3.

7. Cole, *How Sex Changed the Internet*, 39–40.

8. David C. Munson Jr., "A Note on Lena," *IEEE Transactions on Image Processing* 5, no. 1 (1996), https://doi.org/10.1109/TIP.1996.8100841.

9. Linda Kinstler, "Finding Lena, the Patron Saint of JPEGs," *Wired*, January 31, 2019, https://www.wired.com/story/finding-lena-the-pa-tron-saint-of-jpegs/.

10. Amanda Lenhart et al., "Teenage Life Online," Pew Research Foundation, June 21, 2001, https://www.pewresearch.org/internet/2001 /06/21/teenage-life-online/.

11. Lenhart, "Teenage Life Online."

12. David Pogue, "Are You Taking Advantage of Web 2.0?," *New York*

Times, March 27, 2008, https://www.nytimes.com/2008/03/27/technology/personaltech/27pogue-email.html.

13. Maureen O'Connor, "Pornhub Is the Kinsey Report of Our Time," *New York*, June 12, 2017, https://www.thecut.com/2017/06/pornhub-and-the-american-sexual-imagination.html.

14. Cole, *How Sex Changed the Internet*, 164.

15. Cole, *How Sex Changed the Internet*, 164.

16. Cole, *How Sex Changed the Internet*, 168.

17. Samantha Cole, "The Ugly Truth Behind Pornhub's 'Year In Review,'" *Vice*, February 18, 2020, https://www.vice.com/en/article/wxez8y/pornhub-year-in-review-deepfake/.

18. Pornhub, "The 2019 Year in Review," news release, 2019, https://www.pornhub.com/insights/2019-year-in-review#celebrity.

19. Cole, "The Ugly Truth Behind Pornhub's 'Year In Review.'"

20. Cole, "The Ugly Truth Behind Pornhub's 'Year In Review.'"

21. University of Montreal, "Are the Effects of Pornography Negligible?," news release, December 1, 2009, https://www.sciencedaily.com/releases/2009/12/091201111202.htm.

22. Shira Tarrant, *The Pornography Industry: What Everyone Needs to Know* (Oxford University Press, 2016), 88.

23. Cole, *How Sex Changed the Internet*, 179.

24. Cole, *How Sex Changed the Internet*, 181 and 184.

25. Cole, *How Sex Changed the Internet*, 181.

26. "Vibe Check," *Business Insider*, December 14, 2023, https://www.businessinsider.com/vibe-check-gen-z-survey-data-2023-12.

27. Bijan Stephen, "Tumblr's Porn Ban Could Be Its Downfall—After All, It Happened to LiveJournal," *The Verge*, December 6, 2018, https://www.theverge.com/2018/12/6/18127869/tumblr-livejournal-porn-ban-strikethrough.

28. Hannah Ellison, "The Book Burning That Wasn't: Thousands of Works of Fiction Destroyed and No One Pays Attention," *HuffPost*, https://www.huffingtonpost.co.uk/hannah-ellison/fanfiction-the-book-burning-that-was_b_1592689.html.

29. Deanna Schwartz and Meghan Collins Sullivan, "Gen Z Is Driving Sales of Romance Books to the Top of Bestseller Lists," NPR, August 29, 2022, https://www.npr.org/2022/08/29/1119886246

/gen-z-is-driving-sales-of-romance-books-to-the-top-of-bestseller
-lists#:~:text=Social%20media%20pushing%20romance%20to%20
younger%20readers&text=Sales%20for%20authors%20whose%20
books,that%20tracks%20U.S.%20book%20sales.

30. David Frederick et al., "Differences in Orgasm Frequency Between Gay, Lesbian, Bisexual, Lesbian, Bisexual, and Heterosexual Men and Women in a U.S. National Sample," *Archives of Sexual Behavior* 47, no. 1, https://doi.org/10.1007/s10508-017-0939-z.

31. Frederick, "Differences in Orgasm Frequency."

32. Justin Lehmiller, "Male Porn Stars Are Hogging All the Orgasms, Too," *Vice*, June 23, 2017, https://www.vice.com/en/article/kzqd4e /women-are-even-being-denied-orgasms-in-porn.

33. Christine Cabrera and Amy Dana Menard, "'She Exploded into a Million Pieces': A Qualitative and Quantitative Analysis of Orgasms in Contemporary Romance Novels," *Sexuality and Culture* 17 (July 2013), http://dx.doi.org/10.1007/s12119-012-9147-0.

34. Lehmiller, "Male Porn Stars."

35. Cabrera and Menard, "'She Exploded into a Million Pieces.'"

36. Frederick, "Differences in Orgasm Frequency."

37. Elizabeth Kastor, "The Broad Sweep of Helm's Arts Amendment," *Washington Post*, August 2, 1989, https://www.washingtonpost .com/archive/lifestyle/1989/08/02/the-broad-sweep-of-helms-arts -amendment/1a5e4a4b-f65d-4643-8e64-bed0c1c7306e/.

38. Justin Lehmiller, "Gen Z Aren't Having the Sex You Think: Here's Why," Lovehoney blog, June 26, 2002, https://www.lovehoney.com /blog/gen-z-are-having-less-sex-here-is-why.html.

39. Sian Cain, "150m Shades of Grey: How the Decade's Runaway Bestseller Changed Our Sex Lives," *The Guardian*, January 15, 2020, https://www.theguardian.com/books/2020/jan/15/150m-shades-of -grey-how-the-decades-runaway-bestseller-changed-our-sex-lives.

40. Debby Herbenick et al., "Sexual Diversity in the United States: Results from a Nationally Representative Probability Sample of Adult Women and Men," *PLoS One* 12, no. 7 (2017), https://doi.org /10.1371/journal.pone.0181198.

41. Herbenick, "Sexual Diversity in the United States."

42. Debby Herbenick et al., "'It Was Scary, but Then It Was Kind

of Exciting': Young Women's Experiences with Choking During Sex," *Archives of Sexual Behavior* 51, no. 2 (2021), https://doi.org/10.1007%2Fs10508-021-02049-x.

43. Herbenick, "'It Was Scary, but Then It Was Kind of Exciting.'"
44. Herbenick, "'It Was Scary, but Then It Was Kind of Exciting.'"
45. Julia Pugachevsky, "Choking Without Consent Is a Gen Z Hookup Trend. Even If It Doesn't Bother You, It Can Be Extremely Dangerous," *Business Insider*, November 9, 2022, https://www.insider.com/choking-gen-z-sex-hookups-consent-assault-2022-10.
46. Herbenick, "'It Was Scary, but Then It Was Kind of Exciting.'"
47. Herbenick, "'It Was Scary, but Then It Was Kind of Exciting.'"
48. Anna Moore and Coco Khan, "The Fatal, Hateful Rise of Choking During Sex," *The* Guardian, July 25, 2019, https://www.theguardian.com/society/2019/jul/25/fatal-hateful-rise-of-choking-during-sex.
49. Moore and Khan, "The Fatal, Hateful Rise of Choking During Sex."
50. Moore and Khan, "The Fatal, Hateful Rise of Choking During Sex."
51. *What Can Be Consented To?* (We Can't Consent to This, 2020), https://static1.squarespace.com/static/5c49b798e749409b-fb9b6ef2/t/5e4da72920c08f54b94d91e4/1582147383202/WCCTT+briefing+sheet+2020+February.pdf.
52. Kaitlyn Tiffany, "How the Snowflakes Won," *The Atlantic*, February 1, 2022, https://www.theatlantic.com/technology/archive/2022/02/tumblr-internet-legacy-survival/621419/.
53. Rachel Leingang and Stephanie Kirchgaessner, "Kevin Roberts, Architect of Project 2025, Has Close Ties to Radical Catholic Group Opus Dei," *The Guardian*, July 26, 2024, https://www.theguardian.com/us-news/article/2024/jul/26/kevin-roberts-project-2025-opus-dei.
54. Aja Romano, "A New Law Intended to Curb Sex Trafficking Threatens the Future of the Internet as We Know It," *Vox*, July 2, 2018, https://www.vox.com/culture/2018/4/13/17172762/fosta-sesta-backpage-230-internet-freedom.
55. *Erased: The Impact of FOSTA-SESTA* (Hacking//Hustling), https://hackinghustling.org/wp-content/uploads/2020/01/HackingHustling-Erased.pdf.
56. *Sex Trafficking: Online Platforms and Federal Prosecutions*, U.S. Gov-

ernment Accountability Office, June 2021, https://www.gao.gov/as
sets/gao-21-385.pdf.

57. *Erased* (Hacking//Hustling).

58. John Hann and Sean Murphy, "Kansas Moves to Join Texas and Other States in Requiring Porn Sites to Verify People's Ages," Associated Press, March 26, 2024, https://apnews.com/article /internet-pornography-age-verification-states-2ad9939bb95c cc15126419b38067be94?ref=404media.co.

59. Samantha Cole, "Pornhub Is Now Blocked In Almost All of the U.S. South," *404 Media*, January 1, 2025, https://www.404media.co/porn hub-is-now-blocked-in-almost-all-of-the-u-s-south/.

60. Adam Gabbatt, "I Tried Mike Johnson's Favorite Anti-Porn App. It Didn't Go Well," *The Guardian*, November 21, 2023, https://www .theguardian.com/us-news/2023/nov/21/mike-johnson-covenant -eyes-anti-porn-app.

61. Gabbatt, "I Tried Mike Johnson's Favorite Anti-Porn App."

62. Samantha Cole, "Popular Porn Sites Warn Texas Users Porn Will 'Impair Brain Development,'" October 12, 2023, https://www .404media.co/popular-porn-site-warns-texas-users-health-and-hu man-services/.

63. Camille Sojit Pejcha, "Jessica Stoya and Samantha Cole on Sex, Tech, and Censorship," *Document*, June 16, 2023, https://www.docu mentjournal.com/2023/06/jessica-stoya-samantha-cole-sex-work-in ternet-censorship-online-pornography-pornhub-onlyfans/.

64. Jennifer S. Hirsch and Shamus Khan, *Sexual Citizens: A Landmark Study of Sex, Power, and Assault on Campus* (W. W. Norton & Company, 2020), xiv.

65. Hirsch and Khan, *Sexual Citizens*, xvi.

66. Hirsch and Khan, *Sexual Citizens*, xvii.

67. Emily F. Rothman et al., "A Pornography Literacy Program for Adolescents," *American Journal of Public Health*, February 2020, https://www.ncbi.nlm.nih.gov/pmc/articles/PMC6951388/pdf /AJPH.2019.305468.pdf.

68. Landen Vandenbosch and Johanna M. F. van Oosten, "The Relationship Between Online Pornography and the Sexual Objectification of Women: The Attenuating Role of Porn Literacy Education,"

Journal of Communication 67, no. 6, (2017), https://doi.org/10.1111/jcom.12341.

69. Alanna Goldstein, "Beyond Porn Literacy: Drawing on Young People's Pornography Narratives to Expand Sex Education Pedagogies," *Sex Education*, 20, no. 1 (2019), https://doi.org/10.1080/14681811.2019.1621826.

5. INTERNET SEXPLORERS

1. Jeffrey M. Jones, "LGBTQ+ Identification in U.S. Now at 7.6%," Gallup, March 13, 2024, https://news.gallup.com/poll/611864/lgbtq-identification.aspx.

2. Anna Brown, "About 5% of Young Adults in the U.S. Say Their Gender Is Different from Their Sex Assigned at Birth," Pew Research Center, June 7, 2022, https://www.pewresearch.org/short-reads/2022/06/07/about-5-of-young-adults-in-the-u-s-say-their-gender-is-different-from-their-sex-assigned-at-birth/.

3. Jean M. Twenge, "How Gen Z Changed Its Views on Gender," *Time*, May 1, 2023, https://time.com/6275663/generation-z-gender-identity/.

4. *Accelerating Acceptance* (GLAAD, 2023), https://assets.glaad.org/m/23036571f611c54/original/Accelerating-Acceptance-2023.pdf.

5. Twenge, "How Gen Z Changed Its Views on Gender."

6. Kim Parker and Ruth Igielnik, "On the Cusp of Adulthood and Facing an Uncertain Future: What We Know About Gen Z So Far," Pew Research Center, May 14, 2020, https://www.pewresearch.org/social-trends/2020/05/14/on-the-cusp-of-adulthood-and-facing-an-uncertain-future-what-we-know-about-gen-z-so-far-2/.

7. Melissa Deckman, *The Politics of Gen Z: How the Youngest Voters Will Shape Our Democracy* (Chicago University Press, 2024), 16.

8. Deckman, *The Politics of Gen Z*, 58.

9. Deckman, *The Politics of Gen Z*, 45.

10. Kimberly J. Mitchell et al., "Accessing Sexual Health Information Online: Use, Motivations and Consequences for Youth with Different Sexual Orientations," *Health Education Research* 29, no. 1 (2013), https://doi.org/10.1093%2Fher%2Fcyt071.

11. Mitchell, "Accessing Sexual Health Information Online."

12. Cultural Currents Institute, "'Am I Gay?' and Similar Google Searches Up Over 1,300%," news release, https://www.culturalcurrents.institute/insights/lgbtq-identity.

13. Kaitlyn Tiffany, "How the Snowflakes Won," *The Atlantic*, February 1, 2022, https://www.theatlantic.com/technology/archive/2022/02/tumblr-internet-legacy-survival/621419/.

14. Jones, "LGBTQ+ Identification in U.S. Now at 7.6%."

15. Cindy M. Meston and David M. Buss, "Why Humans Have Sex," *Archives of Sexual Behavior*, July 2007, https://labs.la.utexas.edu/mestonlab/files/2016/05/WhyHaveSex.pdf.

16. *2023 U.S. National Survey on the Mental Health of LGBTQ Young People* (The Trevor Project, 2023), https://www.thetrevorproject.org/survey-2023/assets/static/05_TREVOR05_2023survey.pdf.

17. *2023 U.S. National Survey on the Mental Health of LGBTQ Young People* (The Trevor Project).

18. Matthew N. Berger et al., "Social Media Use and Health and Well-being of Lesbian, Gay, Bisexual, Transgender, and Queer Youth: Systematic Review," *Journal of Medical Internet Research* 24, no. 9 (2022), https://doi.org/10.2196/38449.

19. Sarah M. Coyne et al., "Analysis of Social Media Use, Mental Health, and Gender Identity Among US Youths," *JAMA Network Open* 6, no. 7 (2023), https://doi.org/10.1001/jamanetworkopen.2023.24389.

20. Coyne, "Analysis of Social Media Use, Mental Health, and Gender Identity Among US Youths."

21. Jessica N. Fish et al., "'I'm Kinda Stuck at Home with Unsupportive Parents Right Now': LGBTQ Youths' Experiences With COVID-19 and the Importance of Online Support," *Journal of Adolescent Health* 67, no. 3 (2020), https://doi.org/10.1016/j.jadohealth.2020.06.002.

22. Fish, "'I'm Kinda Stuck at Home with Unsupportive Parents Right Now.'"

23. *Fast Facts: HIV in the United States*, CDC, April 22, 2024, https://www.cdc.gov/hiv/data-research/facts-stats/index.html.

24. Phillip L. Hammack et al., "Making Meaning of the Impact Pre-Exposure Prophylaxis (PrEP) on Public Health and Sexual Culture: Narratives of Three Generations of Gay and Bisexual Men," *Archives of Sexual Behavior* 48, no. 4 (2019), https://doi.org/10.1007%2Fs10508-019-1417-6.

25. Hammack, "Making Meaning of the Impact Pre-Exposure Prophylaxis."

26. Erik D. Storholm et al., "Risk Perception, Sexual Behaviors, and PrEP Adherence Among Substance-Using Men Who Have Sex with Men: A Qualitative Study," *Prevention Science* 18, no. 6 (2017), https://doi.org/10.1007%2Fs11121-017-0799-8.

27. Gabrial Arana, "PrEP: The Story of a Sexual Revolution," *Them*, March 16, 2020, https://www.them.us/story/prep-the-story-of-a-sexual-revolution.

28. Sakina Z. Kudrati et al., "Social Media and PrEP: A Systematic Review of Social Media Campaigns to Increase PrEP Awareness and Uptake Among Young Black and Latinx MSM and Women," *AIDS and Behavior* 25, no. 12 (2021), https://doi.org/10.1007/s10461-021-03287-9.

29. Andrew Hartman, *A War for the Soul of America: A History of the Culture Wars*, 2nd ed. (University of Chicago Press, 2019), 21.

30. Aja Romano, "The Demise of a Social Media Platform: Tracking LiveJournal's Decline," *Daily Dot*, June 2, 2021, https://www.dailydot.com/culture/livejournal-decline-timeline/.

31. Aja Romano, "Puritanism Took Over Online Fandom—and Then Came for the Rest of the Internet," *Vox*, May 24, 2023, https://www.vox.com/culture/23733213/fandom-purity-culture-what-is-proship-antiship-antifandom.

32. Angela Nagle, *Kill All Normies: Online Culture Wars from 4Chan and Tumblr to Trump and the Alt-Right* (Zer0 Books, 2017), 69.

33. Nagle, *Kill All Normies*, 70.

34. Adrienne Rich, "Compulsory Heterosexuality and Lesbian Existence," *Journal of Women's History* 15, no. 3, Autumn 2003, https://posgrado.unam.mx/musica/lecturas/Maus/viernes/AdrienneRichCompulsoryHeterosexuality.pdf.

35. Rich, "Compulsory Heterosexuality."

36. Lindsay Kang-Miller, "How Tumblr's 'Am I a Lesbian?' Google Doc Became Internet Canon," *Vice*, June 25, 2020, https://www.vice.com/en/article/am-i-a-lesbian-tumblr-google-doc-internet-canon/.

37. Jones, "LGBTQ+ Identification in U.S. Now at 7.6%."

38. Ryan J. Waston et al., "Evidence of Diverse Identities in a Large

National Sample of Sexual and Gender Minority Adolescents," *Journal of Research on Adolescence* 30, suppl. 2 (2020), https://doi.org/10.1111/jora.12488.

39. *PRRI Generation Z Fact Sheet* (PRRI, 2024), https://www.prri.org/spotlight/prri-generation-z-fact-sheet/.

40. *Newsweek* Staff, "What Is Queer Nation?" *Newsweek*, August 11, 1991, https://www.newsweek.com/what-queer-nation-202866.

41. Alessandra Stanley, "Militants Back 'Queer,' Shoving 'Gay' the Way of 'Negro,'" *New York Times*, April 6, 1991, https://www.nytimes.com/1991/04/06/nyregion/militants-back-queer-shoving-gay-the-way-of-negro.html.

42. Stanley, "Militants Back 'Queer,' Shoving 'Gay' the Way of 'Negro.'"

43. Cathy J. Cohen, "Punks, Bulldaggers, and Welfare Queens," *Journal of Lesbian and Gay Studies*, May 1997, https://doi.org/10.1215/10642684-3-4-437.

44. Cohen, "Punks, Bulldaggers, and Welfare Queens."

45. Cohen, "Punks, Bulldaggers, and Welfare Queens."

6. THE FUCKABILITY TRAP

1. Kari Paul, "'It Spreads like a Disease': How Pro-Eating-Disorder Videos Reach Teens on TikTok," *The Guardian*, October 16, 2021, https://www.theguardian.com/technology/2021/oct/16/tiktok-eating-disorder-thinspo-teens.

2. Paul, "'It Spreads like a Disease.'"

3. Carolina Public Health, "Survey Finds Disordered Eating Behaviors Among Three out of Four American Women," news release, September 26, 2008, https://sph.unc.edu/cphm/carolina-public-health-magazine-accelerate-fall-2008/survey-finds-disordered-eating-behaviors-among-three-out-of-four-american-women-fall-2008/.

4. Emily Weinstein and Carrie James, *Behind Their Screens: What Teens Are Facing (and Adults Are Missing)* (MIT Press, 2022), 18.

5. Amia Srinivasan, *The Right to Sex* (Farrar, Straus and Giroux, 2021), 103.

6. *Social Media and Youth Mental Health: The U.S. Surgeon General's Advisory* (Office of the Surgeon General, 2023), 9, https://www.hhs.gov/sites/default/files/sg-youth-mental-health-social-media-advisory.pdf.

304 | NOTES

7. Vivek Murthy, "Surgeon General: Why I'm Calling for a Warning Label on Social Media Platforms," *New York Times*, June 17, 2024, https://www.nytimes.com/2024/06/17/opinion/social-media-health-warning.html.

8. Sophia Choukas-Bradley et al., "The Perfect Storm: A Developmental-Sociocultural Framework for the Role of Social Media in Adolescent Girls' Body Image Concerns and Mental Health," *Clinical Child and Family Psychology Review* 25, no. 4 (2022), https://doi.org/10.1007/s10567-022-00404-5.

9. Choukas-Bradley et al., "The Perfect Storm."

10. Weinstein and James, *Behind Their Screens*, 41.

11. Elizabeth A. Daniels et al., "Becoming an Object: A Review of Self-Objectification in Girls," *Body Image* 33 (2020), https://doi.org/10.1016/j.bodyim.2020.02.016.

12. Lara Winn and Randolph Cornelius, "Self-Objectification and Cognitive Performance: A Systematic Review of the Literature," *Frontiers in Psychology* 11 (January 2020), https://doi.org/10.3389%2Ffpsyg.2020.00020.

13. Srinivasan, *The Right to Sex*, 103.

14. Choukas-Bradley, "The Perfect Storm."

15. Salomé Wilfred and Jennifer Lundgren, "The Double Consciousness Body Image Scale," *International Disorder of Eating Disorders* 54, no. 10 (2021), https://doi.org/10.1002/eat.23581.

16. Srinivasan, *The Right to Sex*, 104.

17. Savannah R. Roberts et al., "Incorporating Social Media and Muscular Ideal Internalization into the Tripartite Influence Model of Body Image: Towards a Modern Understanding of Adolescent Girls' Body Dissatisfaction," *Body Image* 41 (2022), https://doi.org/10.1016/j.bodyim.2022.03.002.

18. Daniels, "Becoming an Object."

19. Daniels, "Becoming an Object."

20. Mariska Kleemans et al., "Picture Perfect: The Direct Effect of Manipulated Instagram Photos on Body Image in Adolescent Girls," *Media Psychology* 21, no. 1 (2018), https://doi.org/10.1080/15213269.2016.1257392.

21. Jia Tolentino, "The Age of Instagram Face," *New Yorker*, December

12, 2019, https://www.newyorker.com/culture/decade-in-review/the-age-of-instagram-face.

22. Choukas-Bradley, "The Perfect Storm."

23. *2022 ASPS Procedural Statistics Release* (American Society of Plastic Surgeons, 2023), https://www.plasticsurgery.org/documents/News/Statistics/2022/plastic-surgery-statistics-report-2022.pdf.

24. Kaitlyn Frey, "Kylie Jenner's Nurse Confirms the Star Gets Lips Fillers, but No Other Cosmetic Injectables," *People*, October 18, 2018, https://people.com/style/kylie-jenners-nurse-confirms-she-only-gets-lip-fillers/.

25. Sophie Caldwell, "Kylie Jenner Admits She Had Breast Augmentation at 19, Would Be 'Heartbroken' if Daughter Did the Same," *Today*, July 27, 2023, https://www.today.com/popculture/kylie-jenner-confirms-breast-augmentation-rcna96644.

26. Rob Haskell, "Bella from the Heart: On Health Struggles, Happiness, and Everything in Between," *Vogue*, April 2022, https://www.vogue.com/article/bella-hadid-cover-april-2022.

27. Haskell, "Bella from the Heart."

28. "Why Are Eating Disorders on the Rise?," Center for Women's Health, Oregon Health & Science University, https://www.ohsu.edu/womens-health/why-are-eating-disorders-rise.

29. Georgia Wells et al., "Facebook Knows Instagram Is Toxic for Teen Girls, Company Documents Show," *Wall Street Journal*, September 14, 2021, https://www.wsj.com/articles/facebook-knows-instagram-is-toxic-for-teen-girls-company-documents-show-11631620739?mod=hp_lead_pos7&mod=article_inline; data from Teen Mental Health Deep Dive, published by *The Wall Street Journal*, September 29, 2021, https://s.wsj.net/public/resources/documents/teen-mental-health-deep-dive.pdf.

30. Wells, "Facebook Knows Instagram Is Toxic for Teen Girls."

31. Wells, "Facebook Knows Instagram Is Toxic for Teen Girls."

32. Wells, "Facebook Knows Instagram Is Toxic for Teen Girls."

33. Mark Zuckerberg, Facebook, October 5, 2021, https://www.facebook.com/zuck/posts/10113961365418581.

34. Ken Dixon, *CT Insider*, "Richard Blumenthal's Net Worth Is Likely Far Ahead of Challenger Leora Levy in U.S. Senate Race," November

5, 2022, https://www.ctinsider.com/politics/article/blumenthal-levy-us-senate-race-wealth-17559050.php.

35. Jessica Strübel and Trent A. Petrie, "Tinder Use, Gender, and the Psychosocial Functioning of Young Adults," *Journal of Social Media in Society* 11, no. 2 (2022), https://thejsms.org/index.php/JSMS/article/view/1025; Alvin Tran et al., "Dating App Use and Unhealthy Weight Control Behaviors Among a Sample of U.S. Adults: A Cross-Sectional Study," *Journal of Eating Disorders* 7, no. 16 (2019), https://doi.org/10.1186/s40337-019-0244-4.

36. Tran, "Dating App Use."

37. Michael J. Rosenfeld and Reuben J. Thomas, "Searching for a Mate: The Rise of the Internet as a Social Intermediary," *American Sociological Review* 77, no. 4 (2012), https://doi.org/10.1177/0003122412448050.

38. Elizabeth F. Emens, "Intimate Discrimination: The State's Role in the Accidents of Sex and Love," *Harvard Law Review* 122, no. 5 (2009), https://harvardlawreview.org/print/vol-122/intimate-discrimination-the-states-role-in-the-accidents-of-sex-and-love/.

39. Elizabeth E. Bruch and M. E. J. Newman, "Aspirational Pursuit of Mates in Online Dating Markets," *Science Advances* 4, no. 8 (2018), https://www.science.org/doi/full/10.1126/sciadv.aap9815.

40. Bruch and Newman, "Aspirational Pursuit of Mates."

41. Alexis Kleinman, "Black People and Asian Men Have a Much Harder Time Dating on OKCupid," *HuffPost*, September 12, 2014, https://www.huffpost.com/entry/okcupid-race_n_5811840.

42. Kleinman, "Black People and Asian Men Have a Much Harder Time Dating on OKCupid"; "Race and Attraction, 2009–2014," September 9, 2014, archived July 3, 2019, https://web.archive.org/web/20190703033241/https://theblog.okcupid.com/race-and-attraction-2009-2014-107dcbb4f060.

43. Jevan Hutson et al., "Debiasing Desire: Addressing Bias & Discrimination on Intimate Platforms," *Proceedings of the ACM on Human-Computer Interaction* 2, no. CSCW (2018), https://doi.org/10.1145/3274342.

44. Christopher T. Conner, "The Gay Gayze: Expressions of Inequality on Grindr," *Sociological Quarterly* 60, no. 3, (2018), https://www.tandfonline.com/doi/full/10.1080/00380253.2018.1533394.

NOTES | 307

45. Ryan M. Wade et al., "Racialized Sexual Discrimination (RSD) and Psychological Wellbeing Among Young Sexual Minority Black Men (YSMBM) Who Seek Intimate Partners Online," *Sexuality Research and Social Policy* 19 (December 2021), https://link.springer.com/article/10.1007/s13178-021-00676-6.

46. Jessica Strübel and Trent A. Petrie, "Tinder Use, Gender, and the Psychosocial Functioning of Young Adults," *Journal of Social Media in Society* 11, no. 2 (2022), https://thejsms.org/index.php/JSMS/article/view/1025/593.

47. Rachel F. Rodgers et al., "In the Eye of the Swiper: A Preliminary Analysis of the Relationship Between Dating App Use and Dimensions of Body Image," *Eating and Weight Disorders—Studies on Anorexia, Bulimia, and Obesity* 25, no. 5, (2019), https://doi.org/10.1007/s40519-019-00754-0.

48. J. Edward Moreno, "Dating Apps Have Hit a Wall. Can They Turn Things Around?" *New York Times*, March 12, 2024, https://www.nytimes.com/2024/03/12/business/dating-apps-tinder-bumble.html.

49. Moreno, "Dating Apps Have Hit a Wall."

50. Megan A. Vendemia, "Objectifying The Body Positive Movement: The Effects of Sexualizing and Digitally-Modifying Body-Positive Images on Instagram," *Body Image* 38 (September 2021), https://doi.org/10.1016/j.bodyim.2021.03.017.

7. "OF COURSE HE'S GONNA SEND YOU DICK PICS"

1. Sheryl Gay Stolberg and Richard Péréz-Peña, "Wildly Popular App Kik Offers Teenagers, and Predators, Anonymity," *New York Times*, February 5, 2016, https://www.nytimes.com/2016/02/06/us/social-media-apps-anonymous-kik-crime.html.

2. Emily A. Vogels, *The State of Online Harassment*, Pew Research Center, January 13, 2021, https://www.pewresearch.org/internet/2021/01/13/the-state-of-online-harassment/.

3. Emily A. Vogels, *Teens and Cyberbullying 2022*, Pew Research Center, December 15, 2022, https://www.pewresearch.org/internet/2022/12/15/teens-and-cyberbullying-2022/.

4. Monica Anderson and Emily A. Vogels, "Young Women Often Face

Sexual Harassment Online—Including on Dating Sites and Apps," Pew Research Center, March 6, 2020, https://www.pewresearch.org/short-reads/2020/03/06/young-women-often-face-sexual-harassment-online-including-on-dating-sites-and-apps/.

5. Anderson and Vogels, "Young Women Often Face Sexual Harassment Online."

6. Kalyani Chadha et al., "Women's Responses to Online Harassment," *International Journal of Communication* 14, no. 1, 2020, https://ijoc.org/index.php/ijoc/article/view/11683.

7. Danielle Keats Citron, "The Continued (In)visibility of Cyber Gender Abuse," *Yale Law Journal Forum* 133 (2023), https://www.yalelawjournal.org/pdf/CitronYLJForumEssay_8ghxwtua.pdf.

8. *The National Intimate Partner and Sexual Violence Survey: 2016–2017 Report on Sexual Violence* (CDC, June 2022), https://www.cdc.gov/nisvs/documentation/nisvsReportonSexualViolence.pdf.

9. *The National Intimate Partner and Sexual Violence Survey* (CDC).

10. Chadha, "Women's Responses to Online Harassment."

11. Chadha, "Women's Responses to Online Harassment."

12. Kate Manne, *Entitled: How Male Privilege Hurts Women* (Crown, 2020), 7.

13. Camille Mori et al., "Are Youth Sexting Rates Still on the Rise? A Meta-analytic Update," *Journal of Adolescent Health* 70, no. 4 (2022), https://doi.org/10.1016/j.jadohealth.2021.10.026.

14. Camille Mori et al., "The Prevalence of Sexting Behaviors Among Emerging Adults: A Meta-Analysis," *Archives of Sexual Behavior* 49, no. 4 (2020), https://doi.org/10.1007/s10508-020-01656-4.

15. Camille Mori et al., "Association of Sexting with Sexual Behaviors and Mental Health Among Adolescents," *JAMA Pediatrics* 173, no. 8 (2019), https://doi.org/10.1001/jamapediatrics.2019.1658.

16. Mori, "Association of Sexting with Sexual Behaviors and Mental Health."

17. Evelyn Thorne et al., "Sexting in Young Adults: A Normative Sexual Behavior," *Archives of Sexual Behavior* 53, no. 2 (2023), https://doi.org/10.1007/s10508-023-02728-x.

18. Lauren A. Reed et al., "How Do Adolescents Experience Sexting in Dating Relationships? Motivations to Sext and Responses

to Sexting Requests from Dating Partners," *Children and Youth Services Review* 109 (February 2020), https://doi.org/10.1016/j.childyouth.2019.104696.

19. Weinstein and James, *Behind Their Screens*, 104.
20. Thorne, "Sexting in Young Adults."
21. Emily F. Rothman et al., "'Without Porn . . . I Wouldn't Know Half the Things I Know Now': A Qualitative Study of Pornography Use Among a Sample of Urban, Low-Income, Black and Hispanic Youth," *Journal of Sex Research* 52, no. 7 (2015), https://doi.org/10.1080/00224499.2014.960908.
22. Rothman, "'Without Porn . . .'"
23. Rothman, "'Without Porn . . .'"
24. Mori, "Are Youth Sexting Rates Still on the Rise?"; Mori, "The Prevalence of Sexting Behaviors Among Emerging Adults."
25. Maria Neomi Paradiso et al., "Image-Based Sexual Abuse Associated Factors: A Systematic Review," *Journal of Family Violence* 25 (2024), https://doi.org/10.1007/s10896-023-00557-z; Anastasia Powell et al., *Image-Based Sexual Abuse: An International Study of Victims and Perpetrators* (RMIT University, Goldsmiths University of London, Monash University), 2020, https://researchmgt.monash.edu/ws/portalfiles/portal/319918063/ImageBasedSexualAbuseReport_170220_WEB_2.pdf; Nicola Henry and Gemma Beard, "Image-Based Sexual Abuse Perpetration: A Scoping Review," *Trauma, Violence, and Abuse* 25, no. 5 (2024), https://doi.org/10.1177/15248380241266137.
26. Powell, *Image-Based Sexual Abuse*.
27. Powell, *Image-Based Sexual Abuse*.
28. Joris Van Ouytsel et al., "A First Investigation into Gender Minority Adolescents' Sexting Experiences," *Journal of Adolescent Health* 85 (2020), https://doi.org/10.1016/j.adolescence.2020.09.007.
29. Dora Bianchi et al., "A Bad Romance: Sexting Motivations and Teen Dating Violence," *Journal of Interpersonal Violence* 36, nos. 13–14 (2018), https://doi.org/10.1177/0886260518817037.
30. Steven Roberts et al., "Navigating the Tensions of Normative Masculinity: Homosocial Dynamics in Australian Young Men's Discussions of Sexting Practices," *Cultural Sociology* 15, no. 1 (2020), https://doi.org/10.1177/1749975520925358.

31. Roberts, "Navigating the Tensions of Normative Masculinity."
32. Roberts, "Navigating the Tensions of Normative Masculinity."
33. Jennifer S. Hirsch and Shamus Khan, *Sexual Citizens: A Landmark Study of Sex, Power, and Assault on Campus* (W. W. Norton & Company, 2020), xvi.
34. Weinstein and James, *Behind Their Screens*, 110.
35. "Frequently Asked Questions," Cyber Civil Rights Initiative, https://cybercivilrights.org/faqs/#current-state-laws.
36. "Frequently Asked Questions," Cyber Civil Rights Initiative.
37. *State Sexting Laws* (Cyberbullying Research Center, 2022), https://cyberbullying.org/pdfs/2022_Sexting_Laws.pdf.
38. Citron, "The Continued (In)visibility of Cyber Gender Abuse."
39. Justin W. Patchin and Sameer Hinduja, "Sextortion Among Adolescents: Results from a National Survey of U.S. Youth," *Sexual Abuse*, 2020, https://doi.org/10.1177/1079063218800469.
40. Monica Anderson and Skye Toor, "How Social Media Users Have Discussed Sexual Harassment Since #MeToo Went Viral," Pew Research Center, October 11, 2018, https://www.pewresearch.org/short-reads/2018/10/11/how-social-media-users-have-discussed-sexual-harassment-since-metoo-went-viral/.
41. "Read Christine Blasey Ford's Prepared Statement," *New York Times*, September 26, 2018, https://www.nytimes.com/2018/09/26/us/politics/christine-blasey-ford-prepared-statement.html.
42. Bryce Covert, "Years After #MeToo, Defamation Cases Increasingly Target Victims Who Can't Afford to Speak Out," *The Intercept*, July 22, 2023, https://theintercept.com/2023/07/22/metoo-defamation-lawsuits-slapp/#:~:text=for%20The%20Intercept-,Years%20After%20%23MeToo%2C%20Defamation%20Cases%20Increasingly%20Target%20Victims%20Who%20Can,out%20in%20the%20first%20place.
43. Citron, "The Continued (In)visibility of Cyber Gender Abuse."
44. *Online Harassment, Digital Abuse, and Cyberstalking in America* (Data and Society Research Institute, Center for Innovative Public Health Research, 2016), https://www.datasociety.net/pubs/oh/Online_Harassment_2016.pdf.
45. *Online Harassment, Digital Abuse, and Cyberstalking in America*

(Data and Society Research Institute, Center for Innovative Public Health Research).

46. Citron, "The Continued (In)visibility of Cyber Gender Abuse."

47. Zack Beauchamp, "Our Incel Problem," *Vox*, April 23, 2019, https://www.vox.com/the-highlight/2019/4/16/18287446/incel-definition-reddit.

48. Laura Bates, *Men Who Hate Women: From Incels to Pickup Artists: The Truth about Extreme Misogyny and How It Affects Us All* (Sourcebooks, 2021), 28.

49. Ruxandra M. Gheorghe, "'Just Be White (JBW)': Incels, Race and the Violence of Whiteness," *Feminist Inquiry in Social Work* 39, no. 1 (2023), https://doi.org/10.1177/08861099221144275.

50. Kayla Preston et al., "The Black Pill: New Technology and the Male Supremacy of Involuntarily Celibate Men," *Men and Masculinities* 24, no. 5 (2021), https://doi.org/10.1177/1097184X211017954.

51. Preston, "The Black Pill."

52. Elizabeth E. Bruch and M. E. J. Newman, "Aspirational Pursuit of Mates in Online Dating Markets," *Science Advances* 4, no. 8 (2018), https://www.science.org /doi /full /10.1126 /sciadv.aap9815.

53. OKCupid, "A Woman's Advantage," *OKCupid Dating* (blog), March 5, 2015, https://theblog.okcupid.com/a-womans-advantage -82d5074dde2d; Bruch and Newman, "Aspirational Pursuit of Mates."

54. Risa Gelles Watnick, "For Valentine's Day, 5 Facts About Single Americans," Pew Research Center, February 8, 2023, https://www.pewresearch.org/short-reads/2023/02/08/for-valentines-day-5-facts -about-single-americans/.

55. Rachel Roubein and McKenzie Beard, "Suicides Are Spiking Among Young Men," *Washington Post*, September 30, 2022, https://www.washingtonpost.com/politics/2022/09/30/suicides-are-spiking -among-young-men.

56. Judy Chu et al., "The Adolescent Masculinity Ideology in Relationships Scale," *Men and Masculinities* 8, no. 1 (2005), http://dx.doi.org /10.1177/1097184X03257453.

57. L. H. Clark et al., "Investigating the Impact of Masculinity on the Relationship Between Anxiety Specific Mental Health Literacy and

312 | NOTES

Mental Health Help-Seeking in Adolescent Males," *Journal of Anxiety Disorders* 75 (December 2020), http://dx.doi.org/https://doi.org/10.1016/j.janxdis.2020.102292.

58. CNN staff, "Transcript of Video linked to Santa Barbara Mass Shooting," May 27, 2014, https://www.cnn.com/2014/05/24/us/elliot-rodger-video-transcript/index.html.

59. Kate Mather and Matt Stevens, "UCSB Sorority Targeted by Isla Vista Shooting Suspect Urges Privacy," *Los Angeles Times*, May 25, 2014, https://www.latimes.com/local/lanow/la-me-ln-sorority-isla-vista-privacy-20140525-story.html.

60. Mather and Stevens, "UCSB Sorority Targeted by Isla Vista Shooting Suspect Urges Privacy."

61. Rachel Janik, "'I Laugh at the Death of Normies': How Incels Are Celebrating the Toronto Mass Killing," Southern Poverty Law Center, April 24, 2018, https://www.splcenter.org/hatewatch/2018/04/24/i-laugh-death-normies-how-incels-are-celebrating-toronto-mass-killing.

62. Hailey Branson-Potts and Richard Winton, "How Elliot Rodger Went from Misfit Mass Murderer to 'Saint' for Group of Misogynists—and Suspected Toronto Killer," *Los Angeles Times*, April 26, 2018, https://www.latimes.com/local/lanow/la-me-ln-elliot-rodger-incel-20180426-story.html.

63. Debbie Ging, "Alphas, Betas, and Incels: Theorizing the Masculinities of the Manosphere," *Men and Masculinities* 22, no. 4 (2019), https://doi.org/10.1177/1097184X17706401.

64. Janik, "I Laugh at the Death of Normies."

65. Bates, *Men Who Hate Women*, 321–24.

66. *Intimate Image Abuse, an Evolving Landscape* (Revenge Porn Helpline, 2020), https://revengepornhelpline.org.uk/assets/documents/intimate-image-abuse-an-evolving-landscape.pdf?_=1639471939.

67. Citron, "The Continued (In)visibility of Cyber Gender Abuse."

68. Tiffany Hsu, "Fake and Explicit Images of Taylor Swift Started on 4chan, Study Says," *New York Times*, February 5, 2024, https://www.nytimes.com/2024/02/05/business/media/taylor-swift-ai-fake-images.html.

69. Hsu, "Fake and Explicit Images of Taylor Swift Started on 4chan."

70. *A Revealing Picture: AI-Generated "Undressing" Images Move from Niche Pornography Discussion Forums to a Scaled and Monetized Online Business* (Graphika, 2023), https://public-assets.graphika.com/reports/graphika-report-a-revealing-picture.pdf?ref=404media.co.

71. *A Revealing Picture* (Graphika).

72. Jason Koebler and Emanuel Maiberg, "'What Was She Supposed to Report?': Police Report Shows How a High School Deepfake Nightmare Unfolded," *404 Media*, https://www.404media.co/what-was-she-supposed-to-report-police-report-shows-how-a-high-school-deepfake-nightmare-unfolded/.

73. Natasha Singer, "Teen Girls Confront an Epidemic of Deepfake Nudes in Schools," *New York Times*, April 8, 2024, https://www.nytimes.com/2024/04/08/technology/deepfake-ai-nudes-westfield-high-school.html.

74. Simon Usborne, "From Bone Smashing to Chin Extensions: How 'Looksmaxxing' Is Reshaping Young Men's Faces," *The Guardian*, February 15, 2024, https://www.theguardian.com/lifeandstyle/2024/feb/15/from-bone-smashing-to-chin-extensions-how-looksmaxxing-is-reshaping-young-mens-faces.

75. American Association of Orthodontists, "Does Mewing Actually Reshape Your Jaw?," news release, January 17, 2024, https://aaoinfo.org/whats-trending/is-mewing-bad-for-you/.

76. Ana Iulia Solea and Lisa Sugiura, "Mainstreaming the Blackpill: Understanding the Incel Community on TikTok," *European Journal on Criminal Policy and Research* 29 (August 2023), https://doi.org/10.1007/s10610-023-09559-5.

77. Solea and Sugiura, "Mainstreaming the Blackpill."

78. Angela Nagle, *Kill All Normies: Online Culture Wars from 4Chan and Tumblr to Trump and the Alt-Right* (Zer0 Books, 2017), 64.

79. Cameron Joseph, "JD Vance Suggests People in 'Violent' Marriages Shouldn't Get Divorced," *Vice News*, July 25, 2022, https://www.vice.com/en/article/jd-vance-suggests-people-in-violent-marriages-shouldnt-get-divorced/.

80. Alec Hernández and Summer Concepcion, "JD Vance Says 2021 Comments About Giving More Votes to People with Kids Were a

'Thought Experiment,'" *NBC News*, August 11, 2024, https://www
.nbcnews.com/politics/2024-election/jd-vance-allotting-votes-peo
ple-children-thought-experiment-rcna166140.

81. Daniel A. Cox, "Why Young Men Are Turning Against Feminism,"
Survey Center on American Life, December 14, 2023, https://www
.americansurveycenter.org/newsletter/why-young-men-are-turning
-against-feminism/.

82. Sam Wolfson, "Young Men in the U.S. Used to Lean Left. Could They
Now Hand Trump the Presidency?" *The Guardian*, August 5, 2024,
https://www.theguardian.com/us-news/ng-interactive/2024/aug
/05/young-men-voters-us-election-trump-harris.

83. Wolfson, "Young Men in the U.S. Used to Lean Left."

84. Van Badham, "When Andrew Tate and the Online Boys Obsess over
a 'Bodycount,' Girls, You Know What to Do," *The Guardian*, November 2, 2023, https://www.theguardian.com/commentisfree/2023
/nov/03/when-andrew-tate-and-the-online-manboys-obsess-over-a
-bodycount-girls-you-know-what-to-do.

85. Liza Miller, "Tate-Pilled," *New York*, March 14, 2023, https://nymag
.com/intelligencer/article/andrew-tate-jail-investigation.html.

86. "Who Is Andrew Tate? The Self-Proclaimed Misogynist Influencer,"
BBC, July 23, 2024, https://www.bbc.com/news/uk-64125045.

87. Miller, "Tate-Pilled."

88. "Andrew Tate's Trial on Charges of Rape and Human Trafficking Can
Start, a Romanian Court Rules," Associated Press, April 26, 2024,
https://www.nbcnews.com/news/world/andrew-tate-trial-charges
-rape-human-trafficking-can-start-court-rules-rcna149562.

89. Oana Marocico and Ben Milne, "'Tate Raped and Strangled Us'—
Women Talk to BBC," *BBC*, September 8, 2024, https://www.bbc
.com/news/articles/cwyje823er4o.

90. Marocico and Milne, "'Tate Raped and Strangled Us.'"

91. Nathan P. Kilmoe and Lilliana Mason, *Radical American Partisan-
ship: Mapping Violent Hostility, Its Causes, and the Consequences for
Democracy* (University of Chicago Press, 2022), 82.

92. Melissa Deckman and Erin Cassese, "Gendered Nationalism and
the 2016 US Presidential Election: How Party, Class, and Beliefs

about Masculinity Shaped Voting Behavior," *Politics and Gender* 17, no. 2 (2021), http://dx.doi.org/10.1017/S1743923X19000485.

93. Theresa K. Vescio and Nathaniel E. C. Schermerhorn, "Hegemonic Masculinity Predicts 2016 and 2020 Voting and Candidate Evaluations," *Psychological and Cognitive Sciences* 118, no. 2 (2021), https://doi.org/10.1073/pnas.2020589118.

94. Nathaniel E. C. Schermerhorn, Theresa K. Vescio, and Kathrine A. Lewis, "Hegemonic Masculinity Predicts Support for U.S. Political Figures Accused of Sexual Assault," *Social Psychological and Personality Science* 14, no. 5 (2023), https://doi.org/10.1177/19485506221077861.

95. Data from Teen Mental Health Deep Dive, published by *The Wall Street Journal*, September 29, 2021, https://s.wsj.net/public/resources/documents/teen-mental-health-deep-dive.pdf.

96. *The Youth Vote in 2024* (Center for Information & Research on Civic Learning and Engagement, Tufts University, 2024), https://circle.tufts.edu/2024-election#economy-was-the-top-youth-issue,-drove-youth-vote-for-trump.

97. Robert Downen, "What to Know About Nick Fuentes, the White Supremacist Who Was Just Hosted by a Major Texas PAC Leader," *Texas Tribune*, October 10, 2023, https://www.texastribune.org/2023/10/10/nick-fuentes-texas-meeting/.

98. Isabelle Frances-Wright and Moustafa Ayad, "'Your Body, My Choice': Hate and Harassment Towards Women Spreads Online," Digital Dispatches, Institute for Strategic Dialogue, November 8, 2024, https://www.isdglobal.org/digital_dispatches/your-body-my-choice-hate-and-harassment-towards-women-spreads-online/.

99. Meredith McGraw, "Donald Trump dined with white nationalist, Holocaust denier Nick Fuentes," *Politico*, November 25, 2022, https://www.politico.com/news/2022/11/25/trump-white-nationalist-nick-fuentes-kanye-00070825.

8. A DISTURBING RITE OF PASSAGE

1. "CMS Board of Education Meeting—March 8, 2022," Charlotte, North Carolina, Facebook video, 3:45:06, https://www.facebook.com/cmsboe/videos/cms-board-of-education-meeting-march-8-2022/952953375583803/.

2. "Silenced: Inside the Alleged Sexual Assault Cover Up in Charlotte Schools," *Vice News*, June 18, 2022, https://www.youtube.com/watch?v=m7I3qyOlFyY.

3. Carter Sherman, "Inside the Sexual Assault Scandal Plaguing a High School District," *Vice News*, June 24, 2022, https://www.vice.com/en/article/v7vg9y/inside-the-sexual-assault-scandal-plaguing-a-high-school-district.

4. Sherman, "Inside the Sexual Assault Scandal Plaguing a High School District."

5. Sherman, "Inside the Sexual Assault Scandal Plaguing a High School District."

6. *National Intimate Partner and Sexual Violence Survey: 2010 Summary Report*, (CDC, 2011), archived June 16, 2023, https://web.archive.org/web/20240509011441/https://www.cdc.gov/violenceprevention/pdf/nisvs_report2010-a.pdf.

7. Sherman, "Inside the Sexual Assault Scandal Plaguing a High School District."

8. *Errata Sheet Explainer for 2017–18 Civil Rights Data Collection Sexual Violence in K-12 Schools Issue Brief*, U.S. Department of Education Office for Civil Rights, December 2022, https://www2.ed.gov/about/offices/list/ocr/docs/sexual-violence.pdf.

9. *Errata Sheet Explainer for 2017–18 Civil Rights Data Collection Sexual Violence*, Department of Education Office for Civil Rights.

10. *Youth Risk Behavior Survey Data Summary & Trends Report: 2011–2021* (CDC, 2023), 13, https://www.cdc.gov/yrbs/dstr/pdf/YRBS_Data-Summary-Trends_Report2023_508.pdf

11. Donna St. Georgia, "Teen Girls 'Engulfed' in Violence and Trauma, CDC Finds," *Washington Post*, February 13, 2023, https://www.washingtonpost.com/education/2023/02/13/teen-girls-violence-trauma-pandemic-cdc/.

12. *Report on the AAU Climate Survey on Sexual Assault and Sexual Misconduct* (Association of American Universities, 2020), https://www.aau.edu/sites/default/files/AAU-Files/Key-Issues/Campus-Safety/Revised%20Aggregate%20report%20%20and%20appendices%201-7_(01-16-2020_FINAL).pdf.
13. *Report on the AAU Climate Survey on Sexual Assault and Sexual Misconduct* (Association of American Universities).
14. Laura P. Chen et al., "Sexual Abuse and Lifetime Diagnosis of Psychiatric Disorders: Systematic Review and Meta-analysis," *Mayo Clinic Proceedings*, July 2010, https://doi.org/10.4065%2Fmcp.2009.0583.
15. Chen, "Sexual Abuse and Lifetime Diagnosis of Psychiatric Disorders."
16. Erin O'Callaghan et al., "Navigating Sex and Sexuality after Sexual Assault: A Qualitative Study of Survivors and Informal Support Providers," *Journal of Sex Research*, October 2019, https://doi.org/10.1080%2F00224499.2018.1506731.
17. O'Callaghan, "Navigating Sex and Sexuality after Sexual Assault."
18. Joseph Shapiro, "Campus Rape Victims: A Struggle For Justice," NPR, February 24, 2010, https://www.npr.org/2010/02/24/124001493/campus-rape-victims-a-struggle-for-justice.
19. Shapiro, "Campus Rape Victims."
20. Shapiro, "Campus Rape Victims."
21. "University Officials Accused of Hiding Campus Homicide," Associated Press, June 24, 2017, https://www.nytimes.com/2007/06/24/us/24university.html.
22. Kathryn Joyce, "The Takedown of Title IX," *New York Times*, December 5, 2017, https://www.nytimes.com/2017/12/05/magazine/the-takedown-of-title-ix.html.
23. Nick Anderson, "Sexual Violence Probes at Colleges Arise from Obama Push on Civil Rights Issues," *Washington Post*, May 3, 2014, https://www.washingtonpost.com/local/education/sexual-violence-probes-at-colleges-arise-from-obama-push-on-civil-rights-issues/2014/05/03/51cf604e-d228-11e3-9e25-188ebe1fa93b_story.html.
24. Anderson, "Sexual Violence Probes at Colleges."
25. Jennifer Steinhauer and David S. Joachim, "55 Colleges Named in Federal Inquiry into Handling of Sexual Assault Cases," *New York*

318 | NOTES

Times, May 1, 2014, https://www.nytimes.com/2014/05/02/us/poli
tics/us-lists-colleges-under-inquiry-over-sex-assault-cases.html.

26. Jessica Roy, "Columbia Student Will Carry a Mattress Everywhere Until Her Alleged Rapist Is Expelled," *New York*, September 2, 2014, https://nymag.com/intelligencer/2014/09/columbia-student-art-proj ect-protests-her-rapist.html.

27. Katie J. M. Baker, "Here's the Powerful Letter the Stanford Victim Read to Her Attacker," *Buzzfeed News*, June 3, 2016, https://www .buzzfeednews.com/article/katiejmbaker/heres-the-powerful-letter -the-stanford-victim-read-to-her-ra.

28. "Stanford Sexual Assault: Chanel Miller Reveals Her Identity," *BBC*, September 2, 2019, https://www.bbc.com/news/world-us -canada-49583310.

29. Jasmine Aguilera, "House Members Unite to Read Stanford Rape Victim's Letter," *New York Times*, June 16, 2016, https://www.ny times.com/2016/06/17/us/politics/congress-stanford-letter.html.

30. Tyler Kingkade, "Males Are More Likely to Suffer Sexual Assault Than to Be Falsely Accused of It," *HuffPost*, December 8, 2014, https://www.huffpost.com/entry/false-rape-accusations_n_6290380.

31. Nicole Bedera, "Moaning and Eye Contact: Men's Use of Ambiguous Signals in Attributions of Consent to Their Partners," *Violence Against Women* 27, nos. 15–16 (2021), https://doi.org/10.1177 /1077801221992870.

32. Jack Noland and Anna Massoglia, "Betsy DeVos and Her Big-Giving Relatives Are GOP Royalty," *Open Secrets*, December 1, 2016, https:// www.opensecrets.org/news/2016/12/betsy-devos-big-giving-rela tives-family-qualifies-gop-royalty.

33. Chase Peterson-Withorn, "Inside Betsy DeVos' Billions: Just How Rich Is the Education Secretary?," *Forbes*, August 1, 2019, https:// www.forbes.com/sites/chasewithorn/2019/07/24/inside-betsy-de vos-billions-just-how-rich-is-the-education-secretary/.

34. Anya Kamentez, "DeVos Family Money Is All Over the News Right Now," NPR, August 2, 2018, https://www.npr.org/2018/08 /02/630112697/devos-family-money-is-all-over-the-news-right -now; Noland and Massoglia, "Betsy DeVos And Her Big-Giving Relatives Are GOP Royalty."

NOTES | 319

35. Kamentez, "DeVos Family Money Is All Over the News."
36. *The Truth About Attacks on Our Kids, Schools, and Diversity* (SIE-CUS, 2022), https://siecus.org/wp-content/uploads/2022/05/The-Truth-about-Attacks-on-Our-Kids-Schools-and-Diversity.pdf.
37. Elizabeth Dias and Lisa Lerer, "The Untold Story of the Network That Took Down *Roe v. Wade*," *New York Times Magazine*, May 28, 2024, https://www.nytimes.com/2024/05/28/magazine/roe-v-wade-christian-network.html.
38. Andy Kroll et al., "We Don't Talk About Leonard: The Man Behind the Right's Supreme Court Supermajority," ProPublica, October 11, 2013, https://www.propublica.org/article/we-dont-talk-about-leonard-leo-supreme-court-supermajority.
39. Erica L. Green and Sheryl Gay Stolberg, "Campus Rape Policies Get a New Look as the Accused Get DeVos's Ear," *New York Times*, July 12, 2017, https://www.nytimes.com/2017/07/12/us/politics/campus-rape-betsy-devos-title-iv-education-trump-candice-jackson.html.
40. Tyle Kingkade, "The Lawyer Who Helped Bill Clinton's Rape Accusers May Have Scored a Top Civil Rights Job Under Trump," *Buzzfeed News*, April 3, 2017, https://www.buzzfeednews.com/article/tylerkingkade/the-lawyer-who-helped-clinton-rape-accusers-may-have-scored.
41. Green and Stolberg, "Campus Rape Policies Get a New Look as the Accused Get DeVos's Ear."
42. Hélène Barthélemy, "How Men's Rights Groups Helped Rewrite Regulations on Campus Rape," *The Nation*, August 14, 2020, https://www.thenation.com/article/politics/betsy-devos-title-ix-mens-rights/.
43. Barthélemy, "How Men's Rights Groups Helped Rewrite Regulations."
44. U.S. Department of Education Office of Civil Rights (DoEd OCR), *Q&A on Campus Sexual Misconduct*, September 2107, archived June 8, 2019, https://web.archive.org/web/20190608061233/https://www2.ed.gov/about/offices/list/ocr/docs/qa-title-ix-201709.pdf.
45. U.S. DoEd OCR, *Q&A on Campus Sexual Misconduct*.
46. Stephanie Saul and Kate Taylor, "Betsy DeVos Reverses Obama-era Policy on Campus Sexual Assault Investigations," *New York Times*, September 22, 2017, https://www.nytimes.com/2017/09/22/us/devos-colleges-sex-assault.html.

320 | NOTES

47. U.S. DoEd OCR *Q&A on Campus Sexual Misconduct*.
48. U.S. Department of Education (DoEd), *Summary of Major Provisions of the Department of Education's Title IX Final Rule*, https://www.ed.gov/sites/ed/files/about/offices/list/ocr/docs/titleix-summary.pdf.
49. U.S. DoEd, *Summary of Major Provisions of the Department of Education's Title IX Final Rule*.
50. Dana Bolger et al., "A Tale of Two Title IXs: Title IX Reverse Discrimination Law and Its Trans-Substantive Implications for Civil Rights," *University of California, Davis Law Review* 55, no. 2 (2021), https://lawreview.law.ucdavis.edu/archives/55/2/tale-two-title-ixs-title-ix-reverse-discrimination-law-and-its-trans-substantive.
51. Bolger, "A Tale of Two Title IXs."
52. U.S. Sentencing Commission, *2022 Annual Report and Sourcebook of Federal Sentencing Statistics*, 49, https://www.ussc.gov/sites/default/files/pdf/research-and-publications/annual-reports-and-sourcebooks/2022/2022-Annual-Report-and-Sourcebook.pdf.
53. Bolger, "A Tale of Two Title IXs."
54. Kenny Jacoby, "Despite Men's Rights Claims, Colleges Expel Few Sexual Misconduct Offenders While Survivors Suffer," *USA Today*, https://www.usatoday.com/in-depth/news/investigations/2022/11/16/title-ix-campus-rape-colleges-sexual-misconduct-expel-suspend/7938853001/.
55. Jacoby, "Colleges Expel Few Sexual Misconduct Offenders."
56. *The Cost of Reporting: Perpetrator Retaliation, Institutional Betrayal, and Student Survivor Pushout* (Know Your IX), https://www.advocatesforyouth.org/wp-content/uploads/2024/06/Know-Your-IX-2021-Cost-of-Reporting.pdf.
57. U.S. Department of Education Office of Civil Rights (DoEd OCR), *Fiscal Year 2017 Budget Request*, https://www2.ed.gov/about/overview/budget/budget17/justifications/z-ocr.pdf.
58. U.S. DoEd OCR, *Fiscal Year 2017 Budget Request*.
59. U.S. DoEd OCR, *Fiscal Year 2017 Budget Request.*
60. Annie Waldman, "DeVos Has Scuttled More Than 1,200 Civil Rights Probes Inherited from Obama," *ProPublica*, June 21, 2018, https://www.propublica.org/article/devos-has-scuttled-more-than-1-200-civil-rights-probes-inherited-from-obama.

61. Erica L. Green, "DeVos Education Dept. Begins Dismissing Civil Rights Cases in Name of Efficiency," *New York Times*, April 20, 2018, https://www.nytimes.com/2018/04/20/us/politics/devos-education-department-civil-rights.html.

62. Waldman, "DeVos Has Scuttled More Than 1,200 Civil Rights Probes."

63. Waldman, "DeVos Has Scuttled More Than 1,200 Civil Rights Probes."

64. Tyler Kingkade, "K-12 Schools Keep Mishandling Sexual Assault Complaints. Will New Title IX Regulations Help?," *NBC News*, https://www.nbcnews.com/news/us-news/k-12-schools-keep-mishandling-sexual-assault-complaints-will-new-n1212156.

65. Naaz Modan, "Duties Deferred: The Price Students Pay When Schools Pass the Buck on Title IX," *K–12 Dive*, December 13, 2023, https://www.k12dive.com/news/title-ix-in-k12-schools-student-harassment-education-department/701814/.

66. Modan, "Duties Deferred."

67. Modan, "Duties Deferred."

68. Daniel Chang, "States Opting Out of a Federal Program That Tracks Teen Behavior as Youth Mental Health Worsens," *KFF Health News*, October 26, 2022, https://kffhealthnews.org/news/article/states-opt-out-federal-teen-mental-health-survey/; Jay Waagmeester, "Parental Permission, Survey Opt Out Will Affect Data on Young Iowans, Advocates Say," *Iowa Capital Dispatch*, June 2, 2023, https://iowacapitaldispatch.com/2023/06/02/parental-permission-survey-opt-out-will-affect-data-on-young-iowans-advocates-say/; Gracie Johnson, "Alabama Discontinues Biennial Youth Behavior Survey: A Step Back in Tracking Health Risks?" *ABC 3340 News*, October 10, 2023, https://abc3340.com/news/local/alabama-discontinues-biennial-youth-behavior-survey-a-step-back-in-tracking-health-risks; Peter Greene, "Idaho Created a Book Ban Bounty. Now a Library Is Adults Only," *Forbes*, May 24, 2024, https://www.forbes.com/sites/petergreene/2024/05/23/idaho-created-a-book-ban-bounty-now-a-library-is-adults-only/; *LGBTQ Curricular Laws* (Movement Advancement Project, 2024), https://www.lgbtmap.org/equality-maps/curricular_laws.

322 | NOTES

69. *Youth Risk Behavior Survey Data Summary & Trends Report: 2011–2021* (CDC), 53.

70. Evie Blad, "Some States Back Away from a Major Student Well-Being Survey. Why, and What It Could Mean," *Education Week*, May 5, 2022, https://www.edweek.org/leadership/some-states-back-away-from-a-major-student-well-being-survey-why-and-what-it-could-mean/2022/05.

71. Jon Brown, "Florida District Drops 'Sexualized' CDC Student Survey After Letter from DeSantis-Backed Education Official," *Fox News*, February 14, 2023, https://www.foxnews.com/politics/florida-district-drops-sexualized-cdc-student-survey-after-letter-desantis-backed-education-official.

72. Brown, "Florida District Drops 'Sexualized' CDC Student Survey."

73. U.S. Department of Education, "U.S. Department of Education Releases Final Title IX Regulations, Providing Vital Protections Against Sex Discrimination," news release, April 19, 2024, https://www.ed.gov/about/news/press-release/us-department-of-education-releases-final-title-ix-regulations-providing.

74. Katherine Knott and Johanna Alonso, "A New Title IX Era Brings Confusion and Frustration," *Inside Higher Ed*, August 1, 2014, https://www.insidehighered.com/news/students/safety/2024/08/01/enforcement-bidens-title-ix-rule-complicated-lawsuits.

75. Zach Montague, "Liberty University Fined $14 Million for Mishandling Sex Assaults and Other Crimes," *New York Times*, March 5, 2024, https://www.nytimes.com/2024/03/05/us/politics/liberty-university-fine-crime-sexual-assaults.html.

76. William Melhado, "U.S. Department of Education Reaffirms Baylor's Religious Exemption in Response to Sexual Harassment Complaints," *Texas Tribune*, August 12, 2023, https://www.texastribune.org/2023/08/12/baylor-title-ix-sexual-harassment/.

77. U.S. Department of Education Office for Civil Rights, *Baylor University Religious Exemption Response*, https://www2.ed.gov/about/offices/list/ocr/docs/t9-rel-exempt/baylor-university-response-07252023.pdf.

78. "Baylor Settles 2016 Sexual Assault Lawsuit with 15 Survivors," *ESPN News Services*, September 18, 2023, https://www.espn.com

/college-sports/story/_/id/38434684/baylor-settles-2016-sexual-as
sault-lawsuit-15-survivors.

79. "Baylor Settles 2016 Sexual Assault Lawsuit."
80. Sherman, "Inside the Sexual Assault Scandal Plaguing a High School District."
81. Sherman, "Inside the Sexual Assault Scandal Plaguing a High School District."
82. Anna Maria Della Costa, "Accused Football Player Wore Ankle Bracelet in Game. In NC, That's Allowed," *Charlotte (NC) Observer*, October 5, 2021, https://www.charlotteobserver.com/news/local/ed ucation/article254750017.html.
83. Anna Maria Della Costa, "Some Olympic High Volleyball Players Benched After Protesting Sexual Assaults," *Charlotte (NC) Observer*, October 5, 2021, https://www.charlotteobserver.com/news /local/article254774757.html.
84. Della Costa, "Some Olympic High Volleyball Players Benched."
85. Nick Ochsner, "A CMS Student Reported Being Sexually Assaulted. Then She Was Suspended," *WBTV*, November 1, 2021, https:// www.wbtv.com/2021/11/01/cms-student-reported-being-sexually -assaulted-then-she-was-suspended/.
86. Anna Maria Della Costa, "'In Over Your Head': Investigation, Performance Review Give Insight into Winston's Firing," *Charlotte (NC) Observer*, April 21, 2022, https://www.charlotteobserver.com/news /local/education/article260563152.html.
87. Ochsner, "A CMS Student Reported Being Sexually Assaulted."
88. Holly McDede, "Hundreds of SF High School Students Walk Out of Class, Demanding More Support for Sexual Assault Survivors," *KQED*, November 11, 2021, https://www.kqed.org/news/11895886 /hundreds-of-sf-high-school-students-walk-out-of-class-demanding -more-support-for-sexual-assault-survivors; Jenny Brundin, "Grandview High School Students, Angered over Delay on Alleged Sexual Assault Case, Walk Out in Protest Amid Review of Title IX," Colorado Public Radio, April 21, 2022, https://www.cpr.org/2022/04 /21/grandview-high-school-student-walk-out-sexual-assault-title-ix/; Alex Bowers and Marc Levy, "Student Walkout Around Sexual Assault Concerns Shows Persistence of Problem Since 2016 Protest,"

324 | NOTES

Cambridge Day, December 2, 2021, https://www.cambridgeday
.com/2021/12/02/student-walkout-around-sexual-assault-concerns
-shows-persistence-of-problem-since-2016-protest/; Brayden Garcia, "Hundreds of Denton ISD Students Walked Out in Protest
After Allegation of Sexual Assault on Campus," *Dallas Morning
News*, October 15, 2021, https://www.dallasnews.com/news/edu
cation/2021/10/15/hundreds-of-denton-isd-students-walked-out
-in-protest-after-allegation-of-sexual-assault-on-campus/; Hannah
Krieg, "Hundreds of Seattle Students Walk Out Demanding Better Treatment of Survivors of Sexual Assault," *The Stranger*, April
29, 2022, https://www.thestranger.com/slog/2022/04/29/72110837
/hundreds-of-seattle-students-walk-out-demanding-better-treat
ment-of-survivors-of-sexual-assault.

89. Haley Ott, "Hundreds of Stories of Sexual Assault at Colleges
around the World Shared on Anonymous Instagram Accounts," *CBS
News*, September 29, 2020, https://www.cbsnews.com/news/st-an
drews-survivors-instagram-scottish-university-sexual-assault/.

90. Anna Maria Della Costa, "This Book Caused a Stir for Some Charlotte Parents. Students Picked It," *Charlotte (NC) Observer*, March
24, 2022, https://www.charlotteobserver.com/news/local/education
/article259503159.html.

91. "CMS Board of Education Meeting—March 8, 2022"; "Silenced,"
Vice News Tonight Investigates.

92. "CMS Board of Education Meeting—March 8, 2022"; Sherman,
"Inside the Sexual Assault Scandal Plaguing a High School District";
"Silenced," *Vice News Tonight Investigates*.

93. Sherman, "Inside the Sexual Assault Scandal Plaguing a High School
District"; "Silenced," *Vice News Tonight Investigates*.

94. "Silenced," *Vice News*; Anna Maria Della Costa, "Myers Park Principal Reassigned After Title IX Complaints, Investigation," *Charlotte
(NC) Observer*, October 13, 2021, https://www.charlotteobserver.
com/news/local/education/article254975572.html.

95. Sarah Delia, "Jury Rules in Favor of CMS in Myers Park High Sexual Assault Title IX Case," *WFAE 90.7*, January 20, 2023, https://
www.wfae.org/crime-justice/2023-01-20/jury-rules-in-favor-of-cms
-in-myers-park-high-sexual-assault-title-ix-case.

96. Anna Maria Della Costa, "Former Myers Park Student Drops Title IX Lawsuit Against Charlotte-Mecklenburg Schools," *Charlotte (NC) Observer*, March 30, 2023, https://www.charlotteobserver.com/news/local/education/article273786170.html.

97. Anna Maria Della Costa, "'In Over Your Head': Investigation, Performance Review Give Insight into Winston's Firing," *Charlotte (NC) Observer*, April 19, 2022, https://www.charlotteobserver.com/news/local/education/article260563152.html#storylink=cpy.

98. Jonathan Lowe, "CMS Superintendent Search, Title IX Improvements Mark First Half of School Year," *WSOC-TV*, January 13, 2023, https://www.wsoctv.com/news/local/cms-shares-accomplishments-first-half-school-year/5PHK763EBBDUNJC7RTOR3KJCXI/.

9. *ROE* V. YOUR SEX LIFE

1. *Abortion Surveillance—United States, 2021*, CDC, 2023, https://www.cdc.gov/mmwr/volumes/72/ss/ss7209a1.htm?s_cid=ss7209a1_w#T3_down.

2. Carter Sherman, "A 23-Year-Old Had an Abortion in Secret After Roe. Here's What It Was Like," *Vice News*, July 8, 2022, https://www.vice.com/en/article/y3pdwb/self-managed-abortion-pills-arizona.

3. *Self-Care, Criminalized: The Criminalization of Self-Managed Abortion from 2000 to 2020* (If/When/How, 2023), https://ifwhenhow.org/wp-content/uploads/2023/10/Self-Care-Criminalized-2023-Report.pdf.

4. *Self-Care, Criminalized* (If/When/How).

5. Isaac Maddow-Zimet and Candace Gibson, *Despite Bans, Number of Abortions in the United States Increased in 2023*, Guttmacher Institute, March 2024, https://www.guttmacher.org/2024/03/despite-bans-number-abortions-united-states-increased-2023.

6. Carter Sherman, "'Tip of the Iceberg': US Self-Managed Abortions Soar Post-Roe, Study Shows," *The Guardian*, March 25, 2024, https://www.theguardian.com/world/2024/mar/25/self-managed-abortions-avoid-bans.

7. Lauren Ralph et al., "Self-Managed Abortion Attempts Before vs. After Changes in Federal Abortion Protections in the U.S.," *JAMA Network Open*, no. 7 (2024), https://doi.org/10.1001/jamanetworko pen.2024.24310.
8. Ralph, "Self-Managed Abortion Attempts."
9. Sherman, "A 23-Year-Old Had an Abortion in Secret After Roe. Here's What It Was Like."
10. Sherman, "A 23-Year-Old Had an Abortion in Secret After Roe. Here's What It Was Like."
11. Sherman, "A 23-Year-Old Had an Abortion in Secret After Roe. Here's What It Was Like."
12. Sherman, "A 23-Year-Old Had an Abortion in Secret After Roe. Here's What It Was Like."
13. Match Group, "SIA 13 *Roe v. Wade*," unpublished data, January 23, 2024.
14. Katrina Kimport and Krystale E. Littlejohn, "What Are We Forgetting? Sexuality, Sex, and Embodiment in Abortion Research," *Journal of Sex Research*, June 2021, https://doi.org/10.1080/00224499 .2021.1925620.
15. Kimport and Littlejohn, "What Are We Forgetting?"
16. Kimport and Littlejohn, "What Are We Forgetting?"
17. Elizabeth Nash and Peter Ephross, *State Policy Trends 2022: In a Devastating Year, US Supreme Court's Decision to Overturn Roe Leads to Bans, Confusion and Chaos*, Guttmacher Institute, December 2022, https://www.guttmacher.org/2022/12/state-policy-trends-2022-dev astating-year-us-supreme-courts-decision-overturn-roe-leads.
18. Carter Sherman, "The Last Summer of *Roe v. Wade*," *Vice News*, September 2, 2021, https://www.vice.com/en/article/m7ew94/roe -wade-legal-abortion-texas-v28n3.
19. Sherman, "The Last Summer of *Roe v. Wade*."
20. Sherman, "The Last Summer of *Roe v. Wade*."
21. "Oklahoma Governor Signs the Nation's Strictest Abortion Ban," Associated Press, May 26, 2022, https://www.npr.org/2022/05/26 /1101428347/oklahoma-governor-signs-the-nations-strictest-abor tion-ban.
22. Margot Sanger-Katz and Claire Cain Miller, "How Many Abor-

tions Did the Post-Roe Bans Prevent?," *New York Times*, November 22, 2023, https://www.nytimes.com/2023/11/22/upshot/abortion-births-bans-states.html.

23. Sanger-Katz and Cain Miller, "How Many Abortions Did the Post-Roe Bans Prevent?"

24. Samuel L. Dickman et al., "Rape-Related Pregnancies in the 14 US States With Total Abortion Bans," *JAMA Internal Medicine* 184, no. 3 (2024), https://jamanetwork.com/journals/jamainternalmedicine/fullarticle/2814274.

25. *The Report of the 2015 U.S. Transgender Survey* (National Center for Transgender Equality, 2016), 205, https://transequality.org/sites/default/files/docs/usts/USTS-Full-Report-Dec17.pdf.

26. Stephanie Coontz, *The Way We Never Were: American Families and the Nostalgia Trap*, rev. ed. (Basic Books, 2016), 175.

27. Coontz, *The Way We Never Were*, 176.

28. Amanda Jean Stevenson and Kate Coleman-Minahan, "Use of Judicial Bypass of Mandatory Parental Consent to Access Abortion and Judicial Bypass Denials, Florida and Texas, 2018–2021," *American Journal of Public Health* 113, no. 3 (2023), https://doi.org/10.2105%2FAJPH.2022.307173.

29. Molly Redden, "This Is How Judges Humiliate Pregnant Teens Who Want Abortions," *Mother Jones*, September/October 2014, https://www.motherjones.com/politics/2014/10/teen-abortion-judicial-bypass-parental-notification/.

30. *Access Denied: How Florida Judges Obstruct Young People's Ability to Obtain Abortion Care*, Human Rights Watch, February 9, 2023, https://www.hrw.org/report/2023/02/09/access-denied/how-florida-judges-obstruct-young-peoples-ability-obtain-abortion.

31. *Access Denied* (Human Rights Watch).

32. *Access Denied* (Human Rights Watch).

33. Gretchen E. Ely et al., "Access to Choice: Examining Differences Between Adolescent and Adult Abortion Fund Service Recipients," *Health and Social Care in the Community* (April 2018), https://doi.org/10.1111/hsc.12582.

34. Caitlyn Myers and Daniel Ladd, "Did Parental Involvement Laws Grow Teeth? The Effects of State Restrictions on Minors' Access

328 | NOTES

to Abortion," *Journal of Health Economics* 71 (2020), https://doi.org
/10.1016/j.jhealeco.2020.102302.

35. "Abortion Law Blamed in Death," *Chicago Tribune*, April 8, 1990,
https://www.chicagotribune.com/1990/04/08/abortion-law-blamed
-in-death/.

36. "Abortion Law Blamed in Death."

37. Tamar Lewin, "In Debate on Abortion, 2 Girls Make It Real," *New
York Times*, October 27, 1991, https://www.nytimes.com/1991/10
/27/us/in-debate-on-abortion-2-girls-make-it-real.html.

38. Lewin, "In Debate on Abortion."

39. Angela Bonavoglia, "Kathy's Day in Court," *Ms. Magazine*, April 1988.

40. Molly Redden, "A New Alabama Law Lets Judges Appoint Lawyers
for Fetuses. Here's What That Looks Like," October 6, 2014, https://
www.motherjones.com/politics/2014/10/alabama-abortion-law-at
torney-fetus-lawyers/.

41. Redden, "A New Alabama Law Lets Judges Appoint Lawyers for
Fetuses."

42. *Pregnancy as a Crime: A Preliminary Report on the First Year After
Dobbs* (Pregnancy Justice, 2024), https://www.pregnancyjusticeus
.org/wp-content/uploads/2024/09/Pregnancy-as-a-Crime.pdf.

43. Carter Sherman, "More Than 200 Pregnancy-Related Prosecutions
in First Year Post-*Roe*," *The Guardian*, September 24, 2024, https://
www.theguardian.com/us-news/2024/sep/24/abortion-prosecu
tions-roe-v-wade.

44. Megan Messerly and Alice Miranda Ollstein, "Dems Split on
Whether Parents Must Know Their Child Is Having an Abortion,"
Politico, May 17, 2023, https://www.politico.com/news/2023/05/16
/democrats-gop-parental-notification-abortion-laws-00097245.

45. Faith Miller, "Colorado Abortion Rights Bill Advances After 14-Hour
Hearing," *Colorado Newsline*, March 10, 2022, https://coloradonews
line.com/2022/03/10/14-hour-hearing-abortion-rights-bill/; Mar-
shall Zelinger, "Colorado Abortion Measure Does Not Take Away
Parental Notification," *9News*, April 4, 2022, https://www.9news
.com/article/news/local/next/colorado-abortion-parental-notification
/73-21f780be-bb7d-47be-a677-d4441432904a.

46. Jo Ingles, "Message in Ads Opposing the Proposed Ohio Abortion

Amendment Is Raising Eyebrows," *Statehouse News Bureau*, March 16, 2023, https://www.statenews.org/government-politics/2023-03-16/message-in-ads-opposing-the-proposed-ohio-abortion-amendment-is-raising-eyebrows.

47. Carter Sherman, "Anti-Abortion Misinformation Mounting Ahead of Key Ohio Vote, Experts Warn," *The Guardian*, November 3, 2023, https://www.theguardian.com/us-news/2023/nov/03/ohio-abortion-vote-misinformation-warning.

48. Sneha Gubbala et al., "How People Around the World View Same-Sex Marriage," Pew Research Center, September 27, 2023, https://www.pewresearch.org/short-reads/2023/11/27/how-people-around-the-world-view-same-sex-marriage/.

49. *Half of All U.S. States Limit or Prohibit Youth Access to Gender Affirming Care* (KFF, 2024), https://www.kff.org/other/issue-brief/half-of-all-u-s-states-limit-or-prohibit-youth-access-to-gender-affirming-care/.

50. Ansev Demirhan, "Abortion Is Still Under Threat by Dark Money Groups That Helped Overturn Roe," *The Guardian*, October 25, 2023, https://www.theguardian.com/us-news/2023/oct/25/abortion-ban-dark-money-roe-v-wade-right-wing.

51. Caroline Kitchener, "Antiabortion Lawmakers Want to Block Patients from Crossing State Lines," *Washington Post*, June 30, 2022, https://www.washingtonpost.com/politics/2022/06/29/abortion-state-lines/.

52. Anne Ryman and Matt Wynn, "For Anti-Abortion Activists, Success of 'Heartbeat' Bills Was 10 Years in the Making," *USA Today*, June 19, 2019, https://www.usatoday.com/in-depth/news/local/arizona/2019/06/19/abortion-laws-2019-how-heartbeat-bills-passed-ohio-missouri-more/1270870001/.

53. Ryman and Wynn, "Success of 'Heartbeat' Bills Was 10 Years in the Making."

54. "Inside the Youth Anti-Abortion Movement in the US: 'Victory is on its way'—video," *The Guardian*, February 8, 2024, https://www.theguardian.com/world/video/2024/feb/08/inside-the-youth-anti-abortion-movement-in-the-us-victory-is-on-its-way.

55. Stephanie Perry et al., "Vast Majority of Republicans Support

Abortion Exceptions for Rape, Incest and Mother's Health," *NBC News*, https://www.nbcnews.com/politics/2022-election/vast -majority-republicans-support-abortion-exceptions-rape-incest -moth-rcna52237.

56. Nellie Bowles, "Jordan Peterson, Custodian of the Patriarchy," *New York Times*, May 18, 2018, https://www.nytimes.com/2018/05/18 /style/jordan-peterson-12-rules-for-life.html.

57. Brian Alexander, "What Is the 'Success Sequence' and Why Do So Many Conservatives Like It?" *The Atlantic*, July 31, 2018, https:// www.theatlantic.com/family/archive/2018/07/get-out-of-poverty -success-sequence/566414/.

58. Alexander, "What Is the 'Success Sequence.'"

59. Kat Stafford, "Why Do So Many Black Women Die in Pregnancy? One Reason: Doctors Don't Take Them Seriously," Associated Press, May 23, 2023, https://projects.apnews.com/features/2023/from -birth-to-death/black-women-maternal-mortality-rate.html#:~:text =Black%20women%20have%20the%20highest,for%20Disease%20 Control%20and%20Prevention.

60. Melissa Deckman, "Is Gen Z Switching Political Direction? Not So Fast," PRRI, March 13, 2024, https://www.prri.org/spotlight/is-gen-z -switching-political-direction-not-so-fast/.

61. Alberto Medina et al., *Republican Youth Are Numerous, Politically Active, and More Moderate than Older Republicans*, Center for Information & Research on Civic Learning and Engagement, Tufts University, September 18, 2024, https://circle.tufts.edu/latest-research /republican-youth-are-numerous-politically-active-and-more-moder ate-older.

62. Melissa Deckman, *The Politics of Gen Z: How the Youngest Voters Will Shape Our Democracy* (Chicago University Press, 2024), 98.

63. Deckman, *The Politics of Gen Z*, 101.

64. Deckman, *The Politics of Gen Z*, 98.

65. Sherman Smith, "'When Is It Going to Be Our Time?' Young Kansas Voters Jilted by Candidates and Election Barriers," *Kansas Reflector*, September 15, 2023, https://kansasreflector.com/2023/09/15/when -is-it-going-to-be-our-time-young-kansas-voters-jilted-by-candidates -and-election-barriers/.

NOTES | 331

66. Paris Raite, "Attention, Young Kansas Voters: You Can Make a Difference. But You Have to Show Up," *Kansas City Star*, July 29, 2024, https://www.kansascity.com/opinion/article290490679.html.

67. Ruby Belle Booth, et al., *The Abortion Election: How Youth Prioritized and Voted Based on Issues*, Center for Information & Research on Civic Learning and Engagement, Tufts University, November 14, 2022, https://circle.tufts.edu/latest-research/abortion-election-how -youth-prioritized-and-voted-based-issues.

68. Christine Filer et al., "Why Ohio Voters Approved Abortion Ballot Measure, According to Exit Polling," *ABC News*, November 7, 2023, https://abcnews.go.com/Politics/ohio-voters-broadly-support-abor tion-access-preliminary-exit/story?id=104696547.

69. *The Youth Vote in 2024* (Center for Information & Research on Civic Learning and Engagement, Tufts University), https://circle.tufts .edu/2024-election#economy-was-the-top-youth-issue,-drove-youth -vote-for-trump.

10. THE *DOBBS* DOMINO EFFECT

1. Virginia Langmaid, "Contraception Demand Up After Roe Reversal, Doctors Say," *CNN*, July 6, 2022, https://www.cnn.com/2022/07/06 /health/contraceptives-demand-after-roe/index.html.

2. Langmaid, "Contraception Demand Up."

3. Tara Law, "21% of Women Reported Switching Their Birth Control Method Post-*Roe*," *Time*, July 27, 2022, https://time.com/6200542 /women-birth-control-switching-methods-abortion/.

4. Jacqueline E. Ellison et al., "Changes in Permanent Contraception Procedures Among Young Adults Following the *Dobbs* Decision," *JAMA*, April 2024, https://jamanetwork.com/journals/jama-health-fo rum/fullarticle/2817438?utm_campaign=articlePDF&utm_medi um=articlePDFlink&_hsenc=p2ANqtz-8H7CWBvbjkR2o3OHp D2pxW3nfTBDC6gwYi7ZaHTs5My3z3koQBeM_4U_Q7bUvo fu4NxFuITxj4H5L89Qz-cDMtggxeKw&_hsmi=302448984&utm _content=jamahealthforum.2024.0424&utm_source=articlePDF.

5. Ellison, "Changes in Permanent Contraception."

6. Grace S. Chung et al., "Obstetrician-Gynecologists' Beliefs About

When Pregnancy Begins," *American Journal of Obstetrics and Gynecology* 206, no. 2 (2012), https://doi.org/10.1016/j.ajog.2011.10.877.

7. Carter Sherman, "Senate Republicans Block Bill to Recognize Legal Right to Contraception," *The Guardian*, June 5, 2024, https://www.theguardian.com/us-news/article/2024/jun/05/legal-right-contraception-senate-vote.

8. *Title X: Three Decades of Accomplishment*, Guttmacher Institute, 2001, https://www.guttmacher.org/sites/default/files/article_files/gr040105.pdf.

9. U.S. Health and Human Services Department Office of Population Affairs, *Title X Family Planning Annual Report 2022 National Summary*, October 2023, https://opa.hhs.gov/sites/default/files/2023-10/2022-FPAR-National-Summary.pdf.

10. Liza Fuentes et al., "Adolescents' and Young Adults' Reports of Barriers to Confidential Health Care and Receipt of Contraceptive Services," *Journal of Adolescent Health* 62, no. 1 (2018), https://doi.org/10.1016/j.jadohealth.2017.10.011.

11. Polina Krass et al., "Adolescent Access to Federally Funded Clinics Providing Confidential Family Planning Following Changes to Title X Funding Regulations," *JAMA Network Open* 5, no. 6 (2022), https://doi.org/10.1001/jamanetworkopen.2022.17488.

12. Brittni Frederiksen, et al, *Rebuilding the Title X Network Under the Biden Administration*, KFF, May 25, 2023, https://www.kff.org/womens-health-policy/issue-brief/rebuilding-the-title-x-network-under-the-biden-administration/.

13. Polina Krass, "Adolescent Access to Federally Funded Clinics."

14. Carter Sherman, "Trump's New Abortion Rules Could Hit Rural Communities Hardest. Just Look at Maine," *Vice News*, July 30, 2019, https://www.vice.com/en/article/trumps-new-abortion-rules-are-going-to-hit-rural-communities-hardest-just-look-at-maine/.

15. Sherman, "Trump's New Abortion Rules."

16. Sherman, "Trump's New Abortion Rules."

17. Victoria M. Li, et al, "Discrepant Abortion Reporting by Interview Methodology Among Men from the United States National Survey of Family Growth (2015–2017)," *Contraception*, August 2022, https://www.contraceptionjournal.org/article/S0010-7824(22)00026-9/abstract.

18. Bethany G. Everett et al., "Male Abortion Beneficiaries: Explor-

ing the Long-Term Educational and Economic Effects of Abortion Among Men Who Report Teen Pregnancy," *Journal of Adolescent Health*, October 2020, https://www.ncbi.nlm.nih.gov/pmc/articles /PMC6755038/.

19. Frederiksen, *Rebuilding the Title X Network Under the Biden Administration*.

20. *Title X Funding* (National Family Planning & Reproductive Health Association, 2023), https://www.nationalfamilyplanning.org/file/Title-X-Funding-Infographic-2023-041323.pdf.

21. Matthew Kacsmaryk, "The Abolition of Man . . . and Woman," *National Catholic Register*, June 14, 2015, https://www.ncregister.com /news/the-abolition-of-man-and-woman-tpnrdgjq.

22. Kacsmaryk, "The Abolition of Man . . . and Woman."

23. Todd Ruger, "Judge Who Said Being Transgender Is a 'Delusion' Nearing Confirmation," *Roll Call*, June 18, 2019, https://rollcall .com/2019/06/18/judge-who-said-being-transgender-is-a-delu sion-nearing-confirmation/.

24. Matthew Kacsmaryk, "The Inequality Act: Weaponizing Same-Sex Marriage," *Public Discourse*, September 4, 2015, https://www.the publicdiscourse.com/2015/09/15612/.

25. Mary Tuma, "Texas Sues Biden Administration to Limit Teenage Access to Birth Control," *The Guardian*, July 26, 2024, https:// www.theguardian.com/us-news/article/2024/jul/26/texas-teen age-birth-control-lawsuit.

26. *LGBTQ Youth: Bans on Transgender Youth Participation in Sports* (Movement Advancement Project, 2024), https://www.lgbtmap.org /img/maps/citations-sports-participation-bans.pdf.

27. Betsy Z. Russell, "House Passes Anti-trans Youth Treatment Bill," *Idaho Press*, March 8, 2022, https://www.idahopress.com/news/local /house-passes-anti-trans-youth-treatment-bill/article_ebb0623c -6df9-5a94-8beb-16d5c7688834.html.

28. Russell, "House Passes Anti-trans Youth Treatment Bill."

29. *2023 U.S. National Survey on the Mental Health of LGBTQ Young People* (The Trevor Project), https://www.thetrevorproject.org/survey -2023/assets/static/05_TREVOR05_2023survey.pdf.

30. David D. Kirkpatrick, "The Next Targets for the Group That

334 | NOTES

Overturned *Roe*," *New Yorker*, October 2, 2023, https://www.newyorker.com/magazine/2023/10/09/alliance-defending-freedoms-legal-crusade.

31. Maggie Astor, "GOP State Lawmakers Push a Growing Wave of Anti-Transgender Bills," *New York Times*, January 25, 2023, https://www.nytimes.com/2023/01/25/us/politics/transgender-laws-republicans.html.

32. Astor, "GOP State Lawmakers Push a Growing Wave of Anti-Transgender Bills."

33. *Behind the Counter: Findings from the 2022 Oral Contraceptives Access Survey* (Advocates for Youth, 2022), https://www.advocatesforyouth.org/wp-content/uploads/2022/09/BehindTheCounter-OralContraceptivesAccessReport-2022-1.pdf.

34. *Behind the Counter* (Advocates for Youth).

35. Ed Komenda and Susan Haigh, "Morning-After Pill Vending Machines Gain Popularity on College Campuses Post-Roe," Associated Press, July 1, 2023, https://apnews.com/article/plan-b-emergency-contraceptive-vending-machine-abortion-00ee797529a855b116a538575790098f.

36. Olivia Marble, "New Law Ensures Medication Abortion Access for Public University Students in Mass.," *GBH*, August 1, 2022, https://www.wgbh.org/news/local/2022-08-01/new-law-ensures-medication-abortion-access-for-public-university-students-in-mass; Johanna Alonso, "New York Governor Signs Campus Abortion Medication Bill," *Inside Higher Ed*, May 3, 2023, https://www.insidehighered.com/news/quick-takes/2023/05/03/new-york-governor-signs-campus-abortion-medication-bill; Mallika Seshadri, "Abortion Pills Will Soon Be Available on California Campuses," *LAist,* July 13, 2022, https://laist.com/news/health/abortion-pills-will-soon-be-available-on-california-campuses.

37. Lesley Cosme Torres, "Wesleyan University Says It Will Pay for Abortions and Emergency Contraception for all Students," *WBUR*, May 12, 2023, https://www.wbur.org/news/2023/05/12/wesleyan-university-pays-abortion-contraception.

38. *Minor Abortion Access Research and Advocacy Project* (Planned Parenthood League of Massachusetts, 2024), https://www.plannedpar

enthood.org/uploads/filer_public/30/9c/309c6baf-cfa7-45b0
-a1ff-c14809075923/aspire_maarap_report_online_version.pdf.

CONCLUSION

1. Alice Evans, "Romantic Love Is an Under-Rated Driver of Gender Equality," *Substack*, March 7, 2024, https://www.ggd.world/p/romantic-love-is-an-under-rated-driver.

ABOUT THE AUTHOR

Carter Sherman is a reproductive health and justice reporter at *The Guardian* who has garnered numerous awards and nominations, including a National Press Club Award, a Scripps Howard Award, and four Emmy nominations. Previously a senior reporter for *Vice News*, Sherman has written for publications such as *Elle, Ms. Magazine*, and *Los Angeles* magazine, and she has been interviewed by outlets such as NPR's *Fresh Air, PBS NewsHour*, and MSNBC. Sherman lives in New York with her husband and two very good cats.